THE HISTORY OF EUROPEAN INTEGRATION

The foundation of the European Union was one of the most important historical events in the second half of the 20th century. In order to fully appreciate the modern state of the EU, it is crucial to understand the history of European integration. This accessible overview differs from other studies in its focus on the major roles played by both the United States and European multinational corporations in the development of the European Union.

Chronologically written and drawing on new findings from two major archives (the archives of the US State Department and the Archive of European Integration), this book sheds crucial new light on the integration process.

The History of European Integration offers a major contribution to our understanding of Europe's postwar history, and will be essential reading for any student of postwar European History, Contemporary History, European Politics, and European Studies.

Ivan T. Berend is Distinguished Research Professor at the Department of History, University of California, Los Angeles, USA.

THE HISTORY OF
EUROPEAN INTEGRATION

A new perspective

Intro, Ch 1+2
3 - 5

Ivan T. Berend

Routledge
Taylor & Francis Group

LONDON AND NEW YORK

First published 2016
by Routledge
2 Park Square, Milton Park, Abingdon, Oxon OX14 4RN

and by Routledge
711 Third Avenue, New York, NY 10017

Routledge is an imprint of the Taylor & Francis Group, an informa business

© 2016 Ivan T. Berend

British Library Cataloguing in Publication Data
A catalogue record for this book is available from the British Library

Library of Congress Cataloging in Publication Data
Names: Berend, T. Ivan (Tibor Ivan), 1930- author.
Title: The history of European integration: a new perspective/
Ivan T. Berend.
Description: New York: Routledge, 2016. | Includes bibliographical references.
Identifiers: LCCN 2015049699| ISBN 9781138654907 (hardback) |
ISBN 9781138654914 (pbk.) | ISBN 9781315622903 (ebook)
Subjects: LCSH: Europe–Economic integration–History. |
European cooperation.
Classification: LCC HC241.2.B358 2016 | DDC 337.1/42–dc23LC record
available at http://lccn.loc.gov/2015049699

ISBN: 978-1-138-65490-7 (hbk)
ISBN: 978-1-138-65491-4 (pbk)
ISBN: 978-1-315-62290-3 (ebk)

Typeset in Bembo
by Sunrise Setting Ltd, Brixham, UK

To the memory of Eric Hobsbawm, my most inspiring
late friend

CONTENTS

ILLUSTRATIONS

Figures

Tables

ACKNOWLEDGMENTS

Having spent my childhood and adolescence in the long shadow cast over the 1930s and 1940s by World War I and the preparation of World War II, and having experienced the terrible suffering of World War II firsthand, I am convinced that the integration of Europe, including the formation of the European Union, is the best transformation ever to have happened to Europe. I want to serve this transformation by narrating and analyzing its more than half-a-century historical road. Therefore, for me, this book symbolizes much more than the culmination of yet another research project.

I have profited tremendously from the extremely rich material of the US National Archive and Record Administration in College Park, MD's (referred in the book as American National Archive) Confidential State Department Central Files; and similarly from the Pittsburg-based European Union's Archive of European Integration. The huge number of documents from these two archives, together with several other primary sources, create the base of the book.

Writing a book is never a "one-person show." Works of the many scholars who have created the rich literature on the European integration process have helped my work. Among the most essential authors on the topic, mentioning only a few here, who had an impact on me is Alan Milward, my late friend. I express special gratitude to him for his illuminating works.[1] I was also inspired by three general works on the European integration. Among them Perry Anderson's impressive volume of essays covering a broad range of problems of the European integration.[2] I sympathize and share the optimistic approaches of Timothy Garton Ash's *Free World* and Luuk van Middelaar's *The Passage to Europe*.[3]

I am also grateful for long talks with friends. Jürgen Kocka made an especially important contribution when he encouraged me to work on the history of the European Union during our walks in London, Los Angeles, and the foothills of the

California Sierra Nevada. Another friend, Bojan Bugarić, also made very useful comments. I am grateful for their help.

To my list of the "supporting cast" of my show, I must add certain institutions and associates. My workplace for the last quarter of a century, the University of California, Los Angeles (UCLA), has played a major role. I could not have written this work without the exceptional collection, including electronic sources and assistance of the Charles Young Research Library; nor could I have undertaken the research without the grant provided by UCLA's Academic Senate. I thank UCLA for all it has provided. I am very grateful to Ellen Wilson who edited and polished my draft manuscript with the greatest professional skill.

Last, but far from least, as always, my wife Kati, who helped to write this book in various ways, providing essential library assistance, critical reading, sometimes sharp comments, and great talks on various topics during our early morning walks and our afternoon "tea ceremonies." To her I express my love and warmest thanks.

Ivan T. Berend
April 8, 2015.

Notes

1   Milward, A.S. (1992) *The European Rescue of the Nation State.* Berkeley, CA: University of California Press; Milward, A.S. (2005) *Politics and Economics in the History of the European Union.* London: Routledge.
2   Anderson, P. (2009) *The New Old World.* London: Verso Books.
3   Ash, T.G. (2004) *The Free World: America, Europe and the Surprising Future of the West.* New York, NY: Vintage Books; van Middelaar, L. (2013) *The Passage to Europe. How a Continent Became a Union.* New Haven, CT: Yale University Press.

INTRODUCTION

This is not a textbook-like comprehensive history of the European Union (EU), but rather it is offering a new perspective. The main goal of this work is to fill certain gaps in the history of the European integration by discussing two less covered or totally neglected factors of this process: the role of the US and the big European corporations. Who built the EU? In recent decades, scholars from history, economics, and most of all political science have created a rich literature on the topic of the European integration process. Still, they have not reached any consensus on the question of "who?" Some have pointed to the strongly federal-Europe-oriented elite politicians who drew the lesson from Europe's penchant for "civil war"—200 of the last 400 years of European history have been marred by major wars, including the most devastating World Wars I and II—that Europe needed to block the road of repetition. Others have called attention to the nation-states that, unable to respond to the difficult postwar economic and political challenges alone, had to turn to cooperation to rebuild and consolidate. Their cooperative attempts died out in the late 1960s, but resumed in the 1970s in the face of cut-throat globalization competition. Others have concentrated their focus on the role of institutions that were created after World War II and that had a spin-off effect. In this narrative, unintended consequences of certain arrangements and institutional innovations generated an automatism towards further integration.[1] Finally, some scholars, beginning with the "father" of European integration, Jean Monnet, have explained the integration process as a series of responses to various crises and have maintained that "Europe was built through crises."[2]

Far from denying roles to these players and factors, this work definitely recognizes their important contribution to the integration process as well as the importance and achievements of the rich literature that discussed their role. Even though it complicates the drama, this book is placing *two more decisively important players* into the spotlight. In the extant literature, these two players—the US and the European multinational corporations—have appeared mostly only as "supporting actors." When they have appeared, in most cases they have been assigned cameo roles.

In the first part of this book, I am going to focus to the central role of the US in building Europe after June 1945. Having emerged from World War II in a position to dictate the basic outlines of the peace settlement (hence the term *Pax Americana*), the US went on to become the leader of the West in the ensuing Cold War decades. The US was also the most powerful and influential among the initiators of the original European Community institutions in the 1950s and 1960s and pushed the European Community enlargement ahead as much as possible. American postwar policy was colored by Cold War hysteria, by the fear of Soviet intrusion into Western Europe. Thus when Stalin started Sovietizing Central and Eastern Europe between 1945 and 1948, the Truman Administration, to counterbalance this Soviet advance, started working on the foundation of a federal Western Europe or, as Winston Churchill suggested in 1946, a United States of Europe. As part of this policy, or better to say in the center of the American policy, was the plan to assist a fast reconstruction and rearmament of Germany, despite strong French opposition. The US offered economic and military aid, including the Marshall Plan with mandatory prerequisite of cooperation of the recipient countries, with a clearly expressed goal to unify Western Europe, including Germany.

Given French wariness of any plan to restore power and might to Germany, the immediate postwar half-decade unfolded as an American–French political chess game, replete with blackmailing, arm-twisting, and compromise. In the end, a methodical American effort from 1945 to the 1950s nudged European political leaders to create an integrated Western Europe as well as a united West European army. Although the project of the integrated army failed, the European Coal and Steel Community and then the European Economic Community, the forerunners of the EU, succeeded. Consecutive American administrations pushed the founding six countries to accept as many anti-communist European countries as possible to strengthen the Western alliance system.

This, of course, would not have happened without both a strong nation-state interest in joining the American initiative and a European federalist political elite ready to fight for it. Nor would it have happened in the absence of widespread popular support for federation. Nor can the trajectory and outlines of the overall integration process be understood without taking into account the fact that the first steps and institutions required others, sometimes in response to unintended consequences. Still, it was the US Government that virtually "dictated" the Monnet–Schuman initiative that set the process in motion.

In the mid-1960s, the forward motion slowed down, and for almost two decades only a very partial and slow integration process followed without further supranationalization. From the end of that decade, and especially in the 1970s, American policy changed towards Europe. The Nixon Administration and its key foreign policy planer, Henry Kissinger, realized that a united Europe is not only an ally, but also a competitor. The alliance also lost part of its importance because the great American design constructed a new world situation by opening towards China and making major agreements with the Soviet Union. Harsh confrontation was replaced by détente. As the US became more inward oriented, Europe emerged as a more independent force. Indeed, conflicts emerged between the allies, and the US stopped pushing European integration ahead.

During this period beginning in the 1970s, and parallel with this change, the world economy was also radically changed by a new technological-communication revolution and the rise of globalization and globalized deregulation of the economy. Hand in hand with this process, especially from the 1970s on, a ruthless global competition was unleashed and the hierarchy of world economic powers was reordered. The corporate strongholds of European economic powers were endangered. Western Europe not only lagged behind the US and Japan in the communication revolution, but also responded slowly to the structural crisis and the sharp decline of the old leading sectors brought on by the technological revolution. In the realms of high-tech and funding for corporate research and development, European businesses felt the ruthless competition of the US and Japan; however, they also suffered competition from the newly industrializing countries of Asia: the four "Small Asian Tigers" (Hong Kong, Singapore, South Korea, and Taiwan) and then the "Big Asian Elephants" (China and India). The latter, with their cheap labor force and similar production structures, made the world economic environment extremely hostile for European corporations who lost ground not only on the world market but even in their domestic markets. American multinational companies started invading the European markets and created an existential danger for their European counterparts.

These two major changes—the American policy towards Europe and the endangered European markets—caused a dramatic change in European integration. As the US stopped pushing integration, the European big corporations and multinational enterprises entered the stage. Their role, unrelated to the American role in the first phase of integration, dominated the second phase, the rebirth of the integration process after the 1980s. Big corporations badly needed a large, domestic market and a Europeanized, closely integrated economy and therefore pushed the realization of the unfulfilled promise of the Treaty of Rome (1957), the real single market with the free flow of goods, capital, and people. These corporate empires, some wealthier and more powerful than nation-states, were facing a new political–economic situation that was substantially changing their position.

An important factor was the loss of their lucrative hunting fields on account of the dissolution of the former West European colonial empires during the first one-and-half postwar decades. The newly independent so-called Third World countries turned to nationalization and economic nationalism and the developing world became extremely unstable and uncertain for business. To get markets and investment possibilities, big business had to turn to other geographical areas.

In this atmosphere of cut-throat international competition, the Western European corporate world turned towards the still underexploited markets and cheap labor of the European peripheries. European multinationals multiplied in number and strength, and started investing in each other throughout Europe, including the peripheral countries.

A stable and politically safeguarded all-European market and cheap labor "backyard" became crucially important to their interests, and thus, in the mid-1980s, movement resumed towards a single market and even common currency, as well as a bold enlargement towards the peripheries in the Mediterranean and the East.

Big business interest became dominant in the European Community. Big European corporations started establishing a dense European network of subsidiaries and value chains throughout the Community. They also indulged in a sort of acquisition and merger mania in the 1980s and 1990s, creating huge business empires and Europeanized banking and manufacturing systems from already big corporations. Their expansion throughout the ever enlarging European Community provided a kind of "reinforced concrete" base for the new structures of an integrated Europe. The supranational European political institutions, in turn, offered essential regulations, laws, and institutions. Member states also contributed to the process in accordance with their own national interests.

Corporate Europe could not have built a closely integrated continent alone. Both collaboration with and support from EU political institutions, such as the European Commission and Parliament, were essential at every step. The corporations built up a huge lobbying apparatus and provided expert advisors, sometimes even initiators of new supranational institutions and further integration. Their interests sometimes met and mingled with the interests of the nation-states who were feeling powerless alone in the transformed world system and were looking for joint solutions.

The collapse of the Soviet Bloc and communism offered an unparalleled new opportunity, and the reemerging German Question in the form of reunification brought some challenges as well. This new situation was exploited by the small but still existing federalist political elite. A coalition was formed by big business, supranational institutions, and politicians of the European Community on the one hand, and the national governments of key member countries on the other, to create a truly single market and enlarge it as much as possible.

If I focus in this book on American postwar policy and European big business, it is because as integrators they were, in my view, equal to or even more important than the other players in the process—the nation-states and the federalist political elite. Still, without the decisive role of the latter group, without the power of the idea of federalism, without some unintended consequences of earlier decisions and the spill-over role of institutions, the EU of today could not have come into being. And without considering all these factors, one cannot understand the historical process underlying that birth.

The 2008 financial–economic crisis generated a political crisis of the Union as well; further economic integration became strongly endangered. This new trauma is still threatening. The crisis has pushed the former peripheries to the brink and is endangering one of the most important and symbolic supranational institutions of the Union, the common currency. For the first time, the possibility that member countries might choose to exit from the euro-zone or even from the Union has appeared on the horizon. Britain, the permanent inside–outsider within the Union, is openly flirting with stepping out. This may easily happen in summer of 2016. Certain groups in some of the most advanced northwestern countries have developed serious doubts about the wisdom of keeping a common currency. Anti-common-currency and even anti-EU political parties have appeared on national political scenes and have even won seats in the European Parliament. The migration crisis in 2014–16 further shocked the Union and caused fission among the member states.

Will the EU survive or disintegrate? Will the integration process halt and turn back the Union to its prior embodiment as a free trade zone? Or will the inertia and strength of established institutions, the new security danger and Russian challenge, the cost of the destruction of common institutions, and the strength of corporate interests conserve and even further develop the achievements of European integration? Will a part of the membership, in a legalized two-tier, two-speed Union, be able to stabilize the achievements and even go further in supranationalization? I will conceptualize and analyze future possibilities in the epilogue to this book. Only the passage of time, of course, will tell which of these possibilities comes to pass.

It is a major challenge today to write a new book about the European integration process. The author of a 2012 study on the EU rightly noted in the first sentences of his work: "Why another book . . . Can anything meaningful be added that has not been written already?"[3] Clearly he thought he had something new to contribute, but all authors since, including myself, argue with conviction that they have something different and important to offer. In this case, the resources of the American National Archive[4] (largely unused for inquiries of this sort) and the Archive of European Integration (40,000 documents posted on the Internet)[5] have been mined, along with an extremely rich set of other primary and secondary sources, to yield a new perspective on the widely discussed topic of the foundation and development of the EU.

Notes

1   A great many political science studies, thus the majority of the literature, apply a theorizing approach to the process. Federalist, neo-functionalist, intergovernmentalist, rational choice, constructivist, and historical institutionalist theories have all been enlisted to explain the outcomes of integration, creating a literature filled with wrestling perspectives. Here I list a few particularly important works: Walter Lipgens, *Europa-Föderationspläne der Wiederstandbewegungen 1940–1945* (München: R. Oldenburg Verlag, 1968); Henri Brugmans, *Prophètes et fondateurs de l'Europe* (Bruges, Belgium: College of Europe, 1974); Alan S. Milward, *The European Rescue of the Nation-State* (Berkeley, CA: University of California Press, 1992); Walter Lipgens, *A History of European Integration, 1945–1947, Vol. 1: The Foundation of the European Unity Movement* (Oxford: Oxford University Press, 1982); David Mitrany *A Working Peace System. An Argument for the Functional Development of International Organization* (Oxford: Oxford University Press, 1943); Ernst B. Haas, *The Uniting Europe. Political, Social, and Economic Forces, 1950–1957* (Notre Dame, IN: University of Notre Dame Press, [1958] 2004); Leon N. Lindberg, *The Political Dynamics of European Integration* (Stanford, CA: Stanford University Press, 1963); Alec Stone Sweet, Wayne Sandholtz, and Neil Fligstein eds. *The Institutionalization of Europe* (Oxford: Oxford University Press, 2001); Stanley Hoffmann *The State of War. Essays on the Theory and Practice of International Politics* (New York, NY: Praeger, 1965); Andrew Moravcsik *The Choice for Europe. Social Purpose and State Power from*

Messina to Maastricht (Ithaca, NY: Cornell University Press, 1998); Perry Anderson *The New Old World* (London: Verso, 2009); Paul Pierson, "The Path to European Integration. A Historical–Institutional Analysis," in *European Integration and Supranational Governance*, eds. Wayne Sandholtz and Alec Stone Sweet (Oxford: Oxford University Press, 1998); Geoffrey Garrett and George Tsebelis, "An Institutional Critique of Inter-governmentalism," *International Organization* 50(2) (1996): 269–99; Wayne Sandholtz and John Zysman, "Recasting the European Bargain," *World Politics* 42(1) (1989): 95–128; Knud Erik Jørgensen, Mark A. Pollack, and Ben Rosamond, eds. *Handbook of European Union Politics* (London: Sage Publications, 2007).

2 Jean Monnet incorporated the association of crisis with decision making into his *Memoirs* (1978): "Men take great decisions only when crisis stares them in the face." He added: "I have always believed that Europe would be built through crisis and that it would be the sum of their solution" (Jean Monnet *Memoirs*, trans. Richard Mayne [Garden City, NY: Doubleday, 1978], 417, 421).

The 2008 financial crisis called the attention of scholars to the role and importance of crises in history. Two economic historians analyzed five global financial crises between 1880 and 2008 as major change-generating challenges of the world eco-nomic–financial system (see Kenneth Rogoff and Carmen M. Reinhart "This Time is Different: Eight Centuries of Financial Folly," NBER Working Paper No. 13882 [2008], available from: www.nber.org/papers/w13882, accessed March 2008). The British Institute of Historical Research organized a conference at the University of Durham in the summer of 2013 called "Re-Evaluating the Role of Crises in Economic and Social History." As the announcement of the conference explained: "The theme of crisis has been a ubiquitous analytical concept for historians from Marxist theories of structural change in society to anthropometric history. Different forms of crisis have been explored in nearly every strand of history, ranging from agrarian famines to epi-demiological outbreaks, and from financial collapses to disasters precipitated by conflict and trade disputes" (https://copingwithcrisisconference.wordpress.com/). Another contribution to the crisis literature, a collection of papers edited by Professor Ludger Kühnhardt, political scientist at the University of Bonn, argued from the idea that "European integration is seemingly driven by the dialectics of paradox and crisis." Using the old Arnold Toynbean "challenge and response" pattern as an "additional explicatory variable," Kühnhardt argued "that the meaning of crises as engines of European integration has been under-researched . . . One can possibly even argue that in the end crises have strengthened European integration" (Ludger Kühnhardt ed. *Crises in European Integration. Challenges and Responses, 1945–2005* (New York, NY: Oxford University Press, 2009), 1–3, 6.

3 Jürgen Neyer, *The Justification of Europe. A Political Theory of Supranational Integration* (Oxford: Oxford University Press, 2012), 3.

4 American National Archive, Confidential US State Department Central Files, *France, Foreign Affairs 1945–1949*. National Archives and Record Administration (based in College Park, MD), hereafter referenced as National Archive, followed by the relevant document number.

5 Archive of European Integration, available from aei.pitt.edu, hereafter referenced as Archive of European Integration, followed by the specific document title.

1

MADE IN THE US?

The origins of European integration from the 1940s

Who built Europe? As the cessation of fighting in May 1945 brought the bloodiest and most devastating of Europe's modern wars to a close, the general idea of integrating the European nations was being considered by a number of different influential individuals and groups. Thus the answer to the question of who should be credited with building Europe is anything but simple. Visionary federalist politicians and the political elite of some extremely vulnerable countries argued for a secure, integrated political structure of Western Europe, based on the bitter lessons of World War II. A vast literature credits the French political economist and diplomat Jean Monnet as the visionary and organizer of an integrated, federal Europe. Henry Kissinger, looking back from the vantage point of 2014 to provide a historical perspective on the current "world order," assigned the credit elsewhere:

> That Western Europe found moral strength to launch itself on the road to a new approach to order was the work of three great men: Konrad Adenauer in Germany, Robert Schuman in France, and Alcide de Gaspari [De Gasperi] in Italy . . . [They had] the vision and fortitude to overcome the causes of Europe's tragedy.[1]

The idea of a united Europe was not entirely new. Enlightenment philosophers, especially those who traveled abroad as Montesquieu did, already recognized the deep similarity of the Western countries, which—as Perry Anderson rediscovered in one of his essays—are essentially like a "single republic."[2] On the other side of the eighteenth-century Atlantic, George Washington was one of the earliest statesmen to speak of a United States of Europe as the natural outcome of processes already at work in Europe. United States of Europe movements spread later, in the last decades of the nineteenth century, with the famous French writer Victor Hugo as one of the movement's high priests. Then in the mid-1920s came pan-European movements maintaining that Europe is one great nation.[3] At the end of that decade, the French Premier Aristide Briand filed an initiative for federal reorganization at the League of Nations. The list of forerunners and variants on the idea of unity in Europe could go on for pages—the idea was clearly alive long before the horrors of World War II added the impetus needed to bring it to fruition.

The long pre-history to which I have just alluded may create an impression that the integration process after World War II was a logical and genuine continuation and realization of these early ideas. In reality, that was not the case. None of these federal dreams and visions ever had the chance to be realized. The spirit of Westphalia (that is, the spirit of the twin treaties signed in 1648), which established the individual state as the legitimate embodiment of sovereignty in Europe, was yet to be really challengeable. Alan Milward went as far as stating, and proving, that even the postwar "saints and prophets," as he sarcastically called the leading advocates of federal Europe, in reality wanted to serve the interests of their own nation-states.[4]

In short, from the passionate federalist advocacy of hundreds of federalist resistance movements, politicians, and organizations, nothing tangible came into being. Federalist ideas hit the thick concrete wall of the resistance of the victorious great powers. The latter had different plans for Europe.

The German Question: postwar ideas about security and peace

With the cessation of formal hostilities in Europe after May 8, 1945, as the full extent of the horror of the second of two twentieth-century total wars came into full view, victors and vanquished alike wondered whether a Europe of fully sovereign nation-states could ever hope to enjoy a lasting peace.[5] Could a political institutional framework be found that would make war obsolete as a mechanism for conflict resolution? And more to the point, could a solution be found to the so-called German Question—could conditions and policies be created that would prevent a repetition of German aggression against neighbors in Europe? What was to be done? What could be done?

The answer seemed at first to lie in a solution based on a continued alliance of the victorious great powers. President Franklin D. Roosevelt dreamed about a world system based on just such an alliance and, at the Tehran summit meeting at the end of November 1943, he spoke about a postwar international order supervised by "four policemen," America, Russia, Britain, and China. Shortly before that, during the Moscow meeting of the foreign ministers of the Allied countries in October 1943, Vyacheslav M. Molotov made a clear and strong statement announcing "that any kind of federation in Europe is unacceptable for the Soviets."[6] Stalin, genuinely paranoid and convinced that any kind of European integration would foster anti-Soviet actions, took a hard line after the war. He instructed the European communist parties to follow and reject any kind of regional integration. Meanwhile, the postwar British Government and its foreign secretary, Ernest Bevin, "did not want to do anything that would exacerbate an increasingly difficult relationship [with the Soviets]." Therefore, in the early postwar years, until the conflict between the victors became manifest, Britain tried to avoid dividing

Europe into two camps by supporting the Western integration plan and instead sought to keep the wartime alliance alive.[7]

All of the victorious powers wanted Germany to pay for the devastation it had caused and to paralyze it so that it would be unable ever to start another war. Before his untimely death in April 1945, Roosevelt had sketched plans to address the German Question—that is, the Prussian German pattern of aggression against neighboring countries that had emerged with national unification in the later nineteenth century and that had spawned the two total wars of the twentieth century. Now, the victors of World War II thought to secure peace by incapacitating, permanently paralyzing, and partitioning Germany. In October 1943, US Secretary of State Cordell Hull agreed in Moscow that the German Question would be handled by the victors acting together. To this end, the Allies established the Allied Control Council in London. In September 1944, the Council suggested creating temporary occupation zones after the war. In February 1945, in Yalta, they agreed to form a new Allied Control Council to run occupied Germany. Then at Potsdam in July 1945, the Allies decided not to establish central government, but nevertheless to handle Germany as a single unit for economic purposes. They also agreed on reparations, including removal of important strategic industrial capacities.

After the fighting ended, because of the rapid emergence of tensions, disagreements, and outright conflict among the Allies, the Potsdam program was never really implemented. In the summer of 1946, Secretary Byrnes suggested the unification of the occupation zones to govern Germany better. Although the French rejected the offer, Britain accepted. By January 1947, the governmental division into four zones was disrupted by the creation of American–British Bizone, or Bizonia, and with this development, the more inclusive economic vision for occupied Germany was dead—at least for the time being. One-and-half years later, a currency reform was introduced by the Western occupation zones, thus introducing another form of division.[8]

Policy making among the Allies, under the best of circumstances, could be a notoriously convoluted business, never more so than when the German Question lay on the negotiating table. The Morgenthau Plan is a case in point. Prepared by President Roosevelt's Secretary of the Treasury Henry Morgenthau Jr, this plan specified the partition of Germany, with either the internationalization or annexation of the German industrial heartland—the Saar, Ruhr, and Upper Silesian regions. The central goal was to dismantle or destroy the heavy industrial base of the country, thereby "converting Germany into a country primarily agricultural and pastoral in character."[9] On September 16, 1944, at their Quebec Conference, Roosevelt and Churchill discussed and accepted the basic ideas contained in this document.

In reality, this plan never became official American policy. In the US, the Departments of State and Treasury were quarreling over policy, as an internal State Department memo makes clear:

> State-war [departments] plan for denazification drawn up in 1944 but vetoed by FDR and the Treasury [Department] crowd . . . The big issue of disagreement . . . at that time was on the broad economic question of how

much and what kind of industries to leave in Germany. The [State] Dept.'s paper of Sept. 4, 1944 entitled Suggested Recommendations on Treatment of Germany from the Cabinet Committee for the President (was discussed by the Cabinet Committee on Sept. 5 but not agreed to). Mr. Morgenthau on Sept. 15 at Quebec got the President and Mr. Churchill to initial a paper embodying his own extreme views on pastoralizing Germany . . . In his reply of October 20 [to the State Department memorandum on the treatment of Germany] the President backed down from the extreme position taken in the Sept. 15 Quebec paper and approved a substantial part of the [State] Department's memorandum.[10]

In April 1945, before the differences could be resolved, Roosevelt died and Harry S. Truman took over the presidency. Two weeks later President Truman called for a meeting to learn about, discuss, and decide how to deal with postwar Germany. Among the participants were Acting Secretary of State Joseph Grew and experts such as William Clayton and John J. McCloy. Morgenthau was also present.[11]

The Morgenthau Plan was shelved, but Morgenthau himself certainly helped to shape the new policy that was accepted just a few days after this meeting. Service Order JCS-1067, the directive that implemented the new policy, did not target the re-agrarization and pastoralization of Germany but was still quite draconian. It gave General Eisenhower explicit orders to enforce its provisions in the American occupation zone and to "urge the Control Council to accept it as a general policy." It stated that

> Germans cannot escape responsibility for what they have brought upon themselves . . . Germany will not be occupied for the purpose of liberation but as a defeated enemy nation . . . The principle Allied objective is to prevent Germany from ever again becoming a threat to the peace of the world.[12]

A policy of "industrial disarmament" targeted the elimination of strategic industries such as ship building, aircraft, synthetic rubber, and oil production, and the limitation of the capacity of other sectors, such as iron, steel, and machine tools, to what was necessary to serve domestic consumption needs. Industrial production, as the directive declared, should only serve to prevent starvation of the population. The order also prohibited scientific research and ordered closure of laboratories and institutes, "except those considered necessary to the protection of public health." The capacities of banned industries were to be dismantled and delivered for reparation, or destroyed. Accompanying these harsh industrial policies was the order for a harsh denazification purge to remove all members of the Nazi Party and military organizations who had been more than nominal participants in the Third Reich. Such individuals were to be "excluded from public office and from positions of importance in quasi-public and private enterprises." Finally, in spite of the fact that Germany was already partitioned, the directive called for establishing a strongly decentralized structure with local responsibilities except in transportation, foreign affairs, and a few other crucial areas.

At the aforementioned Potsdam meeting of the victorious powers, the agreement made on August 4, 1945 largely followed this American directive on the "policies of military, industrial, and scientific disarmament for Germany and directed the Allied Control Council to negotiate and execute programs effectuating these policies."[13] In October, the US State Department finally prevailed over Treasury; Morgenthau was excluded from policy decisions about the German Question and the State Department became responsible for policy making or research on the subject of disarmament.[14] In early 1946, a punitive plan called the Level of Industry Plan, specified setting the maximum allowable output of the German steel industry to 25 percent, the car industry to 10 percent, and heavy industry to 50 percent of prewar levels. Accordingly, 1,500 industrial plants were destroyed or removed. The plan even ordered extensive deforestation.[15] On February 2, 1946, General William Henry Draper Jr reported about the progress "in converting Germany to an agricultural and light industry economy."[16]

The French, victimized by three German attacks since 1870, and motivated by fear as much as by the desire for revenge, sought to go much further.[17] They wanted an unlimited military occupation of Germany, but also a dismembering that would replace greater Germany with several smaller German states— a return to conditions resembling those before the creation in 1871 of the unified German state.[18] Jean Monnet, then a principal spokesman for this French policy but eventually a mastermind of European integration and the so-called Father of Europe, gave an interview to *Fortune* magazine on this subject before the war ended. As he later claimed, he was thinking at that time of "a system whereby the former Reich would be stripped of part of its industrial potential, so that the coal and steel resources of the Ruhr could be placed under a European authority and used for the benefit of all the nations involved."[19]

General Charles de Gaulle, leader of liberated France in the immediate postwar years, described the French plans similarly at a dinner party on April 11, 1945, with invited American guests, Assistant Secretary of War John J. McCloy and Major General Ralph C. Smith, military attaché of the US Embassy in Paris. As Ambassador Jefferson Caffery and General Smith reported to Washington to the secretary of state: "De Gaulle expressed the opinion that in order to safeguard French security, the German portion of the left bank of the Rhine must be broken up into small, semi-independent states operating under French influences." He clearly stated that

> France desires to control left bank from Cologne to Swiss frontiers. It should be made up of small, semi-independent units . . . The Ruhr industrial area, he [De Gaulle] believes should be under international control. Its mines and industries would be operated for the benefit of all Western European countries.[20]

De Gaulle spoke about an International Commission with the participation of France, Belgium, the Netherlands, and probably others. General Smith added: "General de Gaulle envisions close cooperation between Belgium, Holland and France, and did not dismiss the possibility of a customs-union." De Gaulle also discussed the coal production of the Saar region and made it clear that France "needs all of this output and some coal from the Ruhr as well."[21]

Around the end of the war, the State Department agreed with essential French demands. A November 11, 1944 office memorandum acknowledged the "official recognition on our part of the vital interest of France in the solution of the German problem" and insisted on inviting France to the European Advisory Commission that was dealing mostly with German problems.[22] Until 1947, this State Department position, including the integration of the Saar region into France, was repeated several times.[23]

French policy towards Germany did not change in the first years after the war. Reacting to Winston Churchill's famous Zurich speech (discussed later) in the fall of 1946, which was proposing French–German reconciliation, de Gaulle angrily declared: "A united Europe [Churchill's recommendation] would become nothing else than an enlarged Germany."[24] In the summer of 1947 the French Government wanted to make a *fait accompli* regarding the future of the Saar region and prepared a constitution for the local Saar Constituent Commission in June 1947. The preamble declared: "The people of the Saar . . . [are] deeply convinced that their existence and development will be assured by the Saar's organic integration within the economic sphere of France."[25]

In the spring of 1948, the US and Britain did not see real security risk in a German revival. France, however, as a report on the meeting of the military governor's conference summed up: "It is obvious that between the two risks their [the French] principal fear continues to attach to Germans rather than to Russians."[26] Beside security considerations, French policy towards Germany also served French economic interests and the dream of establishing French economic superiority in Europe. Controlling the Ruhr industry also would have provided "protection against commercial competition from the German steel industry."[27]

The Cold War and new American policy towards Germany

Unlike French policy, American policy towards Germany shifted 180 degrees; the "German Question", as it was seen at the end of the war, simply lost its importance for the US. This happened gradually between the Ottawa meeting of Roosevelt and Churchill (Morgenthau Plan) in the summer of 1943 and the announcement of the Marshall Plan in the summer of 1947. During the four intervening years, the US dropped the program of debilitating and fatally weakening Germany and gradually turned to rehabilitating its former enemy to help its economic recovery and foster its robust development and rearmament.

The Germans naturally welcomed the prospect of an American policy change that was favorable to their own national interest, and German politicians, especially Konrad Adenauer, then president of the Christian Democratic Union in the British occupation zone, used various methods and forms of advocacy to ensure that such change came about. Their main goal was to stop the dismantling of war industrial capacities. Adenauer provided a memorandum to the military governors in December 1946, proposing "a complete cessation to any further dismantling of factories."[28] Nearly a year later, on September 24, 1947, at a private lunch with US Consul General Maurice W. Altaffer, Adenauer bitterly complained about the British authorities who want "to eliminate [German industry] as a competitor in the world markets in the future."[29] French actions also came in for criticism.[30]

In his campaign against deindustrialization, Adenauer did not hesitate to call up the specter of totalitarianism, left and right alike. Thus, in September 1948, in his speech opening the Congress of the Christian Democratic Union, just as the change of American policy towards Germany was becoming manifest and public, he actually went so far as to portray the Morgenthau plan as "a crime against humanity which could well compare with National Socialist crimes."[31] Nor did he hesitate to play the "communist card," especially with representatives of the US State Department. Altaffer's report on the aforementioned 1947 lunch with Adenauer noted that Adenauer "informed me that representatives of Soviet-Russian government approached him . . . [also that there is] a school of thought [in Germany] favoring close relations . . . between Germany and Russia."[32] On another occasion, Adenauer complained about a vast "communist infiltration" in the Ruhr, which is not fully recognized by the American authorities, that due to the problems with food supply and the "unfortunate psychological effect of General Clay's recent statement on dismantling . . . he feared that the communists would go a long way towards the achievement of their objectives."[33] The American ambassador, McCloy, also reported in 1949:

> Adenauer stated he did not want to gain the reputation that he was black-mailing the Council . . . on the basis of Soviet moves, but that if action were not taken along the lines he suggested, all of Western Europe would fall in Soviet orbit.[34]

The Western allies worried about alienating the German population and pushing them, as a consequence, into the arms of Russia. American consular reports were warning of a "proletarianized" Germany where "to freeze to death" was a real threat to the population. Such a situation, so frighteningly similar to the 1930s, would pose a danger to the West, particularly because in such conditions, Germany could become a "hotbed for Neo-National Communism."[35] British consular reports expressed their concerns with the same alarmed tone. Germans, they noted, were beginning to believe that the Western occupation powers wanted to "destroy the German nation."[36] Responding to these concerns, General Lucius D. Clay, the US military administrator of Germany, sent a secret cable on July 19, 1946, suggesting an open break with the restriction policy. He had already suspended dismantling German industrial plants in May of that year.

Although the Pentagon and some State Department officials were still advocating harsh measures, the Truman Administration elected to shift policy and to go open with that fact. In Stuttgart in September 1946, Secretary of State J.F. Byrnes addressed the Germans directly and presented the American "Restatement policy on Germany." The media quickly dubbed the new policy the Message of Hope.

In his milestone speech, Byrnes recalled the Potsdam Agreement's goals on demilitarization and reparation, including the removal of some strategic war industries, adding that whatever the policy, the German living standard had to be tolerable and the nation's industry capable to supply the population. Carefully avoiding naming names, Byrnes blamed the Allied Control Council as a whole for failing

> to take the necessary steps to enable the German economy to function as an economic unit . . . The American Government is unwilling to accept responsibility for the needless aggravation of economic distress that is caused by the failure of the Allied Control Council . . . [that] is neither governing Germany nor allowing Germany to govern itself . . . Germany is a part of Europe and recovery in Europe . . . will be slow indeed if Germany with her great resources of iron and coal is turned into a poorhouse . . . The purpose of the occupation did not contemplate a prolonged foreign dictatorship of Germany's internal political life.[37]

The secretary of state also condemned the attempts by the victors to gain political domination of the Ruhr and Rhineland and declared that the "American people want to return the government of Germany to the German people. The American people want to help the German people to win their way back to an honorable place among the free and peace-loving nations of the world."[38] As Max Beloff remarked, Byrnes "buried the specter of Morgenthauism."[39]

From Stuttgart, Byrnes went to Paris where he repeated the essence of his message for the French in early October. Two weeks later he had a radio broadcast about the topic. Byrnes's speech echoed tremendously around the world. *Time Magazine* stated that "Europe and Asia recognized [the Stuttgart speech] as America's boldest move yet towards leadership of the world."[40] The international press published the entire text of the speech. American embassies and consulates reported on the worldwide reaction, including the interpretation of the speech as a "declaration of war."[41]

Winston Churchill, one of the first to suggest French–German reconciliation in 1946, provided invaluable support for the policy change, and propaganda on its behalf. Several times he noted the necessity of policy that would allow the "re-entry of Germany into the family of European nations." Churchill argued, "A united Europe cannot live without the help and strength of Germany." Elsewhere he declared that "for us the German problem is to restore the economic life of Germany and revive the ancient fame of the German race." To avoid the danger of "exposing their neighbours and ourselves to any reassertion of their military power . . . United Europe provided the only solution."[42]

Despite the public announcement of the Truman Administration's intentions, actual policy implementation occurred incrementally over the next several years; therefore, American policy after the Byrnes speech is best described as somewhat corrected, not as dramatically and suddenly changed. A March 1948 letter of Charles Bohlen, one of the chief Soviet experts of the Truman Administration and a close advisor of the president, illustrates the point well. Bohlen, answering Representative

John M. Folger, who had criticized the change, explained that Europe was still properly protected and that the demilitarization of Germany would continue for decades. Bohlen also explained that American policy allowed for faster German economic reconstruction progress only because their slow growth would "retard the whole effort for European recovery . . .." He noted also that "there is a necessity for the revival of German production to make Germany self-supportive."[43] More proof of the gradualism of the policy change can be found in the fact that the order to dismantle major German industrial plants, including the I.G. Farben and all of the Berlin industries, dates only from 1949, as does the American insistence that the mines of the Saar region were the property of the German nation.[44]

Within a year of Byrnes's speech, the Truman Administration actually took a much more radical step when it halted the denazification project. They realized that the process was being partly exploited by left-wing elements who wanted to nationalize private industries.[45] It was apparent that the process being practiced was doomed to failure. Under the March 1946 denazification law all adult Germans had been screened, either by the military government or under military government supervision, and objectionable individuals had been excluded from posts of influence or leadership.[46] Using the criteria of seriousness of crime and/or participation in the Nazi movement, every adult had been assigned to one of five groups, ranking from "major offender" to "follower." The affected individuals numbered in the tens of millions. In the American occupation zone alone, 25 percent of the adult population belonged to one of those categories.[47] The investigation of just one case could take several years and cause permanent tension and deep dissatisfaction among many people. A telling example is the case of Emil Standow, a Stuttgart inhabitant who wrote a letter to President Truman because "his case has been before the Denazification Tribunal for about two years during which time his old age pension, in accordance with the denazification law, has been held up."[48] As early as December 1946, American Consul Maurice W. Altaffer reported to the US secretary of state, that "the present state of denazification has become unbearable for all concerned."[49] Witnesses for the prosecution were not really available whilst witnesses for the defense waited in unlimited numbers. The *New York Times* published an article, also in December 1946, discussing the failure of denazification.[50] Christian Democratic Union President Adenauer placed a proposal before the British Military Governor in the same year, asking amnesty for innocuous party members.[51] Given the practical difficulties and concerns about the possibility that harsh policies would play to the Russian advantage in the war for German public opinion, the political decision was made virtually to end denazification and turn to rehabilitating and rebuilding instead. The first step, as described in an American consular report of October 1947, removed the task of denazification from the jurisdiction of the occupational authorities and assigned it instead to German authorities. The order stipulated "that after December 31st no more persons shall be removed from their posts except in quite exceptional cases."[52]

The political outcome was more than controversial. Now, some American consuls sent alarming reports to Washington about the *renazification* of Germany and the return of ex-Nazis to public life. According to one 1948 report, 60 percent of the judges and 76 percent of prosecutors in Bavaria were former Nazis, and some were even former SS members.[53] More than a year later, in November 1949, another American consul sent a forty-four-page report that mentioned that even "big Nazis" are reemployed.[54] Another report described the rehabilitation of former Nazis that was allowing their return to "influential positions."[55] On January 17, 1949, the *Washington Post* published the "Nazi Comeback," an article based on statements by Charles M. La Follette, the outgoing American military governor of Württemberg-Baden and a former prosecutor at the Nuremberg Trial. The article reported that La Follette "said today that American backed German industry is a potential breeding ground for a Nazi comeback in Germany ... America's emphasis on reindustrializing Germany may encourage a new National Socialism."[56] Still the policy stayed in place. Neither the scandal of a military government having to step in and remove repositioned Nazi war criminals, as the American consul in Stuttgart reported, nor neo-fascist action against Jews, sometimes involving the German police, stopped the Nazi reintegration.[57]

The change of American policy had a mixed echo in democratic circles of Western Europe and even in America. The consular report from Brussels described a conversation with Luxembourg's foreign minister Beck who said that he was

> depressed and anxious ... [because it] seems German mind now completely ignores any responsibility for plunging Europe into chaos distress, etc. In fact some Germans now suggesting they have legitimate basis claims for restoration war damages caused their people by allied bombardment ... Many Germans hope for war between Russia and US that will increase the importance of Germany.[58]

The Society for the Prevention of World War III, a liberal organization based in New York, harshly criticized the State Department's German policy for not fulfilling the Potsdam Agreement and for failing to dismantle German heavy industry before Byrnes's new approaches could be implemented.

With the benefit of hindsight, Jean Monnet, the *éminence grise* of postwar French policy, clearly summarized the gradual steps that produced the change of American policy:

> Quite early on, the Allied [Powers] had renounced the idea of dismembering occupied Germany into a number of small states; then, they had decided to annex no territory, including the Saar; now, finally, they were even preparing to give up internationalizing the resources of the Ruhr.[59]

Monnet was correct. "It has become a paramount objective of US foreign policy," a State Department document summed up in 1948,

> *to endeavor to reinforce Western Europe through the integration with it of a democratic Germany* ... [It is] important that the US Government not ... count itself

[*sic*] to any permanent economic and political restriction upon the prospective German government which will make it impossible to carry out the economic and political rehabilitation of Germany.[60]

The American foreign policymakers, of course, had to consider European fears about German revival, especially those of the French. One of the most effective American arguments was the Soviet danger.

> Western powers have attained impressive 'lead' over Soviet Communist rivals in Germany, and it would be tragic if Kremlin forged ahead now due to continued French conception of their German policy largely in terms of justified fears of another German aggression, overlooking fact that continued French intransigence toward German people will advance Soviet design.[61]

Since a strong Germany had a crucial role in the Western alliance against Russia, the medicine offered by the US Administration was *integration*. In the State Department confidential files, hardly a document can be found that leaves open any question about the American objective. An internal State Department document on concerns that a revived Germany might again try to dominate Europe, noted: "It is argued that to counterbalance this danger, the Western countries *must associate themselves much more closely and include Germany* within their community."[62] American policy arguments stressed that a federal Europe would be the best way to control Germany.[63] The object of the American political program, as the military commissioners were instructed, was *the integration of Germany with other democratic nations of the West*.[64]

For the politicians of Western Europe, the direction of American policy was readily evident. Summing up that policy in retrospect, a Commission of the European Community document from 1956 stated:

> One of the most consistent aspects of postwar United States foreign policy has been steadfast support of economic and political integration . . . of Europe. This policy took shape soon after the war and has continued until the present day . . . European integration within the framework of an expanding Atlantic Community remains the cornerstone of its [American] western European policy.[65]

What kind of new development led to the cancellation of those early plans to eliminate the "German Danger"? Basically another war—this one, however, is lacking in battlefields and bombs. This was the Cold War, which was already taking shape as the hot war drew to a close. Although there are several connected points in the huge literature on the Cold War, I am not going to discuss its history or its literature,[66] but concentrate on its aspects that are the closest connection to the European integration. One of the first to *openly* express a different point of view and to argue for a dramatic policy change was the celebrated Atlantic-Western politician Winston Churchill. In 1946, Churchill delivered two extremely influential speeches, one before Byrnes's famous address, and the second afterwards. The first, delivered on March 5 in the presence of President Harry Truman, was the famous "Iron Curtain" address at Fulton College in Missouri:

> From Stettin in the Baltic to Trieste in the Adriatic an iron curtain has descended across the Continent. Behind that line lie ... what I must call the Soviet sphere, and ... [an] increasing measure of control from Moscow. The safety of the world ... *requires a unity in Europe*, from which no nation should be permanently outcast ... The Communist parties ... are seeking everywhere to obtain totalitarian control ... [These] constitute a growing challenge and peril to Christian civilization.[67]

Stalin answered in *Pravda* in the same tone: "I do not know whether he and his friends will succeed in organizing a new armed campaign against Eastern Europe ... but if they do succeed ... they will be thrashed."[68] Churchill delivered the second speech, in Zurich in September of the same year. Speaking in terms of "Teutonic" aggression and destruction, he warned that the Dark Age might return, but he also offered a remedy. The way to prevent such a development, he suggested, "is to re-create the European Family ... and provide it with a structure under which it can dwell in peace, in safety and in freedom. We must build a kind of *United States of Europe*."[69] Churchill recommended French–German reconciliation as the axis of a new European design built on recognition of a new postwar political conflict between East and West.

The Cold War, a political, economic, military, and diplomatic confrontation, pitted Western capitalist democracy against Soviet communism in its Stalinist form. More than any other development, it *changed American policy* towards Germany and the European integration. Nowadays a library can be filled with books and studies, often debating and opposing each other, about the origins and history of this new form of "war."[70] Without going into details I am going to sum up the main process of rising confrontation that pushed the Truman Administration to initiate European integration. Both the Soviet Union and the US—former allies—wanted to establish long-term security for their own countries, a goal that, despite several points of common interest, often conflicted with the one of continuing cooperation. Besides, old ideological and political differences and conflicts between the two countries had never died. Lack of trust and deeply rooted suspicions led each country to see the other as a threat and to search for long-term guarantees of their individual security at the expense of alliance.[71] Each power, therefore, took controversial steps that irritated and frightened the other. One wrong step from one side generated a response, often another wrong step, from the other side.

One of the first conflicts arose out of Stalin's policy towards Poland. The Big Three had accepted the Soviet leader's argument about borders and had agreed to shift Poland towards the West by giving the former Eastern territories of that nation to the Soviet Union and compensating Poland with territories confiscated from Germany. Stalin, however, did not even wait for a formal agreement, but instead acted unilaterally to create a *fait accompli* by setting up the communist Polish transitory government's civil administration in Danzig and other occupied former German territories, thus virtually attaching those territories to the rest of Soviet-controlled Poland. The American government immediately opposed this step by a memorandum dated May 1945.[72]

Stalin still wanted more—a "friendly government" in Poland. The Polish government-in-exile in London did not fit that description and thus he refused to recognize it. In July 1944, he created a Polish Committee of National Liberation in Lublin under communist leadership. When the Red Army liberated Poland in December 1944, this committee became the provisional government of that nation. Explaining his Polish policy in a message to Roosevelt in December 1944, Stalin said: "The Soviet Union is interested [in Poland] more than any other power . . . because Poland is a border state with the Soviet Union and the problem of Poland is inseparable from the problem of security of the Soviet Union."[73] "I am disturbed," answered Roosevelt, "and deeply disappointed over your message on December 27 in regard to Poland."[74]

The West, however, could not really object to the Soviet claim of a right to its security. A writer for the conservative British daily, *The Times*, in the fall of 1944, explained the problem as follows: "What Russia seeks on her western frontier is her own security . . . ." But that is not the end of the story. The writer goes on to observe that Britain and the US also want to secure interests in the Suez Canal and Central America, regions they have

> always properly considered vital to their own security. It would therefore be inconsistent to ask Russia today to give up a wholly identical right to security, and it would be . . . hypocritical to see in the exercise of that right a symptom of a policy of aggression.[75]

Evan Luard, French historian of the Cold War, assumes "that Stalin interpreted his wartime discussions with Western allies as implying that he would have a predominant influence in Eastern Europe in exchange for American and British influence in Western Europe."[76] Certainly his October 1944 meeting with Churchill could have generated his view of a postwar Europe divided between East and West. Churchill visited Stalin in Russia before the summit meeting and the two allied leaders met at a dinner party in the Kremlin. To recover what happened, let's quote briefly Churchill's later description of that event:

> [I said,] Let us settle about our affairs in the Balkans . . . How would it do for you to have 90 percent predominance in Romania, for us to have 90 percent of the say in Greece and so fifty–fifty about Yugoslavia? While this was being translated, I wrote out on a half-sheer of paper . . . [actually on a napkin, the proposed sphere of interest percentages, including, for the Soviet Union, a 75 percent interest in Bulgaria and 50 percent in Hungary]. I pushed this across to Stalin . . . he took his blue pencil and made a large tick upon it, and passed it back to us. It was all settled in no more time than it takes to sit down.[77]

Stalin probably believed that this agreement would provide the foundation for any permanent postwar arrangement. At least he clearly expressed this belief during a several-hours-long dinner with Churchill on July 18, 1945 in Potsdam. There were just the two of them, with their translators. Stalin, Churchill later stated in his book, "said that he had been hurt by the American demand for a change of government in Romania and Bulgaria. He was *not meddling in Greek affairs*, and it was unjust of them."[78] In other words, Stalin recalled his "percentage agreement" with Churchill in October 1944 when Churchill "offered" Romania and Bulgaria to Stalin for Greece to Britain. Now, Stalin noted that he kept his word about Greece.

Whatever the cause, between 1944 and 1947, Stalin gradually started Sovietizing Central and Eastern Europe, placing the half of the European continent east of the River Elbe under communist regimes. Until 1947–48, however, he tolerated democratic coalitions in Czechoslovakia and Hungary. Given his perspective on Soviet security, one cannot exclude the possibility that he might have accepted the "finlandization" of these two countries[79], but when in 1947 it became clear that the wartime coalition was dead, he quickly opted instead for brutally Sovietizing them. The February 1948 *coup d'état* in Prague completed the construction of the massive Soviet Bloc. In effect, Stalin created a huge buffer zone of countries ruled by communist satellite governments closely controlled by and connected to the Soviet Union through political, economic, and military ties. He was, in fact, merely following a traditional Russian military doctrine that was in place since the invasion of the country by Napoleon. The greater the distance between the West and Russia, it was assumed, the greater the security of Russia.

Just as Stalin's expansionist policy frightened the Western powers, so Stalin was frightened by Western actions. In February 1945, he received an intelligence report about a secret American–British–German meeting in Bern on the subject of German surrender, initiated by Karl Wolff, the commander of the German SS forces in Italy. The Allies had not notified the Soviet Union of their intention to accept the invitation. Stalin, having been briefed of the meeting by Soviet military intelligence, angrily informed Roosevelt that the Soviet Union knew of the meeting from which it had been excluded and, more to the point, that it knew of the British–American agreement with Marshal Kesselring "to open the front and permit the Anglo-American troops to advance to the East."[80]

Other incidents followed. The Soviet Union asked for a US$6 billion lend-lease loan in May 1945 for reconstruction; their request was rejected.[81] The Truman Administration stopped wartime lend-lease to the Soviet Union in mid-May 1945, although it continued the program for a few more months for other nations. Repayment was forgiven for Britain, but not for Russia. To Stalin, all these American actions seemed hostile and frightening.

Worse was the construction of a worldwide American network of air and naval bases in the immediate postwar years "in Greenland, Okinawa and many other places thousands of miles from our shores," as Henry Wallace, vice president of one of the Roosevelt Administrations and secretary of commerce in the Truman Government, stated in a confidential letter to President Truman in the summer of 1946. Wallace continued: "To the Russian all of the defense and security measures of the Western powers seem to have an aggressive intent . . . going far beyond the requirement of defense."[82]

On July 16, 1945, the first atomic bomb was exploded in a test at the Alamogordo Air Base in New Mexico, thus unmasking the fact of yet another American program kept secret from the Soviet ally. Roosevelt and Churchill had agreed on this strategy in September 1944 at a meeting in Roosevelt's Hyde Park home. Harry Stimson, secretary of war in both the Roosevelt and Truman Administrations, wrote a memorandum to Truman on September 11, 1945, noting the need of an agreement with the Soviet Union about

> a partnership upon a basis of cooperation and trust . . . a satisfactory international agreement respecting the control of this new force . . . For if we fail to approach them now . . . having this weapon . . . their suspicions and their distrust of our purposes and motives will increase.[83]

The Cabinet discussed the Stimson memorandum, but only three members supported it. Truman rejected the warnings of both Wallace and Stimson, and dismissed the two men from his government. Instead of trying to keep an alliance alive, as had been done during the war and planning (by Roosevelt) on keeping it afterwards, Truman and Churchill took a different lesson from history and concluded that Chamberlain's "appeasement policy" in 1938 had encouraged rather than contained the aggressor. In other words, that policy had failed. The only sensible and effective policy for the future seemed to be one of firm strength and resistance against the potential enemy.

Cold War hysteria and the containment policy

As the fighting in Europe was coming to a close, anti-communist hysteria quickly took over in American and Western intelligence and government circles. In this atmosphere, the ultimately self-sustaining Cold War rapidly emerged. Churchill sent the message to Truman to hold the American–British military line in Europe lest "communism should dominate and control all of Western Europe."[84] The fear that Stalin wanted to occupy the entire European continent began to color policy making. The US Government, particularly the military, calculated from assumptions that a World War III was entirely likely. American military plans for the next European war invoked three possible scenarios:

> Boiler was the code name for war in 1949 or earlier . . . 'Bushwhacker', the term used to denote war occurring after June 30, 1949. But both these possibilities were thought unlikely owing to the American nuclear monopoly . . . It was the third case, 'Charioteer,' meaning war in 1955 or 1956, that most concerned the American military.[85]

The main foreign policy effort of the Truman Administration was to prepare for a possible new war, and as part of this preparation, strengthen a united Western alliance system against the Soviet danger. Hysterical anti-communism, the moving force of America's European policy, is well documented by a series of small but very characteristic events. I am listing a few of them.

By 1947, the State Department, the American Federation of Labor (AFL) and the Central Intelligence Agency (CIA) were cooperating to fight communism in Europe. The AFL had "opened a European office to combat Communist influence on European labor movements late in 1945 . . . A formal liaison was established between them [State Department, AFL and CIA] in 1947."[86] Washington's paranoia was fed by diplomatic and military intelligence.[87] From France comes a typical case:

> On March 8, 1946 American army sources reported a conversation between [French communist leader] Maurice Thorez and Russian Ambassador Bogomolov in which the latter detailed Soviet plans for a Russian parachute drop of fifty divisions in Southern France and Northern Spain to seize the Pyrenees and foil American plans for a defense against invasion of Western Europe. The French Communist party was to assist Soviet forces with an internal insurrection carried out by its own paramilitary units.[88]

Two months later, on May 3, 1946, US military intelligence reported that the party "would attempt a coup" in France.[89] Secretary of War Robert P. Patterson proposed to Truman that US troops move to France "in case of serious disturbance there." General Joseph McNarney, military commander in Europe, received the authorization from Truman. At the same time, the CIA prepared a plan "to organize potential resistance groups or 'stay-behind nets' in the various West European nations to be activated in the event of Soviet military occupation of Western Europe."[90]

American intelligence even closely observed the meetings of communist German and East European émigré organizations and especially their plans in Latin America. The archives contain multiple examples of this hysterical fear. Edgar J. Hoover, the director of the FBI, informed the State Department about the *Alamania Libre* organization: "With respect to German Communists and other nationality Communist in Mexico," he stated in February 1946,

> reliable Source E indicated that during the evening of June 2, 1946, a meeting was held . . . The prominent German Communist would first return to the Russian occupied part of Germany and from there would infiltrate to the British, American, and French occupied zones for the purpose of carrying on Communist propaganda among the Germans.[91]

Naval Intelligence even sent over the strikingly insignificant information to the State Department that Aladár Tamás, executive secretary of the *Hungaria Libre* organization, "embarked on the Russian ship 'Gogol' from Manzanillo, Mexico for Vladivostok Russia."[92] Between 1945 and 1948, American consular reports were full of news about communist penetration in France and Germany.[93] In 1948, the secretary of state received the information that "we know today that Stalin has at his disposal a Nazi army under Marshall Paulus in Russia and is in very close touch with the Nazi underground inside Germany."[94]

After the failure of the Moscow meeting of the Allied ministers of foreign affairs in the spring of 1947, American consuls reported that "an all-time high" war panic erupted.[95] Even as late as 1949, McCloy thought to report to the secretary of state a seemingly crazy bit of information he received from a certain Dr Müller, the chairman of the Saarbrücken CSU organization, who had actually heard it from a certain Dr Singer, an East German politician from Leipzig said to be close to the Russian Colonel Tulpanov. McCloy quoted "that the Russians were favorably considering a revision of the Oder-Neisse line . . . [Russia wants] a common boundary with Germany . . . As soon as Russian domination over Poland is complete, Germany and Russia will partition Poland again. Germany's share will be a reward for siding with Russia against the Allies."[96] This rumor spread wide. Richard Coudenhove-Kalergi, the famous founder of the pan-European Movement, sent a letter to the director of the Office of European Affairs at the State Department in the spring of 1948, calling attention to the "danger of a Russo-German Union . . . by a new partition of Poland, accompanied by a deportation of the Polish population to Siberia."[97]

The most influential cold-warrior, Winston Churchill, masterfully spread the fear. In one of his powerful speeches in 1949, he said:

> In ten days perhaps the Soviet armour might be in Brussels . . . [they will] liquidate all outstanding personalities in every class . . . and they have got lists here but they might find quite a lot in this room . . . There is terrible danger and peril.[98]

A few months later, addressing a British audience, he declared:

> I tell you with the utmost earnestness that my own anxieties about the safety not only of the free world, but of our own hearts and homes, often remind me of the summer of 1940 . . . At the present . . . [the Soviets] have very few atomic bombs . . . [In] two or three years . . . they will be building up a large stock of them.[99]

The general fear of a Russian invasion blanketed the West from the end of the war. The state of mind was well expressed by General de Gaulle already in the spring of 1945. American ambassador Jefferson Caffery reported to the State Department after his talk with de Gaulle on April 10, 1945, that the latter feared Russia because of its policy in Eastern Europe. On May 5, the ambassador reported again that "General de Gaulle was unusually pessimistic and expressed the opinion that Russia might take over the entire continent of Europe in due course."[100] Fears increased significantly after the final collapse of postwar cooperation among the Allies in the spring of 1947.

The European fear of Soviet invasion spawned panic over the possibility that America would choose to defend Europe only at the line of the Pyrenees.

[Georges] Bidault, the leading French politician, minister of foreign affairs or prime minister during the postwar years, spoke with General Douglas MacArthur and General Bull on January 29, 1948, telling them "of the fear and 'psychosis' existing in France over the belief that the US did not plan to defend Europe in case of Soviet aggression but would rather establish a defensive perimeter at the Pyrenees and England.[101]

As with the American policy shifts—and the two developments are of course linked—the final collapse of postwar Allied cooperation happened gradually. The meeting of the Council of Allied Foreign Ministers in Moscow, March 10–April 24, 1947 proved to be the straw that broke the camel's back. The council, established at the Potsdam Conference of the victorious great powers as the forum for exploring and hammering out joint agreements, had basically functioned well up until this point. During the 44 plenary sessions of the Moscow meeting, however, it became clear that joint agreement on a peace treaty with Germany would never be obtained. "Agreement was made impossible at Moscow," George Marshall wrote in his report on the meeting,

> because, in our view, the Soviet Union insisted upon proposals which would have established in Germany a centralized government, adapted to the seizure of absolute control of a country which would be doomed economically through inadequate area and excessive population, and would be mortgaged to turn over a large part of its production as reparations, principally to the Soviet Union. In another form the same mortgage upon Austria was claimed by the Soviet Delegation.

A few lines later, Marshall added, "Charges were made by the Soviet Delegation and interpretation given the Potsdam and other agreements, which varied completely from the facts as understood or as factually known by the American Delegation."[102] Stalin, it seemed, wanted to paralyze Germany and exploit it on a permanent basis. This was rejected by the US. With the great powers unable to agree about the peace treaty with Germany and Austria, cooperation failed for good and the wartime alliance ended.

American policy now took a new turn, reflecting the ideas of the Soviet expert George Kennan, then posted to Moscow as chargé d'affaires for Secretary of State George Marshall. On February 22, 1946, in his famous "long telegram" to Marshall, Kennan gave an analysis of Soviet foreign policy and specific recommendations for countering it. It pays to quote at length from the telegram since its views became the official program of the Truman Administration. In the first part, Kennan summarized the premises of postwar Soviet ideology as

> put forward by official propaganda machine . . . A) The USSR still lives in antagonistic "capitalist encirclement" with which in the long run there can be no permanent peaceful coexistence . . . B) Capitalist world is beset with

internal conflicts, inherent in nature of capitalist society. These conflicts are insoluble by means of peaceful compromise . . . C) Internal conflicts of capitalism inevitably generate wars. Wars thus generated may be of two kinds: intra-capitalist wars between two capitalist states, and wars of intervention against socialist world. Smart capitalists, vainly seeking escape from inner conflicts of capitalism, incline toward the latter . . . .

Kennan pointed out that Stalin still believed what he had said in 1927 to a delegation of American workers:

In course of further development of international revolution there will emerge two centers of world significance: a socialist center . . . and a capitalist center . . . battle between these two centers for "command of the world economy will decide fate of capitalism and of communism in entire world."

After describing Soviet ideological premises, Kennan outlined the resulting Soviet policies:

(A) Everything must be done to advance relative strength of the USSR as factor in international society . . . (B) Soviet efforts, and those of Russia's friends abroad, must be directed toward deepening and exploiting of differences and conflicts between capitalist powers. If these eventually deepen into an "imperialist" war, this war must be turned into revolutionary upheavals.

In Part Two of the telegram, Kennan critiques the Soviet view, but he also notes that the Soviet psychology was in part a product of Russian experience stretching back for centuries: "At bottom of Kremlin's neurotic view of world affairs," the document remarks, "is traditional and instinctive Russian sense of insecurity," especially with respect to the more economically advanced countries of the West. As a consequence, "they [the Russians] have learned," Kennan states, "to seek security only in patient but deadly struggle for total destruction of rival power, never in compacts and compromises with it." Kennan offered a portrait of a genuinely antagonistic Soviet stance that would adopt subversive political techniques in foreign countries in order to secure total destruction of a rival. But Kennan also believed the problem could be solved without open war, not least because

Soviet power, unlike that of Hitlerite Germany, is neither schematic nor adventuristic . . . It does not take unnecessary risks . . . [and] it is highly sensitive to logic of force. For this reason it can easily withdraw—and usually does—when strong resistance is encountered . . . Thus, if the adversary has sufficient force and makes clear his readiness to use it, he rarely has to do so.[103]

The concept of containment, which would govern American foreign policy regarding the Soviet Union until the collapse of communism and the Soviet state, was now on the table. After it was accepted, Kennan repeated his analysis and rec-ommendations in an anonymous article (signed "X") in the influential journal *Foreign Affairs*. That article appeared in the summer of 1947.[104] In a 1996 interview Kennan clarified his position: "I didn't suspect them [the Soviets] of any desire to launch an attack on us. This was right after the war, and it was absurd to suppose [such a step]."[105] Nevertheless, he did not say *that* in 1946–47, and from 1947 onwards, the determinant factor of US policy became the Cold War competition, economic, political, and armament warfare in a time of fragile peace.

From Moscow, Kennan also sent an important memorandum to the State Department about the American policy in France. This archival document, dated April 1, 1946, reveals what the long telegram only implies, that Kennan was think-ing of anti-Soviet policy and Western integration as related issues:

> Russian influence in French affairs must be considered a major impediment in the path of American policies toward France ... The basic Soviet aim is to weaken the power-potential of all of Western Europe, in order to increase the relative power of Russia in Western European affairs ... [keep Western Europe] *unintegrated* ... [and block the road of any power] capable of pulling *Western European countries together into an effective regional society*.[106]

One of the major formulations of this new policy, the so-called Truman Doctrine, was presented by President Truman in a speech before a joint session of the US Congress on March 12, 1947. On February 21, 1947, the British Government had officially notified the US of the decision to suspend British financial aid to Greece and Turkey. This was a historic message, the recognition of the end of British world power and leadership that was handed over to the US as the manifestation of a new bipolar world order.[107] At the time Greece was fending off a strong communist guerrilla army and was threatened by the possibility of a second civil war, while Turkey faced Russian pressure to share control of the Dardanelles. The Greek Government had formally requested assistance from the US. Truman's speech to Congress was addressing this issue. It outlined the policy of assisting countries endangered by communist "armed minorities or by outside pressures." "The seeds of totalitarian regimes," Truman said, "are nurtured by misery and want ... They reach their full growth when the hope of a people for a better life has died. We must keep that hope alive." Arguing that assistance was imperative, Truman requested US$400 million (about US$40 billion today) for that program. He said that Greece needed assistance "to survive as a free nation."[108]

Undersecretary of State Dean Acheson explained that if either Greece or Turkey were to fall, a "domino effect" would be generated, especially in Asia, and from that moment on the idea of a "domino effect" determined American foreign policy.[109] Winston Churchill, employing this concept in 1950, to build support for war in Korea, took it a step further, suggesting that local communist victories would encour-age the Soviets to start World War III: "What the Communists have begun in Korea should not end in their triumph. If that were happen a third world war ... would certainly be forced upon us."[110] The important think tank, the Brookings Institutions in Washington DC, had spoken that time about a "piecemeal or wholesale absorption [of Western Europe] by the Soviet Union."[111] The Korean War led to an acceleration of fear from Soviet invasion.

President Truman declared on June 27, 1950 that "the attack against Korea makes it plain beyond all doubt that Communism has passed beyond the use of subversion to conquer independent nations and will now use armed invasion and war."[112] The fear of spreading communism generated the attempt to create a strong and large anti-communist alliance.

This same political understanding motivated the most important postwar American initiative in Europe, the Marshall Plan. Secretary of State Marshall, having returned from Moscow in the summer of 1947 with the conviction that further cooperation with the Soviet Union would be futile, asked Kennan to set up what became the Policy Planning Staff at the State Department. The Kennan group presented a memorandum to the also newly established Foreign Aid Committee suggesting "to combat not communism, but the economic maladjustment which makes European society vulnerable . . . and which Russian communism is now exploiting." A group of policy makers shared this view, among them State Department Undersecretary for Economic Affairs William Clayton. On March 27, 1947, after having returned from Europe, Clayton wrote an influential memorandum to Marshall and Acheson, recommending an aid package of US$6–7 billion per year for three years to cope with the "economic, social and political chaos" of Western Europe. "This three-year grant to Europe," the memo argued, "should be based on a European plan which the principal European nations, headed by the UK, France and Italy, should work out. Such a plan should be based on a *European economic federation.*"[113]

US officials decided to go public with their advocacy of European unification. A kind of turning point was the influential speech on American interest in European unification given by John Foster Dulles at the Waldorf Astoria Hotel, on January 17, 1947. Dulles introduced the famous slogan that "Europe must federate or perish." Quickly, leading journals began publishing major articles on the topic. On January 27, a *Christian Science Monitor* commentary on the speech stated: "The rapidly developing concept of European federation is running head-on into the colossal East–West struggle for world power and influence." Benjamin Sumner Welles, diplomat and former undersecretary of state, argued in the *Washington Post* on February 5, "Europe desperately needs some effective form of political and economic federation." In the *New York Herald Tribune*, on March 20, one of the most influential journalists of the era, Walter Lippmann, called for a march for a European Economic Union. On April 5, in the same daily, he painted a highly exaggerated picture of the European economic situation:

> The crisis is developing because none of the leading nations of Europe— Great Britain, France, Italy, Germany—is recovering from the war, or has any reasonable prospect of recovery . . . The truth is that political and economic measures on a scale which no responsible statesman has yet ventured to hint

at will be needed in the next year or so. To prevent the crisis which will otherwise engulf Europe ... the measures will have to be very large—in Europe no less than an economic union and over here no less than the equivalent of a rival of lend-lease.[114]

Members of the US Congress and the British Parliament added their voices to the chorus. Senators William Fulbright and Elbert Thomas moved a resolution to the American Senate, and a similar one by Hale Boggs moved to the House on March 21: "The Congress favors the creation of a United States of Europe." On April 7, Senator Fulbright argued in the Senate that "this country cannot tolerate the expansion of Russia to the point where she controls, directly or indirectly, all the resources and manpower of Europe, Asia and Africa." The Congress issued a bipartisan call for the State Department "to take active steps to promote European union."[115] The British Parliament echoed the same idea in the summer of 1947: Anthony Eden's colleague Peter Thorneycroft and the Labor representative R.W.G. Mackay equally spoke about "defeating communism by building up a great area of prosperity," adding that to work out "a political structure for Europe ... We can build up ... [in the next two years] a *Federation of Western Europe.*"[116]

The Cold War hysteria dominated American policy from the second half of the 1940s until the early 1960s. The former Secretary of State Dean Acheson, at his speech at the University of Connecticut, repeated even in 1963: "The division of Germany and the continued occupation of East-Germany by Soviet troops ... is for the purpose of bringing all Germany under Soviet influence. Such a result would ... make Russia's will dominant in Europe."[117]

The Marshall Plan and the first steps towards European integration

The political soil had been well-prepared. Charles Bohlen, the special assistant who drafted Secretary Marshall's famous commencement speech delivered June 5, 1947 at Harvard University, stressed that the necessary condition of any aid would be its capacity to contribute to "an overall plan for economic cooperation by the Europeans themselves, perhaps an *economic federation* to be worked out over three or four years." Bohlen had derived his position from his reading of the memoranda by Kennan and Clayton.[118] The speech, which of course was announcing what came to be known as the Marshall Plan, used a diplomatic language.[119] I quote:

> It is logical that the United States should do whatever it is able to do to assist in the return of normal economic health in the world, without which there can be no political stability and no assured peace. Our policy is directed not against any country or doctrine but against hunger, poverty, desperation and chaos. Its purpose should be the revival of a working economy in the world so as to permit the emergence of political and social conditions in which free institutions can exist ... Any governments ... political parties, or groups

which seek to perpetuate human misery in order to profit from it politically or otherwise will encounter the opposition of the United States. It is already evident that, before the United States Government can proceed much further in its efforts to alleviate the situation and help start the European world on its way to recovery, there must be some agreement among the countries of Europe as to the requirements of the situation and the part those countries themselves will take in order to give proper effect to whatever action might be undertaken by this Government. It would be neither fitting nor efficacious for this Government to undertake to draw up unilaterally a program designed to place Europe on its feet economically. This is the business of the Europeans. The initiative, I think, must come from Europe. The role of this country should consist of friendly aid in the drafting of a European program and of later support of such a program so far as it may be practical for us to do so. The program should be a joint one, agreed to by a number, if not all European nations.[120]

The US until the spring of 1947 already provided more than US$11 billion grants, loans, food, and other kinds of shipments to Europe. Now the Marshall Plan offered a four-year major aid program to any of the twenty-two European countries willing to accept its conditions, the principle of which was cooperation in joint planning under the auspices of a new, American-initiated entity called the Committee of European Cooperation (renamed the Organisation for European Economic Cooperation, or OEEC, in April 1948). Seventeen countries accepted the invitation to join the program. They estimated that they would need US$29 billion in aid, a figure that the State Department scaled down to US$22 billion. Speaking to Congress on December 19, 1947, President Truman formally requested US$17 billion to finance the European Recovery Program, as the aid program was officially called; in the end, Congress approved US$13 billion (today about US$130 billion). The program became law on April 3, 1948. At the official celebration, Truman said, according to the *New York Times*, that "this measure is America's answer to the challenge facing the free world."[121]

The Marshall Plan consumed 2.1 percent of the American GNP in 1948, 2.4 percent in 1949, and then declined to 1.5 percent between 1948 and 1951. It averaged 1.8 percent of US national income (GNP). Britain received 23 percent and France 20.6 percent of all Marshall Aid. Although the total amount of aid over all the years of the program's existence equaled just 2 percent of the combined European GDP over the same period, in the crucially important first year the aid actually contributed 5–14 percent of GDP.[122]

Although this financial aid helped to cover the huge trade deficits that accumulated in Europe in the postwar years, nevertheless, over time that outcome would prove to be less important than the positive effects of cooperation among receiver countries, and such cooperation was the main prerequisite for receiving aid. All reconstruction plans had to be coordinated through the OEEC. Restrictions to trade with OEEC members had to be gradually abandoned. After the first three months,

60 percent of trade within the OEEC had already been liberalized; by June 1959, the figure was 89 percent.[123] That was revolutionary news after more than half-a-century of tariff wars and trade restrictions in Europe.

One of the most important steps on the road of European cooperation, also generated by the Marshall Plan, was the Agreement for European Payments and Compensations signed on October 16, 1948, and transformed into the European Payment Union in September 1950. This institution existed for more than eight years until currency convertibility was reestablished and the European Monetary Agreement was put into place. The Payment Union multilateralized bilateral trade by creating an automatic mechanism for the settlement of net surpluses and deficits within the OEEC. To handle the transactions, the Bank of International Settlement was revitalized.[124] With its assistance, the increase of trade among Marshall Plan recipient countries grew by leaps and bounds, from US\$10 billion in 1950 to US\$23 billion in 1959.[125]

A few months after the declaration of the Marshall Plan, Allen Dulles, former Swiss Director of OSS, the American intelligence agency and predecessor of CIA, published a book on the Marshall Plan and replaced the diplomatic language with plain talk:

> If the Marshall Plan is realized, we will be acting in a broader field to contain the advance of communism in Europe . . . We adopted that policy not out of charity but for our own protection . . . [We do not want to allow] a great power, with a system incompatible with ours, to overrun Europe . . . Europe today is particularly vulnerable to communism . . . Separately they will not be strong enough, even with American aid, to work out a livable future . . . The United States is the only country . . . which can really help to bring the European states together in a union which will be a defensive bulwark against the advance of communism . . . [The Marshall Plan] is not a philanthropic enterprise . . . It is an integral part of American policy. It is based on our view of the requirement of American security . . . This is the only peaceful course now open to us which may answer the communist challenge to our way of life and national security.[126]

Dulles articulated the hope and goal of the Truman Administration that if the European countries "sat down together . . . [they might] step nearer to the *establishment of a United States of Europe*."[127]

Behind the scene, in the mind of its founders, as Allen Dulles openly declared, the Marshall Plan indeed had a definite political goal to establish a West European federation. According to the most vehement representatives of this idea, the outcome of the Marshall Plan has to be political integration. This idea was openly debated six times at the United States Congress, which discussed the various problems of the Marshall Plan. Senator J. William Fulbright, who belonged to the extremist wing "thought that the E[uropean] R[ecovery] P[rogram] should be used as an instrument of European political unification . . . There was a sharp clash between [Secretary] Acheson and Fulbright on February 11, 1949 about the necessity of political unification. Acheson emphasized that there had to be more progress on an economic level before true political integration could be achieved."[128] This idea of economic integration as a road to political integration was already present during the formation of the program that was later called the Marshall Plan. When Undersecretary Clayton returned from Europe in May 1947 and first suggested the initiation of an aid program for three years that Europe has to work up together and at the end has to lead to a federation, his idea was based on the Benelux customs union. George Kennan, the most influential head of the Policy Planning Staff at the State Department, suggested the establishment of the formation of a West European customs union and a multilateral clearing system in his memorandum of 1947.[129]

On October 31, 1949, Paul Hoffman, the head of the Marshall Aid Program Administration, addressed the OEEC Council in Paris. He openly stated that aiding the economic recovery

> means nothing less than an integration of the Western European Economy . . .
> the building of an expanding economy in Western Europe through economic integration . . . a single large market within which quantitative restrictions on the movement of goods, monetary barriers to the flow of payments, and eventually, all tariffs are permanently swept away . . . This would make it possible for Europe to improve its competitive positions in the world . . . This is a vital objective . . . This brings me to our final suggestion, which has to do with the path by which this goal of integration may be reached. I have repeatedly referred to the creation of a single European market . . . I have made a number of references to the urgency of starting immediately on this program of integration.[130]

This was a clear program realized by the Treaty of Rome in 1957.

"There were parts of the speech," concludes Ernst van der Beugel, secretary to the Dutch national delegation at the Paris conference on the Marshall Plan and then minister of foreign affairs in 1957–58, "which could lead to the belief that integration in the political and institutional sense was the ultimate aim . . . In short America has the power, if it will be patient to impel Europe along the road of real integration."[131]

During the preparatory meeting of the countries that accepted the invitation, thirteen countries made a statement that they are going to establish a Study Committee to analyze the possibility of the customs union. The US Paris embassy, Ambassador Caffery and Undersecretary Clayton who arrived in Paris in July 1947, permanently consulted with the delegations of the participating countries and tried pushing them to create the common market. An influential American group, including Kennan and Clayton, arrived in Paris in August 1947 and concluded that the European countries have reached a disappointing agreement. The US strengthened its push, especially between April 1948 (foundation of OEEC) and September 1950 (the signature of the European Payment Union). "It is this period that the impact of the US on every phase of European cooperation was the strongest than in any other period." The US waited for joint recommendations, prepared by the OEEC. They introduced the "restricted committee principle," giving the authorization for four members of the Commission to make the final decisions, i.e. a "denationalized group" gained a "major and delicate responsibility." They have to analyze the national plans, evaluate them and then decide upon the allocation of American aid. Economic sovereignty, concluded Beugel, was essentially broken.[132]

The first jointly prepared annual program was presented to Paul Hoffman in 1948 who called it an unprecedented achievement. "This is the first time in history that the free people of Europe have cooperated in the preparation of an economic program embracing nineteen separate political units."[133] The House Committee on Foreign Affairs reported on the extension of the Recovery Program in March 1949 and also agreed "The participating nations have moved toward stronger and wider cooperation." Nevertheless, the Committee also expressed some doubts: "The only question in the Committee's mind was this: is the rate of development rapid enough?"[134] Although restrictive quotas were removed on 30 percent of trade and, most of the quantitative restrictions were eliminated on raw materials and other essential supplies, by January 1950 the decision was made on 50–60 percent trade liberalization and, Beugel concluded, "it fell again short of American expectations . . . [Although] it brought intra-European economic cooperation to an unprecedented level in an extremely short span of time. It made the participating countries," Beugel continued,

> extremely sophisticated in the problems of each other's economies and politics. They began to think in European terms . . . Germany was brought back as a partner at the conference table of Western Europe . . . The Marshall Plan and the work of OEEC have made an indispensable contribution, even if the immediate results of their work were disappointing against the light of initial expectations . . . However, OEEC has not lived up to many hopes and expectations . . . The intimate union of economies . . . had not materialized under the OEEC.[135]

Europe, after decades of economic nationalism, confrontation, and warfare was not ready yet to resign major elements of national sovereignty and going down the road of integration. United Europe was not created, particularly because the leading participant who had the biggest share of the American aid and was singled out by the US administration as leader of European integration, Britain, resisted the most. "No single fact has been so harmful to the possibility of the development of OEEC as an instrument for integration," stated the insider former Dutch foreign minister, "as the British refusal to commit itself to full partnership with the continent of Europe."[136]

Between 1947 and 1953, the Cold War and US assistance for a West European integration process were the *leit motifs* of the foreign policy parts of President Truman's State of the Union speeches. His January 8, 1951 address portrayed the

Korean War as "part of the attempt of the Russian Communist dictatorship to take over the world, step by step . . . . The Soviet imperialists," Truman continued,

> have two ways of going about their destructive work. They use the method of subversion and internal revolution, and they use the method of external aggression . . . All free nations are exposed and all are in peril. Their only security lies in banding together. No one nation can find protection in a self-ish search for a safe haven.

The following year's address warned that "the Soviet Union is increasing its armed might . . . The world still walks in the shadow of another war . . . We should do all we can to help and encourage the move toward a *strong and united Europe*." Truman's last State of the Union speech, on January 7, 1953, looked back to the rise of Cold War conflict and explained that the

> Soviet atomic explosion in the fall of 1949 . . . [was responsible for] stimulating the planning for our program of defense mobilization . . . In July of 1950, we began our rapid rearmament . . . We also needed strength along the outer edges of the free world . . . Now the countries of Europe are moving rapidly towards political and economic unity, changing the map of Europe in more hopeful ways than it has been changed for 500 years.[137]

Just months after taking office, President Dwight Eisenhower expressed exactly the same interest in European integration when, on June 15, 1953, he wrote in his letter to the chairmen of the Foreign Affairs Committees of the Congress:

> While in Europe, I watched with keen interest the efforts to work out the first steps toward *European federation* . . . This Community seems to me to be the most hopeful and constructive development so far toward the economic and political integration of Europe.

Chairman Alexander Wiley, in his answer of June 16, 1953, recalled: "It was in 1949 that the Economic Cooperation Act was amended to state that it was the policy of the 'people of the United States to encourage the unification of Europe.'" He added that in 1950, the act had been amended again to emphasize the American policy "to encourage the further unification of Europe." Robert B. Chiperfield, chairman of the House Foreign Affairs Committee, also responding to the president, underlined "that the nations of Europe must pull together to achieve not only military integration but political federation." In its resolution of June 16, 1953, the House Foreign Affairs Committee stated: "The Congress has repeatedly expressed its belief in the paramount importance of such integration, having stated in the Mutual Security Act of 1952 . . . The Congress welcomes the recent progress in political federation, military integration, and economic unification in Europe."[138]

According to American view, the Marshall Plan failed. As the economist and soon presidential adviser Walt Whitney Rostow summed up in 1960: "The Marshall Plan did not succeed in moving Western Europe radically towards unity."[139]

Dangerous conflicts from 1948

The fronts were now frozen. Europe was divided into two separate and hostile parts, a democratic capitalist West and a communist Soviet-controlled East. This division, after 1947–48, seemed permanent. Violent confrontation became an everyday possibility and danger. Nowhere was this more evident than in defeated Germany where, when the Western powers, in connection with their decision to establish an independent and equal West German state, initiated the West German currency reform, Stalin answered, on June 24, 1948, with the bold provocation of closing the surface roads from West Germany to the Western zones of Berlin.[140] For two million West Berliners, an American airlift delivered food, coal, and all kinds of supply. This rescue began on June 26, with the delivery of food and coal by two cargo planes. In one year 200,000 flights delivered 13,000 tons of goods daily to West Berlin. An American Embassy report described this situation as follows:

> The supply of the most essential necessities to the Berlin population depends almost exclusively on deliveries from outside. The total coal, about one-third of the required electric power, and approximately 99 percent of food requirements are imported from the rest of Germany or from abroad.[141]

Any Soviet military action, even accidental, against American planes and deliveries could have triggered World War III.

The original punitive stance of the US towards German industry had already started shifting, as has been noted. In the summer of 1947, the Level of Industry Plan, which until then had strictly limited German heavy industrial output in the previous years, allowed German output to reach the prewar level. Then, on November 8, 1948, American–British Bizonal Law No. 75 included a commitment to revitalize the industries of the Ruhr. Finally, on January 12, 1949, 163 German plants, including the Thyssen steel works in Hamborn, were removed from the list of factories slated for dismantling.

Tensions continued mounting in 1949. In April, the US, with Canada and fifteen European countries, established a new Western military association, the North Atlantic Treaty Organization (NATO). In May of that year, from the three Western occupation zones in Germany the German Federal Republic was created. The Soviet Union and its satellites bitterly attacked the US for dividing Germany. The American answer blamed the Soviet Union for deliberately destroying great power cooperation and sabotaging former joint decision-making.[142] The world was shifted to the brink of military confrontation.

The danger became imminent with the shocking surprise of 1949, the *Pervaya Molniya*, or First Lighting, the August explosion of the first Soviet atomic bomb.

The American monopoly of the most devastating weapon of mass destruction had come to an abrupt end. Less than a year later, on June 25, 1950, Stalin's North Korean ally crossed the 38th parallel and launched a powerful military attack against South Korea. On June 30, Truman ordered American military intervention in Korea and sent over nearly 90 percent of the 340,000 troops that comprised the United Nations Command. China intervened to help North Korea and the resulting three-year fight pushed the world to the brink of a third world war. Four weeks after the American intervention in Korea, John J. McCloy, the American high commissioner in Germany, announced the need for German rearmament. The War Department warned American commanders in Europe within days of the outbreak of hostilities that the North Korean attack "may indicate [a] riskier Soviet policy henceforth of using Satellite armed forces in attempting to reach limited objectives for the expansion of Communism."[143]

Panic flooded Europe. Konrad Adenauer, now chancellor of West Germany, told McCloy: "The fate of the world will not be decided in Korea, but in the heart of Europe. I am convinced that Stalin has the same plan for Europe as for Korea. What is happening there is a *dress rehearsal* for what is in store for us here."[144] Indeed, the attack "was widely viewed as a rehearsal for a comparable effort in Europe."[145] Churchill called for "the immediate creation of a unified European army, under the authority of a European minister of defense."[146] The idea of organizing joint defense, already in the air in Europe since the beginning of the Cold War, acquired new urgency.

The question of British leadership of integration

American efforts to push the West European countries into a united, federal state were based on the understandable belief of British leadership. Britain, after all, enjoyed the greatest prestige after the war. The country's lone, unbending, and self-sacrificing fight against Hitler, coupled with her spectacular past as the first industrial nation and world economic leader, had made her a natural leader in Western Europe. Europeans, peoples, and governments alike, asked: "Was she not a center of an immense Empire . . . Was the sterling area not the biggest currency area in the world?"[147]

Consecutive American administrations attempted to convince the island nation to take over the lead in integrating Europe. The British Embassy in Washington reported: "All [US] administration leaders cherished the vision of a Europe with British leadership."[148] Scholarly work confirms the accuracy of that point of view: Secretary of State Acheson is reported to have said that he "had made it a personal mission to convince Britain to join the European Coal and Steel Community . . . Together with President Truman, he was convinced long-term US national interests required that Britain be a founding member of an integrated Europe."[149] The Truman Administration "in the early post-war years . . . pressed for UK leadership in Europe." Averell Harriman and Paul Hoffman even urged bringing pressure on the Attlee Government.[150] President Eisenhower continued this effort, and he did not hesitate to lecture the British political elite on the great advantage of the establishment of a workable European federation.[151] The Eisenhower Administration urged a "federalist solution." Once such a Europe was built, Eisenhower said in November 1955, at a meeting of the US National Security Council, that the US would be able to "sit back and relax somewhat."[152]

American attempts to pressure Britain to join the integration process already under way, and to lead it, started at the preparation of the Marshall Plan and continued into the 1960s, but with little success. The diplomat George W. Ball, not long before he became undersecretary of state, indirectly expressed American disappointment with British hesitancy in a speech in New York on January 1960: "I think it clear that most Americans would have been happier if other European nations had joined with the Six in the creation of the Common Market."[153]

Two years after the Treaty of Rome bound many of those European nations into the European Economic Community (EEC), President John F. Kennedy stressed that the interests of the US would be served best if Britain were also to join the EEC. At a meeting, he said that the US would even accept economic loss for the sake of great political coherence, such as would be given by British accession.[154] As the well-informed Arthur Schlesinger recalled, the Kennedy Administration believed that if Britain were to join, "the Market could become the basis for a true political federation." Kennedy urged Prime Minister Harold Macmillan to join the EEC.[155] Moreover, he pushed Britain "by refusing to support British requirements [. . .] the Kennedy Administration placed Macmillan in a political bind." The US expressed hostility towards the European Free Trade Association (EFTA), the British-initiated rival European free trade zone, and they made it clear that the British policy may endanger Churchill's continuously nurtured "special relationship" with America. In his review on North Atlantic problems, Dean Acheson, who returned to active politics as advisor for President Kennedy in European affairs, expressed the view that American pressure will work, "particularly if the United States [i]s dealing ever more closely with growing strength on the continent" and help any pro-European trend in Britain. Indeed, in early 1960, Macmillan established an interdepartmental committee to reexamine British orientation. The committee, headed by Sir Frank Lee, suggested a fundamental policy change in May 1960: pursuit of membership in the European Community.[156] William Fulbright, the influential senator, reiterated the American position in 1962: "Only Britain [. . .] has the long experience, the ancient institutions and the over-all political maturity for leading Europe into a new era."[157] In July 1966, top officials of President Johnson's State Department asked Ball, then responsible for European affairs, to advocate "a presidential push on [British Premier Harold] Wilson toward UK membership of the Common Market."

The US was not alone in dreaming of British leadership of an integration process. The Benelux countries also strongly wanted Britain's participation, and they tried several times to convince the British Government to sign on. Paul-Henri Spaak, the leading Belgian politician and member of the government-in-exile in London who later served as minister of foreign affairs and prime minister of Belgium, had several meetings and talks with Churchill both during and after the war. He recalled: "The idea of an organization of Western Europe did not appeal to [Churchill]. My plans for economic integration seemed to him, I believe, a pipe-dream."[158] Ernest Bevin, foreign secretary in the postwar Labour Government, also rejected Spaak's initiative at the end of 1945. *The Economist* rightly mentioned in December 1951: "In French and Benelux eyes, Britain is still regarded as the missing component, without which the Schuman community [ECSC] is in danger of German domination."[159] Even Germany wanted its former arch-enemy to join the Community. In 1960, Walter Hallstein, the German president of the European Commission, spoke in his address to the European Parliament of the "historical importance" of opening the door to "other European states, and in particular Great Britain." In his speech, he publicly pressed Britain "to accept this standing invitation."[160] Six years later, Chancellor Kurt G. Kiesinger of Germany, speaking at the Bundestag stressed again that "the Community of Six is open for all European states that accept its goals. We would especially welcome the joining of Great Britain."[161] Britain, however, resisted.

Churchill, among the first to suggest forming a United States of Europe in his famous Zurich speech of September 1946, nevertheless qualified his call with the statement that "we are with Europe, but not of it. We are linked, but not comprised. We are interested and associated, but not absorbed." Britain, he promised, would help the United States of Europe from outside, not as a member from within.[162] His specific positions on European integration varied according to the political situation. Before the war erupted, he proposed a union with France, and he was definitely integrationist between 1940 and 1943. One of his letters to Eden during the war spoke about the European family of nations that might act together under a Council of Europe and "looked forward to a United States of Europe."[163] Three months after his Zurich speech, he published an article outlining a program towards unification that started with the removal of tariffs and continued with the introduction of a common currency and defense. He even spoke of common passports and postage stamps[164] and initiated the Hague Conference of May 1948, from which emerged the Council of Europe Assembly in the summer of 1949. And on August 11, 1950, at the Consultative Assembly of the Council, he called for "the immediate creation of a unified European army, under the authority of a European minister of defence, subject to European democratic control."[165]

Arguing from the content of several of Churchill's speeches, his biographer Roy Jenkins, a dedicated Europeanist and former president of the European Commission, rejects the view that Churchill was not a firmly "committed British European": "Was he merely telling others to unite, or was he willing to do so too? The evidence is generally held to be against a Churchill commitment to full British participation. I find it conflicting."[166] In support of his position Jenkins highlights, for example, the fact that Churchill, in his Hague Conference speech, treated Britain as part of the core of Europe in the formation of economic and military relationships: "It would have been difficult in these circumstances to add, or even to harbour the thought, but of course I am only talking for others and not of Britain's unique position outside."[167]

This is not convincing. Churchill's British ego counterbalanced his clear recognition of the necessity of European unification and of British participation in it. On November 28, 1949, Churchill said:

> Britain is an integral part of Europe, and we mean to play our part in the revival of her prosperity and greatness. But Britain cannot be thought of as a single state in isolation. She is the founder and centre of a worldwide Empire and Commonwealth. We shall never do anything to weaken the ties of blood, of sentiment and tradition and common interest which unite us with the other members of the British family of nations.

Quoting this statement and Churchill's explanation that *together* with the associated Commonwealth Britain still might be an integral part of Europe, Jenkins argues for Churchill's firm European commitment, and yet Jenkins also acknowledges that the same Churchill developed the concepts of Britain's Atlantic commitment and of its special relationship with the US and the "English speaking people." Speaking about the Schuman Plan in June 1950, he flatly clarified his preferences: "Everyone knows that that [the entity composed of the Empire and the Commonwealth] stands first in all our thoughts. First, there is the Empire and Commonwealth; secondly, the fraternal association of the English-speaking world; and thirdly . . . the revival of united Europe . . . ."[168]

The Empire was in the state of dissolving, of course, but Churchill, along with the majority of the British political elite, still imagined Britain with its Commonwealth as an equal in the "three larger groupings of the Western democracies": Europe, the Commonwealth, and the US.[169] The postwar Labour Government and its foreign secretary Ernest Bevin basically shared the same views and flirted with an independent British role in their own European politics. "In three important meetings held between 10 and 17 August 1945, Bevin revealed to his own advisers and to representatives of the Treasury and the Board of Trade what has been called his Grand Design."[170] Bevin described a British-led alliance plan from the Aegean Sea to the Baltic, from Greece and the Mediterranean to the Low Countries and Scandinavia. He spoke about the foundation of a "Western Union." At the end of 1945, he thought, the postwar world would consist of "three Monroes," or spheres of interest.[171] Beside the American and Soviet "Monroes," Britain would have its own as well. This "middle-of-the-planet" sphere would be a British-led Europe.

Whatever his dreams of empire, Bevin's ideas about Britain's leadership role in Europe actually often changed. In the summer of 1946, he ordered a Cabinet paper on a Western European customs union, and he even broached the idea of such a union with his French counterpart, Georges Bidault. Britain signed the Dunkirk Treaty with France in March 1947, and Bevin planned to form a British–French economic committee. In September of that year he visited French premier Paul Ramadier in Paris and described an even more grandiose dream: France and Britain with their "vast colonial possessions . . . could, if they acted together, be as powerful as either the Soviet Union or the United States . . . [and] occupy in the world a place equivalent to that of Russia and of the United States."[172] Speaking on the Western European defense pact in the House of Commons on January 22, 1948, he stated:

> I believe therefore that the moment is ripe for consolidation of Western Europe . . . We in Britain can no longer stand outside Europe and insist that our problems and position are quite separate from those of our European neighbors . . . [N]ow we should be able to carry out our task in a way which will show clearly that we are not subservient to the United States of America.[173]

A defense pact was thus quite acceptable, but when the subject was a form of integration that could have given outside control over British economic policy, Bevin was more cautious. Thus the record of a closed cabinet meeting a few years later documents him calling Robert Schuman's European integration plan a *Schumania* and urging action against it: "If we do nothing," he said, "Schumania will spread. Better that we shd. [sic] take initiative."[174]

From the summer of 1945 until 1948, Bevin was enthusiastic in planning, or better to say, improvising a grandiose British European design, but in reality, nothing was done. "An obvious possibility is that Bevin was never fully serious about European integration and that the 'Grand Design' was little more than impractical pipe-dream of a dilettante in foreign affairs."[175] Nevertheless, there certainly were more serious considerations behind inaction. Regardless of party affiliation, from the end of the war until the early 1960s, Churchill, Bevin, and other leading British politicians had ambiguous, oft-conflicting views about their relationship with the continent. A telling episode happened after the US launched the Marshall Aid program. Bevin, at a meeting with the plan's American representative, William L. Clayton, protested "that the new policy of providing aid to western Europe as an integrated bloc rather than individual countries would mean that Britain would now be *'just another European country.'"*[176] Bevin considered Britain *primus inter pares* in Europe and also a special Atlantic partner of the US. He supported a European customs union in the second half of 1947, as noted earlier, but later he opposed this idea. Similarly to Churchill, he held perennially mixed and ambivalent views.[177]

Probably more important, the economic ministers of the British Cabinet and the British Board of Trade genuinely opposed any kind of economic unification with the European continent. They considered Britain a great power, winner of the war, center of the Commonwealth and the Empire. The Board of Trade lived in the past, in a world of trade relations between industrial countries, on the one hand, and food and raw material producers, on the other, and it did not realize that the modern, postwar economy was bringing a changing division of labor. "A Customs Union," the board maintained, "consisting of a number of primary producing countries with a wide diversity of unexploited resources would be likely to be to the advantage of the United Kingdom." Bevin, in a letter to Prime Minister Attlee on September 5, 1947, clearly expressed his goal "to reestablish Britain's position in the world and to free Britain from financial dependence on the United States. One way to do this was . . . drawing on the raw-material resources of the Commonwealth and Empire." The British Cabinet, accordingly, set up an Interdepartmental Committee on September 25, "to consider the feasibility of a customs union with the colonies or even with the Commonwealth."[178] But a customs union with Europe was off the table. In fact, a governmental committee concluded in the summer of 1947 that "it is not our interest to encourage the idea of a European Customs Union of which the United Kingdom would be a member . . . A general West European customs union is out of the question."[179]

Even Harold Macmillan, the "most Europeanist" Tory, was reported to have stressed that "the Empire must always [have] first preference for us: Europe must come second in a specially favoured position."[180] The National Executive Committee of the British Labour Party published a fifteen-page statement entitled "European Unity," prepared before the Schuman Plan was announced, but reedited and published exactly after it happened. This paper clearly expressed the governing party's views: "Britain herself is unwilling to join such a union for fear of losing her independence outside Europe. But it is already obvious that if European unity is built without Britain it will be dominated by Germany." Britain, it declared, is

> the nerve center of a world wide Commonwealth . . . [and] we in Britain are closer to our kinsmen in Australia and New Zealand . . . than we are in Europe . . . The economies of the Commonwealth countries are complementary to that of Britain to a degree which those of Western Europe could never equal.[181]

Oliver Harvey, British ambassador to Paris, having mentioned a customs union in a speech in Paris, received a message from London in January 1950: "The Board of Trade was scared even if any mention of a European customs union [was uttered] by British representatives . . . In fact the present view of Ministries is that we must remain completely uncommitted."[182] The chronicler of the British rejection of the formation of the European Coal and Steel Community concluded: "Britain was bankrupt of ideas. Creativity was left to others."[183] In fact, not only the politicians but the majority of the British people also opposed joining continental Europe. As Sir Oliver Franks, British ambassador to the United States between 1948 and 1952, stated in his BBC Reith Lectures in 1956: on Europe the British people "have thought less and cared less."[184]

Britain, in reality, had inadequate economic, financial, and military power to form a "third power" between the two superpowers. Moreover, she actually needed American military shield and financial assistance in her weakened postwar state. Consequently, from 1948 on, Britain gave up its great power dreams and joined the American-led Western alliance. But membership in alliance was as far as she was willing to go. In January 1949, an informal meeting of senior representatives of the Foreign Office, Dominions Office, and Treasury developed a joint resolution that was accepted by the Cabinet. "According to the minutes of the meeting . . . We hope to secure a special relationship with USA and Canada . . . for in the last resort we cannot rely upon the European countries."[185] In October 1949, in a Cabinet paper presented jointly by the secretary of state and the chancellor of exchequer, the British concept was finalized: "We must remain, as we have always been in the past, different in character from other European nations and fundamentally incapable of wholehearted integration with them."[186] The finality of the British decision became clear to Secretary of State Acheson in September 1949 when he consulted Bevin and Chancellor of the Exchequer Stafford Cripps. The State Department, and especially Kennan, already realized that the deep federal integration of Western Europe would not be possible with Britain rejecting any kind of federative solution. Consequently Kennan suggested in July 1949 that France would be a better leader.[187]

And so the US turned to France and suggested that the French take the initiative to form an integrated West European Community, as will be discussed later. When Schuman invited Britain on May 9, 1950 to join in preparatory discussions on a plan to form the European Coal and Steel Community, the British Government declined. This decision was strengthened by the decision of Schuman and Monnet to consult with Germany in advance, but not with Britain. That was much more than a diplomatic mistake. After their plan had been unveiled, Schuman and Monnet claimed that they had wanted Britain to join. At a meeting with a British delegation in 1952, Monnet stated: "There was nothing that our countries wanted or hoped for more than that Great Britain should come in with the venture of ours. But Britain did not feel able to join."[188] The British, however, insisted that in fact, France had never wanted to include Britain in what was essentially a French–German construction. From the British point of view, the polite words of Schuman and Monnet to convince Bevin to join were meant only to provide cover for their real plan: to establish French leadership in the architecture of a new Europe.

Through the Consultative Assembly of the Council of Europe, Britain put forward an alternative to the Schuman Plan, which suggested placing the planned European Coal and Steel Community under the sponsorship of the Council of Europe to minimize its supranational character. That idea, however, was not supported by the Six, who proceeded to sign the Paris Treaty (1951) founding the European Coal and Steel Community, without Britain. Britain was sidelined by itself.

The British position did not change when the Conservatives won the elections and Churchill returned to 10 Downing Street. He spoke as a devoted European in his influential speeches and, as opposition leader, criticized the Labour Government for blocking the road of European unification. In his major speech in the House of Commons on the Schuman Plan, he flatly declared "that the British Socialist Government was no friend to the process of the unification of Western Europe." He went so far as to declare on behalf of the Conservative and Liberal Parties "that national sovereignty is not inviolable."[189]

However, Churchill did not change the British policy regarding Europe at all. In November 1951, with the European Coal and Steel agreement not yet signed and the door still open for Britain, he stated at a Cabinet meeting: "I am not opposed to a European Federation . . . But I never thought that Britain and the

British Commonwealth should . . . become an integral part of a European federation, and have never given the slightest support to the idea."[190] In 1952, Anthony Eden, who became foreign secretary again in the new Tory Government, presented his "Eden Plan," a proposal for an alternative organization lacking a supranational character. In January 1960, still by choice outside the EEC of the Six, Britain even established a rival organization, the European Free Trade Association (EFTA), with Austria, Denmark, Sweden, Norway, Switzerland, and Portugal.

During the 1950s and 1960s, however, both the psychology and imperial identity of the Brits steadily changed. During that time, the empire gradually disintegrated. The humiliating experience of the Suez Canal crisis in 1956 was a central part of this change. Gamal Abdel Nasser's new revolutionary Egyptian Government nationalized the Canal. In response, the British organized and took part in a British–French–Israeli military action against Egypt. This action, one of a type that would have been a usual step and a certain winner in the nineteenth century, met with the denunciation of President Eisenhower and failed. "Gunship diplomacy," which had made Britain great in the previous centuries, was over forever. As the European Community's *Bulletin* phrased it in December 1956, after the Suez failure, France and Britain "have suddenly realized their weakness." The Western nations

> have no chance of being accepted as great powers except by presenting to the world a united, unbroken front . . . The unfortunate Suez affair demonstrates more clearly than ever our isolation and our weakness . . . No other [way] exists than that of building a united Europe.[191]

By 1960, the dissolution of the mighty British colonial empire was completed. The 1960s consequently became the decade of changing British policy towards Europe. On July 31, 1961, Prime Minister Macmillan announced Britain's application for membership in the EEC. His speech at the House of Commons used a compelling Cold War-rooted political argument to explain his new policy: Britain's joining the EEC would have

> capital importance in the life . . . of all of the countries of the free world. This is a political as well as an economic issue . . . It has an important political objective, namely, to promote unity, stability in Europe which is so essential a factor in the struggle for freedom . . . throughout the world.[192]

When this new policy failed because the British application met with the veto of French President Charles de Gaulle, Britain's Labour Government led by Harold Wilson resubmitted the British application along with its Cold War argumentation. On July 4, 1967, British Secretary of State for Foreign Relations George Brown explained again his Government's policy in a speech at the Council of the Western European Union, which was meeting in The Hague:

> Unless Europe is united and strengthened she will not be able to meet the challenge of the world today . . . The European Communities are developing

on an economic base. But we in Britain . . . do not see the issues only in economic terms . . . Some of the most decisive considerations for us have been political.[193]

De Gaulle vetoed this second application as well. Only after his resignation did his successor, President Pompidou, and Prime Minister Edward Heath reach an agreement in a secret meeting on May 1971.[194] After years of British rejection to join, and then years of failed attempts to do so, in 1973, Britain finally joined the EEC. It was too late for the US to realize its plan to secure British leadership in an integrated Europe.

US efforts to gain French leadership for integration

Having failed to secure British leadership in Europe, American policy, as has already been indicated, turned to France, the other major power of Europe. French political elite and governments, however, had a great power psychology somewhat similar to Britain's. France was also in the process of losing a colonial empire. Henri Bonnet, the French ambassador in Washington, clearly expressed this attitude:

> Our American friends appear to have an extremely simplistic conception of the unity of Europe . . . ignoring the seriousness of the problem faced by the European states, particularly France, a power having worldwide responsibilities . . . The French Union and the construction of a Federal European state were mutually exclusive.[195]

The American embassy in Paris summed up in a memorandum called "What worries the French" by quoting the concerns of several famous and influential people. One mentioned the fear "that American imperialism will swallow up some of our colonies." Another accused the US of seeking "to block the road for France to control the Rhineland." French sensibilities, commented the embassy, "have taken an almost pathological turn."[196]

Georges Bidault, as the US Embassy reported to Washington in a telegram, had complained already, before the end of the war, on February 15, 1945 that "the Big Three put France in the same class with China . . . I don't like often the way your government treats us. I don't like the secondary position . . . ."[197] France's political elite considered the country a world power, weakened, and therefore faced with the necessity of rebuilding it. When Bidault visited Truman in May 1945, he expressed his hopes for American support "in enabling France to return to his former position . . . A strong France was needed in the interest of all." De Gaulle even offered French military contributions to the Americans to aid in the war against Japan. In his talk with Bidault, Truman mentioned "that he received a message from General de Gaulle to the effect that France would be glad to participate in the war against Japan."[198]

Archival materials clearly demonstrate that an American–French political chess game about postwar German policy played out between 1945 and 1950. The various

French governments tried blackmailing the US with the communist danger and their turn towards Russia if American aid to fail to help revive France as a world power. Similarly, the American administrations blackmailed France by threatening to stop economic and military aid. It pays to quote from the memorandum of May 12, 1945, written by the American ambassador to France, Jefferson Caffery, to the secretary of state:

> Ever since liberation . . . French foreign policy has followed a very uncertain course and has been marked by recurring efforts to draw closer to the Soviet Union, Great Britain, or the United States, depending on external developments at the time. In the early part of the period the emphasis was toward the Soviet Union.[199]

On May 5, 1945, the US ambassador reported his conversation with General de Gaulle, who said: "I would rather work with the United States than any other country . . . If I cannot work with you I must work with the Soviets."[200] In August 17, 1945, de Gaulle tried blackmailing the US by stating to the American ambassador:

> The decision about Germany's western frontiers would have far-reaching repercussion on French international policy . . . [If] Germany was permitted to retain those areas [the Ruhr, the Rhineland and the Saar as] part of a strong central Germany . . . France might be obliged to orient her policy toward Russia.[201]

In March 1946, Bidault's statement on the possible reorientation of French foreign policy towards Russia was displayed on the front page of the *New York Times*.[202]

France was hardly ready to give up plans for ensuring her security against Germany, and yet she was unable to operate without major American assistance. As early as November 1944, Monnet had indicated that by January 1946 his country would need imports from the US to supply 50 percent of the country's food, 25 percent of its coal and other raw materials, 80 percent of its semi-finished goods, and 90 percent of finished goods. France requested financing from the US for the Monnet Plan, the postwar program of reconstruction and building up of French economic leadership on the continent. France even established the French Supply Council in New York with 1,200 employees.[203] In January 1946, the veteran French socialist politician, Leon Blum, preparing to meet with Secretary of State Byrnes, sent a message to Ambassador Jefferson Caffery about the need of a reconstruction loan.[204] During the discussions, as a prerequisite for the aid, Secretary Byrnes suggested that France reconsider its German policy, i.e. calls for the separation of the Rhine area, internationalization of the Ruhr, and economic integration of the Saar with France. The French Government immediately responded that if the Blum assignment fails, France "almost inevitably . . . would be constrained to organize our economic policy in different directions."[205]

With his Washington superiors, Caffery argued for a "generous credit" for France "on political rather than economic grounds." If the US lost interest, he argued, the French would feel abandoned and turn to communism.[206] At the National Advisory Council in Washington, William Clayton argued in the same way: a decision against a substantial loan would be a "catastrophe." However, instead of the French request of US$2 billion, he suggested an Export–Import Bank loan of US$650 million. At the end of the Blum–Byrnes meeting, this US$650 million was indeed provided and, in addition, France's US$2.8 billion lend-lease obligations were cancelled. At last, American aid began flowing to France: first a reconstruction loan in 1946, and then budgetary aid, Marshall Aid, and military assistance totaling US$1 billion per year between 1945 and 1954. France would become one of the main beneficiaries of the Marshall Aid, receiving 21 percent of the total.[207] France also depended on American aid in her colonial war in Indochina. Ultimately, the US supported (and later took over) the French struggle in Vietnam, having linked it—by virtue of the fact that the Vietminh was led by Ho Chi Minh and the communists—to the Cold War struggle.

The Marshall Plan gave the Americans some leverage over French policies in Europe. In particular, it became a good weapon to force the French Government to drop its calls for German reparations and ceilings on German industrial output. At the Paris meeting on the German peace treaty in 1947, the US, seeking to prevent the French from walking out, made a concession by agreeing to the idea of forming an international Ruhr coal authority. But at the London conference in early 1948, an American–British draft of a German constitution also took a further step towards creating an independent West Germany as an equal partner in all of the treaties concerning the West. The previous French plans of an unlimited military occupation of Germany, as well as those put forth by the British for a forty-year occupation were shelved for good. To eliminate French resistance to the new policy towards Germany, the Truman Administration actually threatened to withdraw Marshall Plan aid to France, resorting like de Gaulle to a form of blackmail to advance his country's interests. De Gaulle was outraged, but he had to bow.[208]

Although the American aid amounted to a permanent bargain between the two governments, in reality, American Cold War policy was focused not on France exclusively, but on Western Europe as a whole. What Ambassador Caffery told de Gaulle in the spring of 1945 was true: "the United States will have a much more active interest in Europe after the war than ever before."[209]

Convincing France to form a community and federal state with Germany was not an easy task. Sometimes the US had to provide carrots along with the sticks of blackmail. Thus, for example, American military deliveries restored French military superiority over the Germans.[210] The French were vulnerable in any of these negotiations, precisely because their needs were great and pressing. In the end this situation gave the American administration the upper hand. The US Embassy in France became an important power base and influential in French politics. As an example it pays to mention that as early as 1947, Ambassador Caffrey, informing Prime Minister Ramadier, Bidault, and Minister of Justice Teitgen about the Truman speech on Greece and Turkey [the Truman Doctrine], could remark: "From now on the situation is clear. One must choose."[211]

American pressure on France for progress in European unification became very strong in October 1949, when Marshall Plan administrator Paul Hoffman, in an aggressive speech, flatly warned that American assistance was going to be tied to progress in integration. The US forced the OEEC members to reduce their tariffs by 50 percent, and also to establish the European Payment Union: 25 percent of Marshall Plan aid subsidized these goals in 1950.[212] With all of these steps the US actually *initiated* the economic integration of Western Europe. America did not give the French much elbow room in which to maneuver. Kennan, for example, in a memorandum dated July 18, 1947, remarked that

> there is a serious gap between what is required of Germany for European recovery and what is being produced there today. Unless this gap can be overcome no European recovery program will be realistic . . . We should place squarely before the French the choice between a rise in German production or no European recovery financed by the US.[213]

The American Government categorically informed "the French that the Ruhr authority could attain legitimacy only if the *coal and steel industries of France and the Benelux were brought under its purview as well.*"[214] This American concept and recommendation was first aired by the American high commissioner for Germany, John J. McCloy, in conversations with his close friend, Jean Monnet. The idea became the core concept of the ECSC when it was founded a few years later.

American initiative to establish a joint West European army

Nothing is more convincing about the direct American role in initiating and forcing West European integration than the American attempt to establish a united West European army. As part of the American plan to push Western Europe towards the formation of a federal state, Henry Byroade, a State Department official at the German Desk, prepared a memorandum in 1950 called "An Approach to the Formation of a European Army." Dean Acheson, secretary of state at the time, learned that Byroade's initiative had been sent over to John McCloy (marked "Eyes only for McCloy"). McCloy subsequently exchanged some cable messages with Byroade and did not wait for long before setting up a meeting with his friend Jean Monnet to discuss the possibility of a joint European army. And so, Monnet later explained, at his country house in Houjarray, not far from Paris, "the eventual framework of the European Defense Community was conceptualized."[215]

Monnet's "conceptualization" of the framework of the European Defense Community was in reality nothing else than a "translation" of the ideas contained in Byroade's draft memorandum to the State Department on the need for a European army into a French initiative. Monnet had learned of the memorandum's contents when he met with McCloy. Monnet drafted the plan of the European Defense Community and presented it to the new French Prime Minister, René Pleven. The "Pleven Plan," as it came to be called, recommended the establishment of a European army by a "complete fusion" of the European armed forces, with German participation, under a European minister of defense, with a supranational command, budget, and general staff. Rather than supporting the independent rearmament of Germany, the plan suggested allowing that nation to rearm under strict European control.

The former Dutch foreign minister Ernst van der Beugel presents a distorted interpretation about the history of the European Defense Community. This plan, Beugel maintains, "was mainly conceived by the French Government, while the United States [later] became exclusively committed to a scheme it originally had opposed." To the contrary to what happened, according to Beugel, McCloy and the US Embassy in Paris *supported* "Monnet's ideas on the European Army project." Moreover, it was Monnet who convinced Eisenhower to accept and support his idea, something that the General originally disliked. Beugel suggests that although the US gave initially a maximum of only "a silent endorsement to go on with the exploration of the possibility of the Pleven Plan," by 1953 this plan became a major American plan.[216] This became clear at the meeting of the North Atlantic Council in December 1953, when John Foster Dulles delivered a frightening speech to force acceptance of the joint army plan. In his speech, as the *New York Times* presented it, Dulles said that if "the European Defense Community should not become effective . . . there would be grave doubt whether continental Europe could be made a place of safety." He even tried to blackmail Europe by stating that the failure of the plan "would compel an agonizing reappraisal of basic US policy" and would remove its forces from Europe. If Western Europe "decide to commit suicide, they may have to commit it alone." In this case, Europe cannot be integrated in freedom, "although it might be that Western Europe would be unified, as Eastern Europe has been unified, in defeat and servitude."[217]

Pleven pushed forward his plan to the French National Assembly on October 24, 1950. Despite strong opposition from more than 200 representatives, including the former Prime Minister Eduard Daladier, Pleven's Plan had already received preliminary approval from the Assembly,[218] but in August 1954 the French Parliament discarded the plan. The idea of a joint European army was shelved.

Monnet was one of the French politicians who realized quite early that France had little choice but to align itself with the US's European and German policy. In April 1948 he went to Washington. This was an official trip, but his main goal was gathering information. "To understand America, its people, and its leaders," he confessed in his *Memoirs*, "one has to go back regularly and form some idea of the changes that ceaselessly carry forward . . . That was the real reason for my regular visits, which always began with calls on well-informed friends."[219] These "well-informed friends" were influential political gurus. Among them were Dean Acheson and George Ball; also Walt Rostow, economist and later presidential advisor; McGeorge Bundy, foreign policy expert and later presidential security advisor; Walter Lippmann and James Reston, influential journalists and political commentators.

Having gathered valuable information in the US, Monnet recalls, he immediately wrote to Schuman, the French foreign minister, telling him that

> America is on the move . . . A great change occurred here recently: preparation to make war has given place to preparation to prevent it . . . [Monnet

adds that] in the same letter to Schuman I broached an idea which was to go on developing at the back of my mind for the next two years: Everything I have seen and reflected on here leads me to a conclusion which is now my profound conviction: that to tackle the present situation, to face the dangers that threaten us, and *to match the American effort, the countries of Western Europe must turn their national efforts into a truly European effort.* This will be possible only through *federation* of the West.[220]

Monnet eventually took over the American ideas and politics of those years and presented them to the French Government.

It pays to mention that Monnet was always presented in the literature and speeches as the "Father of Europe," the initiator of integration. Former Dutch Foreign Minister Beugel also misinterprets Jean Monnet's role and presents him not as an arm of American policy or as the well-informed European by his American connections who translated the American plans to present them as a genuine French initiative, but rather as *influencing* American policy. "American policy towards European cooperation and integration cannot be fruitfully analyzed . . . [without] the position and influence of Jean Monnet . . . [without] his most remarkable capacity . . . his great influence on the formulation of US policy towards Europe." Key American politicians, in this interpretation, had only some assisting role. Undersecretary Clayton, the initiator of the Marshall Plan, was "one of the men who helped to clarify his [Monnet's] ideas which resulted in the Coal and Steel Community."[221]

France complies "at gun point"

As has already been indicated, the US and France were unequal allies in the delicate game of postwar negotiations about the postwar structure of Europe. From the very beginning, American diplomats and politicians categorically told the French what was going to happen in Europe. They flatly said that France would not be receiving reparations from Germany, that the US wanted a united Germany. Bidault's protest was not accepted. Truman also told de Gaulle that the Ruhr was not going to be internationalized.[222] The US could go it alone; the French could not. And so, as the confrontation between the US and the Soviet Union became manifest in the spring of 1947, the French had to choose sides. Bidault "told to [Secretary] Marshall that America could rely on France, France simply needed support and time in order to avoid civil war."[223]

Meanwhile, as Monnet portrays it, a

> financial crisis in Paris brought the French to their knees. On September 10, the Ministry of Foreign Affairs notified Washington that all imports of needed raw material . . . must be ceased by the end of October 1947, because French currency reserves would by then be totally exhausted . . . The French needed at least $100 million per month to live through July 1, 1948 . . . In exchange . . . the French government also declared that it

recognized the necessity of the economic integration of Europe and was ready for negotiations with any European nations to achieve it . . . On September 23 Bidault appropriately concluded that the German question had become a "lost cause" for France . . . On August 8, 1948, Bidault told American officials that publicly he still supported the harsh terms of the Morgenthau Plan, but privately we know that we have to join in the control of Germany and reorganization of Western Europe, but please *don't force us to do so at the point of a gun.*[224]

In September, Acheson told Bevin that if the French were not to cooperate "he would have to consider going ahead with German rearmament anyway." This idea was enough to frighten Schuman. On September 26 he told Acheson that France would take the initiative, but he pleaded that this country could *not be dragged on the end of a chain."*[225]

France was indeed forced "by gun point" or "dragged on the end of a chain" during the late 1940s and throughout the 1950s.

> While visiting Paris [in 1953], [John Foster] Dulles announced that if the ancient enmity between France and Germany were not ended and European Defense Community not ratified, Washington would be forced to undertake an "agonizing reappraisal" of its European policy. The implicit threat in these words was that Washington would revert to a peripheral strategy and abandon hope of defending Western Europe in case of a Soviet attack.[226]

War-torn France needed and accepted the financial assistance of the Marshall Plan in 1948, and the military shield offered by the US in 1949. Both forms of assistance came at a price: a strong dependence on America and the acceptance of America's European policy. Meanwhile, the still unanswered German Question required a new approach as well, and the assumption of Soviet danger, so rooted already in Western perceptions, made vital the strengthening of the West European countries. All of these problems called for a coordinated European response. At last, the US succeeded in realizing its new European policy, including its German policy. The West European countries had to comply and so they started their journey on the road of integration towards a federal Europe.

In the spring of 1948, the American ambassador in Paris triumphantly reported: "According to Paris, the French are as desirous as we are of bringing about the integration of Germany with Western Europe."[227] In April 1949 in Washington, Acheson, Schuman, and Bevin openly stated their agreement to address the German Question according to the American plan: "We want assurance on security, we want economy of Germany to be put on proper footing to play her part in integrating European economy with other democratic nations of the West."[228]

The draft of the letter of the US secretary of state to the French minister of foreign affairs clearly and strongly sent the *order:* "[This] is time for French initiative and leadership of the type required to integrate the German Federal Republic promptly and decisively into Western Europe. Delay will seriously weaken the possibility of success." There are several guarantees to control Germany,

> but a strong and effective safeguard is the growth in Germany of a whole-hearted desire to participate in the political and economic development of Western Europe . . . Unless we move rapidly the political atmosphere will deteriorate and we shall be faced with . . . dangerous personalities in the German government . . . The USSR is actively abetting the development of anti-democratic and aggressive tendencies in Germany and is prepared to exploit them to the full . . . The Germans are psychologically and politically ripe to take measures for genuine integration with Western Europe [because of] their fear of Communism and the Soviet Union . . . French leadership is essential and will ensure success.[229]

The author of the letter, Henry A. Byroad, in another message of December 15, 1949, described the crucial event: "It should be remembered that the Secretary in a personal message to Schuman just before the Paris Conference of Foreign Ministers strongly developed the necessity of closer German–French relations and stressed the importance of the French taking the lead towards this end." A copy of this message was sent to Bevin to inform the British Government. The State Department official also noted the possibility of "appropriate retaliatory action" against Britain if she wants to block such a move.[230] That was clear speech. The French Government had just been given its homework.

Notes

1 Henry Kissinger, *World Order* (New York, NY: Penguin Press, 2014), 87.
2 Perry Anderson, *The New Old World* (London: Verso, 2009).
3 Count Richard Nikolaus von Coudenhove-Kalergi, the founder of the pan-European movement, stated: "It is an undeniable fact that, in spite of its dismemberment into thirty-four states and more than forty language groups, Europe constitutes one great cultural community . . . For this reason the conception of a European nation is . . . justified . . . Tomorrow the European sense of nationality will be awakened . . . This discovery of Europe as a great nation . . . will open a new chapter in world history, as did the discovery of America." (Count R.N. Von Coudenhove-Kalergi, *Europe Must Unite* (Glarus, Switzerland: Paneuropa Editions, 1939), 18–20.
4 See Alan S. Milward, *The European Rescue of the Nation-State* (Berkeley, CA: University of California Press, 1992). Milward's sarcastic remark referred to Henri Brugmans's *Prophètes et fondateurs de l'Europe* (Bruges, Belgium: College of Europe, 1974).
5 Between the seventeenth and twentieth centuries, five major "European civil wars," brought on by the operations of dynastic and diplomatic alliances, by conflict over religion as well as territory, visited death, injury, disruption, and destruction on Europeans: the Thirty Years War of 1618–48, which killed one-quarter of the population of the Holy Roman Empire; the Seven Years War of 1756–63; the French revolutionary and Napoleonic wars of 1792–1815; and finally, in 1914–1945, the two modern World Wars. Altogether in nearly 400 years between 1560 and 1945, only 190 years had been more or less peaceful, although even these years had been marred by localized fighting. Europeans seemed inured to settling their differences "by the sword."

6 Ibid., 75.

7 Edmund Dell, *The Schuman Plan and the British Abdication of Leadership in Europe* (Oxford: Oxford University Press, 1995), 65–66.

8 National Archive, Information Memorandum No. 28, 862.00/1–749.

9 Warren F. Kimball, ed., *Churchill and Roosevelt, The Complete Correspondence. Vol. III: Alliance Declining. February 1944–April 1945* (Princeton, NJ: Princeton University Press, 1984), 317; Robert Dallek, *Franklin D. Roosevelt and American Foreign Policy, 1932–1945* (Oxford: Oxford University Press, 1995), 475.

10 National Archive, US Initial Post-Defeat Policy Relating to Germany, March 23, 1945. From E.A. Lightner Jr to Robert D. Murphy on early denazification plan, 862.00/8-1749. Roosevelt said he "disliked making detailed plans for a country we do not yet occupied."

11 National Archive, Meeting About How to Deal with Postwar Germany, April 27, 1945, 862.00/4-2745. President Roosevelt died on April 12 of that year.

12 Directive to Commander-in-Chief of United States Forces of Occupation Regarding the Military Government of Germany, April, 1945, JCS-1067, http://usa.usembassy.de/etexts/ga3-450426.pdf.

13 National Archive, Committee Report on foreign economic administration, October 22, 1945, 862.60/10-2245.

14 Ibid.

15 Nicholas Balabkins, *Germany Under Direct Controls. Economic Aspects of Industrial Disarmament, 1945–1948* (New Brunswick, NJ: Rutgers University Press, 1964), 119.

16 James Stuart Martin, *All Honorable Men* (Boston, MA: Little Brown, 1950), 191; Frederick H. Gareau, "Morgenthau's Plan for Industrial Disarmament of Germany," *The Western Political Quarterly* 14, no. 2 (June 1972): 242–69.

17 For the position that fear of Germany has driven French politics since the war, see André Gauron, *European Misunderstanding* (New York, NY: Algora, 2000), 3.

18 In the Holy Roman Empire, 234 sovereign units existed, including 51 free cities. The Congress of Vienna in 1815 created 32 German state units in the framework of the German Confederation.

19 Jean Monnet, *Memoirs*, trans. Richard Mayne (Garden City, NY: Doubleday, 1978), 222.

20 National Archive, Confidential US State Department Central Files. France. Foreign Affairs, 1945–1949, 711.51/4-2045.

21 Ibid.

22 National Archive, Office Memorandum, 711.51/1-245.

23 James F. Byrnes, in a letter to Georges Bidault, President of the French Provisional Government in September 1945, although opposed unilateral measures, still stated: "I shall be happy to support the position of the French government that certain immediate steps be taken toward integration the economy of the Saar with France" (National Archive, James F. Byrnes Letter to Georges Bidault, President of Provisional Government, Against French Unilateral Action to Annex the Saarland, September 25, 1945, 862.014/9-2546). In December 1947, the acting Secretary of State telegrammed: "we approve French proposal on economic integration of Saar territory into that of France" (National Archive, Acting Secretary of State Telegram of December 23, 1947, 862.00/12-1747).

24 Roy Jenkins, *Churchill. A Biography* (New York, NY: A Plume Book, 2002), 814.

25 National Archive, Ernest de W. Mayer US Consul's Report of October 10, 1947, 862.00/10-1047. At the end of the year, the US Embassy report from Paris described the French Saar policy as follows: "Saar Constitution, December 15, 1947 independent from Germany, France takes over defense and foreign relations, French frank is the legal currency" (National Archive, Embassy Report from Paris to Secretary of State, September 3, 1949, 862.00/9-349).

26 National Archive, Report of Ambassador Murphy on Governor Conference in Berlin, April 1, 1948, 862.00/4-148.

27 National Archive, Material Prepared for the Secretary's Press Conference, November 30, 1948, 862.014/11-3048. The briefing material clearly phrased it: "The French also raised

formally at the London Conference [in 1948] the question of giving the future Ruhr Control Authority supervision over management of the Ruhr industries in addition to control of Ruhr exports" to protect France from German economic competition.

28 National Archive, Consul General Richard M. Groth's Report from Hamburg, December 5, 1946, 862.00/12-546.

29 National Archive, Consul General Altaffer's Message to the Secretary of State, September 24, 1947, 862.00/9-2447.

30 The American consul in Stuttgart reported that strong anti-French feelings were evident in Württemberg because the French occupation authorities had taken 20,000 modern machines from the German watch industry alone (National Archive, Frederick J. Mann, Consul in Stuttgart, Report of August 20, 1948, 862.00/8-2048).

31 National Archive, Report of the American Consul in Bremen about the Congress of the Christian Democratic Union, 862.00/9-848, September 8, 1948. Adenauer made this complaint in a speech that opened the Christian Democratic Union Congress.

32 National Archive, Consul General Maurice W. Altaffer's Report on his Meeting with Adenauer, Bremen, January 5, 1947, 862.00/6-547.

33 National Archive, Report of Consul Martin J. Hillenbrand, Attached to Consul General Altaffer's Letter, October, 13, 1947, 862.00/10-1447. In October 1947, Adenauer told Hillenbrand about his fear.

34 National Archive, McCloy's Report on an Informal Meeting Between the Federal Chancellor and the Council of the Allied High Commission, October 27, 1949, in Bonn-Petersberg, September 27, 1949, 862.00/9-2749. Adenauer "insisted that the dismantling program was being speeded up [in British and French occupation zones] and that he could not be responsible for the consequences in terms of public distrust . . . France and the UK were making the same psychological errors they had made since 1933 and with respect to Nazi regime."

35 National Archive, Consul General Edward M. Groth's Report from Hamburg, January 17, 1947, 862.00/1-1747; see also National Archive, Consul Maurice W. Altaffer's Report from Bremen, February 5, 1947, 862.00/2-247.

36 Consul Martin J. Hillenbrand sent a dramatic report on the situation in North Rhine Westphalia in October 1947. He spoke about a "general mood of hopelessness among the people," about a great crisis that may "explode into a general catastrophe." If the next six months, he stated, "could be survived without complete breakdown, then the Ruhr would be saved for Western Europe" (National Archive, Consul Hillenbrand's Report Attached to Consul General Altaffer's Message to Washington, October 14, 1947, 862.00/10-1447). In May 1947, Ambassador Robert W. Murphy sent a British memorandum from London to the State Department about the "steady deterioration in German morale and an increasing dislike . . . the occupying authority. It is no exaggeration today to say that we are hated by the vast majority . . . who now believe that it is our intention to destroy the German nation" (National Archive, Robert Murphy's Report on May 2, 1947, 862.00/5-2147).

37 For the entire speech, see "Speech by J.F. Byrnes, United States Secretary of State Restatement of Policy on Germany, Stuttgart September 6, 1946," usa.usembassy.de/ etexts/ga4-460906.htm.

38 Ibid.

39 Max Beloff, *The United States and the Unity of Europe* (Washington, DC: The Brooking Institutions, 1963) 8.

40 *Time Magazine*, September 16, 1946; see also "Speech of Hope," (germany.usembassy. gov/speech-h . . .) United States Ambassador to Germany by US Embassy–2012.

41 National Archive, US Embassy Report from Mexico City on the Echo of Byrnes Speech, September 9, 1946, 862.00/9-946. A report from Uruguay mentioned a lead article in *La Cuarta Republica* with the title "France Alone." This stated that the speech "closed all doors" to French hopes for the "solution of the German problem." Germany became a "pawn in the world diplomatic dispute." (National Archive, Embassy Report on the Media Reaction on the Byrnes Speech, Montevideo, October 4, 1946, 862.00/10-446).

42 Winston Churchill's speech in New York March 25, 1949; in Strasbourg August 17, 1949; and in London, November 28, 1949; see Randolph S. Churchill, ed., *In the Balance. Speeches 1949 and 1950 by Winston Churchill* (London: Cassel, 1951), 35, 81, 153.

43 National Archive, Charles Bohlen's Letter to Representative John M. Folger, March 1, 1948, 862.00/3-148. Bohlen said: "Europe and the world will be adequately protected against the danger of future German domination." He also spoke about the policy of "continued demilitarization of Germany for 40 years." "The Ruhr area," he repeated, "will be utilized for the good of European community as a whole."

44 National Archive, Telegram from Wiesbaden to Secretary of State, April 5, 1949, 862.00 (W)/4-1549. "Washington announcement Western Allies agreement removes 150 West German plants from dismantling list." The High Military Commission signed an agreement with the new German Federal Government: further dismantling of I.G. Farben in Ludwigshafen "will not take place . . . All dismantling in Berlin will cease"; see National Archive, High Commission and Federal Government Agreement, signed by Adenauer, McCloy, B.H. Robertson, and A. François Poncet, November 24, 1949, 862.00/11-2449. The French Government in 1949 was trying to find a way to prevent the Saar region from being returned to German control, as might be expected to arise with the American policy change. When Adenauer reported on the French efforts to the American ambassador, he was rewarded with the unequivocal support of the US Secretary of State Acheson who immediately declared: "Dept. would share Adenauer's concern . . . mines were property of Reich." On the Saar issue, see National Archive, McCloy's Report on December 22, 1949, 862.014/12-2249. Acheson also ordered to clarify the issue with Schuman.

45 National Archive, Consul General Altaffer's report from Bremen, November 17, 1947, 862.00/11-1747. The consul called attention to left-wing exploitation of the "Law for Liberation from National Socialism and Militarism." Denazification boards, Altaffer Consul General reported in November 1947, are "composed chiefly of very radically inclined persons . . . [Communist elements on the boards] using their positions in a destructive manner for political purposes" and for socialization of companies. "The methods are simple: serious charges are brought against owners or managing directors of profitable industrial and other private enterprises."

46 National Archive, Charles E. Bohlen's Answer to La Follette's Article, 862.00/1-1749.

47 National Archive, "The evolution of US denazification policies in Germany," Report of the Political Advisor of the Military Government in Germany, May 5, 1948, 862.00/5-1148.

48 National Archive, From the State Department to US Consular Officer in Charge, Stuttgart, 862.00/3-248.

49 National Archive, Consul Maurice W. Altaffer's Report on Denazification to Secretary of State, December 24, 1946, 862.00/12-2446.

50 National Archive, From Mr. Oppenheimer to Mr. Fahy, December 10, 1946, 862.00/12-1046. The *New York Times* article is mentioned in this letter.

51 National Archive, Consul General Richard M. Groth's Report from Hamburg, December 5, 1946, 862.00/12-546.

52 National Archive, Consul Altaffer's Report from Bremen, October 8, 1947, 862.00/10-847; National Archive, Report of the US Consulate in Hamburg, January 13, 1948, 862.00/1-1348.

53 National Archive, Consul General B. Tomlin Bailey's Report from Munich, August 16, 1948, 862.00/8-1648. "In Landkreise Krumbach and Dinkelsbuehl, the percentage of reelected ex-Nazi bürgermeisters is 71 percent and 60 percent respectively . . . Nazis have returned to position within government agencies throughout Bavaria."

54 National Archive, Some Aspects of Renazification in Bavaria, Clarence M. Bolds, Acting Land Commissioner, to J. McCloy, Munich, November 1, 1949, 862.00/11-149. "The failure of the program of denazification led to an evident renazification in many fields of Bavarian life . . . 30 percent of top civil servants are former Nazis. They reemploy the 'big' Nazis." In the summer of 1948, the reelection of the Nazi mayor of

Schwabish Gmuend, Franz Konrad, caused a major scandal. At first, Konrad was categorized as Major Offender in Class I, the highest category for Nazi criminals, but he was later recategorized to Class IV, and then to Class V as a "Mitlaufer." The Military Government stepped in and suspended him. See National Archive, Frederick J. Mann, Consul in Stuttgart, report of July 26, 1948, 862.00/7-2848.

55 National Archive, Robert Murphy's Report to the Secretary of State, July 28, 1948, 862.00/8-648: "Spruchkammer trials . . . qualifying persons for employment and other activities on all levels. Besides serving as a more rapid rehabilitation of persons affected by the denazification law, this action has also served . . . to make possible the re-entry into influential positions of ex-Nazis." The report complained that in some local places, German officials want to exclude ex-Nazis who were elected to certain office. This phenomena "would be reversing a trend which Military Government itself has supported in the past year and one half."

56 *Washington Post*, "Nazi Comeback Chance Seen," January 17, 1949.

57 National Archive, Frederick J. Mann, Consul in Stuttgart, Report on July 26, 1948, 862.00/7-2848. Mann wrote that scandal "has had no effect in slowing down the rapid pace of 'renazification' of public life." For neo-fascist action, see National Archive, Report on the Danger of Neo-Nazism, Berlin, June 17, 1948, 862.00/6-1748. In the summer of 1948, an editorial titled "Against Neo-Nazism" in the *Nürnberg Nachrichten* reported that "there are now a continuing number of desecrations of Jews graves. In a short period recently there were twelve such cases in Bavaria alone." The *New York Herald Tribune* reported on August 11, 1949 that the German police in Munich opened fire upon 1,000–1,500 Jewish demonstrators who protested against the *Suddeutsche Zeitung*'s article (actually a letter to the editor) that suggested that all Jews be committed to gas chambers and put to death.

58 National Archive, From Brussels to Secretary of State, August 24, 1948, 862.00/8-2448.

59 Monnet, *Memoirs*, 293.

60 National Archive, Proposal for Meeting Anglo-French Security Desires with Respect to Germany, December 9, 1948, 862.00/12-948. The US policy with regard to security measures against Germany was set forth in the draft Byrnes Four Power treaty for the disarmament and demilitarization of Germany. This proposal was warmly greeted by the British and French when it was made; however, now "the French was told that the Byrnes treaty proposal should be regarded for the time as a '*dead duck*'."

61 National Archive, Barbour's Message to Secretary of State, October 20, 1949, 862.00/10-2049.

62 National Archive, From Wayne G. Jackson to J.D. Hickerson, March 25, 1/949, 862.00/3-2549.

63 National Archive, Consul General in Hamburg to the Secretary of State, January 23, 1948, 862.011/1-2348. "European federation would also be the best and actually the only effective way of dealing with the fears of France. In a European federation it would be much easier to control Germany."

64 National Archive, The Allied High Commissioners' Meeting with Representatives of the German Federal Government on November 15. McCloy's Report of November 16, 1949, 862.00/11-1549.

65 Archive of European Integration, "The Community's Relations with the Outside World," *Bulletin from the European Community for Coal and Steel*, no. 20 (December 1956): 3.

66 A huge literature on the Cold War could fill an entire library. Several elements of the rising confrontation were closely connected with Europe and Germany and thus works on the Cold War have close connection with the topic of this chapter. Without going into endless details, let me mention a few closely connected books: Marc Trachtenberg, *A Constructed Peace: The Making of the European Settlement, 1945–1963* (Princeton, NJ: Princeton University Press, 2000) that put the German Question and the nuclear confrontation into the center of the work; Kenneth Weisbrode, *The Atlantic Century: Four Generations of Extraordinary Diplomats Who Forged America's Vital Alliance with Europe* (Boston, MA: De Capo Press, 2009) is also connected with this topic whilst

focusing on key personalities such as Dean Acheson, Averell Harriman, Henry Kissinger, and others. It is also important to note the book of W.R. Smyser, *From Yalta to Berlin: The Cold War Struggle Over Germany* (New York, NY: St Martin's Press, 1999).

67 Winston Churchill, *His Complete Speeches 1896–1963, Vol. VII: 1943–1949,* ed. R. Rhodes James (London: Chelsea House Publisher, 1974), 7290–2.

68 Quoted from *Pravda* in André Fontaine, *History of the Cold War. From the October Revolution to the Korean War, 1917–1950* (New York, NY: Pantheon Books, 1968), 1: 267–77.

69 "Something to astonish you!" The Churchill Society, May 8, 1945, www.churchill-society-london.org.uk/astonish.html.

70 The literature is strongly split and often heatedly controversial: during the Cold War decades it was heavily influenced by political considerations and biases. Several works, by repeating official American Government views of the era, one-sidedly accused the Soviet Union of sole responsibility for the conflict. On the other hand, several Soviet Bloc historians reflected the official Soviet interpretation by blaming the US. After the Vietnam War, an American "revisionist" school of thought challenged the orthodox American interpretations and gradually developed towards a balanced evaluation.

71 In August 1944, Eleanor Roosevelt read Churchill's memo of September 1919 about the Western military efforts against Soviet Russia. Mrs Roosevelt sent a copy of two paragraphs from Churchill's memo to her husband and commented: "It is not surprising if Mr Stalin is slow to forget" (see Kimball, ed., *Churchill and Roosevelt*, 3: 288). When Roosevelt died, Stalin, who had good working relations with the American President, sent a cable to the State Department with questions about the circumstance. He was immediately suspicious and asked for "an autopsy ... to determine if the president had been poisoned" (see Kimball, *Churchill and Roosevelt*, 3: 631).

72 The State Department telegram to George Kennan, then posted to the Moscow Embassy, stated: "Please, seek an early interview with Vishinsky and deliver a written memorandum: 'The government of the USA has received the communication setting forth the status of the Free City of Danzig and certain pre-1937 German territory under Soviet military occupation which was addressed on April 7, 1945 by Vishinsky to Mr Harriman. The US Government fails to understand the statement of Mr Vishinsky's letter to the effect that the establishment and competence of the Polish civil administration set up in the Free City of Danzig and certain occupied German territory has no relation to the question of the future boundaries of Poland." The US warned against the "unilateral action of the occupying power without prior consultation and agreement." (see National Archive, Telegram from the State Department to Moscow (Kennan), May 8, 1945, 862.00/5845).

73 Kimball, ed., *Churchill and Roosevelt*, 3: 476.

74 Ibid., 3: 482.

75 Cited in Fontaine, *History of the Cold War*, 1: 217.

76 Evan Luard, *The Cold War. A Reappraisal* (London: Thames and Hudson, 1964), 52.

77 Winston Churchill, *The Second World War, Vol. VI: Triumph and Tragedy* (Boston, MA: Houghton Mifflin, 1953), 227–28.

78 Ibid., 543, italics added.

79 The term "finlandisierung" was introduced by the German scholar Richard Lowenthal in 1961. Finland, a small neighboring country of Russia, after having lost two wars with the Soviet Union between 1939 and 1944, still was allowed by Stalin to keep its sovereignty in internal affairs. The country avoided a communist takeover, although it had to adjust its foreign policy to the Soviet demands that it stay out of Western international agreement systems and practice self-censorship regarding its relationship with the Soviets. The country also had to keep a balance in economic connections between the Soviet Union and the West.

80 Kimball, ed., *Churchill and Roosevelt*, 610.

81 The Lend-Lease Act (1941) was accepted by the American Congress in March 1941 to lend or lease war supplies to a country "whose security was vital to the defense of the

United States"; see National Archive, Records of the US House of Representatives, HR-77 A-D13, Record Group 233, www.ourdocuments.gov/doc.php?doc=71. The Lend-Lease program was introduced to help Britain, but was later extended to the Soviet Union as well.

82 "Letter of Wallace to Truman, July 23, 1946," in *The Truman Administration. A Documentary History*, eds. Barton J. Bernstein and Allen J. Matusow (New York, NY: Harper and Row, 1966), 240–2.

83 Bernstein and Matusow, eds., *Truman Administration*, 22; reprinted from the Stimson Papers, Yale University Library.

84 Report by J. Davis to Truman, June 12, 1945, in Bernstein and Matusow, eds., *Truman Administration*, 177.

85 Irwin M. Wall, *The United States and the Making of Postwar France, 1945–1954* (Cambridge: Cambridge University Press, 1991), 131.

86 Ibid., 96.

87 National Archive, Walter R. Sholes's Consul General Report "The Communist Threat in Germany" from Basel, August 28, 1945, 862.00/8-2845: "It is no use to close our eyes to the realities: Communism (in the end in the shape of National Bolshevism) is developing in Germany."

88 Wall, *The United States and the Making of Postwar France*, 301.

89 National Archive, 851.00/5-346.

90 Wall, *The United States and the Making of Postwar France*, 48.

91 National Archive, John Edgar Hoover, Director of the FBI, to the State Department, February 7, 1946, 862.01/2-746.

92 National Archive, Chief Naval Intelligence to State Department, July 3, 1946, 864.01/7-346.

93 National Archive, Sam E. Wood, Consul General in Munich, Report of October 16, 1947, 862.00/10-1647. The report maintained that the Communist Party had only 36,596 members in Bavaria, but spoke also of the "considerable number of sympathizers and fellow travelers" and the dangerous penetration of local government agencies by communists. The consul reported that in the Housing Office there were five communists, and four in the welfare office. In an early fall of 1949 report on communist penetration in the Mannheim area, it was stated that "of the 209 members of the Worker Council . . . 60 members or 28.7 percent are KPD adherents" (National Archive, Communist Penetration in the Mannheim Area, September 14, 1949, 862.00/9-1449).
  In August 1946, the American legation in Bern, Switzerland, based on information from a Swiss communist, reported that the *Nationale Zeitung* recounted that "sooner or later there will be two new Soviet republics: Poland and East Germany" (National Archive, Report of the American Legation in Bern, August 26, 1946, 862.00/8-2646). In the spring of 1947, the American consul in Stuttgart reported information about the Russian organized *Freies Deutschland* (Free Germany) movement that had already recruited 350,000 former Wehrmacht soldiers (National Archive, Dana Hodgen, Consul General in Stuttgart, Report, May 23, 1947, 862.00/5-2347).

94 National Archive, Letter to the Secretary of State, March 30, 1948, 862.01/3-3048.

95 National Archive, James Wilkinson, Consul General in Munich, Report of May 6, 1947, 862.00/5-647. "During the past three weeks, rumors of war have multiplied tremendously among the population here . . . Don't return to Munich [they say] Russian panzers have already entered the city by the autobahn from Salzburg . . . these rumors . . . indicate a widespread belief in the imminence of war."

96 National Archive, McCloy's Report to Secretary of State, October 26, 1949, 862.00/10-2649.

97 National Archive, Coudenhove-Kalergi's Letter to John D. Hickerson, Director of the Office of European Affairs, March 11, 1948, 862.00/3-1148. The US envoy in Lisbon, according to the report of a French diplomat, said that "the United States has no plans to defend France in case of Soviet invasion of Western Europe. The Americans would rather fall back to a defensive line in the Pyrenees because they regarded only Britain, Spain and Portugal as reliable allies." Irwin M. Wall, author of the study from which

I have taken this quotation stresses the accuracy of the report, and adds that "American military plans were predicated on the idea that France and Germany could not be defended successfully against a Soviet attack" (report cited in Wall, *The United States and the Making of Postwar France*, 57–58).

98 Winston Churchill speech at a dinner at the Ritz-Carlton Hotel, New York, March 25, 1949, in Randolph S. Churchill, ed., *In the Balance. Speeches 1949 and 1950 by Winston Churchill*, 36.

99 Ibid., 328. Speech in Plymouth, July 15, 1950.

100 National Archive, Memorandum for the Secretary of State from Ambassador Jefferson Caffery, May 12, 1945, 751.00/5-1245.

101 Cited in Wall, *The United States and the Making of Postwar France*, 132. Wall also wrote that "on April 8, 1948, he [French ambassador in Washington, Henri Bonnet] reported that the 'highest military authorities' did not believe that the Russian army could be stopped short of the Pyrenees in the event of war." In the spring of 1948, the American consul in Hamburg reported that German views had radically changed. Before, "German masses [blamed] the Occupying Powers for all the hardships which they had to endure . . . However the situation now changed . . . The general reaction to the Russian menace is of extreme fear which is shared by practically everybody . . . [Germans recognized that] fate has given them only one choice: the Anglo-Saxons or the Russians" (National Archive, Consul General Edward M. Groth Report from Hamburg on the Change in German Mentality, April 6, 1948, 862.00/4-648).

102 George Marshall's report "Fourth Meeting of the Council, of Foreign Ministers in Moscow," March 10 to April 24, 1947," Yale Law School Lillian Goldman Law Library, Avalon.law.yale.edu/20th_century/decade23.asp.

103 George Kennan, "Long telegram" from Moscow to George Marshall, February 22, 1946. In Harry S. Truman Administration File, Elsy Papers, www.trumanlibrary.org/whistlestop/study_collections/ . . . /6-6.pdf.

104 George Kennan, "The Source of Soviet Conduct," *Foreign Affairs* 25, no. 4 (July 1947).

105 David Gergen's interview with George Kennan, April 18, 1996, www.pbs.org/newshour/gergen/kennan.html.

106 National Archive, George Kennan's memorandum, April 1, 1946, 711.51/4-146, italics added.

107 See Joseph M. Jones, *The Fifteen Weeks, (February 21—June 5, 1947)* (New York, NY: The Viking Press, 1955), 7; John W. Spanier, *American Foreign Policy since World War II* (New York, NY: Praeger), 1960, 29–30.

108 Harry S. Truman, *Memoirs*, 2 Vols. (New York, NY: Doubleday, 1955–56), 2: 106.

109 President Eisenhower addressed the domino effect at a press conference on the French war in Indochina on April 7, 1954: "You have a row of dominoes set up, you knock over the first one, and what will happen to the last one is a certainty that it will go over very quickly." French loss of the war would lead to disintegration in Southeast Asia, with the "loss of Indochina, of Burma, of Thailand, of the Peninsula, and Indonesia following" (see "Eisenhower gives famous 'domino theory' speech," This Day in History, April 7, 1954, www.history.com/this-day-in-history/eisenhower-gives-famous-domino-theory-speech).

110 Winston Churchill's speech at the Independence Day dinner of the American Society in London, 4 July, 1950, in Randolph S. Churchill, ed., *In the Balance. Speeches 1949 and 1950 by Winston Churchill*, 312.

111 The Brookings Institution, *Major Problems of the United States Foreign Policy, 1949–50* (Washington, DC: The Brookings Institution, 1949), 406.

112 US Department of State, *Bulletin*, July 3, 1950.

113 The Clayton memo is cited in Alan S. Walter Lipgens, *History of European Integration 1945–1947, Vol. 1: The Formation of the European Unity Movement* (Oxford: Oxford University Press, 1982) 474.

114 *Christian Science Monitor*, January 27, 1947; *Washington Post*, February 5, 1947; *New York Herald Tribune*, March 20, 1947, and April 5, 1947. Cited in Lipgens, *History of European Integration*, 468–72.

115 Lipgens, *History of European Integration*, 468–72, 492–3.

116 Peter Thorneycroft's statement is in UK Parliament, *House of Commons Parliamentary Debates Weekly Hansard* 438, 19.6.1947, 2280; R.W.G. Mackay's statement in UK Parliament, *House of Commons Parliamentary Debates Weekly Hansard* 443, 28.10.1947, col. 753. Both cited in Lipgens, *History of European Integration*, 492–93, italics added.

117 For Acheson speech: *The New York Times Magazine*, December 21, 1963

118 Michael J. Hogan, *The Marshall Plan. America, Britain and the Reconstruction of Western Europe, 1947–1952* (Cambridge: Cambridge University Press, 1987), 41–43.

119 The planners of the program, Kennan, Clayton, Acheson, and Bohlen, strongly suggested offering the assistance to the Soviet Union as well. "It was realized that they [the Russians] were unlikely to agree to lay open their economy in this way, but it was important to make them come into the open so that the US should not bear responsibility for dividing Europe." They also noted that "it would be essential . . . that the Russian satellite countries would either exclude themselves by unwillingness to accept the proposed conditions or agree to abandon the exclusive orientation of their economies." For this, see the Memorandum to the Foreign Aid Committee, Interim report of 21.4.1947, cited in Lipgens, *History of European Integration*, 473, 477; italics added.

120 www.oecd.org/ . . . /themarshallplanspeechatharvarduniversity5june194.

121 "Aid Bill is Signed by Truman as Reply to Foes of Liberty," *New York Times*, April 4, 1947.

122 In 1948–49, Austria's share was equal to 14 percent of the country's GNP; for the Netherlands 10.9; France 6.5; West Germany 2.9; Italy 5.3, and Britain 2.4 percent. The aid made a significant contribution to recovery and growth, except in Belgium (0.6) and Sweden (0.3 percent). American aid's contribution to European capital formation after the first two years was less than 10 percent, but for Germany, between 1948 and 1951, that aid contributed 31, 22, 11, and 7 percent per year. In Italy, the contribution figures were 27, 34, 10, and 9 percent. American shipments between April 1948 and December 1951 consisted of food, feed, and fertilizers (32.1 percent); fuel (15.5 percent); cotton and other raw materials (32.8 percent); and machinery (14.3 percent). Investment goods represented a significant part of the shipments: for Belgium 36.8 percent; for Norway 25.7; for the Netherlands 24.2; for Italy 20.6; for France 23.4; for Austria 11.3; for Germany 3.3; and for Britain 8.8 percent. The goal of the Marshall Plan was a 30 percent increase in European industrial output. Actual output was 35 percent, and without Germany, 45 percent by 1951 (see Alan S. Milward, *Reconstruction of Western Europe 1945–1951* (London: Methuen, 1984), 94, 96, 101.

123 Lucrezia Reichlin, "The Marshall Plan Reconsidered," in *Europe's Post-War Recovery*, ed. Barry Eichengreen (Cambridge: Cambridge University Press, 1995), 42, 44, 52–3, 96, 101–2.

124 This bank was established in 1930 by seven European countries to handle German reparation payments. At Bretton Woods, the powers decided for its liquidation, but the Truman Administration suspended the execution, and in 1948, the Bretton Woods decision was reversed and the bank started serving the Marshall Plan countries.

125 Barry Eichengreen and Jorge Braga de Macedo, *The European Payments Union: History and Implications for the Evolution of the International Financial Architecture* (Paris: OECD Development Center, 2001).

126 Allen W. Dulles, *The Marshall Plan* (Oxford: Berg [1948] 1993), 111, 116–25. During World War II, Dulles joined the Office of Strategic Services (OSS), the forerunner of the CIA, and served as the OSS Chief in Bern, Switzerland. In 1953, he was appointed Director of the Central Intelligence Agency (CIA).

127 Ibid., 39, italics added.

128 Ernst H. van der Beugel, *From Marshall Aid to Atlantic Partnership. European Integration as a Concern of American Foreign Policy* (Amsterdam: Elsevier, 1966), 73, 75.

129 Ibid., 43, 47.

130 "The Hoffman Speech (1949)," October 31, 1949, www.let.leidenuniv.nl/pdf/geschiedenis/eu-history/EU_03.doc.

131 Beugel, *From Marshall Aid*, 186.

132 Ibid., 79, 137, 146–7.

133 European Cooperation Administration, *Bulletin*, no. 232 (October 18, 1948): 156–7.

134 Beugel, *From Marshall Aid*, 177.

135 Ibid., 205–6, 219, 221–3.

136 Ibid., 224.

137 State of the Union addresses by United States Presidents, www.hn.psu.edu/faciulty/ . . . / suaddresshtruman.pdf); (www.infoplease.com> . . . >Documents>State of the Union Addresses. Italics added.

138 Archive of European Integration, Exchange of letters between President Eisenhower and the chairmen of the Foreign Affairs Committees of the United States Congress relating to the European Coal and Steel Community and the unification of Europe, June, 1953.

139 Walt W. Rostow, *United States in the World Arena, an Essay in Recent History* (New York, NY: Harper & Row, 1960), 216.

140 Berlin, located in the middle of the Soviet occupation zone, was divided into four zones, each one controlled by a different country: Britain, the US, France, and the Soviet Union. According to an agreement, surface road connections were guaranteed from the Western zones of Germany to Berlin's three Western-controlled zones.

141 National Archive, Report of Robert Murphy, September 15, 1948, 862.00/9-1548.

142 National Archive, American Embassy in London, October 4, 1949, 862.01/10-449. "The USSR was never willing to deal with GER as a single ECON unit. Its REPS at Berlin, through systematic use of veto, gradually reduced Allied Control Council to impotence . . . In 1948 they deliberately destroyed the Control Council and four-power Berlin Kommandatura by walking out of these bodies."

143 David Coleman, "The Berlin–Korea Parallel: Berlin and American National Security in Light of the Korean War," *Australasian Journal of American Studies* 18, no.1 (July 1999): 19–41.

144 Monnet, *Memoirs*, 338, italics added.

145 David E. Murphy, Sergei A. Kondrashev, and George Bailey, *Battleground Berlin: CIA versus KGB in the Cold War* (New Haven, CT: Yale University Press, 1998), 86.

146 Churchill's address at the Consultative Assembly of the Council of Europe, in Richard Mayne and John Pinder with John Roberts, *Federal Union. The Pioneers. A History of Federal Union* (Houndsmills, UK: Macmillan, 1990), 106.

147 Ibid., 86.

148 For the American positions during the Johnson Administration, see Helen Parr, *Britain's Policy Towards the European Community. Harold Wilson and Britain's World Role 1964–1967* (London: Routledge, 2006), 76. This Embassy report was written before Prime Minister Wilson visited Washington DC in the 1960s.

149 Sarwar A. Kashmeri, "The Sun Never Sets on Britain's Eternal Question: To Be or Not To Be European," review of David Hannay, *Britain's Quest for a Role. A Diplomatic Memoir from Europe to the UN* (London: I.B. Tauris, 2015); kashmeri.com/category/european-union/.

150 Edmund Dell, *The Schuman Plan*, 50–1.

151 Eisenhower speech in London on July 3, 1951 at the English-Speaking Union, an organization to cultivate the special relationship between the US and Britain. The speech was printed in the Department of State, *Bulletin*, July 30, 1951, cited in Jean Monnet, *Memoirs*.

152 The 267th meeting of the National Security Council, November 21, 1955, in Nancy E. Johnson, Robert J. McMahon, and Sherrill B. Wells, eds. (William Z. Slany, general ed.), *Foreign Relations of the United States 1955–1957, Vol. 4: Western European Security and Integration* (Washington, DC: US Government Printing Office, 1988), 348–9; cited in Leopoldo Nuti, "A Continent Bristling with Arms: Continuity and Change in Western European Security Policies after the Second World War," in *The Oxford Handbook of Postwar European History*, ed. Dan Stone (Oxford: Oxford University Press, 2012), 343.

153 Archive of European Integration, George W. Ball, The Common Market—the Period of Transition, 400th Meeting of the National Industrial Conference Board Inc., New York, 21 January, 1960, aei.pitt.edu/14940/.

154 George Wilkes, ed., *To Enter the European Community 1961–1963. The Enlargement Negotiation and Crisis in European, Atlantic and Commonwealth Relations* (London: Frank Cass, 1997), 199.

155 Ibid., 200.

156 Stuart Ward, "Kennedy, Britain and the European Community," in *John F. Kennedy and Europe*, ed. Douglas Brinkley and Richard T. Griffiths (Baton Rouge, LA: Louisiana State University Press, 1999), 319, 320, 332).

157 Quoted by George M. Tuber, *John Kennedy and a United Europe* (Bruges, Belgium: College of Europe, 1969), 49.

158 Paul-Henri Spaak, *Continuing Battle. Memoirs of a European 1933–1966* (London: Weidenfeld and Nicholson, 1971), 164.

159 *The Economist*, December 15, 1950.

160 Archive of European Integration, The address of the president of the Commission of the European Economic Community [Walter Hallstein] to the Joint Session of the European Parliament and the Consultative Assembly of the Council of Europe, 24 June, 1960, 20.

161 13 Dezember 1966, *Aus der Regierungserklärung der Bundeskanzlers Kiesinger vor dem 5 Deutschen Bundestag. Dokumente zur Deutschlandpolitik*, V. Reihe, Band 1, 1 Dezember 1966 bis 31 Dezember 1967. Bearbeitet von Gisela Oberländer, Bundesministerium für Innerdeutsche Beziehungen (Frankfurt: Alfred Metzner Verlag, 1968), 59.

162 Winston Churchill, speeches (available at www.winstonchurchill.org/resources/speeches).

163 Winston Churchill, *The Second World War, Vol. IV: The Hinge of Fate* (London: Cassel & Co, 1948–54), 504.

164 *Daily Telegraph*, January 30, 1946.

165 Mayne and Pinder with Roberts, *Federal Union. The Pioneers*, 106.

166 Jenkins, *Churchill*, 814–16.

167 Ibid.

168 Winston Churchill's speech in the House of Commons on June, 27 1950 in Churchill, *In the Balance*, 299.

169 Jenkins, *Churchill*, 817–18.

170 Sean Greenwood, *Britain and European Cooperation Since 1945* (Oxford: Blackwell, 1992), 9.

171 Bevin clearly had in mind American President James Monroe's early nineteenth-century doctrines and policies on Latin America.

172 Victor Rothwell, *Britain and the Cold War 1941–1947* (London: Cape, 1982), 448.

173 Alasdair Blair, *The European Union since 1945* (Harlow, UK: Pearson Longman, 2005), 96.

174 Cabinet Minutes C.C.(52)101st Meeting – CC(54)12th Meeting, www.nationalarchives.gov.uk/documents/transcript-cab195-11.pdf; italics added. Minister of State Kenneth Younger, deputy of Bevin, clearly expressed his biases and suspicions about Schuman. "I would not . . . pin too much faith to him as he is an odd personality . . . A bachelor and a very devout Catholic who is said to be very much under the influence of the priests" from K. Younger's diary, May 14, 1950, cited in Dell, *The Schuman Plan*, 65.

175 Greenwood, *Britain and European Cooperation*, 12.

176 FRUS 1947, III, 271, in Milward, *Reconstruction of Western Europe*, 62, italics added.

177 National Archive, Caffery's Report from Paris to Secretary of State, May 10, 1949, 862.00/5-1049. Bevin's habit was certainly well-known because Schuman told the American ambassador in 1949 that "I do not want to be pressured by Bevin especially because Bevin changes his mind so very often and he might change it again."

178 Lipgens, *History of European Integration*, 555, 556.

179 T 236/808 London Committee, Sub-Committee on Integration of Europe, July 23, 1947, cited in Milward, *Reconstruction of Western Europe*, 239.

180 Manchester Dispatch, October 11, 1950, cited in Dell, *The Schuman Plan*, 64.

181 Walter Lipgens and Wilfried Loth, eds., *Documents on the History of European Integration. Vol. 3: The Struggle for European Union by Political Parties and Pressure Groups in Western*

European Countries 1945–1950, European University Institute, Series B (Berlin: Walter de Gruyter, 1988), 746–53.

182 Dell, *The Schuman Plan*, 87.
183 Ibid., 88.
184 Ibid., 65.
185 Ibid., 68.
186 Greenwood, *Britain and European Cooperation*, 30.
187 Dell, *The Schuman Plan*, 11.
188 Archive of European Integration, Monnet statement at the meeting of the Joint Committee of the High Authority and the British Delegation to the High Authority, November 17, 1952.
189 Winston Churchill's speech in the House of Commons on June 27, 1950 in Churchill, *In the Balance*, 288, 303.
190 The record of the Cabinet meeting (Public Record Office, CAB 129/48) cited in Greenwood, *Britain and European Cooperation*, 40–1.
191 Archive of European Integration, "The Community's Relations with the Outside World," *Bulletin from the European Community for Coal and Steel*, no. 20 (December 1956).
192 www.cvce.eu/content/publication/2002/9/3/ . . . aca0 . . . /publishable_en.pdf. The Labour document also expressed the leftist view that any "representative body in Western Europe would be anti-Socialist or non-Socialist in character . . . No Socialist Party . . . could accept a system . . . surrendered to a supranational European representative authority, since such an authority would have a permanent anti-Socialist majority . . . "
193 British Information Services, New York, July 5, 1967, aei.pitt.edu/view/eusubjects/HO17001.html.
194 www.margerettchatcher.org/archive/heath-eec.asp. This site presents the records of this meeting and agreement, which were released by the Margaret Thatcher Foundation. The president and the prime minister, among others, agreed to keep the intergovernmental character of the community's decision-making process.
195 Wall, *The United States and the Making of Postwar France*, 266.
196 National Archive, Memorandum "What Worries the French," March, 1945, 711.51/3-2145.
197 National Archive, Memorandum to the Secretary by Ambassador Caffery, May 12, 1945, 751.00/5-1245.
198 National Archive, The Acting Secretary's Report on the Meeting of Truman, Bidault, Admiral William D. Leahy, and Acting Secretary Grew, May 2, 1945, 711.51/5-1845.
199 National Archive, Ambassador Caffery's Memorandum to the Secretary of State, May 12, 1945, 751.00/5-1245.
200 National Archive, Caffery's Report to the Acting Secretary of State, May 5, 1945, NIACT 2381.
201 National Archive, Ambassador Caffery's Telegram for the Secretary of State, August 17, 1945, 751.00/8-1745.
202 National Archive, Paris Embassy's Report, March 22, 1946, 751.00/3-2246.
203 Wall, *The United States and the Making of Postwar France*, 36–37.
204 National Archive, Leon Blum Message to Ambassador J. Caffery, January 23, 1946, 851.00/1-2346.
205 Wall, *The United States and the Making of Postwar France*, 50.
206 National Archive, Ambassador Caffery's Message to the State Department, 851.00/4-446.
207 Wall, *The United States and the Making of Postwar France*, 2, 6, 4, 54–5: "American influence in France was unusually strong, powerful, direct, felt more concretely from day to day than at any previous time . . . or in any period since." In the early years this was based on economic aid, but "from 1950 on, French dependence on the United States appeared less a reflection of painful economic reality than the consequence of cold war policies and unbridled colonial warfare."
208 Helge Berger and Albrecht Ritschl, "Germany and the Political Economy of the Marshall Plan, 1947–52: A Re-revisionist View," in *Europe's Post-War Recovery*, ed. Barry

Eichengreen (Cambridge: Cambridge University Press, 1995), 218–19; Milward, *Reconstruction of Western Europe*, 147–8.

209 National Archive, Ambassador Jefferson Caffery's Report to the Secretary of State, May 8, 1945, 711.51/4-2045.
210 Wall, *The United States and the Making of Postwar France*, 191.
211 Ibid., 65.
212 Ibid., 191.
213 FRUS, 1947, III, 332, cited in Berger and Ritschl, "Germany and the Political Economy of the Marshall Plan," 217.
214 Wall, *The United States and the Making of Postwar France*, 192, italics added.
215 National Archive, John J. McCloy, Telegram No. 962, for Acheson and Byroade, August 3, 1950, in Record Group 466, Top Secret General Records, Box No.2, File August 1950, J.J. McCloy Papers; Henry Byroade Telegram No. 943, August 4, 1950, Ibid. Both telegrams are cited in Manfred Görtemaker, "The Failure of EDC and European Integration," in *Crises in European Integration. Challenges and Responses, 1945–2005*, ed. Ludger Kühnhardt (New York, NY: Berghahn Books, 2009), 38–9.
216 Beugel, *From Marshall Aid*, 268, 272.
217 *The New York Times*, December 15, 1953.
218 "Pleven Plan for a European Army," *Cairns Post*, October 27, 1950, trove.nla.gov.au/ndp/del/article/42703850.
219 Monnet, *Memoirs*, 271.
220 Ibid. 272, italics added.
221 Beugel, *From Marshall Aid*, 242, 245.
222 Ibid., 39.
223 National Archive, 504/4-2347, April 23, 1947.
224 Monnet, *Memoirs*, 80, 88–9.
225 Ibid., 199.
226 Ibid., 272.
227 National Archive, Caffery Report on March 27, 1948 to Secretary, 862.00/3-2748.
228 National Archive, Report on Bevin's Foreign Affairs Speech, by Douglas, November 17, 1949, 862.00/11-1849.
229 National Archive, Draft Letter to Foreign Minister Schuman Concerning German Development from H.A. Byroade to Secretary of State, October 28, 1949, 862.00/10-2849.
230 National Archive, Bureau of German Affairs. From Henry A. Byroade to Mr. Joce, December 15, 1949, 711.5162/12-1549.

2

BEGINNING OF THE EUROPEAN INTEGRATION AND ENLARGEMENT

Who helped the American project?

Even with the consent of the French, mighty America could not have realized its Cold War pet project—European federation—without the positive reception of its plans by several nation-states and a great part of the population of Europe. In the state of shock caused by the unprecedented destruction, occupation, and brutality of the long war, a great number of politically active Europeans developed the conviction that in order to avoid repeating the tragic mistakes of the past, their countries should unite into a federal state. They believed that the nation-state as an institution had lost its legitimacy when, during two wars, it had proven unable to provide minimal security to its citizens. The struggle against Fascism and Nazism had convinced a great part of the people that the catastrophe of World War II was directly rooted in the wrongful policy of the victors after World War I, and in the extreme forms of nationalism that flooded the continent. In particular, economic nationalism, which had ruled a great part of Europe in the interwar decades, had created a condition of permanent economic warfare in peacetime that in turn had paved the way for new confrontations. These convictions, which first emerged during the war years, were most prevalent among active opponents of the regimes of Mussolini and Hitler who had participated in the various resistance movements in Nazi-occupied Europe.

The German historian Walter Lipgens collected and published 176 manifestos and statements issued by Italian, French, Belgian, Dutch, British, German, and other wartime, anti-Nazi resistance organizations. All of them argued for the foundation of an integrated, federal Europe. They revealed that quite suddenly the isolated and uncommon prewar ideas of a few idealist visionaries on European integration gained relatively broad recognition.[1] In Italy, Alcide De Gasperi's program for the reconstruction of the Christian Democratic Party of Italy argued in the spring of 1943 for an integrated European market, harmonized legal systems, and integrated citizenship. It was followed on July 25, 1943, by the Milan Program of the Italian Christian Democratic Party, which embraced the ideas of a federation of the European states and European citizenship. Several socialist groups also expressed their support for a federation, and the journal of one of them, *Libérer et Fédérer*, published a federalist manifesto in France in the spring of 1944, and after the liberation of Europe, resistance organizations established the *Europeesche Actie* in The Hague to work for the creation of the United States of Europe.

One of the first and best known federalist programs, the so-called Ventotene Manifesto, emerged from an Italian island prison where it had been penned by Altiero Spinelli and Ernesto Rossi in June 1941. The document argued against reconstructing the prewar order with its balance of power policy:

> The question which must first be resolved ... is that of the abolition of the division of Europe into national, sovereign states ... The general spirit today is ... a federal reorganization of Europe ... The multiple problems which poison international life on the continent [such as mixed population, minorities, the Irish question, the Balkan question] ... would find easy solution in the European federation ... the single conceivable guarantee ... of peaceful cooperation.[2]

Three years later, on May 20, 1944, came the Geneva Declaration, the product of three meetings held in Geneva between the fall of 1943 and the spring of 1944 by representatives of resistance groups. The call for the creation of a federal Europe was clear:

> The peoples of Europe are united in their resistance to Nazi oppression. This common struggle has created among them solidarity and unity ... During the lifetime of one generation Europe has been twice the centre of a world conflict whose chief cause was the existence of thirty sovereign States in Europe. It is the most urgent task to end this international anarchy by creating a European Federal Union.[3]

The federal idea was widespread and was embraced in Britain as well as on the European continent. The leader of the British Labour Party, Clement Atlee, formulated his famous slogan "Europe must federate or perish" in November 1939. William Beveridge, head of the British Federal Union Research Institute in Oxford published his "Peace by Federation" study in May 1940.[4] Various political parties and politicians, new organizations, and even some Christian churches, as the Geneva-based World Council of Churches (WCC) documented, found in the federalization of Europe the best answer to the war. The Federalists Conference in Paris in March 1945 sharply criticized "the dogma that the nation state is the highest political form of organization of mankind," and went on to declare that "only the establishment of federation solves the problem of Europe." After the war, federalist politicians headed newly formed governments in Belgium, Italy, and the Netherlands. Lipgens points out that, as early as 1945, "the Belgian government under Paul-Henri Spaak and the Italian government under Alcide De Gasperi had made proposals aiming at European unification, which had been rejected in London and Paris."[5] Liberated peoples, exhausted and desperate, were prepared to accept the federal idea in several countries. When the French Polling Institute asked about rebuilding Europe on a federal basis, with autonomy for police, schools, and court in the former nation-states, 73 percent of the answers were positive.[6] History offers numberless examples of the power of ideas. Isaiah Berlin phrased it in a convincing way: "philosophical concepts nurtured in the stillness of a professor's study could destroy a civilization."[7] Ideas could also build one.

Nevertheless, to interpret postwar European integration as primarily a consequence of an enthusiastic wartime and postwar federalist movement would be as mistaken as to neglect the positive influence on integration projects of this postwar atmosphere. Even though earlier federalist dreams did not in fact have a direct and immediate impact on European political development, the ideal of federation certainly did influence the postwar generation of politicians, as well as the politically very active elite. Series of impressive national referenda in postwar Europe clearly reveal how the ideas of integration and limited national sovereignty penetrated the way of thinking in Europe and acquired the political efficacy to nudge Europeans towards the idea that giving up major elements of national sovereignty could be the best answer to the challenges of war and its postwar consequences.

Foundation of a new international institutional system

The attempt of the victorious powers to build international institutional guarantees to prevent a repetition of post-World War I mistakes definitely strengthened the appeal, among victors and vanquished alike, of ideas such as cooperation and limited national sovereignty. In particular, the initiative to create institutional protections against the reappearance of economic nationalism became an important factor in postwar European transformation. In the post-World War I situation, a leadership vacuum—the withdrawal of the US into isolationism, the lack of a responsible European hegemon, and the impotence of the League of Nations (LN)—opened the door for chaos in Europe and led to the renewal of revenge and struggle among nation-states. In contrast, after World War II, the US assumed the responsibilities of hegemonic power and initiated several major agreements to create a new world order. As a first step, in Dumbarton Oaks between August and October 1944, the representatives of the US, Britain, the Soviet Union, and China worked out the charter of a new institution—the United Nations (UN)—to replace the defunct LN. The UN Charter was signed in the summer of 1945 by fifty-one countries and the new international organization started its work in October 1945.

More importantly, the Americans led the initiative to create a regulated international economic system. In July 1944, representatives of forty-four countries gathered together in Bretton Woods, New Hampshire to establish a stable international financial system. The leading British interwar economist John Maynard Keynes and his American counterpart Harry Dexter White recommended introducing a strictly regulated multilateral capital market with convertible currencies and fixed exchange rates. To support this system, the International Monetary Fund (IMF) and the International Bank for Reconstruction and Development (World Bank) were founded. The member countries agreed to finance these institutions by contributing according to a quota system based on relative GDP and share in world trade.[8] Voting right was determined by the relative financial contribution. In other words, the IMF and World Bank were practically under Anglo-Saxon leadership. The formal purpose of the IMF was to assist member countries by providing loans in the event of short-term balance of payment difficulties, thus to facilitate the operations of the international financial system and to avoid crises. The World Bank, on the other hand, served to provide credits to governments and private enterprises for reconstruction and development.[9] Supported by these new international institutions, the postwar years became the formative period in the rise of an organized world economic system.

As a strategy to prevent the continuation of economic nationalism, the US also initiated the return to a free trade system. Due to this American initiative, twenty-seven countries gathered in Geneva in 1947 and agreed to reduce tariffs, import quotas, and other trade barriers gradually. After one hundred and twenty-three sets of negotiations and agreements on about fifty thousand items, twenty-three countries signed the General Agreement on Tariffs and Trade (GATT) in October 1947. The number of member countries gradually increased and half-a-century later, it had 123 countries. In the 2010s, the successor of GATT—the World Trade Organization—had 161 member countries. The West European countries joined the international regime and the danger of return to nationalist, autarchic economic policy was minimized. The new system bound its member countries together into a "Western" international economic establishment.[10]

The fatigued, ensanguined, weakened nations of Europe also faced the possibility of a new military confrontation on their soil, this one between the victorious superpowers, the US and the Soviet Union. In this environment, the West European nation-states were ready to fasten on the American safety belt as they set out on the drive of postwar recovery. Thus came into being a new Atlantic association with the US. The Marshall Plan was only the beginning, but it did not provide for military defense in a Europe where the Soviets controlled the East, and the Americans the West. Therefore, the nation-states of Western Europe happily accepted American leadership and the defense shield of American military and nuclear strength, relinquished the central function of defending their citizens, and escaped into the American-led North Atlantic Treaty Organization (NATO).

The roots of this agreement go back to March 1948 when representatives of Belgium, France, Luxembourg, the Netherlands, and the UK met in Brussels and, frightened by the sharpened Cold War crisis, signed a mutual assistance treaty providing for a common defense system. The treaty declared that if any of the signatories attacked the other signatories, the members would provide "all the military aid and assistance in their power." But in the event of an attack by Russia, they would have been helpless. In June 1948, the American Congress adopted a resolution recommending that the US join the West European countries in a defensive pact. The resulting North Atlantic Treaty signed on April 4, 1949 in Washington, DC, established NATO, the first US peacetime military alliance since 1778.[11] In October 1949, the American Congress authorized US$1.3 billion military aid for the new alliance. In 1952, Greece and Turkey joined the organization. A rearmed Germany followed in 1955.[12]

All these policies impinged on the sovereignty of the nation-states of Western Europe. The Bretton Woods agreement and GATT both required countries to give up important aspects of their sovereign monetary and foreign trade policy. The Atlantic association created a tight framework and required Europe to adjust to the new American Cold War-shaped strategy regarding Germany. Among its programs, the Marshall Plan did not necessitate a formal resignation of sovereign national rights, but in a real sense, it subordinated the European countries to the US and kicked off economic integration, whilst the North Atlantic military pact not only absorbed European national defense directly into an American-led military organization but also subordinated Europe to the US in a most essential area of national sovereignty: military power and military self-defense. The countries of Western Europe continued to be called France, Germany, Belgium, Italy, and so forth, but the political meaning of those names in 1949 had already moved significantly away from the conditions that had provoked two terrible wars. The American plan for moving towards a federal Europe had already begun to break through. A structure had been established that would push the French to abandon their punitive stance towards Germany and instead to formulate and propose a *substitute solution* based on cooperation among Western European nations.

Beginning of the realization of the American integration plan: the European Coal and Steel Community

A breakthrough in economic cooperation came with the establishment of the European Coal and Steel Community (ECSC) in 1951; a step that integrated the strategically critical coal, iron, and steel industries of France and Germany, but also of the three Benelux countries and Italy. Although naked national interests, not communitarian ideals, provided the primary impetus for this step, it could not have happened without a strong American initiative and push. Nor could it have happened without the broad international regulatory system and the North Atlantic military cooperation that already had placed the West European nation-states into a kind of international straitjacket. The idea that relinquishing some of the rights of sovereign nations might best guarantee future peace and stability in Europe had already been accepted in the West. Now the related idea of cooperation took root, with the French in the lead.

Given that sectoral integration was going to allow the six countries collectively to control coal, coke, and steel—the raw materials essential to the production of arms—the acceptance of such integration required the prior acquiescence of the French to the possibility of a rearmed Germany. The French took this necessary step in September, 1950 at the meeting of the Atlantic Council (NATO) in New York. French Minister of Foreign Affairs Robert Schuman spoke with Dean Acheson before the meeting started. "Dean Acheson told him [Schuman] and Bevin that America would send reinforcements to Europe only when the Europeans themselves had armed sixty divisions—ten of which might be German."[13] In the meeting on September 16, Schuman was politically isolated and the French anti-German policy rejected. Jean Monnet, who was not at the meeting, wrote a letter to Prime Minister Maurice Couve de Murville on the same day. We are

> forced to take short cuts. Now, the federation of Europe would have to become an immediate objective. The army, its weapons, and basic production would all have to be placed simultaneously under joint sovereignty. We could no longer wait, as we have once planned, for . . . a gradual process . . .[14]

In Monnet, the American policy already had an influential representative. Monnet had seen some Allied documents already in August 1947, sent to him by a friend, and the information he had gathered during his trip to America in the spring of 1948 harmonized with their content. He would recall in his *Memoirs* that it was evident that the Marshall Plan would be including the German economy in its production targets:

> I found some disturbing facts. The German steel industry would soon be absorbing all the coke production of the Ruhr, with the result that steel production in France and the rest of Europe would have to be limited . . . Economically and politically, this would be unacceptable; and I saw no solution except to propose linking the growth of German steel production to an increase in Ruhr coke exports . . . Only in this way could we maintain France's steel production targets, which were the key to the whole French Plan.[15]

What this meant was that Monnet recognized that his original plan for a postwar French modernization, which envisioned an independent and highly developed French steel sector surpassing a strictly controlled and strongly decreased German sector, was endangered.[16] "The French could not become modern or great themselves, alongside European neighbours and competitors . . ." Monnet recollected.

> Tomorrow our steel production might be at the mercy of German coke deliveries; later, our agriculture might depend on the whims of European importers. Disquieting signs began to appear on all sides . . . The removal of controls over the German economy would have meant renewed uncertainty about our vital supplies of coal, and especially coke, and would thereby have made our steel industry very much weaker than its powerful German rival.[17]

It was already obvious that the Americans intended to return control of the Saar and Ruhr to Germany, removing these two regions and their rich resources from joint French and international administration. By mid-1949, the limits placed after the war on German steel output had been broken and surpassed, and iron ore resources were being used for German production. Furthermore, the German coal allocation to France had actually been reduced in mid-1947. When the London conference on Germany decided in 1948 to establish an independent West Germany, French policy adjustments had to be made.[18]

> From the French point of view, there was the fear of a Germany ultimately freed from any control at all ... In the confused state of Franco–German relations, the neurosis of the vanquished seemed to be shifting to the victor: France was beginning to feel inferior again as she realized that attempts to limit Germany's dynamism were bound to fail. France's continued recovery will come to a halt unless we rapidly solve the problem of German industrial production and its competitive capacity ... From this unsuccessful experiment ... [and from all the threatening signs and endangered plans, Monnet concluded:] I had rapidly to draw positive and practical conclusion.[19]

That positive and practical solution turned French policy 180 degrees, from domination of critical German resources to a form of cooperation that guaranteed French access. It also creatively aligned French interests and policy with American plans. Monnet and his associates offered a draft proposal to the French Government on April 15, 1948—two-and-a-half years before Schuman's change of position at the NATO meeting gave the green light to move ahead:

> Europe must be organized on a federal basis ... The establishment of common bases for economic development must be the first stage in building Franco-German union. The French Government proposes to place the whole of Franco-German coal and steel production under an international Authority open to the participation of the other countries of Europe.[20]

Ernst H. van der Beugel (former Dutch foreign minister who had intimate knowledge about postwar American policy towards European integration), in his previously quoted 1966 book that presented an excellent analysis about the role of the Marshall Plan in European integration, mistakenly maintained that the "Schuman plan was the result of European initiative." Quoting Paul Hoffman's speech in 1950, he goes as far as noting that Schuman, "a European, goes much further than any American would have dared to propose at this time." In this interpretation, the US had no direct role behind the Schuman Declaration, but when it happened, "wholeheartedly welcomed the European initiative." This happened, because this plan "met four policy objective of the United States at the same time" and Schuman knew that "his bold move ... [would] almost certainly win strong support from the American government."[21]

Beugel also misinterprets Jean Monnet's role and presents him not as an arm of American policy, or as the well-informed European by his American connections who translated the American plans to present them as a genuine French initiative, but he present Monnet's role as *influencing* American policy. "American policy towards European cooperation and integration cannot be fruitfully analyzed . . . [without] the position and influence of Jean Monnet . . . [without] his most remarkable capacity . . . his great influence on the formulation of US policy towards Europe." Key American politicians, in this interpretation, had only some assisting role. Undersecretary Clayton, the initiator of the Marshall Plan, was "one of the men who helped to *clarify* his [Monnet's] ideas which resulted in the Coal and Steel Community."[22]

The resemblance between Monnet's proposal and American policy is hardly accidental. Monnet's idea was actually a rephrasing of an earlier American suggestion: that if the French wanted to control the Ruhr mining and heavy industrial centers and keep the Ruhr authority alive, the only way is that "*the coal and steel industries of France and the Benelux were brought under its purview as well.*"[23] After nine revisions, the final draft stated: "By the pooling of basic production . . . this proposal will lay the first concrete foundation of the European Federation which is indispensable to the maintenance of peace." Monnet actually recommended the acceptance of the US State Department's earlier, quoted concept. In his memorandum of May 1950, Monnet repacked the American idea as central to French interest to convince the French Government to accept the plan for a French–German coal and steel union:

> At the present moment, Europe can be brought to birth only by France. Only France is in a position to speak and act. But if France fails to speak and act now . . . Germany will develop rapidly, and we shall not be able to prevent her being armed. France will be trapped . . . and this will inevitably lead to her eclipse.[24]

Monnet was repeating the American recommendation: France has to act now.

Monnet's draft was a clear expression of French national interest to control the German resources and industrial capacities in a different way compared to their postwar attempt. Founding the Coal and Steel Community was a weaker and more limited form of European integration than the customs union, the American administration, wanted to achieve through the Marshall Plan. It was immediately accepted by the French Government and became the basis of the French Declaration on May 9, 1950, which came to be called the Schuman Plan. In his speech in the Salon de l'Horloge of the Quai d'Orsay, Schuman argued that pooling the French and German coal and steel resources under a supranational authority would open a new chapter in European history:

> Europe will not be made all at once, or according to a single plan. It will be built through concrete achievements which first create a de facto solidarity. The coming together of the nations of Europe requires the elimination of the

age-old opposition of France and Germany. Any action taken must in the first place concern these two countries. With this aim in view, the French Government proposes that action be taken immediately on one limited but decisive point. It proposes that Franco–German production of coal and steel as a whole be placed under a common High Authority, within the framework of an organization open to the participation of the other countries of Europe. The pooling of coal and steel production should immediately provide for the setting up of common foundations for economic development . . . The solidarity in production thus established will make it plain that any war between France and Germany becomes not merely unthinkable, but materially impossible. The setting up of this powerful productive unit, open to all countries willing to take part and bound ultimately to provide all the member countries with the basic elements of industrial production on the same terms, will lay a true foundation for their economic unification.[25]

Schuman explicitly stated that "by pooling basic production and by setting up a new higher-authority . . . these proposals will build the first concrete foundation of the European Federation."[26]

The ECSC came into being the following year with the signing of the Treaty of Paris. Federation had won the day. Two years later, in a statement before the Randall Committee, Monnet declared unambiguously that the ECSC's "ultimate object is to contribute essentially to the creation of the United States of Europe."[27]

This passionate Europeanism, however, probably still concealed the strong French interest in the arrangement.[28] André Gauron, advisor of two French prime ministers, did not hesitate to say as much in his 1998 book: "under the cover of Europe, France hoped to use Germany's power to benefit its own economy . . ." He went on, however, also to note the self-interest behind the German position: "Germany was not fooled by the French machinations. But it *found them to be in its own interests*, temporarily. Chancellor Adenauer's priority was to attain sovereignty with equal rights."[29]

Germany, Italy, and the Benelux countries are joining

Understandably, then, the Schuman Plan was enthusiastically welcomed in Germany. "In his personal letter to me," Adenauer recalled in his memoirs,

Schuman wrote that the aim of his proposal was not economic but highly political. There was still fear in France that when Germany had recovered she would attack France . . . I immediately informed Robert Schuman that I agreed to his proposal with all my heart.[30]

Adenauer's Germany was ready to accept any solution to regain its face, to recover from the heavy burden of the Nazi past and re-establish herself as an equal part of the European family of nations.

Adenauer clearly recognized at the end of the war that Germany had no other option but to subordinate herself to France's security interests. One of his letters from October 1945 demonstrates this point clearly: "The only way to fully satisfy the French desire for security must in the long run lie in the economic interlocking of West Germany, France, Belgium, Luxemburg and Holland."[31] Just a few months earlier, he had presided over the founding of a new German political party, the Christian Democratic Union, and he was steering that party towards the idea that the road to German rehabilitation lay through European integration. In 1946, he attended the secret meeting of European Christian Democratic leaders, among them Robert Schuman and George Bidault, held in Switzerland, where one topic of discussion was the possibility of a European economic system, based on the free market with a social dimension.[32] Adenauer also participated at The Hague Congress of the Union of European Federalists that united several federalist movements. Together with Churchill, De Gasperi, Spaak, Schuman, and Richard Nikolaus Eijiro von Coudenhove-Kalergi, Adenauer was elected honorary president of the European Movement.

During the immediate postwar years, Adenauer consistently worked to realize his ideas and closely collaborated with the US to achieve them. Among his actions were private conversations to pave the way for French–German reconciliation. He kept the Americans up-to-date about his meetings with leading French politicians: "Adenauer informed me," the American military governor of Germany reported to Washington, that "he had secret meeting with Bidault and also with Schuman to reach a Franco–German understanding . . . Schuman and Adenauer are old friends from before 1933."[33] Adenauer used the usual Cold War rhetoric to support his integration plans. In a speech at Heidelberg University he urged Germany to join the rest of Europe to "construct a wall against Asia."[34] Adenauer fully understood the American policy on reconciliation. His article in *Rheinische Merkur* in the spring of 1948[35], welcomed the American concept of a united West: "A renaissance of the conception of the 'West' can rise only as a result of a fruitful understanding between Germany and France."[36] His opening speech at the congress of the CDU in September 1948, presented "the European Union as the only hope of saving Christian Occident." The same speech declared that "France now seems to consider the consolidation of Europe as a guarantee for its security . . . this would represent a basic change in the relationship between Germany and France."[37]

Even before he became chancellor, Adenauer was trying to convince France that Germany had given up militarism. "In public address . . . [he] declared that he was against remilitarization of Western Germany. In his view the Allies were legally obliged to defend W.G. against invasion."[38] In the fall of 1949, Adenauer wanted Germany to join the Council of Europe. To this end, and to secure assurances that a German application would be accepted, he met with McCloy on October 2, 1949. McCloy reported: "He wanted High Commissioners' approval of proposed action as well as some indication as to Germany's chances of being admitted."[39]

Acheson immediately answered, expressing his absolute support for the German request. He also directed McCloy to ensure that France be informed about the American position:

> DMPT accordingly favors GMR admission to Council of EUR at earlier possible moment and favors Adenauer's proposal to make application before November MTG . . . Shld (sic) be made clear to FR that our interest in this matter springs . . . from deep conviction that future EUR security depends upon successful POLIT incorporation of GRM into EUR Community.[40]

Among German politicians, it was Adenauer who properly understood and cooperated with European pro-federation policy. The US recognized his value, even when his advanced years brought challenges. Consul General Altaffer's message to the secretary of state described Adenauer as follows:

> Dr. Adenauer is gradually assuming the character of his age (72 years): he [is] becoming more and more capricious, impatient, and runs full tilt at everything, thus more and more isolating himself from the rank and file of the party . . . [Also under] heavy personal strain due to the long illness and death of his wife.[41]

Nevertheless, as American consul Martin Hillenbrand said about him: "Adenauer [is] one of the few Germans who at the present enjoy a European reputation."[42] "I am impressed by him," McCloy summed up. "I think he is a man who firmly believes in the necessity of a French–German rapprochement."[43]

The new Bonn Government identified itself with Adenauer's policy: "By overwhelming majority within government [in Bonn]," the report informed the secretary of state, it "would promote establishment thorough-going federation Western Europe, including political, economic, and military integration when and if Germany allowed participate these activities."[44]

In the August 1949 West German elections, the Christian Democratic Union emerged as the strongest party, and in September 1949 Adenauer became the first chancellor of the newly established Federal Republic of Germany. A few weeks later he repeated the American view: "I should agree to an authority that supervised the mining and industrial areas of Germany, France, Belgium, and Luxembourg." In an interview in the spring of 1950, he suggested establishing a union between France and Germany by merging their economies, parliaments, and citizenships. This was too much and not well received in France.[45] Nevertheless, the German political elite and government recognized that their national interest would be served by joining the Schuman Plan.

In addition to Germany, Italy and the three Benelux countries jumped onto the bandwagon of integration with France. Accepting the French invitation could serve a variety of national motivations. In an Italy with a past marred by fascism and a wartime alliance with Hitler, it was possible to argue that national interest, similar to Germany's, lay in following policies that would ensure the country's return as an *equal* to the family of European nations. Prominent members of De Gasperi's Christian Democratic Government—among them De Gasperi himself, Luigi Einaudi, deputy premier and minister of finance, and Count Carlo Sforza, foreign minister—thought that European federalization would offer the surest means of attaining this desired status. At a cabinet meeting on July 15, 1947, Sforza is reported to have stated that "no national sacrifice was too great for a united Europe . . . [that a united Europe was] a supreme necessity."[46] Italy, therefore, immediately accepted the French invitation to join the Coal and Steel Community.

In the three Benelux countries, with their bitter war experience of defenselessness, accepting the invitation served the elemental national interest of maintaining close relations with friendly great powers. The establishment of a federal state seemed the ideal means to this end. In the fall of 1944, Paul-Henri Spaak, representing Pierlot's Belgian Government-in-exile, had actually tried to persuade the British Government of the wisdom of pursuing unification. The British, however, had rejected Spaak's proposal. In the Netherlands, similarly to Italy and Belgium, the post-liberation government included federalists such as Henri Brugmans and Sicco Mansholt. Foreign Minister Eelco Van Kleffens, declared in the Dutch Parliament on October 30, 1945 that his government supported "regional unions in Europe."[47] In the fall of 1947, the Belgian and Dutch ambassadors sent a joint Benelux memorandum to the occupying powers' foreign ministers' meeting in London that "pointed out the dependence of the recovery program in the three Benelux countries upon the economic revival of Germany."[48] They wanted Germany, the past and potential economic powerhouse of Europe, to be included in any such union.

In 1946, when the French Government of de Gaulle suggested founding a joint French–Benelux "economic area," that is, a customs union, the Dutch would have been ready to join had Britain and Germany been invited too. Given that these two countries were not included, the Dutch, like their counterparts in Belgium, worried about French dominance and chose to remain outside. The American embassy in Brussels correctly explained this situation when it reported that de Gaulle

> is seeking to gain over Low Countries' foreign policy to embrace them in his vision of a new and powerful France, but that Belgium prefers to cling to her traditional pro-British policy . . . There is an intense desire in Belgium to string along with two great English-speaking powers and corresponding distrust of those who do not.[49]

The Benelux countries warmly supported the new American policy towards Germany and the federalization of Western Europe. "This new method of going to work is obviously the fruit of growing realization that 'colonialism' is past and that Germany must as far as possible be treated as an equal if the West wishes to be assumed of whole-hearted German cooperation."[50]

The Benelux countries were working together as early as 1948 within a functioning Benelux Customs Union. They started developing a political integration plan in 1950. When that failed, they started advocating for a broader customs union with the potential to develop into an economic and political union. Small wonder that they immediately accepted Schuman's invitation to join the Coal and Steel Community.

In April 1951, six signatories, representing the six countries that found West European integration in their preeminent national interest, signed the Treaty of Paris that established the ECSC for fifty years. The Community started its work in July 1952. For its governance, a unique institutional system was created. The so-called High Authority, headed by Monnet, was a supranational institution with broad authority to decide upon production and trade and to make binding decisions and directives. The market of the six founding-member countries was liberalized, but also regulated. The trade of steel products among the six members would increase by four times in the first decade of the Community's existence. Monopoly institutions such as cartels were abolished, and prices were closely regulated and kept at low level. The supreme power of the High Authority was somewhat controlled by a Council of Ministers consisting of representatives of the member countries, and by a Common Assembly with seventy-eight delegates sent to the assembly by the member countries' parliaments. A Court of Justice was responsible for settling disputes. Inspired mostly by the need to solve the German Question within the framework of American Cold War European policy, a first step had been taken and a milestone reached: European economic integration had begun.

Nevertheless, a coal and steel community arising primarily out of French security needs and consisting of just six members was definitely not the full and satisfactory answer to the Cold War challenge. The German Question, for all its centrality and urgency, was also not the only postwar problem that required a definite answer. The ECSC guaranteed neither a high degree of European prosperity nor the rebuilding of Europe's economic position in the world. It did not do enough to strengthen the weakened West European economic potential and social fabric against communism. It was not complex enough and provided insufficient ties among the relevant countries. The Community was also far away from the solution that the US advocated: the creation of a United States of Europe.

Further step to realize the American initiative: the European Economic Community

True, the builders of European integration did not want to stop at this early stage. Monnet believed that economic integration would spread to other sectors, probably first to transportation and the atomic energy program. However, as the entire further history of the European integration proved, the logic of sectoral integration just did not apply in reality. The later successes of this type were the Euratom agreement to bind the research and progress of the new energy sector and the Common Agricultural Policy that integrated European agriculture. Both were expressions of par excellence French interests. Atomic energy figured in Monnet's French modernization plans as a means of securing the strong, independent energy base necessary to the return of France to great power status. Here, as with the ECSC, Monnet found that by reorienting French policy, he could combine American goals with French national interests. It was his special skill at convincing people and making deals that earned him the well-known moniker "Father of Europe."

Most other Western European countries, and a great many other leading postwar politicians, however, were genuinely much more integrationist than Monnet. In fact, it was not so much the Franco–German reconciliation, as primarily emphasized in the scholarly literature, but rather the Benelux countries that drove the engine of European integration towards a deeper and closer political and economic merger. I argue that the small Benelux countries—following their own recognized national interest—learned the lessons of the war the fastest and the best.[51] In 1944, before the war ended, their governments-in-exile in London held a joint customs convention to discuss postwar policy. At that forum they established the Benelux Customs Union. This institution started its work in 1948, and in ten years it was deepened into the Benelux Economic Union. After the war, the three countries definitely wanted to move even further along the road of integration. They realized that they could not defend their security alone and that they needed a broader political union to protect and foster their economic goals. Small countries have naturally the most open economies. Nowadays, foreign trade represents about two-thirds of the Belgian and Dutch GDP, more than twice the average percentage in the most advanced OECD (Organisation for Economic Co-operation and Development) countries. For small countries, export is the oxygen for economic breathing.

The Benelux countries wanted a united customs area in Western Europe; they were also highly interested in close economic connections with a dynamically developing Germany, and in being part of a political integration. As it happened, the particular national interests of these small, defenseless, open-economy countries best expressed the general interest of the European continent. The Benelux integration plans thus met with the acceptance of Germany and Italy, and the two defeated and humiliated big countries of the continent. Both countries recognized that their best chances for acceptance as equal partners in the family of the European nations lay in the policy of integration. Postwar Italy had the most federalist-oriented government in Europe, and Adenauer's Germany, dissatisfied with a partial, sectoral integration, wanted deeper integration and stronger guarantees of its eventual return to equal status.

The sectoral approach, as some experts soon recognized, was not actually the best approach to integration. Bela Balassa, the Hungarian-born American economist, analyzing the problems in 1961, noted that sector-by-sector integration needs a quasi-permanent readjustment of the equilibrium of prices, costs, resource allocation, and balance of payment changes. He concluded that "these theoretical objections suggest the inadvisability of integration sector by sector."[52] Balassa was right. Later economic history analysis proved that the Coal and Steel Community was unable to reach even its limited goals because national price control and subsidies remained in place. Steel tariffs were not eliminated but only harmonized, and a real common market was not created. The High Authority did virtually nothing to stimulate technological and organizational changes. The real historical achievement of the Coal and Steel Community lay mostly in initiating integration, and in the acceptance of Germany as an equal partner in Europe, steps that started the process of building common institutions and that created the conditions that would allow the Treaty of Rome.[53] The Benelux initiative should therefore be seen as the real practical engine of further European integration. The approach fits better with US European policy, and was therefore a more appropriate answer in the determinant international environment to the postwar challenge.

The Benelux countries first gained a central role in the integration drive between 1950 and 1952. The year 1950 saw panic in Europe on account of the outbreak of the Korean War. In August that year, at the Consultative Assembly of the Council of Europe, Winston Churchill proposed forming a joint West European Army. But the Council, which had been established in May 1949 as an intergovernmental, consultative, cooperative institution of sovereign nations, based on the initiative of Churchill's Zurich speech, did not have the authority to follow through on such proposals. The assembly did, however, vote to accept the resolution. A few months later, the French Government of René Pleven suggested creating a common European defense for a united Europe. In May 1952, the six signatory countries of the Coal and Steel Community met in Paris and signed a treaty to create a European Defense Community (EDC) with an army of forty mixed divisions (fourteen French, twelve German, eleven Italian, and three Benelux) in the same uniform and under one flag.

The foreign ministers of the Six, pushed by the Benelux countries, Italy, and Germany, wanted to combine the formation of the EDC and the ECSC with the creation of a federal Europe under a European Political Authority. An "Ad Hoc Assembly" consisting of the ECSC Assembly and nine additional members of the Consultative Assembly, headed by Spaak, met in the fall and winter of 1952–3 in Strasbourg. A draft treaty was adopted in March 1953 by this ad hoc group. The details were worked out in the Assembly's Constitutional Committee under Heinrich von Brentano, who would become foreign minister of Germany in 1955. In September 1953, the draft treaty was presented to an Intergovernmental Conference.

This treaty proposed establishing a European Community of a supranational character founded upon a union of peoples and states. It would have been governed by a bicameral Parliament. The 268 members of the proposed Peoples Chamber (lower house) would have been directly elected by the people in every fifth year, whilst the eighty-seven members of the Senate (upper house), as representatives of member countries, would have been appointed by their national parliaments.[54] The Community's executive power would have been placed in the hands of a powerful body, the European Executive Council. Council members—the ministers of the European Community—would have had to be accepted by both chambers of the Parliament, which also would have had the right to dismiss them. The Council would have had the additional right to issue regulations. A Council of National Ministers, with rotating presidency, would have been responsible for harmonizing the actions of the Executive Council with the governments of the member countries.

This new Community would have assumed the powers and functions of both the Coal and Steel Community and the planned European Defense Community. Moreover, it would have targeted the establishment of "a common market among the member states, based on the free movement of goods, capital and persons." The organization would have had a budget, funded by contributions of member states according to their own income. Member countries would have financed their individual contributions by, amongst other things, levying new taxes. This plan for a genuine European federation, however, proved overly ambitious and did not survive the planning phase. It failed not least because the EDC, essential to its structure, was vetoed by the French Parliament in 1954.[55]

The Netherlands did not stop advocating a closer and more general integration agenda. In June 1950, in connection with the Marshall Plan program, the Dutch foreign minister, Dirk Stikker, suggested his "Plan of Action," which was a tariff reduction and trade liberalization program for the Organisation for European Economic Cooperation (OEEC), the organization of the receivers of the Marshall Aid. When this plan failed on British opposition, the Netherlands joined the Coal and Steel Community, believing that the "Six" would be a better community for tariff reductions and a customs union. In 1952, about the time the Coal and Steel Community was being formed, Johan Willem Beyen was appointed minister of foreign affairs of the Netherlands. He had worked previously at the IMF and the Bank for International Settlements, the latter a Marshall Plan institution that served the European Payment Union. He had an immense knowledge about the integration plan of the Marshall Aid organization, the OEEC, and found the progress of integration under the Marshall Plan insufficient. Beyen created and published his own supranational integration plan in 1952. Instead of the sectoral integration concept of Monnet's Coal and Steel Community—which he did not find to be the best way to further integration—he suggested a common market and customs union, comprising the six ECSC countries. Just as Monnet's plan expressed direct French interests, Beyen's reflected the interests of the Netherlands and the small, open-economy countries of the Benelux, which preferred multilateral deals over bilateral agreements with their large and strong neighbors. In 1952, however, Beyen's initiative was unable to break through.

When the political integration plans, the EDC, and the European Political Community failed in 1954, Beyen renewed his market integration plan in a memorandum of 1955. He still rejected the approach of sectoral integration, preferring "to create a supranational community with the task of bringing about the economic integration of Europe in the general sense, reaching economic union by going through a customs union as a first stage."[56] Beyen gained the support of his Belgian and Luxembourgian colleagues, Paul-Henri Spaak and Joseph Beck. His plan for a common market with a customs union became popular in the new situation and was accepted by and found an additional sponsor in the influential Monnet. The Benelux initiative became the centerpiece of new negotiations in 1955–6.

The existing institutions of the six partner countries had an impact on further development. A kind of spill-over automatism—discussed by a large corps of political science studies on the subject—worked. The caravan of Western Europe increased its speed. On April 2, 1955, Spaak sent Beyen's suggestion to the foreign ministers of the six Coal and Steel Community countries. An ad hoc committee was formed, chaired by Spaak. Adenauer, ever mindful of German political interest, supported pushing integration ahead, and France favored the same, as furthering its economic modernization plan.[57] On May 5, Spaak, Beyen, and Beck presented to Monnet a joint Benelux memorandum, which combined the Belgian and Dutch ideas of a sectoral and common market approach. On May 9, the assembly of the ECSC unanimously adopted the resolution to form an intergovernmental committee of the Six. The foreign ministers of the Six met accordingly in Messina on June 1–3, 1955, and established the intergovernmental Spaak Committee to work out a draft plan. This committee met again one month later near Brussels. In May 1956, the committee's report was drafted, presented, and accepted in Venice by the foreign ministers of the Six.[58] On March 25, 1957, representatives of the six ECSC countries met in the Palazzo dei Conservatori in Rome and signed two treaties establishing the European Economic Community (EEC) and the European Atomic Energy Community (EAEC or Euratom). Both entered into force on January 1, 1958. The preamble of the Treaty of Rome makes clear the intentions of the signatories:

> Determined to lay the foundations of an ever closer union among the peoples of Europe, resolved to ensure the economic and social progress of their countries by common action to eliminate the barriers which divide Europe, affirming as the essential objective of their efforts the constant improvements of the living and working conditions of their peoples, recognizing that the removal of existing obstacles calls for concerted action in order to guarantee steady expansion, balanced trade and fair competition, anxious to strengthen the unity of their economies and to ensure their harmonious development by reducing the differences existing between the various regions and the backwardness of the less-favoured regions, desiring to contribute, by means of a common commercial policy, to the progressive abolition of restrictions on international trade, intending to confirm the solidarity which binds Europe and the overseas countries . . . resolved by thus pooling their resources to preserve and strengthen peace and liberty, and calling upon the other peoples of Europe who share their ideal to join in their efforts, [we, the signatories] have decided to create a European Economic Community . . .[59]

The central goal of the treaty establishing the EEC was to gradually abolish tariffs and other restrictions on trade amongst member countries over twelve years. This target was actually reached in ten years and the Community then took further integrative steps.

As the pioneering work of Bela Balassa illuminates, economic integration may have various forms and stages. Balassa differentiates five stages: in the first, the loosest, the free trade area eliminated tariffs and other restrictions among the participating countries, but each of them retained their own tariffs against non-member counties. With the second stage, reached in 1968, the customs union unified the external tariffs at the exterior border of the member countries. With the third stage came the common market with elimination of restrictions on free movement of labor and capital. The Treaty of Rome actually declared these principles, but that stage was fully achieved only in the 1990s. Despite having begun to travel the road of gradual economic integration, the EEC needed three more decades to reach the fourth stage, the economic union that, according to Balassa, combined all the results of the previous three stages of integration. The crowning fifth stage, the achievement of complete economic integration, however, requires several further steps, including monetary, fiscal, and social integration with common economic policies, directed by supranational institutions. That stage has been reached only partly with changes instituted in the crises in the 1970s–80s.[60]

The Treaty of Rome, a kind of "constitution" of the EEC, had 248 articles, four annexes, thirteen protocols, four conventions, and nine declarations that established the institutional network of governance. At the heart of the new Community stood the European Commission, courier of the supranational "European Idea." The Commission functioned as a quasi-executive branch, originally with nine members and a German, Walter Hallstein, as president. It had 13,000 staff members and became the engine of the Community with the right to recommend policies and initiatives. The other central institution, the Council of Ministers representing the member states, was an intergovernmental institution with decision-making responsibility that was limited, however, by the demand for unanimous consent. The Parliamentary Assembly, with 142 representatives delegated by the member countries' parliaments, was given only a consultative role, not real decision-making power. The European Court of Justice (ECJ), with seven judges who adjudicated disputes amongst member countries, emerged as the most federal institution, especially after its decision in 1964—unopposed by the member countries—that national laws and constitutions are subordinate to European Community law.

With the Treaty of Rome, Europe laid down a real framework and road to economic union—in short, an agenda for European integration and unification. Combining markets, tariff policies, and other policy areas of the six West European countries made possible their export-led growth, a new trade orientation, and a much more modern division of labor. The member countries became more active in each other's markets. Their trade dramatically increased—by six-and-half times during the 1950s and 1960s. (After another two decades, the increase stood at fourteen times, compared to1958.) Trade expansion was greater than at any time in history. By 1973, some of the countries had increased their exports by ten to fifteen times over prewar years. In 1938, 53 percent of imports and 64 percent of exports of the West European countries originated from other West European countries. Over half a century of integration, these shares increased to nearly 75 percent of exports and imports (see Figure 2.1).

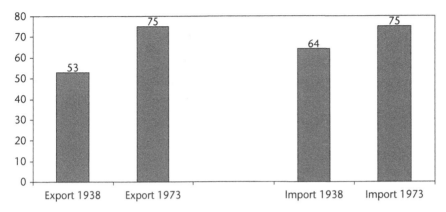

FIGURE 2.1   Trade among the countries of the European Economic Community

These new trade relations went hand-in-hand with a spectacular change of the structure of trade. Before the war, the traditional division of labor was characterized by trade between agricultural and raw material producers on the one hand, and processed industrial goods producers on the other. Imports of raw materials and food from other continents dropped from the prewar figure of 33 percent to 18 percent of the total by 1970. Industrial exports to non-European, non-industrialized countries declined from more than 30 percent to 17 percent. Trade between the member countries of the EEC was gradually dominated by exchanges of industrial products amongst the more highly developed countries. Several such products were produced in cooperation; different countries manufactured different parts that were then assembled to create the product. The EEC countries enjoyed an advantage of scale that helped to increase productivity and growth. France, the Netherlands, and other countries reached economic growth rates three to four times greater than during the prewar regime of economic nationalism. Germany and Italy, as well as several other West European countries, experienced their economic miracles, substantial answers to the challenges of wartime destruction and frightening postwar economic decline. For the time being, Europe certainly had found a way to avoid the danger of economic nationalism.

In the same period, the welfare state was introduced throughout Western Europe to offer social security to citizens: free health care, schooling, and pensions. Welfare regulations, however, remained the responsibility of the nation-states, and the EEC did not take over this task. (The concept of "Social Europe" became part of the European agenda only in later decades.) Rapidly increasing living standards and the rise of the consumer society elevated Western Europe to a much higher level of living. In 1950, an average German and French citizen spent 43 to 45 percent of income for food and basics. By 1971, this share had dropped to 27 percent. The housing situation improved tremendously and car ownership spread. In 1950, only 20 percent of French households owned a car. By 1972, this share was 60 percent. The number of TV sets in Western Europe increased from 177,000 in 1950 to nearly twenty-four million by 1973. In the latter year, 60 to 80 percent of households were mechanized and West Europeans were spending 44 percent of their income for household, health, culture, and leisure, nearly twice as much as in 1950.[61] This increasing richness and the emergence of the welfare state became a significant factor in Cold War competition, able to take the wind out of the sails of communism in Western Europe. Europe, pushed by the US, gave an innovative answer to the deep and complex postwar challenge.

American policy towards enlargement of the European Community

With the first major steps of West European integration the realization of the American Cold War strategy in Europe began. The US's strategic program, however, included more than just forcing Western European federalization. Cold War confrontation required the broadest possible anti-communist alliance within Europe. To achieve that, because communist dictatorship was the defined enemy, American administrations were ready to make alliances with right-wing, anti-communist dictatorships on the peripheries of Europe. Various American administrations did not hesitate eliminating democratically elected governments if it endangered geopolitical American interests. The Eisenhower Government organized to overthrow the governments of Iran and Guatemala in 1953 and 1954, respectively. In 1960, President Eisenhower expressed his understanding that "dictatorships of this type [the Salazar dictatorship in Portugal] are something *necessary* in countries whose political institutions are not so far advanced as ours."[62] Communist dictatorships were bad; anti-communist dictatorships understandable and acceptable. Winston Churchill, who condemned communist regimes from a high moral stand of freedom and human rights, expressed a similar understanding about the bloody Franco dictatorship in Spain. In his speech about the North Atlantic Treaty in May 1949, Churchill praised Franco's Spain for services and a "most fertile trade" during the war. Moreover, he maintained that "the conditions under which people live in Spain give far greater freedom to the individual than those under which they live in Russia." What was the reason of this understanding? Churchill clearly answered this question: "The absence of Spain from the Atlantic Pact involves, of course, a serious gap in the strategic arrangements for Western Europe."[63] The cynical President Nixon accepted as fact that Latin America, Africa, and Asia were not well suited to democracy, which is inappropriate in the Third World. Both the pragmatic Henry Kissinger and the Nixon Administration did not even attempt to find explanations for collaboration with anti-democratic regimes. Kissinger, stated one expert, was "very unconcerned with human rights" and his "indifference to domestic conditions in foreign societies permitted him to forego judgments about indecencies or inequalities of other national systems, as long as repressive governments renounced their revolutionary aims."[64] He maintained that human rights in other countries were not America's business. Nixon explicitly expressed his disinterest in Soviet domestic policy. "We cannot gear our foreign policy to transformation of other societies."[65] As White House tapes proved, his administration would therefore happily aid dictators, Nixon said, "if it is in our interest . . . I won't lecture him on his internal structure . . . Our concern is foreign policy."[66]

In the American view, integration of countries into the European Community would strengthen and stabilize NATO and would create strong political cohesion amongst member countries. In a speech in Frankfurt, President Kennedy clearly expressed this traditional American concept: "*It is only a fully cohesive Europe that can protect us all against fragmentation of the alliance.*"[67]

The strategically important Mediterranean countries Spain, Portugal, Greece, and Turkey were all governed by right-wing authoritarian and/or military dictatorships after World War II. Some of these regimes had existed since the 1930s; some, such as Franco's Spain, even in alliance with Hitler and Mussolini. After World War II, these countries did not participate in the democratic transformation of the continent and they became political pariahs in Europe, closed, isolated.

The logic of the Cold War, however, led the American administrations to incorporate them into the "Western world" and its alliance system. On the same basis, the US wanted these countries included in the emerging European Community. The strong human rights rhetoric against dictatorial communism was not used against these countries even though, as Helen Graham and Alejandro Quiroga have argued, Spain, Portugal, and Greece "replicated the structural violence and coercion of the Cold War enemy, which meant that they actively undermined the idea of western political superiority and civility . . . ." "Cold War fears," they continue, "caused the western allies to support repressive regimes on the southern boundaries of 'free' Europe . . . These international priorities determined the eventual outcomes of civil wars, guaranteeing the survival [of those regimes] . . . ."[68] The authors elaborate: "Spain was excluded from Marshall Aid . . . However, by 1953, Spain had got its own US aid package, which underwrote the dictatorship and led [the bloodstained leader,] Franco, himself to declare: at last I have won the Spanish civil war."[69]

For the Americans and British, what mattered most was that these right-wing dictatorships were strongly anti-communist. In their civil wars, Spain and Greece defeated communist challengers, the latter with American assistance. The first part of the Greek civil war ended in late 1944 with the defeat of the communist partisan army by a powerful British intervention, a defeat that liberated most of the country. When the British informed President Truman that they were unable to keep control of Greece in 1947, Truman announced the American takeover of Greece both by massive financial assistance to the dictatorial regime and heavy US military involvement. William Harris, an American military expert, clearly explained: "The US interest in Greece was preventing the Soviet Union from controlling Greece, which would deny the United States access to the strategically important Aegean and eastern Mediterranean seas and grant it to the Soviet Union." The same author described that, due to Public Law 75 an American Army-Group-Greece was established on April 14, 1947. The Truman Administration then decided to increase the Royal Greek forces from forty-two to one hundred battalions, financed by the US. In December of that year, the American Military Advisory and Planning Group-Greece were established. As the

American military chief of the Greek organization later declared, I have been "a military dictator in every meaning of the word." The US army improved the combat capacity of the nationalist, anti-communist army "through persistent training, mentorship, direction and disciplinary advice [. . .] [and] contributed to victory over the communists through its material and operational assistance."[70]

The second chapter of the Greek civil war between 1947 and 1949 therefore ended by means of strong American participation, and US interests increasingly set the tone for the policy of the West at large with regard to Greece. In 1953, the first Greek–American defense cooperation agreement was signed. American military installations, among them a base in Crete, were established. Both during and after the civil wars, Greece was controlled by dictatorial military and right-wing governments. Nevertheless, pushed by the US Government, the European Community started negotiations with Greece in the fall of 1959, concluding in March 1961. The European Community signed an agreement "based on customs union to be established . . . over a transition period and intended to enable Greece to become at a later day, when its economic progress allows, a full member of the Community."[71] In 1965, George Papandreou's Centre Union Party won the elections and formed the government. After eighteen months, however, King Constantin II removed Papandreou. The so-called Apostasia 1965 constitutional crisis was targeted to be resolved by new elections in May 1967. Before the elections, however, as it became clear that Papandreou was going to win again and that he might establish a coalition government with the United Democratic Left, which was assumed to be a legal organization of former communists, the king asked the American ambassador, Philip Talbot, about the US attitude towards an "extra-parliamentary solution." He did not get a straight answer. Nevertheless, on April 27, 1967, a few weeks before the elections, a military coup created a *tabula rasa*. The Junta of Colonels took over and introduced a ruthless dictatorship. About one hundred thousand people were executed, imprisoned, or exiled. The State Department was not very happy with this solution, but accepted it.[72] The Junta, led by Colonel George Papadopulous, ruled the country until 1974.[73]

Behind the scenes, however, Greece's Western connections remained strong.[74] "Our first VIP visitor after the coup was Richard Nixon," noted Robert Keeley, the former diplomat at the US Embassy in Athens. "The former Vice-President who was in his campaign for presidency, arrived in mid-June and met, among others, the bloody handed Brigadier Stylianos Pattakos, interior minister of the regime."[75] In 1970, when the Tory Party regained power in Britain and Edward Heath formed the government, the military regime's mouthpiece *Nea Politia* triumphantly declared that the British elections "show that the swing towards the left in Europe is being halted . . . [These developments] vindicate the 1967 Revolution and show that the Greek officers who launched it were the first to understand the message of [the] time."[76] Indeed, in September 1970, the British Government decided that the "co-operation with Greece in the military field was particularly important." The Greek foreign minister visited London and met with Sir Denis Greenhill, undersecretary of foreign affairs. He stated that Britain wished to do "as much business as possible with Greece."[77] In the middle of the military dictator-ship, Spiro Agnew, vice president of the US under Nixon, also visited Greece and signed an agreement establishing an American naval base in Athens.

The assertive anti-communist Cold War rhetoric used by the governments of these Southern European dictatorships helped to convince the West European population that an alliance with undemocratic regimes was justified, and it also guaranteed essential political support and economic aid from the West. Earlier, Spain, for example, was isolated by the US and excluded from the Marshall Aid program. The Franco regime was also under a diplomatic boycott. This policy, however, soon changed dramatically. The US Joint Chief of Staff had already expressed military interests in Spain in 1947. American Military planners argued in mid-1947 that the US "should furnish economic aid to Spain . . . in order to strengthen her capacity for military resistance." In October, the State Department decided to modify policy towards Spain. In December 1947, the National Security Council's "Report on US Policy toward Spain"[78] made this reorientation official, beginning in January 1948. In August 1950, a few weeks after the Korean War started, US$62.5 million aid was sent over to Franco. The regime isolation ended and, with US assistance, Spain joined the OEEC in late 1950.[79]

On September 26, 1953, the preamble of an agreement between the two gov-ernments on establishing American military facilities in Spain stated:

> Faced with the danger that threatens the western world, the Governments of the United States and Spain, desiring to contribute to the maintenance of international peace and security through foresighted measures which will increase their capability and that of the other nations which dedicate their efforts to the same high purposes, to participate effectively in agreements for self-defense.

In exchange for four American military bases in Spain, the US agreed to support

> Spanish defense efforts for agreed purposes by providing military end item assistance to Spain during a period of several years to contribute to the effec-tive air defense of Spain and to improve the equipment of its military and naval forces, to the extent to be agreed upon in technical discussions in the light of the circumstances, and with the cooperation of the resources of Spanish industry to the extent possible.[80]

Between 1953 and 1961 Spain received US$1.4 billion aid and became the third largest recipient of American assistance in Europe.

Turkey's postwar situation was different from that of other Mediterranean countries. Its political position was good because it was neutral in the earlier phases of the war and it then aligned with the Allies. Its location on the Dardanelles Straits, which control access from the Black Sea to the Mediterranean, and between the Soviet Union and the Middle East, made it a key country in Cold War politics.

As the Soviets stepped up their aggressive attempts to control the Dardanelles, the Turks became frightened. The Soviet actions generated a strong American reaction and even military demonstration. Stalin withdrew. The popular *Time Magazine* informed the American public about Turkey's genuine anti-Russian attitude: "Turkish history in the last three hundred years," the article stated, "was a history of war against Russia." "Some estimate as many as 22 [wars] . . . . If Turkey were not in the way, no substantial military force would stand between Russia and its dreams of domination of the Middle East and its oil riches . . ."[81] As a consequence, Turkey aligned itself over time with the West rather than with the West's former ally, the Soviet Union.

Although Turkey was not a democracy and its political system was based on one-party rule, free elections were held in 1950, 1954, and 1957. Five Menderes Governments followed, one upon the other; however, as in any delicate political situation, the army never hesitated to launch a military coup, as happened in 1960, 1971, and 1980. The 1970s saw violent right–left confrontations and massacres in, for example, Bahçelievla, Taksim, and Kahramanmaraş where thousands of people were killed. From the 1960s onwards, after Cyprus became independent, Turkish confrontations with Greece over Cyprus became a permanent source of political crisis and aggression. Regardless of these problems, the US included Turkey in its military defense strategy and pushed Europe to build a close alliance with the country. As George McGhee, American ambassador to Turkey, stated in his article in *Foreign Affairs*:

> The successful visit to the United States in February of this year [1959] of President Bayar of Turkey, at President Eisenhower's invitation, has high-lighted one of the most significant political events of our times—Turkey's emergence as a full and responsible member of the Western alliance.[82]

Turkey's inclusion in the Western alliance system occurred in steps, beginning with the Truman Doctrine, the US–Turkish Ankara Agreement, and then the Marshall Plan. NATO membership failed in 1950 because Norway and Denmark voted against it, but was realized after the Korean War. In 1951 there was an invitation to join the Middle East Command to preserve the Western position at the Suez Canal. In 1954, the Balkan Pact, signed by Turkey along with Greece and Yugoslavia, set up protections against a potential Soviet aggression, and in July 1958, the IMF rushed a US$359 million economic stabilization program to assist the country.

On January 5, 1957, soon after the Suez Crisis, President Eisenhower sent a message to the American Congress about the policy of protecting the countries of the Near East from Soviet danger. In March, Congress accepted this "Eisenhower Doctrine" as well as the formation of the so-called Central Eastern Treaty Organization (CENTO) with the participation of Turkey, Iran, and Pakistan. Turkey served as a bridge between the NATO and CENTO and became a main player in Western Cold War policy. Ankara became the location of the headquarters of the NATO's Allied

Land Forces in Southeastern Europe. Eisenhower invited the Turkish President Bayan to visit the US in 1959, and he visited Turkey at the end of the same year, the year of the American–Turkish Bilateral Treaty.[83]

This close connection did not suffer any setback after the Turkish military coup of May 1960. It was launched by the so-called National Unity Committee, a group of US-trained officers. The coup occurred just as Prime Minister Adnan Menderes was planning a visit to Moscow, thereby raising the prospect of a potential reorientation of Turkish foreign policy. The coup not only eliminated the democratically elected Bayan–Menderes civil government, but also ousted the Democratic Party and executed Menderes along with two other leading members of his government.

America's prime concern was to maintain its alliance with Turkey. General Eisenhower stressed the strategic value of Turkey when he briefed President Truman in 1951. Four years later, in his own presidency, Eisenhower repeated that the alliance with Turkey is "the best possible way to buttress US security interest in the Near East." Secretary of State Dulles told the Turkish ambassador in 1955 "Turkey is our No.1 exhibit." After the shocking success of the Soviet Sputnik, which validated the Soviet long-range missile threat, Turkey's importance increased even further in the eyes of the US, and the two countries signed an agreement on the deployment of Jupiter missiles in Turkey.[84] "The Americans did not oppose the undemocratic military regime in Turkey, which came to power on 27 May 1960. Instead they extended recognition to it three days after the military coup and promised more economic and military aid."[85] Turkey, which badly needed financial and military assistance and wanted to join Europe, made good service for the West:

> We saw it as our duty to support France, America and Britain in their dealing with Algerian, Vietnam and Suez problems. We also felt it our responsibility to defend Western colonialism in the Bandung Conference . . . In the United Nations voting, we look at the arms of American representative.[86]

Turkey, however, was then—and remains today—a highly controversial country for the European Community.[87]

In general, during the 1950s and 1960s, in the years of harsh Cold War confrontation, American administrations built military–political–economic connections with the Mediterranean dictatorships and military regimes, and never ceased urging the EEC to enlarge by admitting those countries: "Successive US Administrations and many Members of Congress," argued the enlargement expert of the Congressional Research Service in a 2013 report,

> have long backed EU enlargement, believing that it serves US interests by advancing democracy and economic prosperity throughout the European continent. Over the years, the only significant US criticism of the EU's enlargement process has been that the Union was moving too slowly, especially with respect to Turkey, which Washington believes should be anchored firmly to Europe.[88]

In the center of another Congressional Research Service document regarding Turkish membership in the European Community is Turkey's NATO membership:

> The United States believes that Turkey's membership in NATO has demonstrated that Turkey can interact constructively with an organization dominated by most of the same European countries that belong to the EU . . . The US has been disappointed that it has not been able to use its influence to help shape a more constructive EU–Turkey relationship.[89]

Portugal, Greece, and Turkey all became Marshall Aid recipients—Portugal was a founding member of NATO in 1949, while Greece and Turkey joined in 1952. Meanwhile, in Spain, after its 1953 military agreement with the US, the Franco regime gave up its isolationist policy and realized a stabilization plan with assistance from the IMF, the OEEC, and the American Government. The West contributed US$420 million to Spanish financial stabilization and dismantled trade restrictions. Spain was opened for foreign investments and this triggered the invasion of the country by Western tourists. The World Bank sent a mission to the country in March 1961 to prepare a development plan. In total, Spain would receive about US$2.5 billion between 1950 and 1970.

One year after the US–Spanish agreement, Helmut Burckhardt, the vice president of the Consultative Committee of the ECSC, in his speech in Pittsburgh spoke of an enlarged Community with "the eventual inclusion of Scandinavia, Spain, Portugal, and possibly Great Britain and Austria."[90] American Cold War policy was having its influence. When Turkey and Franco's Spain in 1959 and 1962, respectively, made their first applications for membership of the EEC, the Community shelved these politically inconvenient applications for a while.

> Without much fanfare, however, the European Community signed a Preferential Commercial Agreement with Spain . . . with highly favorable terms. European tariffs were immediately and substantially reduced by 60 percent . . . The goal was to establish completely free trade, and all quantitative restrictions against Spanish exports were removed . . . Spain . . . [became] an 'external' member of the European Community.[91]

In 1963, Turkey and the EEC also signed the Ankara Agreement, an association agreement, thus beginning the process of building closer economic ties. This agreement was supplemented by an Additional Protocol signed in 1970 that prepared the way for a customs union.

The Treaty of Rome (1957) stipulated that the Community "may conclude with one or more third countries . . . agreements establishing an association involving reciprocal rights and obligations."[92] That was what actually happened. Greece applied for associate membership in 1959. Association partnership agreements were signed with Greece in 1961 and with Turkey in 1963. Cold War enlargement in the form of informal associations, as represented by the semi-concealed partnerships with Spain, Portugal, Greece, and Turkey, together brought seven additional countries into the orbit of an integrating Europe. Although the association agreements did not guarantee subsequent formal admission, they paved the way towards that goal. Greece, Portugal, and Spain became full members of the EEC in the 1980s. Turkey's acceptance remained more problematic and uncertain, subject to endless delay. Despite the country's application for membership in 1959, Turkey had to wait until 1999 to be recognized as an official candidate.[93]

In every case, at least in the Mediterranean, enlargement (see Figure 2.2) served twin purposes: advancing European integration and US Cold War aims. And so, once again, European integration successes owe a debt to US pressures and policies.

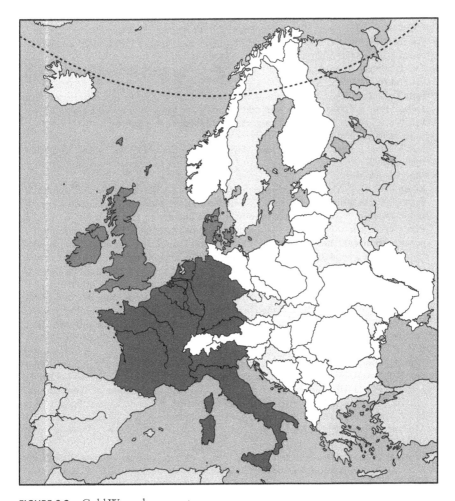

FIGURE 2.2   Cold War enlargement

Notes:
Dark gray: France, Germany, Belgium, the Netherlands, Luxembourg, Italy.
Medium gray: Britain, Ireland, Denmark.
Light gray: Spain, Portugal, Greece, Turkey.

Notes

1 Walter Lipgens, *Europa-Föderationspläne der Wiederstandbewegungen 1940–1945* (München: R. Oldenburg Verlag, 1968).
2 "The Ventotene Manifesto by Altiero Spinelli and Ernesto Rossi", reprinted in *The European Union*, eds. Brent F. Nelsen and Alexander C-G. Stubb (London: Lynne Rienner, 1998), 4–6.
3 Draft Declaration of the European Resistance Movement, May 20, 1944, ucparis.fr/index.php/download_file/view/748/235/.
4 Winston Churchill, *The Second World War. Vol. IV: The Hinge of Fate* (London: Cassell and Co, 1964), 504.
5 Walter Lipgens, *A History of European Integration 1945–1947. Vol. 1: The Formation of the European Unity Movement* (Oxford: Oxford University Press/Clarendon Press, 1982), 19, 41, 56, 85, 115, 126, 134, 142–3, 159, 248, 259, 269.
6 Walter Lipgens, *Europa-Föderationspläne*, vii.
7 Isaiah Berlin, *The Power of Ideas* (Princeton, NJ: Princeton University Press, 2000), ix.
8 For the IMF, the US's quota was US$2.8 billion and Britain's US$1.3 billion; France's quota was US$450 million and India's US$400 million.
9 The Bank had an initial capital of US$10 billion, which increased to US$21 billion by the end of the 1950s.
10 Ivan T. Berend, *The Economic History of Twentieth-Century Europe: Economic Regimes from Laissez-Faire to Globalization* (Cambridge: Cambridge University Press, 2006), 192–3.
11 In 1778, a Franco–American alliance was established.
12 www.nato.int/history/nato-history.html.
13 Jean Monnet, *Memoirs*, trans. Richard Mayne (Garden City, NY: Doubleday, 1978), 342.
14 Ibid., 342–3.
15 Monnet, *Memoirs*, 274.
16 In August 1945, Monnet recalls meeting and talking with de Gaulle and explaining France's backwardness and the need of modernization. Monnet described this episode in his *Memoirs*: "From that moment onward, the underlying philosophy of the French Plan was clear in my mind . . . At the beginning of December 1945 I was already in a position to meet General de Gaulle's deadline, and I sent him a five-page Note entitled 'Proposals for a Modernization and Investment Plan.'" On January 3, 1946, the French Government established the Commissariat-General of the French Modernization and Investment Plan, chaired by the prime minister, consisting of twelve other ministers, and run by Monnet as planning commissioner. The institution was attached to the prime minister's office. The first French plan concentrated on six sectors and set production targets. In 1946, the planners worked out the main modernization program and it became national policy by 1948 (Monnet, *Memoirs*, 228, 232–3, 236–7, 240, 249, 257).
17 Ibid., 277, 284.
18 Alan S. Milward, *Reconstruction of Western Europe 1945–1951* (London: Methuen, 1984), 468; Ruggero Ranieri, "Unlocking Integration: Political and Economic Factors Behind the Schuman Plan and the European Coal and Steel Community in the Work of Alan Milward," in *Alan S. Milward and a Century of European Change*, ed. Fernando Guirao, Frances M.B. Lynch, and Sigfrido M. Ramírez Pérez, (London: Routledge, 2012), 304.
19 Monnet, *Memoirs*, 292, then 277.
20 Ibid.
21 Ernst Hans van der Beugel, *From Marshall Aid to Atlantic Partnership. European Integration as a Concern of American Foreign Policy* (Amsterdam: Elsevier, 1966), 232–4, 238, 240.
22 Ibid., 242, 245.
23 National Archive, Memorandum "What Worries the French," March, 1945, 711.51/3-2145.
24 Irwin M. Wall, *The United States and the Making of Postwar France, 1945–1954* (Cambridge: Cambridge University Press, 1991), 294–5, 298.
25 europa.eu/about-eu/basic . . . /europe . . . /schuman-declaration/index_en.htm.

26 Archive of European Integration, Declaration by French foreign minister Robert Schuman, Paris, 9 May, 1950.
27 Archive of European Integration, Jean Monnet's statement before the Randall Committee, 11 November 1953.
28 Jean Monnet was considered to be a prophet of European integration. George Orwell characterized him as someone who had "done more to unite Europe on a permanent basis than all the emperors, kings, generals and dictators since the fall of the Roman empire." Quotation from George Orwell, *The Lion and the Unicorn* (Harmondsworth, UK: Penguin Books, 1982), 35. On the other hand, Alan S. Milward in his *The European Rescue of the Nation-State* (Berkeley, CA: University of California Press, 1992) strongly criticizes the decisive role of federalists, the "prophet founders" of integrated Europe. Milward sarcastically entitles one chapter of his book "The lives and teachings of the European saints." He maintains that the chief goal of each of these "saints"—including Schuman and Monnet—was to rescue their own nation-states, and their security and economies.
29 André Gauron, *European Misunderstanding* (New York, NY: Algora Publishing, 2000); (original French "Le Malentendu Européen," Éditions Hachette Littératures, 1998), 5–6, emphasis added.
30 Konrad Adenauer, *Erinnerungen, Vol. I, 1945–53* (Stuttgart: DVA Verlag, 1965), 314–15.
31 Adenauer quoted his letter of October 31, 1945 in Adenauer, *Erinnerungen*, 39.
32 Fernando Guirao, Frances M.B. Lynch, and Sigfrido M. Ramírez Pérez, eds. *Alan S. Milward and a Century of European Change* (London: Routledge, 2012), 200.
33 National Archive, Maurice Altaffer, American Consul General's Report from Bremen, October 22, 1948, 862.00/10-2248.
34 National Archive, Consular Report to the Secretary of State, May 22, 1949, 862.00/5-1549.
35 Konrad Adenauer, *South European Society and Politics* 17(1), (2012).
36 National Archive, Ernest de W. Mayer Consul's Report from Baden-Baden, March 31, 1948, 862.00/3-3148.
37 National Archive, Consular Report from Bremen about the Congress of the CDU, September 8, 1948, 862.00/9-848.
38 National Archive, Altaffer Consul Reports from Bremen, January 31, 1949, 862.011/1-3149.
39 National Archive, McCloy to Secretary of State, October 26, 1949, 862.00/10-2649.
40 National Archive, Acheson's Message to McCloy, October 28, 1949, 862.00/10-2849.
41 National Archive, Consul General Maurice Altaffer's Report from Bremen, May 5, 1948, 862.00/5-548.
42 National Archive, Consul Martin J. Hillenbrand Report from Bremen, March 29, 1948, 862.00/3-1548.
43 National Archive, High Commissioner McCloy's Letter, October 28, 1949 to James E. Webb, 862.00/10-2849.
44 National Archive, Memorandum of Riddleberger, August 18, 1949, 862.00/8-1849.
45 Monnet, *Memoirs*, 283, 285; Thomas Pedersen, *Germany, France and the Integration of Europe. A Realist Interpretation* (London: Pinter, 1998), 76. The French daily, *L'Aube*, issued by the governing French Christian Democratic Mouvement Républicain Populaire (MRP), rushed to reject Adenauer's ideas: "Adenauer wants to build Europe around Germany and for Germany."
46 Carlo Sforza, *Cinque anni a Palazzo Chigi. La politica estera Italian dal 1947 al 1951* (Rome: Atlante, 1952), 51–53, quoted in Lipgens, *A History of European Integration*, 501.
47 Lipgens, *History of European Integration* 264, 267.
48 National Archive, Robert A. Lowett's Message on November 26, 1947, 862.00/11-2647.
49 National Archive, Brussels Embassy Reports, February 1, 1945, 862.014/2-145.
50 National Archive, US Embassy in The Hague Reported (Baruch) on March 8, 1949, 862.011/3-349.
51 Today, in the early twenty-first century, the three countries, Belgium, the Netherlands, and Luxembourg, together occupy a nearly 75,000 square kilometer territory with more than 23 million inhabitants.

52 Bela Balassa, *The Theory of Economic Integration* (Westport, CT: Greenwood Press, 1961), 184–5.
53 See Barry Eichengreen and Andrea Boltho, "The Economic Impact of European Integration," in *The Cambridge Economic History of Modern Europe. Vol. 2: 1870 to the Present* ed. Stephan Broadberry and Kevin H. O'Rourke (Cambridge University Press, 2010), 279–81.
54 France, Germany, and Italy would have sixty-three deputies and twenty-one senators each, and France would have seven additional for the overseas departments.
55 See Richard T. Griffiths, *Europe's First Constitution: The European Political Community 1952–1954* (London: Federal Trust, Kogan Page, 2000); Jean-Claude Masclet, *L'Union politique de l'Europe* (Paris: Presses Universitaires de France, [1973] 2001).
56 Pierre Gerbert, *La Construction de l'Europe* (Paris: Notre Siècle, 1983), 197.
57 See Milward, *The European Rescue of the Nation-State*, 180–201.
58 Manfred Görtemaker, "The Failure of EDC and European Integration," in *Crises in European Integration. Challenges and Responses, 1945–2005*, ed. Ludger Kühnhardt (New York, NY: Berghahn Books, 2009) 41–2.
59 See eur-lex.europa.eu › . . . › EU law and publications › EUR-Lex.
60 See Balassa, *Theory of Economic Integration*. 1961.
61 See Berend, *Economic History of Twentieth-Century Europe*, 238–51.
62 Quoted in Kenneth Maxwell, *The Making of Portuguese Democracy* (Cambridge: Cambridge University Press, 1995), 96, emphasis added.
63 Winston Churchill's speech in the House of Commons about the North Atlantic Treaty on 120 May, 1949, in Randolph S. Churchill, ed. *In the Balance. Speeches 1949 and 1950 by Winston Churchill* (London: Cassel, 1951), 61–2.
64 Argyris G. Andrianopoulos, *Western Europe in Kissinger's Global Strategy* (New York: St Martin's Press, 1988), 17.
65 Daniel J. Sargent, *A Superpower Transformed. The Rethinking of American Foreign Relations in the 1970s* (New York, NY: Oxford University Press, 2015), 209.
66 Nixon tapes quoted by Sargent, *A Superpower Transformed*, 69.
67 Ernst H. Van der Breugel, *From Marshall Aid to Atlantic Partnership. European Integration as a Concern of American Foreign Policy* (Amsterdam: Elsevier, 1966), 369, emphasis added.
68 Helen Graham and Alejandro Quiroga, "After the Fear Was Over? What Came After the Dictatorships in Spain, Greece, and Portugal," in *Oxford Handbook of Postwar European History*, ed. Dan Stone (Oxford: Oxford University Press), 502.
69 According to Graham and Quiroga, the position of Greece, "as the frontline against the nascent eastern bloc, brought a level of US support . . . that was sufficient to win them the civil war": Graham and Quiroga, "After the Fear Was Over," 507.
70 William D. Harris, *Installing Aggressiveness. US Advisors and Greek Combat Leadership in the Greek Civil War, 1947–1949* (Fort Leavenworth, KS: Combat Studies Institute Press, 2012).
71 Archive of European Integration, "Athens Ceremony for EEC-Greek Associations." Bulletin from the European Community, no. 48, July 1961.
72 For the entire story, reported by the authentic US diplomat at the Athens' embassy, see Robert V. Keeley, *The Colonels' Coup and the American Embassy. A Diplomat's View of the Breakdown of Democracy in Cold War Greece* (University Park, PA: Pennsylvania State University Press, 2010).
73 Alexandros Nafpliotis, "Britain and Greece: 40 Years Ago," accessed December 12, 2015, www.academia.edu/242029/Britain_and_Greece_40_years_ago. See also Alexandros Nafpliotis, *Britain and the Greek Colonels: Accommodating the Junta in the Cold War* (London: I.B. Tauris, 2012).
74 See Eirini Karamouzi, *Greece, the EEC and the Cold War, 1974–1979*. (London: Palgrave Macmillan, 2014).
75 Keeley, 2010, 127–9.
76 Nafpliotis, "*Britain and Greece: 40 years Ago*."
77 Ibid.
78 https://history.state.gov/historicaldocuments/ . . . /ch6.

79 Oscar Calvo-Gonzales, "Neither Carrot nor Stick: American Foreign Aid and Economic Policy Making in Spain during the 1950s," *Diplomatic History* 30, issue 3 (June 2006): 409–38, here 410–11, 412, 416.
80 The text of the agreement can be found in the Law Library of Yale University, September 26, 1953, Avalon.law.yale.edu/20th_century/sp1953.asp.
81 *Time Magazine,* February 3, 1958.
82 George McGhee, "Turkey Joins the West," www.foreignaffairs.com/ . . . 07 . . . /turkey-joins-west.
83 Hikmet Özdamir, "The Turkish–American Relation Toward 1960 Turkish Revolution," dergiler.ankara.edu.tr/dergiler/44/671/8549.pdf.
84 Bruce R. Kuniholm, "Turkey's Jupiter Missiles and the US-Turkish Relationship," in *John F. Kennedy and Europe,* eds. Douglas Brinkley and Richard T. Griffiths (Baton Rouge, LA: Louisiana State University Press, 1999), 117–18.
85 Nasuh Uslu, *The Turkish–American Relationship Between 1947 and 2003. The History of Distinctive Alliance* (New York, NY: Nova Science Publisher, 2003), 23.
86 Ahmet Ş. Esmer, "Uyduluk Siyasetine Son," *Milliyet,* December 24, 1965 quoted by Uslu, *The Turkish–American Relationship,* 29.
87 See the studies of Mehmet Dosemeci, "How Turkey Became a Bridge between 'East' and 'West': The EEC and Turkey's Great Westernization Debate, 1960–1980," in *The East–West Discourse: Symbolic Geography and its Consequences,* ed. Alexander Maxwell (Bern: Peter Lang, 2010), 169–90; "Turkish Opposition to the Common Market: An Archeology of Nationalist Thought, 1964–1988," *South European Society and Politics,* 17, issue 1, (2012).
88 Kristin Archick, "European Union Enlargement," Congressional Research Service, February 19, (2014): 1, 10, www.fas.org/sgp/crs/row/RS21344.pdf.
89 Vincent Morelli, "European Union Enlargement: A Status Report on Turkey's Accession Negotiations," Congressional Research Service, www.fas.org/sgp/crs/row/RS225.
90 Archive of European Integration, Speech [on European unity] by Mr Helmut Burckhardt, Vice President of the Consultative Committee of the European Community for Coal and Steel, at the Duquesne Club, Pittsburgh, October 22, 1954.
91 Ivan T. Berend, *An Economic History of Nineteenth-Century Europe* (Cambridge: Cambridge University Press, 2006), 259.
92 Article 217, Treaty of Rome (1959).
93 Turkey was unable to accomplish the required reforms regarding the rule of law, human rights, gender equality, a new, democratic constitution, and other issues. France and some other countries are strongly against its acceptance, arguing that historical, cultural, and religious differences separate Turkey from Europe. Not only the member countries and their populations, but even some of the governments are sharply divided. It is symptomatic that the German parliamentary parties and even the Angela Merkel Government have conflicting and conflicted opinions about the relationship with Turkey. The Social Democrats and Greens are for acceptance, stressing economic and security considerations as well as bridge building to the Muslim Middle East. However, the governing Christian Democratic and Christian Social Parties are against it and recommend "privileged partnership" instead. Even within the German Government, Foreign Minister Guido Westerwelle is for acceptance, whilst Chancellor Merkel opposes full membership. Moreover, Turkey's relationship with the West is also changing. The followers of Kemal Ataturk's policy orientation looked to EU membership as the "final step towards becoming a fully accepted part of contemporary civilization." During the last decade, however, the ruling Adalet ve Kalkinma Partisi (Justice and Development Party) strongly reoriented the country's foreign policy orientation. The Recep Erdoğan Government does not accept the characterization of Turkey as a Western state and society, and stresses instead that the country's multiple identities—European, Middle Eastern, Black Sea, and Caucasian—are rooted in Muslim traditions. (Indeed, only five percent of Turkey's population is living on European territory.) The new political and government elite, in the words of Yavuz Baydar, a leading Istanbul journalist, has shifted

"towards a conservative-nationalist ground," highly suspicious about the West and this elite prefers a regional power status for the country: "Turkey," Baydar notes, "can no longer be taken for granted as automatic follower of Western policies." The relations between the EU and Turkey, quoting Baydar again, are "at best on stand-by mode, or, at worst brain-dead." See Heinz Kramer, "The Future of Turkish Western Relations," *Südosteuropa Mitteilungen* 01 (2013): 57, 59; Yavuz Baydar, "Turkish–European Relations and the Importance of Visa Liberalization," *Südosteuropa Mitteilungen* 01 (2013): 90, 91.

3

CHANGE OF GUARD IN THE 1970s

European corporations step into America's role

Changing relations between America and Europe

In the first quarter of a century after World War II, transatlantic relations were one-sided. America was strong, Europe was weak, and this difference characterized every aspect of the relationship—economic, military, and political. Under both the Truman and Eisenhower Administrations, during the emerging and then sharp Cold War confrontation between East and West, American leadership was dominant and unquestionable. The US had a "seat at the European table," assisted Western Europe by keeping a security umbrella over the continent with its army and nuclear power through NATO, provided economic assistance, and determined the direction of European policy towards integration. Europe, although it sometimes resisted, was basically "expected to follow" the US leadership (discussed in Chapter 1).

After the spectacular reconstruction, unparalleled economic growth and consolidation of Western Europe, transatlantic relations started to change. During the 1960s, under the Kennedy Administration, US–European Community relations became more balanced, and Europe gradually became an equal partner rather than a subordinated client. This happened in the time when the main motivation of previous American policy towards Europe, the Cold War, also started losing its sharp edge and imminent danger. President John F. Kennedy outlined his new policy for peace in his Commencement speech at the American University in June 10, 1963. It is important to quote it in length because it was a call to "re-examine our attitude towards the Cold War." For the first time in about one-and-a-half postwar decades, Kennedy clearly recognized the need of policy change: "We are both caught up in a vicious and dangerous cycle with suspicion on one side breeding suspicion on the other, and new weapons begetting counter-weapons." Hostility has to end between the US and the Soviet Union, "the tide of time and events will often bring surprising changes in the relations between nations and neighbors . . . Among the many traits the peoples of our two countries have in common, none is stronger than our mutual abhorrence of war."

The "Peace Speech" also clearly expressed the will to abandon postwar American dominance and dictate:

> What kind of peace do I mean and what kind of a peace do we seek? Not a Pax Americana enforced on the world by American weapons of war, not the peace of the grave . . . I am talking about genuine peace—the kind of peace that makes life on earth worth living . . . I speak of peace because of the new face of war. Total war makes no sense in an age where great powers can maintain large and relatively invulnerable nuclear forces . . . It makes no sense in an age where a single nuclear weapon contains almost ten times the explosive force delivered . . . in the second world war . . . The two strongest powers are the two in the most danger of devastation. All we have built, all we have worked for, would be destroyed in the first 24 hours . . . In short, both the United States and its allies, and the Soviet Union and its allies, have a mutually deep interest in a just and genuine peace and in halting the arms race.

President Kennedy also made clear that the US, although it wanted to change postwar policy, would still keep its commitments "to defend Western Europe and . . . the United States will make no deal with the Soviet Union at the expense of other nations and other peoples, not merely because they are our partners, but also because their interests and ours converge."[1]

Kennedy also offered "a true partnership" for Europe and created "two pillars of democracy of equal weight with leaders of equal voice." He made his proposal about a "transatlantic partnership of equals" in a symbolic way in the Independence Hall, Philadelphia, where he made the "declaration of interdependence" on July 4, 1963.[2] He announced a new Atlantic Partnership "between the new union now emerging in Europe and the old American union founded here 175 years ago."

He prepared for this new opening with the initiative of a changed trade relation. Kennedy asked the Congress for authorization to reduce tariffs by 50 percent on a reciprocal basis and eliminate tariffs in areas where the US and the European Economic Community (EEC) conduct 80 percent of the world trade. In June 1962, the Trade Act was passed.

Kennedy's triumphant visit in Europe in June–July 1963 successfully popularized his new "grand design" of world strategy and new Atlantic approach. In his speech at Frankfurt he stressed the importance of European unification, but underlined the role of European self-determination when he stated:

> It is only a fully cohesive Europe that can protect us all against fragmentation of alliance. Only such a Europe will permit full reciprocity of movement across the Ocean . . . With only such a Europe can we have a full give-and-take between equals an equal sharing of responsibility, and an equal level of

sacrifice . . . It is Europeans who are building Europe . . . the choice of path to the unity of Europe is a choice which Europe must make.[3]

Europe enthusiastically received the new American policy opening. However, the relations with the Soviet Union started changing slowly and the Atlantic relations still exhibited US hegemony, especially because Kennedy had been assassinated and did not have the time to realize the new relations in concrete actions.[4]

His vice president and then successor, Lyndon B. Johnson, wanted to continue and fulfill Kennedy's initiatives, including the "Thaw," the gradually emerging détente. In his October 1966 speech, "Making Europe Whole: An Unfinished Task," he stressed the goal of "peaceful engagement" with the Soviet Bloc, liberalizing trade, eliminating travel restrictions, and promoting cultural and scientific exchange. He changed the language of political discourse when speaking about American–Soviet relations, and signaled the acceptance of the Oder-Neisse border. He also wanted to further balance the relations with the West European allies by introducing the Multilateral Force policy, first considered by Kennedy to share the responsibility for strategic decision with NATO allies on using atomic weapons, or to create a European controlled strategic nuclear force. In the summer of 1967, Johnson praised Germany's *Ostpolitik* in a conversation with German journalists, advocated the "German bridge-building towards the east" and added that the German Government did not need his approval for new initiatives in this area.[5]

These attempts, however, were not successful. First of all, President Johnson turned to domestic policy. In his January 1964 State of the Union address, he declared "war on poverty." In May of that year, in his speech at the University of Michigan, he described his vision of the Great Society: promoting full employment, civil rights for African-Americans, and government guarantee of adequate health care, education, and housing for all. The next year, he succeeded to enact major laws to realize his projects: the Voting Right Act, Medicare, and Aid to Education Act. Very soon, the US declined deeply into the Vietnam War, which totally preoccupied Johnson's attentions and efforts. Europe and transatlantic policy were shifted to the background. The Vietnam War heavily damaged the reputation of the US and its president. Johnson, understandably, was totally preoccupied with his domestic policy breakthrough and foreign policy troubles. Moreover, he had very limited knowledge of Europe and would have been worried about going there after Kennedy's highly successful visit. He knew he was unable to compete with his brilliant predecessor. He did not even go to the burial of Winston Churchill in 1965. President Johnson had very limited diplomatic skills, his style was hardly appropriate to refined international negotiations, and he therefore missed several opportunities in foreign policy. Most of the European leaders did not like or respect him. President Charles de Gaulle made nasty hostile remarks, maintaining that Johnson "doesn't take the trouble to pretend he's thinking," and he is the "very portrait of America. He reveals the country to us as it is, rough and raw."[6] "Foreign policy," concluded Schwartz (the historian of Johnson's European policy), "appeared to be LBJ's Achilles' heel."[7]

American–European relations consequently did not change radically in the 1960s. Significant change started during the crisis-ridden 1970s. Several factors contributed to this alteration of the relationship. One of them was the gradual decrease of security danger after the Kennedy–Khrushchev summit in Vienna and the start of negotiations between the two hostile superpowers. From the second half of the 1960s, the frightening danger of a coming nuclear war—so vivid during the Cuban crisis—started to disappear. As defense secretary Robert McNamara reasoned, "both superpowers by the mid-1960s possessed so many weapons that each could absorb a preventive nuclear strike while retaining sufficient offensive capabilities to retaliate against the other. The predicament," McNamara contended, "made nuclear war improbable."[8]

American–Soviet rivalry started losing its heat and the two superpowers' interests met in stabilizing the arms race by signing the Treaty of Non-Proliferation of Nuclear Weapons. Negotiations started in 1965 in Geneva and agreement was reached by 1968. This situation gradually changed the American and West European attitude and also the US pressure upon the allied countries. There was much less urgent need to strengthen the Western allies against the Eastern Bloc. The Cold War-induced need to unite and federalize Western Europe faded away. Parallel with these changes, Europe had risen as a strong economic power. As a consequence of the common market with its common outside tariffs, the EEC started negotiating with outside partners, including the US, as a single economic unit. Europeans were able to protect the subsidies that they paid in agriculture and thus maintain low agricultural prices, which assured advantages in the world market. They managed to lower tariffs of imported US industrial products. This situation unavoidably harmed American interests.

From the mid-1960s, America's *relative* economic superiority gradually melted down. Between 1949 and 1960, America's share of the output of the advanced-industrialized countries decreased from 59 to 45 percent, and its share in world exports from 25 to 15 percent. The US dollar, an unquestionable world currency, also declined on foreign exchange markets. Moreover, the circulating dollar currency in the world surpassed the gold reserves of the US, which endangered the existing agreement about exchanging dollars to gold by America. A dollar crisis forced President Johnson to introduce temporary measures such as mandatory capital control and tax increase. From 1964–65, the US's current account balance also started deteriorating and in 1971, the country started running trade deficits for the first time since 1893. Richard Nixon, former vice president, stated in a speech that in 1967 "the deficit in our balance of payment is matched by a mounting deficit in our balance of influence."[9]

Relative American economic strength continued to diminish. From the mid-1980s, the US, instead of being an international creditor since the 1920s, became an international debtor. The EEC's economy gradually strengthened to match the American economy, and in one-third of a century, in certain areas it even surpassed it. By the 1990s, as one of the analysts stated, although the prospect that the

EU is "becoming a major military superpower is uncertain, its status as an economic superpower is no longer in doubt."[10]

Recognition of interdependence—instead of Pax Americana

From the 1960s on, a broad recognition emerged that Pax Americana became obsolete and the world system became characterized by *interdependence*. Pope John XXIII in his only encyclical, *Pacem in Terris* (Peace on the Earth) in 1963, interestingly combined the progress of globalization—not yet a widely recognized phenomenon—with the need for replacing the arms race by agreements: "There is also a growing economic interdependence between States. National economies are gradually becoming so interdependent that a kind of world economy is being born." In this new situation "Men's common interests make it imperative that . . . a world-wide community of nations be established." Differences among states "must be settled in a truly human way, not by armed force." Therefore "we are deeply distressed to see the enormous stocks of armaments that have been, and continue to be, manufactured in the economically more developed countries." The charismatic Pope denounced the arms race:

> if one country increases its military strength, others are immediately roused by a competitive spirit to augment their own supply of armaments. And if one country is equipped with atomic weapons, others consider themselves justified in producing such weapons themselves, equal in destructive force . . . The stock-piles of armaments which have been built up in various countries must be reduced all round and simultaneously by the parties concerned. Nuclear weapons must be banned. A general agreement must be reached on a suitable disarmament program, with an effective system of mutual control.[11]

These ideas gradually became broadly accepted. In the late 1960s and 1970s, scholars published influential works about interdependence. Stanley Hoffman, the leading American political scientist, had spoken about irrelevant concepts of superpower domination in the more complex and balanced world system, and economist Richard Cooper published his book, *The Economics of Interdependence. Economic Policy in the Atlantic Community* in 1968. Futurologist Alvin Toffler in his bestseller *Future Shock* (1971) spoke about the rise of a "worldwide super-industrial society." The political scientist Raymond Vernon, in his *Sovereignty at Bay. The Multinational Spread of U.S. Enterprises* (1971), pointed to the conflict between the nation-states and the emerging transnational capitalist system. Ecologist Lester Brown concluded in his 1972 book, *World Without Borders*, that national sovereignty has to be sacrificed for affluence.[12] The spread of this view was excellently expressed a few years later on Independence Day, July 4, 1976 when *The New York Times* called to mind the economic interdependence with other industrial nations and in nuclear stability with the Soviet Union, and suggested to reinvent Independence Day as *Interdependence Day*.[13]

Radical change in American policy towards Europe in the 1970s

Small wonder that in the spreading international recognition of the hopeless arms race and of interdependence that newly elected President Richard Nixon in his inaugural speech in January 1969 also stressed that

> man's destiny on Earth is not divisible . . . For the first time, because the people of the world want peace, and the leaders of the world are afraid of war, the times are on the side of peace . . . We are caught in war, wanting peace. We are torn by division, wanting unity . . . After a period of confrontation, we are entering an era of negotiation . . . With those who are willing to join, let us cooperate to reduce the burden of arms, to strengthen the structure of peace.[14]

The new Nixon Administration turned to negotiation and agreement to end the arms race and confrontation. The strong military and political Cold War alliance with integrated Western Europe—the core American foreign policy imperative before—definitely lost its importance. Meanwhile, America started realizing that a united Europe was not only an ally, but also a rising *competitor*. This recognition first emerged during the General Agreement on Tariffs and Trade (GATT) Kennedy Round of negotiations (held between 1964 and 1967 in Geneva) in relation to US and EEC tariffs. From that time on, Henry Kissinger, at that time a Harvard University professor, started criticizing the previously dominant American policy towards Europe maintaining that "the United States is in fact creating its own rival." He was probably the first person who recognized the danger that a strengthened and united Europe would challenge American hegemony not only in economy, but also in Atlantic policy. In his 1965 book, *The Troubled Partnership*, Kissinger expressed his view, for the first time in postwar American politics, that an integrated and united federal Europe may be harmful for the US and advocated the return to de Gaulle's initiated Fouchet Plan, which was a "confederated Europe [that] would enable the United States to maintain an influence at many centers of decision rather than be forced to stake everything on affecting the views of a single, supranational body." Kissinger also worried that a strongly united Europe may follow an independent policy.

> The assumption that a united Europe and the United States would evidently conduct parallel policy . . . runs counter to historical experience. A separate unity has usually been established by opposition to a dominant power . . . [Europe] will challenge American hegemony in Atlantic policy.[15]

It is not true, he noted, that "united Europe would ease Atlantic relations."[16]

A few years later, Kissinger's criticism about American policy gained critical importance. On January 20, 1969, Richard Nixon became president of the US and appointed Henry Kissinger as his main foreign policy advisor and later secretary of state. Kissinger became the key architect of American foreign policy and immediately started the realization of his concept on European policy. He argued against pushing further European integration. He urged the president to "make clear that we will not inject ourselves into intra-European debates on the forms, methods, and timing of steps toward unity."[17] He also advised Nixon (and practiced himself) not to deal with "Brussels," but instead deal directly with head of states and governments of the member countries. As the French minister of foreign affairs Michel Jobert recognized, and told Kissinger in June 1973, "you wish to divide Europe to strengthen your mastery."

The Nixon Administration, as Daniel Sargent pointed to his classical historical paradox, looked back and wanted to restore and stabilize Pax Americana with American primacy and world dominance. Nixon wanted to save the US position, but the outcome of his policy changed the world system. Although both Nixon and Kissinger were the products of the Cold War, they virtually ended it and replaced it with détente.[18] The first victim of this new architecture was the strong Cold War alliance system with integrating Western Europe. American policy radically changed towards Europe and particularly European integration. In his major report to Congress on foreign policy in 1970, President Nixon spoke about a new chapter of America's European policy:

> For two decades after the end of the Second World War, our foreign policy was [. . .] based on the fact that the United States was the richest and most stable country without whose initiative and resources little security or progress was possible [. . .] The world has dramatically changed since the days of the Marshall Plan. We deal now with a world of strong allies [. . .] [and] America has the chance to move the world close to a durable peace [. . .].

Western Europe became strong and flourished, the Western military alliance—NATO—became stable, and the European Community was secure. That was enough, as Nixon expressed it, for the US, even without the realization of its original goal of a federal Europe.[19] The American business community also realized that Europe had become a major economic rival and demanded the administration assure that American interests be protected. President Nixon echoed this view in his 1971 report to Congress on foreign policy when he stated that "European unity will also pose problems for American policy, which it would be idle to ignore." When he announced his European policy, he argued against direct intervention to European affairs.[20] In 1973, Nixon expressed this thought in a quite brutal way:

> The Europeans cannot have it both ways. They cannot have United States participation and cooperation on the security front and then proceed to have confrontation and even hostility on the economic and political fronts . . . The day of the one-way street is gone. We are not going to be faced with a situation where the nine countries of Europe gang up against the United States which is guarantee of security.[21]

The European policy of the Nixon–Kissinger tandem turned out to be the opposite to their predecessors, differing from both the Truman and Eisenhower Administrations' approach to Europe. Let's recall that President Eisenhower enthusiastically supported the rise of Western Europe as a "third great power." He

> strongly encouraged his cabinet to endorse European integration both privately and publicly: with even greater emphasis the President repeated his view on the desirability of developing Western Europe a third great power bloc, after which development the United States would be permitted to sit back and relax somewhat.[22]

The US acted as a major integrating force of the European unification from the late 1940s and during the 1950s. This activity virtually stopped from the 1960s–70s on. In a discussion on Europe in the spring of 1973, Nixon and postwar European expert John J. McCloy agreed that "from an American point of view, additional European unity was no longer desirable." Kissinger, in a discussion with Arthur Burns, Chairman of the Federal Reserve, flatly stated:

> what we had to do adroitly is to throw a monkey wrench into the Common Market machinery, for European unity in economic areas would definitely work against US interests . . . Kissinger and Nixon agreed long before that one of the worst mistakes we made was to push Britain into the Common Market."

Nichter, who quoted these statements from archival documents, added: "The old generation of Americans who believed in European integration simply for integration's sake was over."[23] The public also turned its back on the Truman Doctrine. As the Chicago Council of Foreign Relations announced, only 36 percent of the population still believe that "defending our allies" should be a national priority; instead, 70 percent was convinced that "fostering international coordination to solve common problems is a "very important foreign policy goal."[24]

The EEC also lost its central importance for the US because the military alliance of NATO was strongly established during the previous decades. Nixon's government turned towards a new grand policy design. Recognizing new opportunities for American world policy, Nixon and Kissinger wanted to exploit the huge cracks in the previously monolithic communist bloc. In the year when Nixon moved into the White House, a rising Chinese–Soviet conflict erupted as a military skirmish in March 1969 when Chinese and Soviet troops opened fire on each other at a border outpost on the Ussuri River, north of Vladivostok. Some of the East European Soviet Bloc countries, such as Romania and Albania, also distanced themselves from the Soviet Union. From the 1970s on, the newly developed "Eurocommunism" in Western Europe also alienated the strongest communist parties of the West from the Soviet Union. They opposed the Soviet one-party system, advocated a democratic political regime, and accepted political pluralism and European integration. West European allies of the Soviet Union disappeared step-by-step or became politically unimportant.

This situation offered a breakthrough for America to play the "Chinese card" and change the US–Soviet relations. In July 1971, Kissinger traveled to Peking. Nixon and Kissinger courageously and skillfully opened their policies towards China, and then in the summer of 1973 they ended the disastrous Vietnam War. This whole new balance of forces made it possible to ease the strained relations with an internationally weakened Soviet Union and to begin a new policy of détente. Nixon visited China and three months later went to Moscow. A competitive cooperation began between the US, China, and the Soviet Union. The US constructed a geopolitical triangle of a new balance of power. Between 1969 and 1975, the US and the Soviet Union signed fifty-eight agreements. In 1972, during Nixon's visit in Moscow and then in the summer of 1973 at the end of Leonid Brezhnev's week-long visit to the US, they signed the Strategic Arms Limitation Treaty (SALT I) and the Agreement on the Prevention of Nuclear War. As an important element of détente, parallel trade relations with the Soviet Union were also reestablished in 1971–72. These landmark agreements radically changed the international atmosphere. The Cold War tension that had already calmed down during the second half of the 1960s was further decreased.

The lack of an immediately dangerous common enemy significantly weakened the US–EEC alliance. For the American Government, Western Europe was not in the center of foreign policy any longer. For Europe, American hegemony became questionable. Nixon and Kissinger hardly consulted with the "forgotten" European allies. "Following a period of intense negotiations with American adversaries, it was as though American diplomats had lost the ability to negotiate with allies."[25]

Rising conflicts between the US and the European Community

From the 1960s and 1970s on, several facts and various statements and analyses reflected a troubled relation between the Western allies. The bipolar era was inching to its end. As an important factor, the era of American—and then American and Soviet—monopoly of nuclear weapons also ended. France tested its nuclear bomb in 1960 and thermonuclear warhead in 1968. China had the atom bomb in 1964. Charles de Gaulle, who returned to power in 1958, challenged Pax Americana. Before Nixon, de Gaulle normalized the relation with China in 1963–64, traveled to Moscow, and signed a joint declaration in 1966. Bipolar structure was also challenged by the Federal Republic of Germany. Willy Brandt, the social democratic minister of foreign affairs from 1966 and then chancellor from 1969, initiated his *Ostpolitik*, which was an opening towards the Soviet Bloc. As a major rapture of previous German policy, he traveled to Warsaw and Moscow and signed an agreement accepting Germany's existing eastern borders. Brandt's "Basic Treaty" also normalized the relation with communist East Germany. Even Britain reevaluated its "special relations" with the US and it applied for membership of the EEC. The pragmatic Kissinger recognized and accepted the fact of rising political multi-polarity and the resurgence of political pressures among the western allies.[26]

At the beginning of Nixon's second term, the Watergate scandal further ruined the relations with Europe. European governments distanced themselves more from the US. Kissinger told the EEC's "messenger," Knud B. Andersen, Danish foreign minister, in September 1973: "Europe must decide if it intends to build Europe or also to build Atlantic relations . . . If the decision is to build Europe when the Atlantic relations [are] collapsing then the European achievement will be at the expense of Atlantic relations."[27] At a staff meeting, he announced in the least diplomatic language: "We are going to try to bust the Europeans . . . We will hit the British, ignore the French, and deal with the Germans and Italians."[28] On November 16, 1971, as the Nixon tapes made it public, Kissinger said in a conversation, "Western Europe is a mess. We've given up our friends to our enemies."[29] Nixon, talking with his own men in the Oval Office as the tapes recorded, used the same language: "It's time for America to look after its own interests . . . Now, in order to play that game, we can perhaps . . . split them up, don't let them get together."[30] In a memorandum sent to the vice president and the secretary of state and defense, Nixon flatly stated: "Although we . . . consult with our allies, we should not permit them to have a veto on our actions . . . "[31]

After the Nixon Administration's first four years of major political shake up of foreign policy and neglect of the European allies, Kissinger realized the troubles in the alliance with Europe and wanted to correct them by a spectacular symbolic "Year of Europe" initiative in 1973. In April of that year, Kissinger delivered a major foreign policy speech at the start of the Year of Europe by calling to open a new chapter in the Atlantic relations with new goals, including a symbolic new Atlantic Charter. However, instead of healing the wounds, his speech further provoked Europe. He spoke specifically on America's "world responsibility," while Europe, as he said, had "regional interests." As the leading French intellectual Raymond Aron noted, "no phrase of Henry Kissinger aroused more indignation in Europe than his remark about the regional interests of Europeans as against global tasks of a world power like the United States." Aron also added that in the economic arena, this statement was not even true. "The European Community constitutes the most important commercial unit in the world."[32] In Germany, a message sent to the chancellor commented that the speech was interpreted by the ministry of foreign affairs as an ultimatum. "The options for Europe are clearly stated – either an agreement with the USA over a common objective or a slow decline of the alliance by neglect, distrust and indifference."[33] The Year of Europe failed miserably. In July, Kissinger stated that "transatlantic relations had now evolved into an adversarial relationship and the so-called Year of Europe is over." He complained that Europe did not react to the initiative for three months and refused to talk to the US.[34]

Together with the Nixon–Kissinger White House, the Congress with its Democratic Party majority also shared a critical view on the European allies and became more self-oriented. In May 1971, Democratic senator and majority leader Mike Mansfield went even further than Nixon and called for a halving of American forces in Europe. At the House Committee of Armed Services, Secretary of Defense Melvin Laird asked, "Why do we need 310,000 troops in Europe twenty-five years after the end of World War II?"[35] The Congress demanded the strongest defense of American trade and economic interests against Europe. This attitude has remained from then on.

Conflicts between the allies appeared in various areas of connections. In the early period of the Nixon Administration, the US, without consulting with its allies, one-sidedly ended the Bretton Woods Agreement. Planned by John Maynard Keynes and Harry Dexter White, and signed as an international agreement in July 1944, the agreement created a stable postwar financial–economic regime by a new world currency system of a fixed but movable gold-based exchange rate and also established an institutional framework, including the International Monetary Fund (IMF) and the World Bank, to keep the world finances and economy in balance. This system was very advantageous for the recovering European countries, which became able to exchange accumulated dollars to gold on a fixed rate of US$35 per ounce. The fixed exchange rate guaranteed stability in trade that significantly helped European reconstruction.

However, troubles started accumulating in the US because this international monetary regime and the American balance of payment situation required rapid change. President Nixon decided to do it and do it alone, without collaboration and even consultation with the allies, and suspended the exchange of dollar to gold after three years in power in August 1971. The main stabilizer of the postwar financial economic system was eliminated and the burden was shifted to the allies. Kissinger realized the unavoidable negative political consequences when he noted, "We can't throw away twenty-five years of what has been built up for Treasury reasons."[36]

The European allies were shocked by the unilateral, unexpected American step and outraged by the breakdown of Western financial cooperation. Conflicts gathered in trade policy and competition. America criticized the European agricultural protectionism. Disagreements became characteristic, even in the most crucial political and security cooperations. During the Arab–Israeli Yom Kippur War in 1973, several European Community countries did not agree with the American policy and made declarations favorable to the Arab position. When the Nixon Administration asked them to place their airbases at their disposal to re-equip the Israeli troops, they refused.[37]

The American Administration did not like Chancellor Willy Brandt's innovative *Ostpolitik*, which actually pioneered the same opening towards Russia as Nixon and Kissinger. Nixon said that "Ostpolitik was a dangerous affair and they would do nothing to encourage it." Kissinger, years later in his memoirs, openly confessed that what bothered them was that Germany became too independent.[38] Kissinger was also skeptical about his European allies' Helsinki Act policy that pushed the "Basket III" human rights issue. He told Gromyko, Soviet foreign minister, that the Western allies were simply "crazy on the subject of human contact." During his talk with Leonid Brezhnev, Kissinger went further and said that he is as angry as Brezhnev is about the human rights policy and mentioned that West European countries failed to change the Soviet regime and "cultural exchange and diplomacy would not now accomplish what the force of arms had not."[39]

Political and economic interests of the US and EEC often conflicted during the 1970s, and from that time on conflicts remained virtually constant. American and West European relations never returned to their earlier state under the Truman and Eisenhower Administrations.[40] In spite of all of the conflicts, the strategic alliance, which was crucial for the security of all of the partners, survived. This is also true for NATO. Its importance, even existence, was questioned as the Cold War confrontation eased,[41] and then from the mid-1980s and especially after 1989–91, it finally ended. The alliance survived, but the US did not force further European integration and stopped being a "builder" of Europe after the 1970s.

Major gaps in European integration—US's multinationals invading Europe

At the time of changed American policy towards further European integration, the development of the EEC arrived at a crossroads. From the mid-1960s on until the mid-1980s, the integration process slowed significantly. Important elements of the Treaty of Rome were realized, such as eliminating tariffs among member countries and unifying the outside tariffs against non-Community countries. In certain areas such as agriculture, the EU implemented a common policy based on strong state intervention. The institutional system of the Community became stable and strong. Nevertheless, the clearly expressed goals of the Treaty of Rome were only less than half realized. (This situation will be discussed in more details in Chapter 4.) Here, it is enough to mention that an internal crisis from 1965 stopped further supranationalization. The roles of the supranational institutions, such as the European Commission, were weakened and a bad compromise in Luxembourg put the member states into the drivers' seat. Huge gaps remained unfilled regarding the creation of a *real* borderless common market where goods, capital, and labor could freely and easily cross borders.

Among the most important gaps I should mention the lack of a harmonized EEC legal system. National legal systems exhibited major differences that created huge obstacles for business activities of companies in other member countries. This activity was eventually banned in some member countries. Major differences also characterized the national industrial standards, which varied broadly across the different countries. This made it difficult and sometimes even impossible to sell products in another member country's market. One of the major gaps was the lack of joint EEC research and development (R&D) activities that remained national and thus fragmented. Consequently, none of the member countries were able to compete with the huge amounts of overseas R&D investments and their outcomes. At last, the separation of national industrial and energy policies, as well as strictly blocked service activities for companies outside the nation-state, conserved the separation of the member countries' markets from each other. The outcome of the elimination of tariffs was consequently limited and even counterbalanced.

Although several nation-states have tried to answer the international challenge of globalization and revolutionary technological development, they all failed because of the highly fragmented resources and activities. That was true for the creation of the so-called "national champions" formed by the merging of several companies, often with state contribution, to enlarge their size in order to be more competitive with overseas companies.

The member states, in other words, were unable to compete separately with the US and Japan in inventing and implementing new technology and defending their international business positions and national markets by producing cheap, modern high-tech products. The unfinished integration program became a huge obstacle for the EEC to adjust to the dramatic changes in the world economy from the late 1960s–70s on. That had a frightening impact on Europe. To understand what kind of prerequisites were missing in the EEC that endangered its positions in the world and even at home, we have to look at the economic changes that made the competitors much stronger and provided great advantage for them in the economic rivalry.

The postwar chapter of the world economy was closed and new trends emerged from the turn of the 1960s–70s. The prime mover behind these changes was a new technological–communication revolution, hand in hand with the breakthrough of globalization and global deregulation. These new trends will be discussed in more details in Chapter 4. Here I am going to summarize only its impact on the European economy along with the rearrangement of a renewed world economic order.

The winners of the changes, the US and Japan, were way ahead in structural adjustment, technological renewal, liberalization, and globalization. Western Europe, after its most successful postwar decades, now suddenly found itself among the laggards. Western European countries during the quarter-of-a-century postwar followed the so-called *extensive development strategy*, which was based on technology imports from the US and labor inputs (1 percent per year as an average for the entire period) at home. Europe, in other words, had a *follower* economic strategy that helped tremendously the postwar reconstruction and growth. Around the end of the reconstruction period, however, the follower strategy has become a major disadvantage in international competition compared to overseas countries. The latter followed an intensive growth strategy based on their own R&D activities, and the European Community did not have its own economic policy because that belonged to the member states. Unfortunately, none of the nation-states had competitive resources to cope with the American and Japanese investments into R&D. The key word in understanding Europe's lacking abilities is *fragmentation*.

The US, an all-round superpower, was the cradle of the new communication revolution and became the first post-industrial society. More than three-quarters of American exports were high-tech products. As a most telling example, in the early years of the new computer age, American IBM installed 75 percent of the computers (in value) in the West and together with three other American computer producers occupied 90 percent of the world market. The American giants had major subsidiaries in Britain, France, Germany, and Italy. In 1980, the American share in the European memory chip and microprocessor market was 64 percent. These products were the heart of data-processing, telecom, industrial automation, consumer electronics, and the modern military industry. Fragmented Europe could not follow this techno-logical transformation, and in one decade, from the late 1970s, Europe's share in this area of production declined from 16 to 10 percent.[42]

American companies started conquering the world market and invested almost 60 percent of world-wide foreign direct investments (FDI). In 1981, almost half of the assets of the world's largest companies were in American hands.[43] Most impor-tantly, the US was the investment leader in R&D, using 2–3 percent of its GDP for this goal, about twice the share in Europe. As early as 1966, an Organisation for Economic Co-operation and Development (OECD) report observed that nearly two-thirds of industrial R&D in the US was connected to programs that invested US$100 million per year or more. As a consequence, 60 percent of significant innovations in the OECD countries—that is in the advanced world—originated from the US. During the 1960s, about 2,000 scientists and engineers per year had already left Europe for better work possibilities and higher income in the US. The OECD report also named the causes of European backwardness: the *fragmentation* of markets, inadequate *size of firms*, and lack of significant state sponsorship.[44]

America's closest partner in the technological transformation was Japan, which had the most miraculous postwar reconstruction and economic renewal. Its GDP increased nearly eight times between the end of the war and 1973, and then three-and-a-half times again in the next three decades. One cannot find a more expressive example than the fact that in 1952, there were 130,000 cars in Japan, 100,000 of them foreign products. By 1980, 26 percent of the top car-making companies were Japanese, nearly equal to Western Europe where the car industry was born. Japan produced 7 million cars, 3.8 million of them for export. The European Commission was alarmed by the fact that although the Japanese car industry increased its produc-tion by 122 percent between 1970 and 1980, and increased its exports by more than four times, the European car industry was stagnating and did not follow the transfor-mation of car technology with computerization and other new innovations. European car exports consequently decreased by nearly one-quarter. This trend called attention to the frightening technological progress in Japan: Toyota, the EC reported, had already started robotization and auto production would be completely automatized by 1984.[45] And that was not the only European industry looking weak in comparison with Japan. Among the top thirty companies in the world computer industry, Japan's share, at 27 percent, was almost twice as big as Western Europe's.

The striking strength of Japan lay in its top performance and innovative strength in the most revolutionary high-tech branches. The country's electronic–telecom sector increased an unparalleled 15 percent per year, almost twice as fast as the comparable sector in the US and more than twice as fast as the European Community's 6.7 percent growth rate. Japan's share in the electronic–telecom sec-tor increased from 26 to 40 percent of the world and its export accounted for one-third of total world exports, up from 12 percent just one decade earlier.[46] Japanese competition in the 1970s–80s genuinely endangered European business. As a European Parliament document warned in 1985, nine out of ten video recorders bought in Europe came from Japan and eight out of ten computers from the US.

Only 40 percent of the European market was covered by Community production in the modern sectors.[47] Japanese firms had also set up production lines in Europe. In 1973, Sony built the first Japanese electronics factory in Europe. In 1987, Sony Europe was established, and in 1991 the company invested £100 million to build a subsidiary in Wales.[48] Japanese companies were also established in Germany, France, Spain, and Portugal

> at the expenses of the European owned firms . . . One by one the British firms left the industry, and by 1987 not one British-owned firm made colour TV sets in Britain . . . In Germany the position was very similar to that in Britain, indigenous firms were absorbed . . . by other firms . . . ".[49]

By 1988, Japan's electronics production equaled that of the US. The Japanese share of the integrated circuit world market elevated to 45 percent, surpassing the American share. The Japanese also dominated the memory chips market and challenged American dominance in the microprocessor field. Japan also conquered a huge part of the final products market of computers, colored TV, and telecom.[50]

The American multinationals, together with their Asian rivals, started swallowing up a huge part of the European markets, especially in autos and computers. Two giants of the American car industry, Ford and General Motors (GM), became leading European carmakers. Ford Europe was founded in 1967; the Ford Fiesta became a "European car," produced in several European countries. Half of Ford's global production and one-quarter of GM's world production was produced in Europe.[51] Over in the computer sector, IBM occupied 40 percent of the British and 50 percent of the French, German, and Italian markets in 1975. "In every branch of telematics . . . Japan and the United States threatened to worsen Europe's already shaky position."[52] George Ball, lecturing on the Common Market in 1960, remarked: "The number of American firms that are now undertaking or planning to undertake, direct investment in the Common Market is growing every day." He underlined the role of the American machinery and transportation equipment industries as the ones "concentrating most heavily on European operations."[53]

The American advantage in the high-tech sector "for a number of European Community policy makers . . . seemed to be [an especially] alarming development. It was feared that US multinationals, after dominating Europe's markets in information technology, would also defeat Europe's telecommunication industry." Indeed, the European share in the information technology market was barely more than one-quarter in 1982, and it generated an increasing trade deficit in these products: in five years until 1982, this deficit increased from US$4.1 to US$7.0 billion. In the mid-1980s, the European Community's share in the semiconductor market declined to 9 percent—against the 56 percent American and 33 percent Japanese shares. Among the world's top thirty companies in the computer business in 1989, the American share of total revenue was 58 percent and the Japanese 27 percent, but the European Community's only 14.5 percent. European telecom equipment production covered only 43 percent of the continent's consumption.

The relative position of European high-tech industries had begun deteriorating around 1970, with performance reaching its nadir in the early 1980s. Additionally, compared to overseas countries, Europe's labor market mobility was low, wage structures rigid and social benefits high. The EEC had no authority in areas that belonged to the member states. The effects of these factors, already seen in the automobile industry, were even more prominent in the information technology market, in which the European share was only 27 percent in 1982. The European Community accumulated huge trade deficit which, for these technology products, increased from US$4.1 billion in the late 1970s to US$7.0 billion by 1985. The situation was similar in the semiconductor market. Europe could only manufacture 43 percent of the semiconductors it actually consumed.

In addition to America and Japan, Europe faced a third competitor in telecommunications in the form of the newly industrializing countries of Asia. Part of the backyard of Japan, these competitors emerged when Japan outsourced several industrial activities to its neighboring Asian region. Hong Kong, South Korea, Singapore, and Taiwan—the "Small Asian Tigers"—rapidly became dominant factors in the world industrial markets. Their main advantages were their close contact with such a technology leader as Japan, but also their work ethic, educational orientation, and last but not least, their low wage levels. Michael Borrus and John Zysman speak about four waves of the rise of Asian competition. After the first two, Japan and the "Small Asian Tigers," a third wave, Thailand, Indonesia, Malaysia, and the Philippines emerged. In the fourth, and one of the most significant waves, China and India joined.[54]

Low and lower wages were exactly the reason why competitors such as the "Small Asian Tigers," and later China, first conquered European labor-intensive industrial markets such as textiles, clothing, and leather production. The apparel manufacturing industry in the European Community, for example, as a European Commission Working Document revealed, paid an average US$12,000 for each laborer per year. The producers of the less developed countries paid only US$2,000 per year. When China entered into the race, the Chinese companies paid only US$600 per worker at the end of the 1970s.[55] The Third World competition also hit the European steel industry hard. In the three years after 1975, this sector dismissed 100,000 employees and another 100,000 became part-time workers.[56] At a later stage, the newly industrializing countries also turned to car, computer, cellphone, and other more advanced technology areas. The European Commission in 1986 prepared a report on international market competition, stating that the rise of the newly industrializing countries is

> the third cause of concern about the future of industry in the Community . . . [because of] the fierce competition aroused by the growth of these newly industrialized countries, which have been specializing in branches of industry similar to the Community far more than to the USA or to Japan."[57]

Although a number of European policymakers were worried about increasing American dominance in European markets, the French editor-journalist Jean-Jacques

Servan-Schreiber was among the very first to set the alarm-bell ringing.[58] In 1967, he published his influential *Le Défi Américain* (*The American Challenge*) about the silent economic warfare in which the US absolutely outclassed Europe in technology, science, and management. "A country which has to buy most of its electronic equipment abroad will be in a condition of inferiority," he warned, "similar to that of nations in the last century which were incapable of industrializing." Servan-Schreiber also called the attention to the American conquest of Europe by establishing a huge network of subsidiaries. He described the American-owned industry in Europe as the second largest industrial force of the world, second only to American industry in the US. The relatively slim volume—hardly more than 300 pages—was translated into fifteen languages. It shocked Europe and cried for both a counteroffensive and European cooperation. In 1980, Servan-Schreiber published another book titled *Le Défi Mondiale* (*The World-Wide Challenge*) that explored the challenges presented by the "Small Tigers of Asia." The French publicist excellently expressed the problem of Europe's relative economic decline and the need for action.[59] Willem Hulsink points out that "the European business community found itself inadequately equipped to cope with the high technology threat from the US and Japan and the low-end technology threat from the Newly Industrializing Countries."[60]

Big European corporations mobilized

In the late 1960s and during the 1970s, European corporations became much more vocal about the threat of overseas competition and they became engaged politically and economically in debates about globalization. The case of one British computer giant is particularly revealing of this trend. Britain was still outside the EEC in the 1960s due to French vetoes. The *London Times* reported the following story on July 1968.

> The British Ministry for Technology stated in 1966: At all cost Britain must maintain an independent and viable computer industry. Since then Britain has learned that she cannot pull this off by herself [. . .] The logical policy for Europe would be to pool all the resources [they have] [. . .] Current disjoined, nearsighted attempts are inexcusable, and doomed to failure."[61]

Indeed, in March 1970, *The Times* already reported that the leading British computer producer, the British International Computer (ICL) proposed unifying the European computer industry. "The eventual aim is the creation of a group strong enough to rival [the American] IBM, the world leader [. . .]. By 1975 design work could start on a gigantic European computer system to be available in the 1980s."[62] In order to assist with and advocate for the corporate initiative, the Parliamentary Labour Party's Science and Technology Group presented a report in the summer of 1968 that urged the rationalization of "European industrial concerns" and the—let me stress again, before Britain became member of the European Community in 1973—the foundation of "supranational European groups." They also called for a unified European patent system and the standardization of the European legal system.[63]

In the fall of 1969, an interesting battle between the American Westinghouse and the German Siemens corporations gained public interest. During the course of the previous year, Westinghouse had worked to establish itself as a multinational European company by buying the French Jeumont-Schneider Company, the Belgian Ateliers de Construction Electrique de Charleroi, and some Italian and Spanish corporations. The German Siemens tried to "beat Westinghouse at its own game." Against the American takeover, the European Commission entered the ring on the side of Siemens. "The Commission injected itself into the corporate drama with a general policy statement on American investments [. . .]. It would be preferable for European electrical-equipment enterprises," the statement declared, "to band together rather than operate under the aegis of Westinghouse [. . .]. It was time European corporations acted on their own to create larger, more competitive units."[64]

Around 1970, it became crystal clear, as *Reuter* reported from Brussels in August 1970 that "companies in the European Economic Community are incapable of competing with giant American corporations under present conditions. [. . .] Effort[s] to foster national mergers are also insufficient. [. . .] American investments in Europe had been running three times that of transitional investments across EEC frontiers."[65]

Europe's competitors have enjoyed several advantages compared to Europe. America and Japan were far ahead in technological research and development of the most modern high-tech industries and services. The American economy was also a pioneer of deregulation from the beginning on the 1980s, paid much less taxes and became much more flexible as a result, and also became very successful and competitive. Although it was not the only successful economic actor in the world, American influence and dominance in international organizations allowed the sweeping neo-liberal deregulatory regime adopted in the US to function as the cultural-ideological companion and driver of globalization.

Japan and especially the newly industrializing Asian countries, over and above their incomparably lower wage level, also developed their "Asian Model," characterized by strong state interventionism, state direction, and even planning and state ownership that has proven to be extremely efficient and successful. China's economic expansion, for instance, was and still is strongly state-driven. The World Bank's 1993 report, *The East Asian Miracle*, underlined the role of the state in successful modernization.[66] The World Bank's 1998 *World Development Report* also stressed the importance of state interventionism in making the region extremely competitive.

The official documents of the European Community during the late 1970s and especially in the 1980s are full of wake-up calls about the dangers posed both by American and Japanese competition and by Europe's lagging positions in the world market and modern technology. Roy Jenkins, President of the European Commission, sharply delineated this fact in an address in Nuremberg in December 1980:

> At present European vitality is low. By comparison with our major industrial partners, we have been relatively unsuccessful both in renewing existing

industries and in introducing new industries based on advanced technologies. I am afraid that we have been more concerned with . . . [the declining] steel, shipbuilding and textile sectors than with the creation of conditions for the new industrial base we need."[67]

In its 1980–81 report, the European Commission noted to the European Council that "the Community's economy has . . . been losing ground in world markets . . . [that we need to] improve the Community's competitiveness, strengthen investment . . . "[68] A Commission memo on biomolecular engineering in January 1980 reads: "the Commission notes that the US and Japan have gained a considerable advance on Europe."[69]

At the end of the 1970s and early 1980s, the world press broadly dealt with this situation. The *Los Angeles Times* in an article called "American Europe" in December 1978 recalled that about "ten years ago Europe was warned that American business was about to take over the continent."[70] *The Sunday Times* in the summer of 1982 explained that behind the current crisis in European and American relations stands the US's competition in high-tech industries, enforcement of "US laws on European soil," and efforts to limit European steel exports.[71] The *Financial Times* described the competition of American chemical companies on the European markets.[72]

But the Community was still frozen in inaction, as it had been since the mid-1960s regarding the full further realization of a real common, integrated market. In the middle of that period, however, the European Commission in 1973 actually worked out an Action Program.[73] Nevertheless, nothing really had happened to thaw the situation because the member states, whose unanimous vote was essential to adopting any action, were not ready yet to collaborate and were instead still advancing their own national programs. At the end of the decade, the European Community warned repeatedly about the dangerous sign of increasing penetration by rivals, but did nothing.[74] The thaw would not set in until the end of the 1980s. Wayne Sandholtz expressed the widespread feelings in Europe at the end of that decade: "A generalized sense of crisis arose . . . The feeling of falling steadily and perhaps irretrievably behind the United States and Japan recalled the panic . . . of the earlier scare."[75]

In this new situation the big European corporations entered the scene. They demanded the realization of the still not accomplished program of the Treaty of Rome to create a real, borderless, single Europe and a single European market for capital, goods, and services, independent from the American dollar and competition. In other words, when America withdrew as a main builder of further European integration, a 'change of guards' happened and the big European corporations *took over the role to build Europe and push European integration forward*. They felt endangered, their international economic position weakened, and their home market invaded. They urged a much more integrated Europe and started cross-border mergers and acquisitions to build a huge all-European network. They could not act alone, however, and needed the European Community's actions to help them.

Notes

1 President J.F. Kennedy's commencement speech at American University on June 10, 1963, www.pbs.org/wgbh/americanexperience/features/ . . . /jfk-university.
2 See US Department of State, *Bulletin*, July 23, 1962, 131–3.
3 Ernst Hans van der Beugel, *From Marshall Aid to Atlantic Partnership. European Integration as a Concern of American Foreign Policy*. Amsterdam: Elsevier, 1966, 382–3.
4 Archive of European Integration, EU Diplomacy Papers, 2/2006, December 2006, Günter Burghardt, "The EU's Transatlantic Relationship"; Archive of European Integration, Frances G. Burwell, "Transatlantic Cooperation and Influence: The Virtue of Crisis and Compromise," (June 5, 1999); Archive of European Integration, IES Working Paper (2/2007), Youri Devuyst, "American Attitude on European Political Integration. The Nixon–Kissinger Legacy"; Douglas Brinkley and Richard T. Griffiths, eds., *John F. Kennedy and Europe* (Baton Rouge, LA: Louisiana State University Press, 1999); *Newsweek*, July 8, 1963.
5 Thomas Alan Schwartz, *Lyndon Johnson and Europe in the Shadow of Vietnam* (Cambridge MA: Harvard University Press, 2003), 150.
6 Ibid., 29, 237.
7 Ibid., 48, 150.
8 Daniel J. Sargent, *A Superpower Transformed. The Rethinking of American Foreign Relations in the 1970s* (New York, NY: Oxford University Press, 2015), 26.
9 Ibid., 37.
10 John McCormick, *Understanding the European Union. A Concise Introduction* (New York, NY: St Martin's Press, 1999), 214.
11 *Pacem in Terris*, Pope John XXIII's Encyclical, http://w2.vatican.va/content/john-xxiii/en/encyclicals/documents/hf_j-xxiii_enc_11041963_pacem.html.
12 Richard Cooper, *The Economics of Interdependence. Economic Policy in the Atlantic Community* (New York, NY: McGraw-Hill, 1968); Raymond Vernon, *Sovereignty at Bay. The Multinational Spread of U.S. Enterprises* (New York, NY: Basic Books, 1971); Alvin Toffler, *Future Shock* (New York, NY: Bentham Books, 1971); Lester Brown, *World Without Borders* (New York, NY: Random House, 1972). All of these works were mentioned and quoted by Sargent, *A Superpower Transformed*, 168.
13 Ibid., 165.
14 Richard Nixon's inaugural speech in January 1969, http://www.presidency.ucsb.edu/ws/?pid
15 Henry Kissinger, *The Troubled Partnership: A Re-Appraisal of the Atlantic Alliance* (New York, NY: McGraw-Hill, 1965), 39, 40, 244.
16 Henry Kissinger, *The White House Years* (Boston, MA: Little, Brown and Co., 1979), 399.
17 Ibid., 88.
18 Sargent, *A Superpower Transformed*, 10, 11, 42.
19 "Nixon's report to Congress on foreign policy, February 18, 1970," *New York Times*, February 19, 1970.
20 US Foreign Policy for the 1970s: Building for Peace, A Report to the Congress by Richard Nixon, February 25, 1971, 29–30, https://history.state.gov/ . . . /frus1969-76v01/d60).
21 Quoted by James Chace, "American Jingoism," *Harper's*, March 1976, 43.
22 Eisenhower Library, NSC Series, Box 7, 267th meeting of NSC, November 21, 1955, 10. Quoted by Archive of European Integration, Stephanie B. Anderson, "Developing Europe into a Third Great Power Bloc: the US, France and the Failure of European Defense Community," 2005, aei.pitt.edu/3269/).
23 Luke A. Nichter, *Richard Nixon and Europe. The Reshaping of the Postwar Atlantic World* (Cambridge: Cambridge University Press, 2015), 123–4.
24 Sargent, *A Superpower Transformed*, 166.
25 Nichter, *Richard Nixon and Europe*, 136.
26 Sargent, *A Superpower Transformed*, 28–9.

27 Nichter, *Richard Nixon and Europe*, 141.

28 Ibid., 140.

29 Nixon Tapes, Executive Office Building 295-14, November 16, 1971, quoted by Nichter, *Richard Nixon and Europe*, 28.

30 On September 11, 1971, discussion with John Conally and Arthur Burns in the Oval Office. Nixon Tapes, Oval Office 570-004, quoted by Nichter, *Richard Nixon and Europe*, 73–4.

31 Nixon's memorandum on February 18, 1969, quoted by Nichter, *Richard Nixon and Europe*, 12.

32 Raymond Aron, "Europe and the United States: The Relations Between Europeans and Americans," in *Western Europe: The Trials of Partnership*, ed. David S. Landes (Lexington, DC: Heath and Co., 1977), 33.

33 Ibid., 118. Quoted from the "Zusammenfassung und Bewertung der Rede Kissinger vom 23 April 1973."

34 Ibid., 135.

35 Quoted by Nichter, *Richard Nixon and Europe*, 29–30.

36 Sargent, *A Superpower Transformed*, 117.

37 Raymond Aron, "Europe and the United States", 30; Archive of European Integration, ACES Working Paper Series, Robert J. Licher, "The European Union and the United States."

38 Mary Elise Sarotte, "The Frailties of Grand Strategies: A Comparison of Détant and Ostpolitik," in *Nixon in the World. American Foreign Relations, 1969–1977*, eds. Frederik Logevall and Andrew Preston (Oxford: Oxford University Press, 2008), 151.

39 Documents on Kissinger–Gromyko and Kissinger–Brezhnev talks, quoted by Michael Coley Morgan, "The United States and the Making of the Helsinki Final Act," in Logevall and Preston, eds., *Nixon in the World*, 172.

40 Let me illustrate the conflicting situation with a few examples from the 1980s on. At the hearing of the US's Congress Joint Economic Committee's Subcommittee on Economic Goals and Intergovernmental Policy in 1983, bitter complaints were made about Europe's competition. The vice president of the Subcommittee, Democratic Senator Lloyd Bentsen attacked the Airbus Consortium of Europe, which produced the A-300 and A-310 air-planes with subsidies and conquered 30 percent of the world market, although its pro-duction costs are 20–25 percent higher than comparable US aircrafts. Senator Bentsen. complained about Europe's unfair competitive practice against McDonnell Douglas and Boeing. The senator also attacked the European Common Market for subsidizing agri-culture by US$2 per bushel of wheat and US$0.5 per pound of beef. "Those subsidies have worked in a spectacular manner to grab markets from our farmers." The US that tolerated EEC's tariff and agricultural policy for decades became dissatisfied and that was clearly expressed in the quoted Congressional committee debate as the US "had just about reached the limit of its patience and talk on the subject of unfair practices" (see *Hearing before the Subcommittee on Economic Goals and Intergovernmental Policy of the Joint Economic Committee Congress of the United States, 98th Congress, First Session, July 25, 1983* (Washington, DC: US Government Printing Office), 39–41). In some way, even the American general public realized the changes in connection with an enriched Europe. In 1980, the *Chicago Tribune* published a characteristic article in which it noted, "In the old day . . . Americans used to go to Europe every summer and look up their relatives . . . but now that Europeans are rich, they are flocking to America to look up their relatives" ("Our Old European Relatives Find us Quaint," *Chicago Tribune*, July 19, 1980). At the time of the German unification in the early 1990s, the EEC initiated major new steps towards a political union to anchor a strengthened Germany closer to Europe. One of the elements of this effort was the initiative of a more independent European Security and Defense Policy. This was interpreted in Washington "as a way to push the United States out of Europe." This skepticism characterized the Clinton Administrations as well. Secretary of State Madelaine Albright warned Europe not to violate the "Three Ds, diminution of NATO, duplication of NATO, or discrimination of NATO members"

(Archive of European Integration, Stephanie B. Anderson, "Developing Europe"). "Every few years" summing up a European analysis in the Archive of European Integration at the end of the 1990s, "concerns are expressed that the transatlantic alliance is on the verge of collapse as disputes overwhelm a host of shared interests and values." This document also quotes from French President Mitterrand from previous years: "France does not know it, but we are at war, an economic war, a war without death . . . The Americans want undivided power over the world" (see Archive of European Integration, Frances G. Burwell, "Transatlantic Cooperation and Influence: The Virtue of Crisis and Compromise," June 3, 1999). Relations became coldest during the George W. Bush Administration when the US started the Iraq war. In 2003 an analyst went as far as stating: "It is time to stop pretending that Europeans and Americans share a common view of the world . . . They agree on little and understand one another less and less . . . The US and Europe have parted ways" (see Robert Kagan, *Of Paradise and Power: America and Europe in the New World Order* (New York, NY: Knopf, 2003), 3–4). A year later another expert added: "It is by no means excessive to ask whether the US and Europe may now be on the verge of a divorce in which their allied of more than half a century collapse . . . " (see Archive of European Integration, ACES Working Paper Series, Robert J. Lieber, "The European Union and the United Sates").

41 The Carter Administration, and its main foreign policy architect, Zbigniew Brezhinski, who put human rights into the center of foreign policy, somewhat renewed Cold War conflicts with the Soviet Union. It was especially true after the Soviet invasion in Afghanistan at the end of 1979 and in the first years of the Reagan Administration in the early 1980s.

42 Wayne Sandholtz, *High-Tech Europe: The Politics of International Cooperation* (Berkeley, CA: University of California Press, 1992), 115.

43 Carl H.A. Dassbach, *Global Enterprises and the World Economy. Ford, General Motors, and IBM, the Emergence of the Transnational Enterprise* (New York, NY: Garland Publishing, 1989), 2–3.

44 OECD *General Report. Gaps in Technology* (Paris: OECD, 1966). See also the same report for 1968, 12–14.

45 Archive of European Integration, Commission Statement on the European Automobile Industry. Structure and Prospects of the European Car Industry, 1981. Commission Communication to the Council, presented on June 1981, COM (81) 317 final, 17.

46 Frank Fishwick, *Multinational Companies and Economic Concentration in Europe* (Aldershot, UK: Gower, 1982), 12, 13, 19.

47 Archive of European Integration, "Europe: a Time to Choose," European Parliament Document, 1985.

48 Alan Cawson, "Interests, Groups and Public Policy-Making: The Case of the European Consumer Electronics Industry," in *Organized Interests and the European Community*, eds. Justin Greenwood, Jürgen R. Grote, and Karsten Ronit (London: Sage Publications, 1992), 109, 111.

49 Justin Greenwood and Karsten Ronit, "Established and Emergent Sectors: Organized Interests at the European Level in the Pharmaceutical Industry and the New Biotechnology," in Greenwood, Grote and Ronit, eds., *Organized Interests*, 102.

50 Wayne Sandholtz and John Zysman, "1992: Recasting the European Bargain," *World Politics* 42, no. 1 (October 1989), 104.

51 John Cantwell, "The Reorganization of European Industries after Integration: Selected Evidence on the Role of Multinational Enterprise Activities," in *Multinationals and the European Community*, eds. John Dunning and Peter Robson (Oxford: Basil Blackwell, 1988), 44.

52 Sandholtz, *High-Tech Europe*, 117, 131.

53 Archive of European Integration, George W. Ball, "The Common Market—the Period of Transition," The 400th Meeting of the National Industrial Conference Board Inc. (New York, January 21, 1960), 10.

54 John Borrus and John Zysman, "Globalization with Borders: The Rise of Wintelism as the Future of Industrial Competition," in *Enlarging Europe. The Industrial Foundation of a*

New Political Reality, eds. John Zysman and Andrew Schwartz, (Berkeley, CA: University of California Press, 1998), 30.

55 Archive of European Integration, EU Commission Working Document. The 1980s: The Decade for Technology? A Study of the State of Art of Assembly of Apparel Products (1979), 1.1.

56 Archive of European Integration, Address by Roy Jenkins, President of the Commission of the European Community to Meeting of the Bundeskommitee Europe-Wahl, Frankfurt (April 24, 1979), 7.

57 Archive of European Integration, Improving Competitiveness and Industrial Structure in the Community. Commission Communication to the Council, COM (86) 40 final (February 25, 1986), 6.

58 The publications of Jean-Jacques Servan-Schreiber are *Le Défi Américain* (Paris: Denoël, 1967) and *Le Défi Mondiale* (Paris: Fayard, 1980). On the concerns of European policy-makers about telecommunications competition, see Volker Schneider, "Organized Interests in the European Telecommunication Sector," in Greenwood, Grote, and Ronit, eds., *Organized Interests*, 50.

59 Jean-Jacques Servan-Schreiber, *The American Challenge*, English trans. of *Le Défi Américain* (New York, NY: Atheneum, 1968), 101.

60 Willem Hulsink, "From State Monopolies to Euro-Nationals and Global Alliances: The Case of the European Telecommunication Sector," in Jules J.J. Dijck and John P.M. Groenewegen, eds., *Changing Business Systems in Europe. An Institutional Approach* (Brussels: VUB Press, 1994), 464.

61 "Computers: battle for the future," *The Times*, July 18, 1968.

62 "ICL urges Europe link in computer to rival IBM," *The Times*, March 9, 1970.

63 "How to meet American challenge in Europe," *The Times*, June 27, 1968.

64 "European Economic Commission is opposing Westinghouse European plans," *New York Times*, October 16, 1969.

65 "Industry link-up in EEC is urged," *New York Times*, August 29, 1970.

66 The World Bank, *The East Asian Miracle: Economic Growth and Public Policy* (New York, NY: Oxford University Press, 1993).

67 Archive of European Integration, Roy Jenkins, President of the European Commission, Address to the Nuremberg Chamber of Commerce and Industry (December 4, 1980).

68 Archive of European Integration, Annual Economic Report 1980–81, Communication of the European Commission of the European Community to the Council (Brussels, October 15, 1980).

69 Archive of European Integration, Commission Proposes Community Research Programme in Biomolecular Engineering, Information Memo P-7/80 (January 1980).

70 *Los Angeles Times*, December 17, 1978.

71 *The Sunday Times*, June 27, 1982.

72 *Financial Times*, August 18, 1982.

73 See Lynn Krieger Mytelka and Michel Delapierre, "The Alliance Strategies of European Firms in the Information Technology Industry and the Role of ESPIRIT," in *Multinationals and the European Community* eds. John H. Dunning and Peter Robson (Oxford: Basil Blackwell, 1988), 7, 113.

74 Archive of European Integration, Eurofocus: A Newssheet for Journalists. Weekly No.7/86 (February 17–24, 1986), 4–5.

75 Sandholtz, *High-Tech Europe*, 113.

4

MADE BY CORPORATE EUROPE?

The "second coming" of the European
integration, 1980s–2000s

This chapter covers roughly two decades between two distinct periods of the history of the European integration. In the first period, the two decades immediately following the war, the destruction and the lessons of World War II strongly influenced devastated nation-states and federalist politicians, motivating them to reorganize Europe. They would not realize their plans, however, without strong American intervention into European political affairs, actions inspired by the rising Cold War, which led to the beginning of West European integration. From the mid-1960s, however, this integration process lost its dynamism and did not go much further towards the end goal of an "ever closer union" by supranationalization.[1]

After a two-decades-long slowing down, a new chapter of dynamic further integration began in the 1980s. During the long period of slower progress in integration, however, major global political and economic changes that characterized that time resulted in a new drive for further integration. From the later 1960s, the American policy towards Europe radically changed (discussed in Chapter 3) but the world's political and economic systems were also dramatically transformed, as discussed later in this chapter. Without these new developments, one cannot understand the new wave of European integration that emerged from the 1980s on, pushed by new players—the big European corporations. These firms felt the world economic transformation in the most direct and painful way because it pushed them into an existential crisis of losing their world positions and even parts of their home markets. Together with the governments of the nation-states and federalist politicians, these firms invested in a new chapter of integration: a "second coming" of Europe.

Slowing down of integration between 1965 and 1985

Walter Hallstein, the German president of the European Commission once was asked at an interview: "How long will it be before there will be a United States of

Europe?" He answered confidently and yet equivocally: "There will be a United States of Europe, but it's certainly premature to say when and what exactly its structure will be."[2] That was in 1959. At the time, the integrative steps initiated with the Treaty of Rome were functioning well to build a tariff-free economic community within the boundaries of Western Europe. Economic integration was thought to pave the way for political integration and federalization, but in 1965, that latter process would come to a very public halt when President Charles de Gaulle of France set off the so-called empty chair crisis. Slow progress of market integration did not realize the explicit plans of the founders and in several areas paralysis would be the rule for the following two decades.

De Gaulle was, at heart, a nineteenth-century nationalist who had always opposed supranational or federal integration. Monnet recalled that de Gaulle was convinced that "only the States, in this respect, are valid, legitimate, and capable of achieving it [cooperation of nations] . . . at present there is and can be no Europe other than a Europe of the States [*l'Europe des états*]." An "integrated Europe" would need a "federator," and the federator, de Gaulle argued, drawing on his postwar experience with the US, "would not be European."[3] Accordingly, from the beginning of his presidency, he promoted a European political alliance system instead of American supported integration. In 1958, he suggested the formation of a global *directoire*, which would include the US, Britain, and France, but exclude Germany.[4] That idea was rejected by the other five countries of the European Community. He tried another tack at the Paris summit of European Economic Community (EEC) heads of state in February 1961 by proposing a more limited political cooperation among the six EEC member countries. A study group was set up explicitly to explore the possible forms of political cooperation and headed by the French diplomat Christian Fouchet, who eventually presented what came to be known as the Fouchet Plan. It proposed a confederation of European states with common foreign and defense policy, as well as cooperation in scientific research and cultural matters. This plan would have subordinated the European Economic Community to a new intergovernmental council. At a press conference on May 15, 1962, de Gaulle suggested: "Let us create a political commission, a defense commission, and a cultural commission, just as we already have a[n] Economic Commission in Brussels."[5]

Although this French plan was considered and rejected in 1961, it was reintroduced and discussed again in January 1962 by the foreign ministers of the EEC countries. Given that the other member countries did not share de Gaulle's opposition to integration and further supranationalization, the plan failed again. At his May 15, 1962 press conference, de Gaulle harshly criticized the Community's federalist policy. In a last attempt to promote the confederative path, he initiated a bilateral Franco–German agreement—the Elysée Treaty or Friendship Treaty—which he signed in January 1963 along with Chancellor Konrad Adenauer. This miniature, two-country version of the Fouchet Plan established periodic meetings of the French and German ministers of foreign affairs, defense, education, and youth, and also the chiefs of staff.[6]

Despite Adenauer's support, Germany, along with the Benelux countries and Italy, turned away from de Gaulle's efforts to replace the European Community with an interstate alliance. Preferring the road of an "ever closer union," these countries wanted to increase the role of the existing supranational institutions—the European Parliament and European Commission. They also suggested introducing qualified majority voting at the Council of Ministers to replace the requirement of unanimity that gave a veto right to each member country. Following a Dutch initiative, the Community proposed establishing its own income source, an automatic tax to be paid to the Community by the member countries, to replace the original system of contributions from governments. In July 1965, de Gaulle vetoed the further integration plans. France left the Council of Ministers, the legislative body of the Community, vacated its chair, and thereafter boycotted Council meetings.[7] De Gaulle followed up with an ultimatum: if member countries' veto rights were to be questioned, France might leave the Community for good. Seven years would elapse before the heads of EEC states convened another summit meeting.

In January 1966, with the so-called Luxembourg Compromise, member countries went ahead and accepted the principle of majority voting, but with a disabling limiting condition: "if [at] any stage, a member state felt that its national interest might be threatened, the voting would simply switch back to unanimity."[8] De Gaulle's "empty chair" tactic had triumphed: the French boycott protected intergovernmental decision-making procedure, allowed de Gaulle successfully to challenge the political authority of the European Commission, and created conditions that effectively stopped the further development of integration until the mid-1980s. As Michael Baun has stated, de Gaulle's triumph appeared to be the death-knell of a supranational Europe and the birth of his "Europe des états."[9] Neither the opposition of various agricultural and industrial interest groups nor the preferences of the other five member countries could save the Community from the paralysis created by the mere existence of the veto power. Consequently, the express train of Europe slowed down, and the station at the end of the line—called Federal Europe—remained out of reach.

But was this EEC failure merely a long shadow of de Gaulle's paralyzing policy? That is hardly possible given subsequent events. On April 28, 1969 "a terse, three-line communiqué from the Elysée presidential palace, issued shortly after midnight," announced the sensational news that, after eleven years in office, de Gaulle had resigned.[10] He had lost a referendum on his planned domestic governmental reforms and had thus decided to leave office. The "empty chair" episode and the Luxembourg Compromise would soon belong to the "dustbin of history" and the first Community summit after de Gaulle's resignation, held in The Hague in 1969, would signal some changes.[11] But the state of inertia still reigned.

What caused stagnation for another one-and-half decades? The rich literature on the history of the European Union fails to provide a convincing answer to this question. Among the contributing factors, I must mention the confusing situation of the world economy. In Europe itself, a new chapter in postwar history opened, as exceptional growth disappeared and was replaced by significant slowing and even decline. Rock-solid international institutions, such as the Bretton Woods agreement on exchange-rate policy and financial control, collapsed in 1971, and two shocking oil crises in 1973 and 1979–80, dramatically changed the international price movement.

These were spectacularly new phenomena, but what were their causes? The world did not have an answer, nor would it find one for some time. EEC governments resorted to short-term measures to protect their declining economies. Meanwhile intergovernmentalism continued to rule the game. In 1974, the founding of a new institution, the European Council, composed of the heads of states and governments of the member countries of the European Union, strengthened the intergovernmental trend. Although informal until 1992, this institution developed into one of the most important European decision-making forums. With its appearance the role of the supranational European Commission was weakened.

The Commission, the institution responsible for initiatives of action, also lacked charismatic and visionary leadership. Although one man—Walter Hallstein—served in the presidency chair in the first decade of the Community's existence (1958–67), four men (Jean Rey of Belgium, Franco M. Malfatti of Italy, Sicco Mansholt of the Netherlands, and François-Xavier Ortoli of France) would occupy the position over the next decade (1967–76). Some of these leaders contributed to further integration in certain areas of cooperation, but none of them put forth major new ideas or initiatives to open a new chapter of the development of integration; they were unable to direct Community policy along new paths, nor were the next two Commission presidents, Roy Jenkins of Britain and Gaston Thorn of Luxembourg. During their four-year terms, the only path-breaking new proposal—for the introduction of the common currency—did not receive preference on the agendas of member countries and the Commission, and it had to wait another thirty years to be realized. Despite this dismal record, the Commission presidents do not deserve to be blamed exclusively. The heads of government with whom they had to work simply were not strongly Europe-oriented.

Although integration slowed down, the world system radically changed. One of the key characteristics of the postwar world system was the dangerous Cold War, which generated a decisive American policy drive towards Europe. The Soviet archenemy of the West, however, in its post-Stalin development, became a less dangerous and less menacing rival, even making efforts to increase domestic standards of living and to keep its military at bay. Although not without contrary trends from time to time, new Soviet leaders became increasingly willing to work with their American counterparts to discuss and even make agreements. The famous Kennedy–Khrushchev meeting in Vienna in June 1961, which ended without an agreement, initiated a 'Thaw,' to use the title of Ilja Ehrenburg's short novel. But this thaw was not permanent. In October 1962, the frightening Cuban missile crisis, a new Soviet provocation, shifted the rivals onto the brink of war. However, after the firm policy of the Kennedy Administration, the Soviet withdrew and a new attitude emerged: discussion of the problems of the relations between the confronting powers—even creating a hot-line for direct connections—led to major agreements. The sharp Cold War ended virtually in 1963. During the 1970s, a new US–Soviet relations emerged (as discussed in Chapter 3), including the emergence of trade and economic connections. The American media started speaking about Soviet "economic or market invasion," especially in the oil markets that were "far more subtle than military threat."[12] Documents from the Foreign and Commonwealth Office of the British Government reflected a new voice in the early 1970s: "It is fair to state as a fact that the expansion of the US/Soviet economic dealings is likely to be at the expense of Western Europe."[13]

Gradually, the Cold War was replaced by détente. The German Government of Willy Brandt, with its new *Ostpolitik,* opened towards Eastern Europe. As a major milestone of this 'opening,' the Helsinki Agreement of 1975 signaled a new international and European environment. The Soviet-initiated agreement targeted the stabilization of the status quo, including postwar borders and the existence of an East German state. In reality, the so-called "Third Basket" on human rights and humanitarian problems particularly helped to legalize the 'dissident' movement, the Soviet Bloc anti-communist opposition such as the Czech Charta 77, or later the Polish Solidarity movement. The agreement also created more elbow-room for increasingly independent foreign policy for reform-oriented Bloc countries. The isolation of the East was broken. Cultural connections improved, which precipitated, in the longer run, a disintegration of the Bloc.

The strict Soviet-dictated unity of the world communist movement—so closely watched and feared by the US in the postwar decades— also ended. Yugoslavia left the Bloc in 1948. In 1960, China turned against the Soviet Union. Eurocommunism in one of the leading West European communist parties, especially the Italian, but also the Spanish and in certain periods the French, openly revolted against the Soviet dictate and rejected Soviet policy and ideology. In postwar West European integration and prosperity, under the shocking impact of the opening of Stalinist crime files, the West European communist parties gave up their traditional communist ideology and embarked on the road of social democratization. They turned to Western values of free markets and democracy. The ideas of "Eurocommunism" were clearly expressed by the head of the Italian Communist Party, Enrico Berlinguer in June 1976:

> We are fighting for a socialist society that has its foundation [. . .] [in] individual and collective freedom and their guarantee, the principle of [. . .] [the] non-ideological nature of the State and its democratic organization, the plurality of the political parties, and the possibility of altering government majorities [. . .] religious freedom, freedom of expression, of culture and arts and sciences.[14]

West European communism dissolved, which strongly influenced East European communist intellectuals and even entire parties. World communism was not as strong, united, or frightening as in the early postwar decades. In this changing international political environment, American policy towards Europe also changed and the US started to realize that a united Europe was not only an ally, but also a rising competitor (discussed in Chapter 3). In 1973, Britain, along with Denmark and Ireland, also joined the Community. The traditionally pro-Atlantic British policy stabilized the American connections with the European Community. Even the British Foreign and Commonwealth Office recognized in the fall of 1973 that there was no need "to any new transatlantic institutional link which might give the Americans the right to intervene concerning Community policies under construction." They confidently stated that the planned European visit of President Nixon "[would] symbolize the progress made in European unity since he last came in 1969."[15] America stopped pushing further integration from the 1960s–70s on.

The world economy also entered into a new chapter of its history in which rapid growth was replaced by decline and stagnation and by skyrocketing oil and raw material prices that generated double digit inflation. A new technological revolution disruption the economy and led to the decline of the old leading sectors. Europe lost its positions and lagged behind its American and Japanese competitors. These changes (discussed in Chapter 3) required a strong and efficient European response and adjustment. The European Community, however, looking like a train wreck, was stopped in its tracks, unable to move.

In this situation, the large European corporations entered center stage. They wanted a rebirth of the Community, a rapid further integration. They needed a real single market, a home base with hundreds of millions of consumers, and a large peripheral area to provide cheap labor, a real economic backyard.

New international economic environment: end of prosperity and oil crises

The postwar quarter of a century was miraculous for Europe, a quality attested to by the metaphors used to describe it: *Wirtschaftswunder* in Germany; *miracolo economico* in Italy; and *les trente glorieuses* in France.[16] During this period of super prosperity, Europe reconstructed its ruined buildings and infrastructure, modernized its economy, created an advanced welfare system, and experienced its highest ever growth with 4–5 percent annual GDP increases.

Corporate Europe flourished. Economic growth was driven by an explosion of consumption, suppressed and delayed for at least a quarter of a century before 1950 and combined with an unparalleled export boom (see Table 4.1).

TABLE 4.1 GDP per capita in three European regions, in thousand million 1990 US dollars

Year	West Europe	%		South Europe	%		East Europe	%	
1950	1,225	100	35	138	100	24	753	100	35
1973	3,503	286	100	570	413	100	2,171	288	100
1985	4,431	362	126	779	564	189	2,694	358	124

Source: Based on Angus Maddison, *Monitoring the World Economy 1820–1992* (Paris: OECD, 1995), 227.

Capital accumulation virtually doubled, compared to the prewar decades, until it accounted for about 25 percent of the GDP by the 1970s. Investments also jumped to new heights and the gross stock of fixed business capital in the leading West European countries increased by more than seven-fold and the stock of machinery thirteen-fold.

These economic miracles, however, vanished from sight during the late 1960s and early 1970s, to be replaced by decline and long stagnation. The annual average growth rate of 4.8 percent in the later EU-12 region before 1973, declined in the first half of the 1980s to an annual rate of only 0.5 percent. Even in Germany, the engine of the West European economy, growth dropped from 5 to 1.6 percent per year in the decade of 1974–83. The West European economy had increased by 300 percent between 1950 and 1973; during the following decade, it increased only by 26 percent, a virtual stagnation. A nearly full employment was replaced by high unemployment, with overall rates skyrocketing from 2 to 12 percent. In the Netherlands and Britain, the rate elevated to 14 and 13 percent, respectively; and in Spain to 20 percent. Europe also lost control of inflation as the former price stability (with 2–3 percent annual increases) gave way to inflation rates of 9–18 percent. Instead of catching up with the US and the spectacularly emerging Japan, Europe lagged dramatically behind. The European corporate world suddenly looked obsolete and unable to keep up with its rivals.

What happened? Above all, the entire world economic environment was radically transformed. The most visible and dramatic change was brought by two politically generated oil crises in 1973 and 1979–80, which increased the world market price of oil ten times.[17] Europe was highly dependent on oil imports. During the postwar prosperity and rising consumerism, the car park of the West European

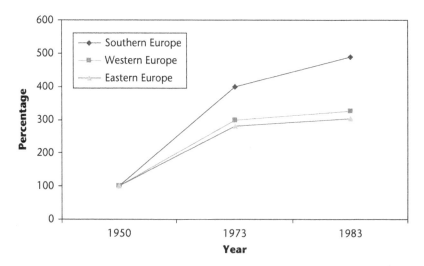

FIGURE 4.1 Slowing growth rate after 1973

Source: Based on *Eurostat Yearbooks* (Luxemburg: Publication Office of the EU).

countries dramatically increased and oil consumption (which increased six times in the world in two decades) jumped more than fourteen times, from less than 1 million barrels in 1949 to more than 14 million barrels by 1970. The sharp price increases and the instability in the oil-producing Middle East contributed to a decade-long inflationary process that elevated the entire price level, especially for raw materials. Between 1973 and 1983, world price level was twice as high as what it had been in 1950–73, and consumer prices in the West more than doubled. The annual price increase in Europe in the 1970s reached more than 9 percent. In the particularly hard-hit Mediterranean region, the price level quadrupled and price increases jumped to more than 18 percent per year. Less developed world regions were hit hard by debt crisis. Twenty-five countries, mostly on the peripheries of the world economy, including a few East European countries, had to reschedule debt repayments in 1983–84.[18]

When the oil crises hit Europe, the Western half of the continent was already struggling with another major and shocking change: the collapse of the centuries-old colonial system. The rise of modern capitalism, and of Western Europe as the core of the modern world economy, had been closely connected with that system. Between the sixteenth and twentieth centuries, about 60 million Europeans had left the old continent to establish the so-called white colonies all over the world. Coming first from Spain and Portugal, and then from the Netherlands, Britain, France, and Belgium, they gradually conquered and settled in the other continents. In 1500, Europe controlled 7 percent of the landed areas of the world. By 1800, Europeans owned 35 percent of it. This process reached its culmination between the 1870s and 1910s, the period Eric Hobsbawm called the "age of empire."[19] Before World War I, Europeans ruled over half of the landed area of the world and one-third of its entire population. The colonies increased the national income of the colonial master countries by 5–6 percent above the domestic GDP and colonial incomes financed trade deficits. They also helped to increase the level of capital accumulation and consumption.[20] "Purely domestic accounts of the 'Rise of the West' . . . are hopelessly inadequate since they ignore the vast web of interrelationship between Western Europe and the rest of the world."[21]

Collapse of colonialism and uncertain Third World markets

The colonial system was the cradle of the world's multinational companies. The first were the British, Dutch, and French East Indian Companies, each of which enjoyed a lucrative state monopoly of trade with various colonies on other continents, possessed a private navy and army, and enjoyed the right, according to home country law, to occupy new territories. These companies often supplemented their legitimate cross-seas trading with forms of piracy by attacking and robbing each other's ships.

The large corporations of modern times emerged in the search for new markets for industrially produced goods set off by the British Industrial Revolution. Britain herself had a great number of "free-standing" companies, an early type of multinational operating enterprises overseas.[22] These were building up large international networks, including plantations and means for extracting and processing raw materials, and all were enjoying the benefits of operating in the relatively safe environments provided by home rule in far-flung non-industrialized lands. The kind of multinational known today began to appear in America and Europe in the late nineteenth century. Among the very first was the Singer Sewing Machine company, which established its first foreign factory in Scotland in 1868. In 1914, thirty-seven American companies already had production facilities in two or more countries. In Europe, Unilever, Nestlé, Philips, and Imperial Chemical belonged to this category.[23] The early Dutch–British multinational giant, Unilever, offers a telling example illustrating the changing interests and orientations of multinational corporations.

James Lever was a partner in a grocery shop that turned to wholesale business in England in 1864. Twenty years later he started producing soap in a rented factory. He began taking over rival companies in order to expand the business. At first, he incorporated companies of raw material production, which allowed him to build up a vertical integration on colonial territories in the early twentieth century. He produced coconut oil in the Solomon Islands, palm oil in the Congo, whale oil in the South and North Atlantic. During the 1900s he started doing business in South Africa, and in the 1930s in India. He also began manufacturing in Black Africa. Expansion to North America began in the late nineteenth century. Before World War I, the company entered into the food business and pioneered margarine production. In 1929, after a series of mergers, Lever made a fusion with the Dutch Margarine Union. Unilever, a giant holding company with two headquarters, one in Britain and the other in the Netherlands, but with identical board members, came into being. In the same year, Lever and his Niger Company joined to establish the United African Company. Unilever also entered into retailing, plastics, packing, chemicals, and several other businesses. By the mid-1970s, the holding company had businesses in forty-three countries, with the twenty in Africa producing one-fifth of the company's profit. At the end of that decade, Unilever was operating in seventy-five countries and employing 318,000 people.[24] More than half of its huge capital was invested on continents other than Europe. Among the twenty largest companies of the world, Unilever ranked twelfth. As one of the chronicler of the company stated:

> This was one of the biggest industrial amalgamations in European history, producing business that employed nearly a quarter of a million people . . . and traded in more places and in more products than any other concern on the planet.[25]

To understand the big corporations' new orientation towards the European markets, Unilever again offers a key. In the mid-1980s the company adopted a new business policy, described by one scholar as "a determination to give a 'high priority' to European business."[26] Sales of the company's African business were dropping and would sink by nearly half before the end of the 1980s. Writing at the beginning of that decade, another scholar of the company's history remarked:

> Europe, by contrast, has been a good home to Unilever . . . and never more so than in the years of high prosperity which followed the signing of the Treaty of Rome [in 1957] . . . The EEC is the kind of unobstructed marketing area . . . Unilever, a child of Europe, has at last been able to reach out towards its full inheritance. In this benign atmosphere Unilever's European operations, always large, have grown steadily larger.[27]

The company's capital invested in Europe increased from 48 to 72 percent of the total and its sales in Europe increased from 59 to 74 percent of the total between 1955 and the end of the 1970s. The creation of the European Community—the replacement of fragmented national markets in Europe with a large market—created conditions favorable to restructuring and rationalizing the business. The company sold about seventy factories and units worldwide, and it also bought new ones in the Mediterranean countries and concentrated production in fewer but much bigger factories to exploit the possible economies of scale. In sum, "Unilever changed greatly between 1984 and 1990."[28] In 1988, it had 180 European factories. In 1990, it established Lever Europe with 10,000 employees assigned just to its headquarters in Brussels.

What was the cause of the reorientation towards Europe exemplified by Unilever? The clue lies in the collapse of colonialism after World War II. The devastation brought by war, the Japanese occupation of several of Europe's Asian colonies, and the dramatic weakening of the former colonial masters all undermined the ability of West European countries to impose their rule on their colonies. Liberation movements and fights for independence made the colonies an expensive burden for colonizers. Foreign assets holding started disappearing during the 1950s; "both France and Great Britain found themselves with net foreign asset holding close to zero."[29] Some countries gradually gave up their empires: Britain's peaceful disengagement led to the liberation of India in 1947, of Burma and Ceylon in 1948. Egypt gained independence in 1952. The Netherlands lost Indonesia in 1950 after a fight of five years. France left Syria and Lebanon in 1946, but launched bloody wars to destroy liberation forces and keep its colonies first in Indochina and then in Algeria. The tactic failed. After nine years of fighting (1945–54) France lost Indochina; the loss of Algeria came after eight years of conflict (1954–62). By the 1960s, the colonial system had collapsed almost entirely in Africa and Asia, and several dozens of new independent states had been formed. The United Nations had thirty-five member states in 1946, but 127 by 1970.

Success in the wars of liberation did not, however, bring political tranquility, especially in the so-called developing world inhabited by newly independent countries. Political regime change, military takeovers, successful *coups d'état,* and coup attempts occurred with extreme frequency. As characteristic examples, let me mention that in Sub-Saharan Africa eighty coups succeeded and 108 failed.

A further 139 coup plots were discovered between 1956 and 2001. There were five coups in Afghanistan between 1973 and 2001, five in Ghana between 1966 and 1981, six in Sierra Leone between 1967 and 1998, five in Uganda between 1971 and 1986, and four in Thailand between 1971 and 2006. This kind of instability remained characteristic and unchanged up to the early twenty-first century. In the early 2000s, coups or serious coup attempts happened in Ecuador, Peru, Guinea-Bissau, Togo, Nepal, Mauritania, and Ecuador.[30] In some countries, relatively liberal governments were replaced by aggressive, nationalist, dictatorial regimes. Bolivia and Thailand introduced dictatorship in the 1950s, and have seesawed since between democracy and dictatorship. Ghana and Pakistan have had four such transitions, Sudan and Honduras five, Guatemala and Peru six, and Argentina eight.[31] Thomas Piketty summed up:

> When a country is largely owned by foreigners, there is a recurrent and almost irrepressible social demand for expropriation. Other political actors respond that investment and development are possible only if existing property rights are unconditionally protected. The country is thus caught in an endless alteration between revolutionary governments . . . and governments dedicated to the protection of existing property owners, thereby laying the groundwork for the next revolution or coup.[32]

Overall, political stability was lacking in the former colonies, and in the Third World or "emerging countries" in general. After their liberation the newly independent states were often fractured and were shocked by murderous civil wars and genocides. The Biafra War from 1967 to 1970 led to the division of Nigeria, and the South Asian crisis ended with the division of Pakistan and the birth of Bangladesh. Several other tribal wars endlessly killed and uprooted millions of people and sometime changed artificially created borders. Political stability episodes were rare in those areas.

The newly independent former countries, with their strong anti-colonial fervor, wanted to establish independent economic regimes and quickly turned against foreign companies, introducing strict restrictions on their activities and in some cases even nationalizing their holdings.[33] In the 1970s, Saudi Arabia, Nigeria, and Venezuela nationalized oil; Chile, copper mining; Ghana, gold and bauxite extraction; and Bolivia took over the tin industry. In 1981, the Malaysian Government took control of the Guthrie Corporation, the largest British rubber and palm oil business.[34]

Over time, however, the danger of nationalization lessened, but it did not entirely disappear. This is well-documented by twenty-first century nationalizations of formerly privatized or foreign established companies in some of the transforming post-communist countries such as Russia or Hungary.[35] However, the effects of various regulations, often retroactively applied, became more harmful. In the late 1970s, for example, the Janata Party in India expelled foreign firms that refused to share their technology with local companies; IBM immediately left the country. A World Bank study revealed in 2004 that 15–30 percent of contracts signed in developing countries (covering US$371 billion of private investments in the 1990s) became the subject of government-initiated renegotiations. "Restriction on the transfer and convertibility of profit, civil disturbances, government failure to honor guarantees, and regulatory restrictions all [proved] to be more significant risks than the potential seizure of assets."[36] The advanced countries warned the Third World that such actions could have consequences and urged them to honor the "international economic order." Roy Jenkins, President of the European Commission, speaking in Brussels in 1980 warned the less developed countries that "it is not good the poor countries thinking that they can change the rules of the international economic order overnight to their advantage."[37]

In addition to the uncertainties that can hamper Western-style business, infrastructure in these regions is often inadequate and bribery the rule. Several multinationals, including ExxonMobile in Kazakhstan, Shell in Nigeria and Russia, and Haliburton in Nigeria, have been charged in bribery cases. Siemens settled a US$1.4 billion corruption case over its actions in Iraq and other places. In 1996, the World Bank initiated an anti-corruption campaign and stated that corruption "distorts the rule of law [and] weakens a nation's institutional foundation."[38] The OECD Convention launched a campaign, "Combating Bribery," the very next year; however, the situation did not change in these non-Western regions or in Eastern Europe. As one participant at the "Investor's Infrastructure Investment Forum" of 2007 in New York stated:

> Our customers found it easier to bribe the Estonian government to change the laws to allow them to use our railroad at below-cost rates than it was to pay freight bills . . . Our consortium was basically forced out of the country after . . . achieving the government's objectives.[39]

Corruption can sometimes oil the machinery of bureaucracy and help foreign business activity, but its overall basic impact is still increased risk and unpredictability. Probably the basic uncertainty in the developing world is an "institutional void," the absence of solid and stable regulatory systems and contract-enforcing mechanisms.[40] One consequence is a relative paucity of investment in such regions. In 2002, for example, only 2.5 percent of total international investments went to the so-called BRICS (Brazil, Russia, India, China, and South Africa)-emerging markets.[41]

Small wonder then, that the rate of return for investments in former colonial and Third World countries dropped from 30.7 percent to 2.5 percent during the 1980s.[42] German multinationals in the 1950s invested heavily in a number of developing countries, especially in Brazil, but also in Argentina, India, and Iran. By 1961, 38 percent of German foreign direct investments (FDI) were in developing countries. But as political and economic problems mounted, German firms shifted their attention to Europe. By 1971, only 20 percent of German FDI were in developing countries. The same was true for all of the advanced countries. Nearly one-third of Norway's investments abroad went to non-industrialized countries in 1986, but half a decade later, it was only 4 percent. In 1991, 89 percent of Norwegian investment targeted the European Community.[43] "During the 1960s and 1970s there was a general exodus from developing countries." In general, given conditions in the regions of their former colonies, European multinational companies had to reorient their business connections between the 1960s and 1980s.[44] This produced a major change in corporate activity within Europe. The new world economic environment, however, had several further new features as well. They all contributed to the shock that hit Europe in the last decade of the twentieth century.

The new technological revolution and structural crisis

The stunning transformation of the world economy in the late twentieth century was closely connected with a new technological–communication revolution, the importance of which can only be compared to the First Industrial Revolution. The first steps were taken at the end of the World War II with major new inventions, such as the first mainframe computer and the discovery of ways to cause nuclear fusion, but also radar, the jet-engine, and the breakthrough of rocket technology. In the 1950s, the core inventions were the transistor and chips (1958) that were able to store thousands, even tens of thousands of transistors in a tiny space. Edward Singer wrote:

> Since the mid-1960s the chip has become increasingly an internal part of the twentieth-century civilization . . . The chip made possible reliable computers, personal computers, lap computers, and calculators. It also made possible digital watches, increased efficiency of automobiles, control robots . . . cellular phones, satellite communications . . . electronic mail . . . home banking and many other new technologies.[45]

All these milestone inventions set off the real explosion of technological change in the 1970s–80s. The symbolic turning point came with the appearance of the personal computer in 1974, which opened the computer age. In 1960, the US, the pioneer of computer technology, had 5,500 installed computer systems, but by 1970 it had 65,000 and 400,000 by 1983. The computer market tripled between 1972 and 1982. The price of a 64K RAM chip was US$50 in 1980, but just US$3.50–$5 two years later. A seemingly endless scientific–technological revolution followed. In 1986, the United States National Science Foundation created a computer network to allow for quick exchange of scientific papers and findings. Once commercialization was legalized, commercial networks followed, and then, in 1991, came the revolutionary World Wide Web. In the 1980s, glass fiber optics with digital transmission revolutionized telephony and generated the digital cellular telephone revolution. The first electronic switch appeared in 1972. The first Atlantic coaxial cable, which started operation in 1956, was able to carry thirty-six simultaneous conversations; the new trans-Atlantic fiber optic cable in 1988 carried 40,000 calls simultaneously. In 1982, the compact audio disc and in the 1990s the digital compact cassettes and digital video discs joined the parade of inventions.

New technology gave birth to new high-tech industries. Information and communication technology production increased by leaps and bounds in the pioneering countries—between 1978 and 1982, in the United States it increased by 17 percent and in Japan by 25 percent.[46] "Telematics technologies," summed up Wayne Sandholtz, "are transforming every segment of the economy, from manufacturing to banking to retailing, health care, and entertainment. The same technologies also provide the 'brains' for modern weapon systems."[47]

Technological revolutions, according to Joseph Schumpeter, generate *structural crises*. New technology makes old sectors based on old obsolete technology, and consequently they decline. Meanwhile, new sectors based on new technology emerge. A structural crisis in this sense is a "creative destruction" that eliminates the obsolete and clears the way for the new. The consequence of these trends to economic growth is a long, sometimes 15–25-year period of stagnation or very slow growth, until the new sectors have grown enough to take over and establish a new prosperity. New technological inventions will cause this process to recur again and again. This fundamental phenomenon thus creates a cyclical pulsation of the economy.[48]

Since the 1970s and 1980s, the world economy has clearly been exhibiting the features of structural crisis. Although the US led the way, restructuring has been occurring all over the advanced world as well. Mining and the fastest growing economic sectors during postwar prosperity (iron and steel, shipbuilding, and still important textile production) suffered the most. In ten West European countries, employment in these ailing industries sharply declined: iron and steel by 58 percent; textiles by 62 percent; shipbuilding by 28 percent between 1974 and 1985. Mining in Belgium, a leading sector, declined by half and eventually all of the famous coal mines of the country were closed. Swedish shipbuilding suffered shutdowns and cutbacks. Only some of these declines were temporary.

De-industrialization, a core element of the current revolution, transformed the Western economic structure the most. Material production sharply declined because the high-tech sectors required much less material content and labor-intensive branches were outsourced to cheap-labor peripheral regions. The British Industrial Revolution had made advancement and industrialization synonymous terms. Two hundred years after the First Industrial Revolution, however, industry stopped being the leading sector of advanced economies. The number of so-called blue-collar workers in the US dropped to less than one-quarter of the labor force. In the EU-15, the total industrial population declined from 41.1 to 29.1 percent in the last three decades of the twentieth century. This phenomenon was especially dramatic in the leading industrial countries: in Britain from 48 to 20 percent; in the Netherlands from 42 to 16 percent; in Sweden from 45 to 18 percent; and in Italy from 40 to 21 percent. The relative decline of manufacturing has continued into the twenty-first century: between 2000 and 2012 the European Union's manufacturing decreased by 3.3 percent per annum to 15.2 percent of the GDP. Since

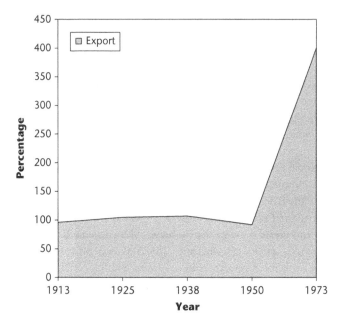

FIGURE 4.2 Export trends of Western Europe

Source: Based on Angus Maddison, *The World Economy,* 363.

agricultural population also declined from nearly 14 to less than 5 percent during the last decades of the twentieth century, and then by an annual decrease of 0.5 percent per annum after 2000 to 1.7 percent of the GDP, services became the dominant sector (see Figure 4.2).

The last third of the twentieth century and the first decade of the new one thus also became the period of a service revolution. Several services that were components of agricultural or industrial processes became separated, highly specialized, and much more efficient and productive. An OECD report in 1987 speaks about the "growing service content of manufactured goods." It speaks of both the "dematerialization of products" and the "industrialization of services." It notes a similar trajectory in agriculture: joining the 2–4 percent of the labor force engaged in agricultural employment was the 10–15 percent employed in specialized services connected with agriculture.[49] In the US, services employed about 75 percent of the labor force and produced a similar share of the GDP. Service employment in Europe increased from 45 to more than 66 percent in the last third of the century. Services produced 52 percent of total value added in Europe in 1973, but 70 percent by 2000.[50] Between 2000 and 2012, market services in the European Union increased by 1.7 percent per year to 50.5 percent of the GDP, and non-market services increased by 1.8 percent per year to 22.9 percent of the GDP. In a short period of time (between 2000 and 2011), actual agricultural employment decreased by 20 percent, mining by 19 percent, and textile by 43 percent, while accommodation and food services increased by 25 percent, real estate by 21, advertisement and market research by 24, administration by 41, health care by 22, entertainments by 25, and computer programming by 39 percent.[51]

The explosion of the service sector was connected with the requirements and gradual progress of infrastructure transformations themselves necessitated by the technological–communications revolution. Every major technological revolution goes hand in hand with the building up of a new infrastructure, and with a new energy system and infrastructure of everyday life. In the nineteenth century the symbols of this new infrastructure were the railroads and the new big cities. During the last third of the twentieth-century and the opening of the twenty-first, rapidly growing highway networks on the ground and dense air transportation networks in the sky were joined by a brand new "information superhighway." High-speed communication was introduced with a nearly 800-mile-long fiber optic cable system on the East Coast of the US in 1982. More recently, "cloud computing" was added to the electric grid, and a new energy system based on wind, sun, biomass, and other reproducible energy sources began slowly to evolve. (See Figure 4.3.)

To this discussion of the changes wrought by the technological revolution must be added the fact that this upheaval opened windows of opportunity for international business. The new electronic communication systems and the radical decrease of communication and transportation costs together created an infrastructure for globalizing the world's formerly fragmented national economies. One consequence was that advanced countries and their big businesses did not really need colonies any longer, and so they began to escape the heretofore deleterious effects of the collapse of the colonial system. In the US in particular, several major corporations, who were already working in several foreign countries, now found their international activities technically much easier and cheaper, and consequently began to spread even farther afield from the home front.

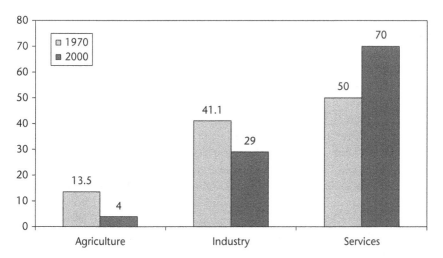

FIGURE 4.3 Change of the economic structure in the EU–15 region

Source: Based on *Eurostat Yearbooks.*

To exploit the new technological opportunities, shifts were needed in the policies that had governed world exchange up to that point. The US, followed by the advanced world in general, started working to eliminate various barriers and policy obstacles to pave the way for free global movement of goods and capital. The world around the turn of the twenty-first century became *globalized*. Economic history literature speaks about a "first globalization" during the half century before World War I.[52] Indeed, there is little doubt that the development of transportation and communication, together with two industrial revolutions (in the late eighteenth century and the turn of the twentieth century) led to a globalization trend. The world was not yet globalized, however, because several regions and even continents had yet to be affected by transnationalization. The globalizing that had occurred had been stopped and its results eliminated by a strong backlash after World War I. Significant globalizing trends did not return until after World War II, when they were fed especially by the free-trade policy and fixed exchange rates introduced by the American-led Western world and by aggressively expanding American multinational companies. The term *globalization* appeared in *Webster's Dictionary* in the early 1960s. The real era of a globalizing world economic system must be dated only from the 1970s and 1980s.

Globalization and globalized neoliberalism: the US and Japan ahead, Europe lagging behind

The commitment to the *laissez-faire* system actually began in 1947, just after World War II, with the signing of the General Agreement on Tariffs and Trade (GATT), which aimed at promoting and enforcing the conditions necessary to free trade. With American-initiated globalization the agreements made under the GATT acquired tremendous importance. International trade increased from US$1.7 trillion in 1973 to US$5.8 trillion by the end of the century; the value of trade of goods and services, which totaled 42 percent of the world's aggregate GDP in 1980, climbed to more than 62 percent of aggregate world GDP by 2007. In the era of globalization, however, international trade statistics no longer presented a complete picture of actual exchange across national boundaries. A much more important signal of the new age is the trade of *intermediaries*—parts and components of products within the networks of huge multinational companies—between the various subsidiaries of the multinational empires. "The increasing spread of global value chains worldwide," stated the European Commission's Directorate-General for Economic and Financial Affairs at the end of 2012, "has been the most prominent features of global economy for the last three decades. Production of goods and services is sliced into stages so that intermediate inputs resourced from most efficient producers often located across the globe."[53] As the World Bank reported in 1992, one-third of the American trade consisted of transactions between US companies and their affiliates abroad.[54] A European Central Bank analysis stated in 2013: "Standard trade indicators do not take at all into consideration that economies are increasingly interconnected at all stages of production chain." In the early

1970s, 45 percent of world trade was already intra-firm trade.[55] In 2011, for example, more than 30 percent of the euro-area's exports were based on imported parts from the region's company's value-chains.[56]

Trade and FDI increased together: the insignificant US$112 billion FDI in 1960 grew to the astronomical US$6,000 billion. The outflow of direct foreign investments was US$714.8 billion per year between 1995 and 2000, but US$1,215.8 billion by 2006. In 1980, these investments represented 6.5 percent of the world's aggregate GDP, and by 2006, it was 32 percent. In the early twenty-first century, between 2000 and 2006, the yearly FDI outflows were about US$1.3–$1.4 trillion. The stock of international claims, mostly bank loans, totaled 10 percent of the world's GDP in 1980, but 48 percent by 2006. Many more trillions in "hot money" flowed all over the globe, entering and leaving countries in hours or days. Financial transactions jumped from US$15 billion to US$1.3 trillion per day in less than a quarter of a century after 1973. Global capital flow trebled between 1995 and 2006, reaching US$7.2 trillion. International financing became a leading business sector in the advanced countries.

During the 1960s, FDI grew at twice the rate of GNP growth in the OECD countries; in the 1980s, it grew four times faster. Over the entire third of a century after 1980, FDI flows increased by leaps and bounds so that before 2010, the amount had reached ten times the 1980 level. The role of investments abroad, however, as a European Central Bank document stated, is "not only limited to a quantitative increase in international capital flow; to the extent that FDI is investment of multinational corporations, it also qualitatively re-structures the production process more and more globally."[57] The cross-border transactions of bonds and equities in the so-called G-7 group of leading economic powers accounted for only 10 percent of their aggregate GDP in 1980, but by the end of the century amounted to 140 percent of their GDP. Financial transactions per day jumped from US$15 billion in 1970 to US$1.3 trillion by 2000. This amount was fifty times higher than the value of world trade.

In conjunction with the spread of trade, the number of multinational or transnational companies operating in two or more countries mushroomed. From 7,000 in the early 1970s, their number reached nearly 80,000 by 2006. In a third of a century, 866,000 subsidiaries and affiliates were established, one-quarter of them in Third World countries. By 2006, the number of employees of multinationals had increased by three-and-half times more than 1982 levels. The assets of foreign affiliates jumped from US$2,206 billion to US$51,187 billion between 1982 and 2006, the latter figure equivalent with 10 percent of the world aggregate GDP. The research networks of multinational companies produced most innovations and their research networks' activities spread through geographical frontiers until three-quarters of the world's manufactured products were traded by multinational companies. In the early twenty-first century, deliveries by the affiliate companies of multinationals represented one-third of the world's exports. The gross product of such affiliates increased from US$676 billion in 1982 to US$4,862 billion by 2006; sales increased by nine times between 1982 and 2006. Some leading American multinational companies built up networks covering the entire globe: before the onset of the 2008 financial crisis, General Electric had 1,184 foreign affiliates, Chevron 106, Procter & Gamble 269, and General Motors 91.[58] With globalization, multinational corporations at the turn of the twenty-first century had become more important players in the world economy than several nation-states. ExxonMobil had higher revenue than Turkey's GDP; Wal-Mart's revenue was bigger than Austria's GDP; General Motors' revenue surpassed GDP in Denmark, Indonesia, and Poland; and Toyota's earnings exceeded GDP in both Venezuela and Finland.[59]

The main motive for creating a huge international network, as a survey of ninety European multinationals reflects, was the desire to reap the benefits associated with having a presence near their foreign consumers, especially when selling and post-sale services were connected. Corporations were also looking for cheap labor, and in several cases for the advantage of good quality local suppliers, know-how, scientific bases, and temporary tax advantages.[60] A great number of industrial companies and a large part of output shifted from advanced to peripheral countries.

As the technical–communication revolution opened the window of new opportunity for the advanced countries, the US Government first and foremost, but also followed by the other advanced countries, shifted overall economic policy in favor of globalization. During the 1980s, a triumphant neoliberal ideology dethroned both demand-side Keynesian economics, the concept and practice of an economic role for the government, and the European mixed economy model, the policy of *Socialpartnerschaft* and welfare state. State intervention was condemned as "the road to serfdom," replaced as the dominant political principle by the undisturbed, self-regulating laissez-faire system, presumed to be the only guarantor of prosperity, as of social and individual freedom. The key words of the age became deregulation and privatization. Total freedom of market and freedom of individuals, the neoliberal ideologues and theorists argued, are inseparable. The argumentation of the Vienna School of Economics and the Chicago School of Economics, embodied by Friedrich Hayek and Milton Friedman, claimed that the self-regulated market has a strong self-correcting automatism. State intervention, that is intervention from outside, disturbs this automatism. For success, the self-regulated market must be undisturbed.

The medicines Friedman advocated were privatizing all state-owned property and functions, and introducing sharp tax cuts. He proposed a 16 percent flat tax rate for everyone together with reductions in government expenditures and the elimination of welfare programs. In this ideal world, everyone is responsible for his/her health care, pension schemes, and their children's schooling in private schools. The laissez-faire economy, the undisturbed and unregulated free market—as the market fundamentalists argued—will solve all the economic *and* social problems of a society.[61] One of Margaret Thatcher's advisors from 1985 has observed: "Ideas from Hayek and Friedman . . . were assimilated precisely because experience had already created [a] place for them by convincing people that neo-Keynesian economics, trade-union hegemony and the permissive society had failed."[62]

In 1989, the equally optimistic Francis Fukuyama, serving as the deputy director of the US policy planning staff of the State Department, went so far as triumphantly to declare the "end of history," "the end point of mankind's ideological evolution," the arrival in reality of the "final form of human government." Liberal free-market democracy, he argued, is "free from fundamental contradictions." If reality still exhibits imperfections, it arises from "incomplete realization . . . rather than flows in the principles themselves."[63]

Ronald Reagan in America and Margaret Thatcher in Britain became the chief propagandists of these ideas and ideologies and realized them with great vigor during the 1980s. Deregulation and privatization became the order of the day. All the major regulatory rules that had been introduced during and after the Great Depression in the 1930s, the crucial years that clearly exhibited severe market imperfection in the capitalist economy, were rapidly eliminated. Some changes had already occurred before the arrival of Reagan and Thatcher on the scene. Mandatory capital reserve requirements for banks had been eliminated in the late 1970s in the US. Now, all kinds of financial firms, including savings and loan institutions, insurance companies, and various types of so-called shadow banking institutions, were allowed to act as investment banks. A new institution—the hedge fund—entered the riskiest investment business. The famous Glass-Steagall Act of 1933, the most important banking regulation in America, was repealed in 1999. Afterwards, the securities business—that is the pooling, slicing, and selling of mortgage loans, derivative business agreements on future transactions, and several other new "financial products"—turned banks into extreme risk-taking, even gambling institutions. The American example was closely followed by Britain. In 1988, ten years before the Glass-Steagall Act was repealed, the leading economic powers (the G-10 countries) had already established the Basel Committee and charged it with harmonizing world banking regulations. Deregulation consequently became general practice in the advanced world, including in Europe, which followed suit from 1992 on.

Deregulated banking activity created cheap and unlimited loans. Real estate sales, supported by unconventional mortgage products requiring zero down or offering low teaser interest rates, flourished and investments jumped dramatically. The stock exchanges ran amok. Neoliberalism triumphed. Its proponents quieted worries about the bubbles that followed one after the other in the financial world, in high-tech sectors, and in real estate. Robert Lucas Jr., leading representative of the Chicago School of Economics, declared in 2003 that neoliberal macroeconomics had solved the problems and found the monetary weapons against cyclical fluctuations. Neoliberal economists, such as Lucas, convinced business and governments that crisis and depression belong to the past.[64]

Three decades of globalized neoliberalism brought not only deregulation but also sharp increases of income disparity. The French economist Thomas Piketty convincingly proved in his monumental scholarly bestseller, *Capital in the Twenty-First Century,* that the famous Kuznets "curve-theory" is wrong. Simon Kuznets's Cold War-influenced thesis holds that inequality historically has a bell-shape curve. It increases at the time a modern economy first emerges, but decreases at maturity.

Piketty argued that the moderation of inequality in the first half or two-thirds of the twentieth century was politically motivated. The two World Wars and the Great Depression generated decreased inequality, the strong need of social solidarity, but not as a permanent trend. Thus, "since the 1970s, income inequality has increased significantly in the rich countries," and has even exceeded the infamous levels of early capitalism in the 1820s.[65] One should add that policy measures against inequality were also strongly influenced by Cold War competition. The collapse of the Soviet Bloc ended that race.

Between 1987 and 2013, the wealth of the top 1 percent of wealth holders of the world increased by 6.8 percent per annum while the average wealth of an adult increased only by 2.1 percent. Top managers' income, 10–17 times of a manufactory worker in 1992, jumped to 13–25 times by 2000. European trends followed those in the US: Britain led with manager earnings at 25 times the average worker, while socially more sensitive Germany and Sweden had manager earnings only 11 and 13 times higher.[66] The world aggregate GDP grew 3.3 percent per year, but the average income of the adult world population only by 1.4 percent. Increased income inequality characterized other world regions too: the per capita world average income (with China's average included) in the early 2010s was 600–800 dollars; in the US, Japan, and Western Europe it was 2,500–3,000 dollars. In India and Sub-Saharan Africa it did not surpass 150–250 dollars.[67]

The representatives of neo-conservatism, the ideological twin of neoliberalism, also gained ground in the last third of the century. They argued that postwar egalitarian ideas are "destructive and counterproductive . . . Inequality is the inevitable (and beneficial) outcome of individual freedom and initiative." The balance between equality and freedom in the social state was broken, they maintained, distorted towards an equality that undermined the self-assurance of private ownership and replaced it with the fear of ownership. From this point of view, liberal democracy had started committing suicide.[68]

Globalization and the globalized deregulation drive eventually created an over-financialized economy as the financial sector took over leadership from manufacturing. This led to the overflow of cheap credits, and created business flexibility and a huge flow of investments abroad. The large corporations of the advanced countries established subsidiaries in low-wage countries. Sharp income disequilibrium replaced moderate income divergence with never-before-seen amounts of bonuses for top managers and profits for entrepreneurs. All these trends made it possible to cope with the oil embargos and the structural crises of the 1970s and early 1980s. The upward trend of the economic cycle began with prosperity based on structural–technological renewal.[69]

Globalization without global governance and the national dead-end roads

Although the economy became global, nearly all economic institutions remained national and oriented towards individual national economies. Under these conditions the phenomenon of globalization rapidly expressed itself as an institutional crisis, specifically as a crisis of governance reflecting the fact that national institutions were losing their importance but had yet to be replaced by international institutions. A number of individuals from several professions began talking openly about the problems arising from this institutional deficit. Harlan Cleveland, American diplomat and author, was among the first to talk about the "nobody in charge" world system. In 1992, an organization called the Commission of Global Governance was established, which in 1995 presented a report on the crisis of global governance. Lawrence Finkelstein, writing in the journal *Global Governance,* argued for the necessity of global governance in an era when "boundaries between national and international arenas" are disintegrating. Such governance would do internationally what governments do at home.[70] George Soros, the Hungarian-born American hedge fund manager who is one of the most successful such investors in the world and therefore a person who has profited enormously from globalization, has called attention to the dangers arising from this absence of global governance. In his 1998 book, *Crisis of Capitalism,* he pointed out that a "collective decision-making mechanism for the global economy simply does not exist." He further argued that giving market forces "complete authority . . . produces chaos and could ultimately lead to the downfall of the global capitalist system."[71]

Although the governance crisis persists to this day, embryonic (and very partial) international governance seems to be in the making. Its origins go back to the crisis of the 1970s. Helmut Schmidt, minister of finance of Germany, suggested to his American counterpart, George Schultz, about organizing a meeting of the ministers of finance of the Western countries. Schmidt remarked on the failure of governments to understand the "complexity of the problems . . . On all sides there have been helpless reactions to the current structural changes, the adjustment problems and the recession . . . There is no unity regarding the assessment of the present world economic crisis, much less the therapy."[72] In June 1975, Schmidt and Giscard d'Estaing agreed to push for a summit meeting of the top five Western countries. In November of the same year, the French Government invited the head of states and governments of the so-called G-5 countries to assemble in Rambouillet, France. According to Emmanuel Mourlon-Druol and Federico Romero, editors of a volume on later twentieth-century summits, "calling the summit in 1975 was a European initiative. It was intended both to resolve the crisis, and to move from American hegemony over the economic system to a regime of collective management, combining Europe, North America and Japan."[73] From 1976, with the participation of Britain, France, Germany, Italy, Japan, the US, and Canada, the Group of Seven (G-7) started holding annual meetings. In 1977, the European Commission and presidents of the EEC Council of Ministers joined in; they were followed in 1998 by Russia: all to little avail. As early as July 1981, Jacques Attali, President Mitterrand's top aid, characterized the institutionalized gathering as "a meeting without any decision, whose sessions are empty, whose declarations are insignificant enough to be accepted by all."[74]

In 1999, seemingly in connection with the Asian financial crisis, several other rich and emerging countries, among them Argentina, Australia, Brazil, China, India, Indonesia, Mexico, Saudi Arabia, South Africa, South Korea, and Turkey, joined the G-7 to create the G-20. These member countries represent 60 percent of the world's population, 85 percent of the world gross product, and 80 percent of the world trade. At the meetings of the new forum, ministers of finance and national bank governors, as well as heads of states and other officials, regularly discuss global issues and policies. Some authors call this "the most important informal group in the 20th century."[75] It is probably more appropriate to say that it may be a beginning of a somewhat better international cooperation. The world has a long way to go before global governance will become a reality, if at all—and because the world has been unable to create an efficient and permanent new institutional system of governance in response to globalization, the importance of the European Union as a creator of European governance has been highly magnified.

In a globalizing world lacking globalized governance, with a European Community struggling with political paralysis, the core nation-states of Western Europe continued to define and implement economic policy from a national perspective. Between 1973 and 1984, their actions—as Helmut Schmidt rightly stated—reflected a failure to recognize the novelty of the problems they were facing. They turned to *old* measures to answer the *new* challenges. Their governments chose to subsidize declining old sectors; or, in the words of Alexandre Lamfalussy, the founding president of the European Monetary Institute, the forerunner of the European Central Bank, they chose to make "defensive investments." The British Government aided the nation's declining steel, mining, and shipbuilding industries. Germany more than doubled the assistance for its old-sector industries, with steel and shipbuilding receiving half of the federal subsidies. The Dutch doubled financial assistance to their declining industries; the Danish increased theirs by four-fold, with half directed to shipbuilding. Swedish state subsidies increased by fourteen times. Overall, during the first half of the 1980s, state aid for declining old industries in the European Community totaled ecu 42.161 billion per year.[76] Concomitantly, European countries increased their export subsidies for the same sectors. Such subsidies, which equaled 1–5 percent of the value of capital goods exports in the 1970s, increased in 1981–3 to 10–28 percent.[77] This upward trajectory reversed during the second half of the 1980s. By 2000, the combined amount of subsidies in fifteen countries had decreased to ecu 25 billion and state aid had dropped from 3 percent of GDP in 1981 (in Italy and Ireland from 5 percent) to 1 percent.[78]

What had happened was that in the mid-1980s, governments started realizing "the failure of the national state in Europe to cope effectively with these new circumstances."[79] The core countries realized that individually they could not solve the problems in the old way and that together they would have to devise new solutions.[80] Among those leading the campaign for such a shift were the big European corporations. Pushed by their multinationals, European governments slowly realized that "regional integration would be the appropriate response to global market competition . . . There remained one way out: an escape by a forward leap—into Europe."[81]

France exhibits the most telling example. Colbertian state-interventionist policy, instituted in the seventeenth century, had persisted in France through revolutions and war into modernity. Such policy continued to dominate postwar French governance into the 1980s, with support from de Gaulle and his successors Pompidou, Giscard d'Estaing, and Mitterrand. Differences of personality and political alignment scarcely affected the commitment to state involvement. The socialist François Mitterrand, who took office in 1981 in a coalition with the French Communist Party, swimming against the liberal stream, attempted to solve his country's economic and social problems with the even more radical state interventionist program of the Union of the Left. A nationalization wave increased the state sector to more than half of the economy. The thirty-nine-hour work week, the paid fifty-six-day annual vacation benefit, and increased minimum wages were all introduced.

Mitterrand also continued the 1960s-era National Champions program, which created huge French companies through various mergers, often with the participation of state-owned firms. The size and oligopolistic dominance of these new giants allowed them to compete successfully with American multinationals, at least in domestic French markets. The 1966 *Plan Calcul,* for example, was a government program to create a French-owned computer company capable of withstanding American competition. The resulting company, Compagnie Internationale pour l'Informatique (CII), supported by state subsidies and other forms of state aid, was the product of a merger of three already large firms in the electricity sector— Compagnie Générale d'Électricité (CGE), CSF, and Schneider. The government also took steps to ensure that CII had access to an indigenous source of electronic components. Under the *Plan Composants,* subsidies were made available to the semiconductor producer COSEM. In 1971, to continue the rise of this high-tech sector, a second *Plan Calcul* was launched. The government also heavily invested in other sectors. Pompidou expanded nuclear power generation. In this case, the state-led project was based on cooperation between two government-owned agencies, CEA and EDF, and two contractors, Framatome (then jointly owned by Schneider and the CEA), and CGE's subsidiary Alsthom. Another major and highly successful state project in the same years was the *Train à Grande Vitesse* (TGV), a project in which a CGE subsidiary cooperated with Alsthom to produce high-speed trains.

State planning in France after the war aimed to modernize the economy. The fifth of French postwar plans (1966–70) added another main national goal, the "reinforcement of [France's] European and world competitive position" by establishing huge companies of "international dimension."[82] France's "grand projects" certainly succeeded in creating huge national champion companies equal to American rivals in size. Just four companies, for example, sold two-thirds of agricultural engineering products, and the 100 largest French industrial firms employed more than one-quarter of the total labor force and produced nearly 29 percent of total industrial sales of the country.

Britain, despite her liberal traditions, also tried creating national champions through state intervention and assistance. The postwar British nationalization drive, which led to government takeover of about one-quarter of the nation's industrial sector, helped British governments to push forward mergers and create giant firms. In 1959, the large airframe groups British Aircraft Corporation (owned by Vickers and English Electric) and Hawker Siddeley (including de Havilland) merged and received huge government grants. In a similar way, the government urged and assisted two computer companies to form the International Computer and Tabulators (ICT) in 1958.

A whole set of institutions were established to run and assist this policy. In 1962 the National Economic Development Office and the Economic Development Committee worked out sectoral modernization plans. In the late 1960s, two government departments were opened, the Department of Economic Affairs and the Ministry of Technology. The Industrial Reorganization Corporation was set up in 1966 with the explicit goal to help concentrate industries so they could enjoy economies of scale.[83] In 1967, with significant government involvement and contribution, the British Steel Corporation was created by the merger of fourteen of the largest domestic companies. The government organized and aided the merger of ICT with the second largest supplier, the computer division of English Electric. As a result, in 1968 the International Computer Limited (ICL) started operation with more than 10 percent government share and nearly £14 million in state grants.[84]

The British Government also assisted the merger of the three largest electrical engineering companies to form the General Electric Company (GEC) with the explicit goal of competing with American General Electric and German Siemens. A similar national champion was formed by merging virtually all the British car and truck manufacturers into the British Leyland Motor Corporation to compete with the two American giants, Ford and General Motors, which occupied a huge part of the British market.

After the mid-1970s, the National Enterprise Board was established and strongly invested in industry. It took over Britain's largest machine tool maker, Alfred Herbert, and the leading electronics company, Ferranti. In 1977, it nationalized the aircraft industry, creating British Aerospace. In addition to pursuing takeovers of existing companies and initiating mergers, the Enterprise Board also established new enterprises such as Celltech in biotechnology and Inmos in semiconductor fields. Over time all these interventions failed to deliver the advantages the British economy needed. As the expert scholar of the national champion programs concluded, the Labour Governments "created national champions on the basis of unrealistic assumptions of what these companies were likely to achieve . . . It [the strategy] failed to inject new dynamism into technically backward industries." Among the problems, decision making was politicized and market adjustment delayed.[85]

Planning, concentration of industry, and establishing large national champions—all these strategies used by the French and British were promoted and assisted by the state in other European countries as well.[86] Spain, during the last decade of Francisco Franco's rule, introduced the Four-Year Plan as organized state interventionist policy. The plan envisioned a huge state-owned sector. However much this might seem to mimic postwar French policy, this Spanish plan was actually copied from Mussolini's policies and built up during the first period of the Franco regime. Between 1964 and 1975, three Four-Year Plans were accomplished in Spain. They used *Acción Concertada,* an organized cooperation between companies and the state, to realize structural–technological modernization. The state provided cheap credit for the corporate realization of state plans and development targets, and government financed up to 70 percent of planned investment projects.[87]

All these national roads eventually became dead-end roads, or as one scholar stated in the 1990s: "National champions of the past are often the lame ducks of the present."[88] Mitterrand was the first to realize that France could not afford the direction his early policies had taken, and therefore he made a policy U-turn. By 1987, he had privatized all the state-owned firms, opened the door for private companies in the communications business, and thus stepped onto the path being taken by the other countries of the West. Aware that France could not proceed alone in the globalizing world, that working within a European structure was going to be necessary, and desiring to leave his fingerprints on that structure, Mitterrand started in the mid-1980s to push further integration to strengthen Europe's position in the world economy.

The French perspective actually differed little from that of countries across the European continent. During the 1980s it was becoming clear that national programs that responded to the international challenge had failed. None of the state-interventionist programs succeeded in making companies or their countries competitive. Not even the turn towards national research and innovations to escape dependence on American technology imports could elevate Western Europe's economic performance. Europe was still losing the race with its main rivals in America and Asia.

There is a broad agreement, although far from unanimous, about the cause of this policy change in the 1980s: the interpretation turns on the history of the high-tech communication sectors, on the fact that even these sectors, new but still organized along national lines, could not compete in the globalized world of internationalized multinationals. It is, therefore, quite natural that the crash of national programs first became evident in the most modern sectors, for example in space technology. "European collaboration in space technologies began after purely national space programs proved untenable. The sheer scale of national investment required to join the space race led national policy-makers to return to cooperation." Space collaboration actually began in 1964, with the ratification of charters for the European Launcher Development Organization and the European Space Research Organization.[89]

Not only the required huge amount of investment, but also the extremely rapid change of technology made a single country's national policy inefficient. No European country could keep up with extremely rapid technological change in sectors that also required a very broad sphere of research. The cost alone was prohibitive. Sandholtz summarized the situation clearly: "No country of Europe has the capacity to cover such a spectrum of technological options, which is the only way to achieve a satisfactory degree of technological flexibility . . . ." Dealing with one of the key areas of the new high-tech sector, the aerospace industry, he concluded: "States turn to collaboration only after national strategies have fallen short . . . ." And on another sector: "The period of national champion strategies [until the 1970s] ended in a crisis for European telematics industries and policies; collaboration emerged in the 1980s."[90]

Meanwhile, the Community's member state governments, virtually in unison, turned from an extensive to an intensive growth model. The *extensive growth model* had been ideal for a postwar Europe ruined and bleeding white. It had tied reconstruction and modernization in West European countries to a system of American technology imports and domestic labor input. The Cold War confrontation between East and West, meanwhile, had made assisting its West European allies a primary goal of the American superpower. Prosperity and modernization were the best weapons against communism, which was, after all, gaining significant ground after the war in several West European countries, especially in Italy, France, and Belgium. Flourishing and technologically modern economies and high standards of living could satisfy the frustrated, war-weary population, one of the keys to building a strong military alliance against the Soviet Bloc. The US had been ready to provide modern technology to Western Europe. The complementarity of European and American needs and goals was the engine of postwar reconstruction and development.

The extensive growth model, however, preserved American leadership and advantage, and as the age of globalization and world-wide competition set in, dependence on America could no longer serve European interests. Europe started to realize that "American coattails . . . are not a safe place."[91] West European governments thus started policies to enhance *intensive growth*. Instead of importing American technology and keeping the follower position, they undertook their own research and development, hoping in this way to regain equal technological-economic status.

Europe, however, was far behind its competitors. In 1963, 1.54 percent of US GDP had been devoted to Research & Development (R&D) expenditures by the government; another 0.36 percent had been contributed by the private sector for a total of 1.9 percent. A full 8 percent of total US Government spending was used to support innovations. Europe lagged far behind. Germany had 1.2 and France 1.0 percent of their GDP expenditure, most of which was government-financed. Sweden, the Netherlands, and Italy spent only between 0.5 to 0.9 percent of their GDP for R&D. In relative terms, none of the European governments spent half the American expenditure to finance R&D. In the computer industry, the US spent five times more on R&D than the West European countries combined. American R&D expenditure soon accounted for 3–4 percent of the GDP and the nearest European figure, in Britain, was only half of that. "There was no way that Europe could match the United States in the development of science-based technologies. The US invested more in general education, especially in the post-gradual level. Its universities had closer links to industry."[92]

In 1973, Western Europe spent 21.6 percent of the world R&D expenditures while North America's share was 33.7 percent. Europe's share gradually increased to 24.2 and then 25.8 percent in 1980 and 1988, respectively. In real terms, Western Europe increased these expenditures by two-and-a-half times during the 1970s. The American share hardly changed in those years and represented 31.1 and then 32.8 percent. The real winners were Japan and South Korea because they (together) spent only 7.9 percent of total world R&D expenditures in 1973, but 10.2 in 1980 and 19.3 percent by 1988. To evaluate these percentage shares one has to consider that in the early 1960s, the world spent US$29 billion for R&D, but in 1977 it spent US$98 billion and in 1988 US$340 billion. At the end of the 1980s, 4.1 million scientists and engineers worked in the R&D industry, 37 percent of them in the US, Japan, and South Korea, and only 17 percent in Western Europe.[93]

New players enter the stage: big corporations

The failure of national responses mobilized big corporations to step in to shape policy according to their interests. In January 1979, an expert group that included representatives of big business issued a report arguing that the European Community should exploit its comparative advantage "by dominating its potential internal market, which presupposes completion of the common market and monetary union . . . [and] internationalizing capital."[94] Community officials did begin addressing the issue that very year. Étienne Davignon, a charismatic Belgian and a newly appointed Commissioner of Industrial Affairs, realized the need of assisting the lagging European high-tech industry. He presented his first proposal on telematics strategy in late 1979 and "invited senior officials from the ten largest computer and telecommunications manufacturers in Europe to meet with him." In February 1980 they discussed the possibility of working out a strategy.

Wayne Sandholtz argues that big business began looking for an ally in the Commission. The chief executives of twelve top European multinationals sent a letter to Davignon stating that Europe's market position is miserable and national programs hopeless, and warning that "unless a cooperative industrial programme of sufficient magnitude can be mounted, more if not all of the current Information Technology industry could disappear in a few years' time." Three French members of this group, GEC, Thomson, and Bull likewise "presented a unified, clear view to the [French] Ministry of Industry, whose minister was persuaded and took up the cause . . . "[95] "A dissatisfaction with the national rout[e] of European policy-making provided incentives for European big business to organize politically at the European level."[96]

In July 1980, when the first microelectronic program was submitted to the European Council, Davignon shepherded it through the political process. In late 1981, at his invitation, the directors of the twelve largest information technology companies met and formed the European Roundtable of Industrialists: "For the technical panels the Twelve sent engineers and technologists. Initially, about

100 people were involved . . . [At last], 400 technologists, 150 people from governments and laboratories and universities worked on the program."[97]

In the 1980s, Wisse Dekker of Philips and Jacques Solvay of the Belgian Solvay Corporation "were vigorously arguing for unification of the European Community's fragmented markets." Philips, a giant multinational, actually published a booklet advocating urgent action on internal markets because "there is really no choice . . . The only option left for the Community," the booklet stated, "is to achieve the goals laid down in the Treaty of Rome. Only in this way can industry compete globally, by the exploiting of economies of scale, for what will then the biggest home market in the world."[98]

The influential Ravenstein Group, a Brussels-based government affairs directors' elite dining group, also argued for a European solution, as did corporations aspiring to become European champions.[99] In October 1983, the Union of Industrial and Employers' Confederation of Europe (UNICE), the peak organization of the European industry, made a strong declaration urging a "fresh start for Europe." In 1989, outlining a scenario for 1992, Sandholtz and Zysman wrote: multinationals

> have taken up the banner of 1992, collaborating with the Commission and exerting substantial influence on their governments . . . European business and the Commission may be said to have together bypassed national governmental processes and shaped the agenda that compelled attention and action.[100]

Adam Harmes goes as far as stating that

> in fact, European big business played the key role in drafting the terms of the Single European Act. In 1983, two years before Jacques Delors called for a Single European Market . . . the European Roundtable of Industrialists drew up a list of proposals that became the basis for the Single European Act. Delors himself, according to Harmes, called the Roundtable 'one of the main driving forces' behind the Single Market.[101]

Multinational companies were not motivated by big political architecture but, as both Adam Smith and Karl Marx agreed, their central motivation as owners of capital is profit making. As Smith phrased it, "the consideration of his own private profit is the sole motive which determines the owner of any capital." Marx said that the capitalists' aim is "the restless, never-ending process of profit making."[102] Paraphrasing the most often quoted lines from Adam Smith's *Wealth of Nations*, corporations that seek to maximize their own gain served the benefit of the further integration of Europe, promoting an "end which was no part of their intention."

In February 1984, the top industrialists of the Roundtable went further and worked out a long list of concrete measures to "unblock the working of the European Community." UNICE, meanwhile, suggested the "establishment of an internal market, eliminating financial, legal and administrative obstacles." Among the recommendations, it also urged "programmes of European research, development and innovation policy." In October 1984, the French Conseil National du Patronat Français and the French Chamber of Commerce and Industry in Paris organized a conference, with the participation of 200 leading representatives of European industry, to campaign for a new "eurodynamism" and a break with the "'Eurosclerosis' of national politicians."[103]

In those years, Davignon's role, especially his success at organizing a political coalition, was instrumental. "He was able," Sandholtz writes, "to take the arguments for cooperation developed within the Commission and sell them first to industry and then, with the help of the powerful business coalition, to national governments."[104] Even the European Council, the representatives of the national governments, finally came round. At its Fontainebleau meeting in June 1984, it appointed an ad hoc committee, headed by the Irish politician James Dooge. The Committee's report started with a statement that the "construction" of the European Community is not finished and therefore "it [the Community] is now in a state of crisis." The Committee recommended a "quality leap" to establish a real political entity, a European Union with "a homogenous internal economic area . . . [and] an economic and monetary union." To achieve this goal, the report specified that a conference of government representatives must be called soon to "negotiate a draft European Union Treaty."[105]

In January 1985, Maria Green Cowles points out, "when French and EC officials proved unable to produce a concrete program for a unified European market," Wisse Dekker, the CEO of Philips, unveiled his own plan for a unified European market—Europe 1990—which he presented at a major Brussels gathering. He also sent the plan to key political leaders in Europe. He had simply tired of waiting for French and EC officials to produce something concrete of their own. Dekker's plan laid out the precise steps needed to create a unified market by 1990 in four key areas: trade facilitation (elimination of border formalities); open public procurement markets; harmonized technical standards; and fiscal harmonization. The European Roundtable of Industrialists, the influential organization of the biggest corporations, publicly endorsed the Dekker plan. "Europe 1990," Cowles tells us, "was viewed by many as the precursor to the Cockfield White Paper, the [Commission's] document that outlined the Single Market or 1992 program issued six months later."[106]

Probably nothing is more characteristic of the interplay between corporate interests and initiatives for further integration than the history of the sacrosanct "national" defense industry during the 1980s–90s. Article 223 of the Rome Treaty allowed defense industrial matters to remain outside EU jurisdiction. The European Defense Industries Group, the representative of the military industry, started lobbying against it in the 1980s. The Group "would like to see Article 223 of the Rome Treaty eliminated or narrowed in scope." An executive of the French firm Thomson-CSF, Europe's largest defense electronics company, argued in the 1980s: "it was unbelievable to put together the words 'Europe' and 'armaments.' It was a taboo . . . Europeans as a whole felt that Europe needed more political integration . . . And more political integration meant more cooperation in defense and armaments." Manfred Bischoff, before assuming chairmanship of Daimler-Benz Aerospace, the dominant company in German defense industry, addressed Europe's disadvantage in that industry: compared to the US, "We cannot wait for full integration of the Single Market," he said in 1995, "why are there no incentives to create optional restructuring in Europe? . . . Why not a European missile company? . . . I don't care if they are German, French or Italian, as long as there's a harmonized approach." In April 1993, Lord Weinstock, managing director of GEC, the British defense electronic company, urged European mergers of defense industry: "We have to respond to the changes in America. They are producing giant companies through these mergers . . . We have to form companies of sufficient size to compete effectively." Serge Dassault, head of the French aircraft company, was "campaigning for an EU rule of *preference européenne* in arms purchase to promote a pan-European defense industrial base."[107]

At the time these initiatives were taken, European big corporations had been organizing themselves within the Community for some time. In 1958, immediately after the foundation of the European Economic Community, they had already created the UNICE, with the somewhat paradoxical charge of creating a "defense mechanism" against the Community's activities. This mentality, however, changed soon enough. By 1965, major pharmaceutical firms, for instance, were backing a Commission directive containing the very first set of transnational regulations issued by that European body. In 1967, the Group of Presidents of Large European Companies was established to discuss European Community issues, followed in 1980 by the European Roundtable of Industrialists. Pehr Gyllenhamar, the CEO of Volvo, spearheaded this last group in cooperation with Commissioner Davignon.[108] By 1985, 654 registered interest organizations were already at work in Brussels. In order to initiate and influence decisions, they built up close connections with the Commission and the Parliament. In 2009, according to certain estimations, that figure had ballooned to 15,000–20,000 such organizations. Today, at least 300 major corporations have their own independent representation.[109]

The British Telecom Office in Brussels, for example, has described its contact with the Commission "as daily [ranging] from formal written papers to informal 'chats' at all levels from Commissioner to lower D[irectorate]G[eneral] staff." Another company's Brussels office had "contact with the Commissioner, the Director General, and the head of section Division. [It] can be weekly, [it] can be two-way."[110] An analysis in the European Union's Archive notes that "some firms were establishing themselves as political insiders through engaging in a high degree of political activity." Among the thirty-four strongest insider companies, we find, among others, the Royal Dutch Shell Company, British Petrol, Daimler Benz, Fiat, Unilever, Siemens, Philips, Bayer, British Aerospace, British Steel, Pirelli, Olivetti, and Thyssen. "The large European firms have had to Europeanise the political action . . . Large French firms, like most of Europe's business, have looked less to national government favours and have . . . to negotiate at the European level."[111]

The coordinated work of Commission, corporations, and nation-states

Given the failure of the national roads and the relative European backwardness in the sharpening global competition, ideas of a European revival gradually emerged from various sources. Big corporations, directly affected as they were by competition from the US and Asia, and sensing that the danger of marginalization was a real one, were the first (as discussed earlier) to suggest finding a new, all-European solution to replace inadequate national policies and economic structures. Almost parallel with this development, the European Community slowly hammered out a strategy for escaping the continent's condition as a place of lagging-behind states; or better to say, the European Community found a way of exiting from the paralysis that had afflicted the two key supranational European institutions—the Commission and the Parliament—since the Luxembourg Compromise of 1966.

At a certain point at the end of the 1970s, the interests and concerns of private and public, the big corporations, and the European Commission and Parliament, converged. The alliance between them had a strong impact on the member countries' national governments. Initiatives from two sides, by the Commission and by the corporations headquartered in the nation-states, influenced the key governments, which of course were also suffering from the crisis and from the failure of their national attempts to find an exit from it. As we have seen, France under Mitterrand was one of the earliest governmental actors to embrace a European solution. Chancellor Kohl's Germany followed just a few years later, at the end of the 1980s. After the collapse of the Soviet Union, Germany, by supporting further European integration even at the political level, was able to quell anxieties among Europeans opposed to German re-unification.

Corporations were very influential and powerful, but they needed the assistance of the European Community to create the legal conditions and standardization necessary for a fully integrated European Community market. The European Union established a High-level Strategy Group, with representatives of various sectors of industries "to oversee standardization at a strategic level and to determine the key requirements for standards in a business context . . . [Standards] must be considered as cooperation between companies and have to be assessed for this reason."[112] A Commission progress report recognized that "business, too, has an important role to play in shaping legislation . . . the Union of Industrial Employers Confederation of Europe have carried out their own surveys and studies and come up with suggested improvements to the regulatory process."[113] The Commission praised the car industry for its cooperation with the Commission in harmonizing technical standards.[114] More than ten years later, the Commission described the collaborative process that was followed by the Association des Constucteurs Européens d'Automobiles (ACEA): the Commission "submitted a list of questions and options . . . [and] ACEA answered with a position paper on desirable policy measures in support of the European automobile industry's structural adjustment process . . . A series of bilateral meetings with representatives EC car manufacturers [followed]."[115]

In some countries, cross-border mergers were legally not even possible. Different national standards impeded the creation of a home-market covering the entire Community. As has been noted already, also disadvantageous for West European core countries of the Community was the lack of a low-wage backyard that was able to provide a pool of cheap labor to produce goods and large numbers of consumers to purchase them. To compete with the US and Japan, Western Europe needed a region that could function as Latin America did for the US and Asia for Japan. The obvious candidates, the peripheral markets in Southern and Eastern Europe, were located in politically and economically unstable regions. The countries of these regions were not original members of the Community. Europe's Mediterranean region had just emerged from their isolated fascist–authoritarian dictatorships in the mid-1970s and had only become members of the European Community in the 1980s; Soviet Bloc Eastern Europe had just started its transformation towards democracy and market economy at the very end of the 1980s. To stabilize these regions politically and bind their economies organically to Western Europe required their inclusion in the European Community. Mergers and acquisitions and strategies for building value chains in low-wage countries were not absolutely safe without Community enlargement to incorporate the peripheral regions of Europe into the institutionalized regional integration bloc. No corporation had the authority to expand the boundaries of the European Community—that was possible only through the bold actions of the Community itself.

Since the 1970s, the dream of realizing the Treaty of Rome's concept of a single market without any internal barriers and with a monetary union had resurfaced from time to time. Now, some enthusiastic Community leaders recognized that the time had come to bring this dream closer to real life, and they were ready to act. However, emerging from "Eurosclerosis," the long stagnation of the integration process from the mid-1960s to the mid-1980s, was not easy. Further integration was opposed by some member states, and thus the supranational Commission was paralyzed and its recommendations often rejected by the Council of Ministers, the representatives of the member states. Moreover, since the "Luxembourg Compromise" of 1966, the veto of a single member state was enough to block implementation of any change. But the integrationist European Commission and Parliament had a powerful ally in the big corporations: the corporations needed the help of these Community supranational institutions as much as the Commission needed the help of the powerful big corporations to counter the resistance of some of the nation-states. It was this mutual dependency that motivated the Commission, the "motor" of integration, to put its weight behind the corporate single market initiative. These two allies, as we have seen, were joined by the French and German Governments of President Mitterrand and Chancellor Kohl. A common ground had finally been found. When, in the mid-1980s, Kohl accepted Mitterrand's suggestion to appoint Jacques Delors, Mitterrand's former minister of finance, to the Commission presidency, a new chapter opened in the history of the Community.

In the new situation, the Commission and its new president Jacques Delors, the committed "militant federalist" (as he once called himself) and congenial organizer and mediator, became ready and able to assist corporate actions and expansions.[116] Delors had the enthusiastic support of the key governments. European integration was reborn. As was discussed in Chapter 3, the Community re-launched the Single Europe project to fully realize the genuine program of the Treaty of Rome and create a real single market without internal barriers. This mission dominated the period between 1985 and 1992, during which nearly 300 directives and new regulations were enacted to eliminate most of the obstacles to further integration.

The enlargement of the Community, which would bring in the additional large markets and low-wage peripheral countries, was also in the making. In this way, the Community's policy helped the building of an economic backyard for the big corporations and core member countries. Enlargement towards the low-wage peripheries translated a genuine corporate interest and ambition, as well as the goals of individual member countries, into the structure of the European Community. The policy of enlargement was rooted in the Community's foundation policy and ideology: to create permanent peace in Europe by anchoring the European countries to each other in the hope of avoiding a repetition of the past. In the decades of the Cold War, strengthening the Western alliance against the assumed Eastern danger was also a genuine motivation of the foundation of the Community. With the challenge of globalization that began in the 1970s in Europe, the goal to further build Europe, including through the bold aggressive enlargement towards the peripheries, assumed center stage.

Notes

1 For a long time, several studies used the term of stagnation regarding the European integration between 1965 and the 1980s. This view was challenged by stressing the institutional, legal development, market integration, and realization of some joint policies (see Joseph H.H. Werler, *The Constitution of Europe* (Cambridge: Cambridge University Press, 1999); Johnny Laursen, ed., *The Institutions and Dynamics of the European Community, 1973-1983* (Baden Baden: Nomos, 2014).

2 Archive of European Integration, Interview of Three European Community Presidents, P. Paul Finet (High Authority of the ECSC), P. Etienne Hirsch (Commission of Euratom) and P. Walter Hallstein (Commission of the EEC), National Pan Club, Washington, DC, June 11, 1959, 12.

3 Jean Monnet, *Memoirs,* trans. Richard Mayne (Garden City, NY: Doubleday, 1978), 441.

4 Jonathan Story and Guy de Carmoy, "France and Europe," in *The New Europe,* ed. Jonathan Story (Oxford: Blackwell, 1993), 187.

5 Éva Bóka, "The Idea of Subsidiarity in the European Federalist Thought. A Historical Survey." Working Paper, 13, 49, accessed December 3, 2011, www.grotius.hu/doc/pub/ECICWF/boka_eva_idea_subidiarity.pdf.

6 See Michael Burgess, *Federalism and European Union: The Building of Europe, 1950–2000* (London: Routledge, 2000); Thomas Pedersen, *Germany, France and the Integration of Europe. A Realist Interpretation* (London: Pinter, 1998), 81.

7 www.cvce.eu/content/publication/1997/10/13/ . . . /publishable_eu.pdf.

8 Andreas Staab, *The European Union Explained: Institutions, Actors, Global Impact,* 3rd ed. (Bloomington, IN: Indiana University Press, 2013), 12.

9 Michael J. Baun, *An Imperfect Union. The Maastricht Treaty and the New Politics of European Integration* (Boulder, CO: Westview Press, 1996), 77. De Gaulle's "empty chair" policy

generated strong reaction among farmers and business people in general. On July 8, 1965, the Committee of Professional Agricultural Organizations expressed deep concern; the French National Federation of Farmers and the German Deutscher Bauernverband defended the Treaty of Rome. The five member countries formulated a common position on the financing of agricultural policy. The Union of Industries (UNICE) issued two communiqués. On October 7, 1965, they strongly defended the common market and cooperation. On July 7, the International Confederation of Free Trade Unions expressed deep concern. A similar statement was made by the International Confederation of Christian Trade Unions on July 15, 1965: "integration is an absolute necessity for the peoples of Europe." Belgian, German, and French industrialists strongly defended the Community. On October 23, 1965, *Le Monde* summed up the results of this session with the headline: "FNSEA urges farmers not to vote for the incumbent in post [De Gaulle] of 5th December." He, indeed, did not get the absolute majority at the first round. On this, see Bóka, "Idea of Subsidiarity," 69–73.

10 http://news.bbc.co.uk/onthisday/hi/dates/stories/april/28/newsid_2500000/2500927.stm.
11 Decision was made on the first enlargement, and the Pierre Werner Committee, which would suggest the unified monetary policy in 1970, was founded. For this, see George Ross, *The European Union and Its Crisis. Through the Eyes of the Brussels Elite* (Houndmills, UK: Palgrave Macmillan, 2011), 13.
12 "Allies in trouble as NATO meets," *Washington Post,* May 9, 1961.
13 Archives Direct, Sources from the National Archive, UK, FCO, 82/287, Political relations between the USA and Europe, (Folder 7) 18 October, 1973.
14 Quoted by Rudolf Tokes, ed., *Eurocommunism and Detant* (New York University Press, 1978), 473.
15 Archives Direct, Sources from the National Archive, UK, 1517452, FCO, 82/287, Political Relations between the USA and Europe, (Folder 7) 15 October, 1973.
16 Nicholas Crafts and Gianni Toniolo, "Les trente glorieuses: From the Marshall Plan to the Oil Crisis," in *The Oxford Handbook of Postwar European History,* ed. Dan Stone (Oxford: Oxford University Press, 2012), 356–78.
17 The 1973 crisis was the outcome of the Yom Kippur War between the Arabic countries and Israel, while the second crisis exploded after the political–religious revolution of Ayatollah Khomeini in Iran. In 1973, the Arab-led Organization of Petroleum Exporting Countries (OPEC) declared a boycott against pro-Israeli Western countries and the consequent severe oil shortages and skyrocketing oil prices stopped economic growth.
18 See The World Bank, *World Development Report 1985. International Capital and Economic Development* (New York, NY: Oxford University Press, 1985).
19 Eric Hobsbawm, *The Age of Empire, 1875–1914* (London: Weidenfeld and Nicolson, 1987).
20 Thomas Piketty, *Capital in the Twenty-First Century* (Cambridge, MA: The Belknap Press of Harvard University Press, 2014), 70.
21 Ronald Findley and Kevin H. O'Rourke, *Power and Plenty. Trade, War and the World Economy in the Second Millennium* (Princeton, NJ: Princeton University Press, 2007), xx.
22 Mira Wilkins, *The Emergence of Multinational Enterprise* (Cambridge, MA: Harvard University Press, 1970); Mira Wilkins and Harm Schröter, eds., *The Free-Standing Company in the World Economy 1830–1996* (Oxford: Oxford University Press, 1998).
23 Donald A. Ball and Wendell H. McCulloch Jr., *International Business* (Plano, TX: Business Publications, 1985), 5.
24 D.K. Fieldhouse, *Unilever Overseas. The Anatomy of a Multinational 1895–1965* (London: Croom Helm, 1978).
25 Brian Lewis, *'So Clean.' Lord Leverhulme, Soap and Civilization* (Manchester, UK: Manchester University Press, 2008), 12.
26 Geoffrey Jones, *Renewing Unilever. Transformation and Tradition* (Oxford: Oxford University Press, 2005), 93.
27 W.J. Reader, *Fifty Years of Unilever 1930–1980* (London: Heinemann, 1980), 91–2.

28 Jones, *Renewing Unilever*, 102.

29 Piketty, *Capital in the Twenty-First Century*, 121.

30 See Valery Besong, "Coup d'etats [sic] in Africa. The Emergence, Prevalence and Eradication," *Stanford University*, Summer 2005 (http://web.stanford.edu/class/e297a/Coup%20d'esats%20in%20Africa%20-The%20Emergence,%20Prevalence%20and%20Eradication.doc).

31 Adam Przeworski, Michael E. Alvarez, José Antonio Cheibub and Fernando Limongi, *Democracy and Development, Political Institution and Well-Being in the World, 1950–1990* (Cambridge: Cambridge University Press, 2000), 47.

32 Piketty, *Capital in the Twenty-First Century*, 70.

33 See Geoffrey Jones, "Multinational Strategies and Developing Countries in Historical Perspective," Working Paper 10-076, Harvard Business School, 2010, hbswk.hbs.edu/item/6407.html. Jones writes: ". . . the dismantling of Western colonial empires, the speed of governmental restrictions on foreign firms in most postcolonial Asia and Africa, and the widespread expropriation of foreign ownership of natural resources during the 1970s, further decimated Western multinational investments in developing countries."

34 Mongolia, meanwhile, canceled international tax treaties and terminated already signed treaties with the Netherlands, Kuwait, the United Arab Emirates, and Luxembourg (see Michael Robinson, "Tax Avoidance: Developing Countries Take on Multinationals," BBC News Business, May 23, 2013 (www.bbc.com/news/business-22638153).

35 This type of uncertainty is also present in post-communist Russia. Yukos, the privatized oil company, was re-nationalized in 2004. TNK–BP started operation on Sakhalin Island in 2003 when British Petroleum (BP) merged with the Russian Tyumenskaya Neftyanaya Kompaniya (TNK). Five years later, however, two British managers of the joint company were arrested, and the state-owned Rosnef Company finally bought the company back. The result of this merger was a company even bigger than ExxonMobile. Regarding Hungary, see Péter Mihályi, *Re-Nationalization in Post-Communist Hungary, 2013–2014* (Budapest: Magyar Tudományos Akadémia, Kozgazdasagtudomanyi Intezet, 2014).

36 Witold J. Henisz and Bennet A. Zelner, "The Hidden Risk in Emerging Markets," *Harvard Business Review*, April, 2010.

37 Archive of European Integration, The Community's Role in the World. Lecture by Mr Roy Jenkins, President of the Commission of the European Community at the Institute Royal des Relations Internationales, Brussels (November 6, 1980).

38 Rob Van Tulder, Alain Verbeke and Liviu Voinea, *New Policy Challenges for European Multinationals* (Bradford, UK: Emerald Insight, 2012), 343.

39 Assessing Risk in Emerging Markets Infrastructure. Institutional Investor's Infrastructure Investment Forum, New York, June 28, 2007 (www.rrdc.com/speech_nyc_Infrstr_Invst_Forum_062807_print.pdf).

40 Since the 1990s, American multinationals have performed better at home and preferred investing in other developed countries. Only one-fifth of the American foreign direct investments targeted Europe in 1960, but by 1983, more than 45 percent of the roughly eight times higher FDI was invested in that region. The American FDI stock in the European Community increased by more than three times between 1972 and 1985 and accounted for US$81.1 billion, compared to US$72.3 billion in the rest of the world. For this, see United Nations, *From the Common Market to EC92. Regional Economic Integration in the European Community and Transnational Corporations* (New York, NY: United Nations Department of Economic and Social Development, 1993), 37; Tarun Khanna, Krishna G. Palepu, and Javat Sinha, "Strategies That Fit Emerging Markets," *Harvard Business Review*, June 2005; Darryl C. Thomas, *The Theory and Practice of Third World Solidarity* (Westport, CT: Praeger, 2001), 147.

41 Khanna, Palepu, and Sinha, "Strategies That Fit Emerging Markets."

42 Thomas, *Theory and Practice of Third World Solidarity*, 147.

43 Geoffrey Jones and Harm G. Schröter, *The Rise of Multinationals in Continental Europe* (Aldershot, UK: Edward Elgar, 1993), 135.

44 Jones, "Multinational Strategies," 16–17.
45 Edward N. Singer, *20th Century Revolution in Technology* (Commack, NY: Nova Science Publisher, 1998), 76–7.
46 Wayne Sandholtz, *High-Tech Europe. The Politics of International Cooperation* (Berkeley, CA: University of California Press, 1992), 48–50, 52; Wayne Sandholtz and Alec Stone Sweet, eds., *European Integration and Supranational Governance* (Oxford: Oxford University Press, 1998), 140–1.
47 Sandholtz, *High-Tech Europe, 2.*
48 Joseph Schumpeter, *Business Cycles: A Theoretical, Historical and Statistical Analysis of the Capitalist Process* (New York: McGraw, [1939] 1981); Joseph Schumpeter, *Capitalism, Socialism and Democracy* (London: Routledge, 1942).
49 OECD, *Structural Adjustment and Economic Performance* (Paris: OECD, 1987), 256.
50 OECD, *Historical Statistics 1970–1999* (Paris: OECD, 2000), 40–1.
51 *Competing in Global Value Chains. EU Industrial Structure. Report 2013 (ec.europa.eu/connect/en/eu_ind_struct_report_2013_en.pdf),* 19, 21.
52 See Kevin H. O'Rourke and Jeffrey G. Williamson, *Globalization and History. The Evolution of a Nineteenth-Century Atlantic Economy* (Cambridge, MA: MIT Press, 1999).
53 Archive for European Integration, European Commission, Directorate-General for Economic and Financial Affairs, Issue 17, December 2012.
54 Quoted in Vincent Wright, "Conclusion: The State and Major Enterprises in Western Europe: Enduring Complexities," in *Industrial Enterprise and European Integration. From National to International Champions in Western Europe,* ed. Jack Hayward (Oxford: Oxford University Press, 1995), 348.
55 C.A. Michalet, *Les firms multinationals et la novella division internationale du travail* (Geneva: International Labour Office, 1973), 32.
56 Filippo di Mauro, Hedwig Plamper, and Robert Stehrer, European Central Bank. Global Value Chains: A Case for Europe to Cheer Up, Component Policy Brief 03/2013 (August 2013) (https://www.ecb.europa.eu/home/pdf/research/compnet/policy_brief_3_global_value_chains.pdf?fcccc5651bee912e1698e1019c8b3969).
57 Archive of European Integration, NO 1614/November 2013: Konstantin M. Wacker: On the Measurement of Foreign Direct Investment and its Relationship to Activities of Multinational Corporations (Frankfurt: European Central Bank, 2013).
58 United Nations Conference on Trade and Development (UNCTAD), World Investment Reports 2004 and 2007 http://unctad.org/en/pages/PublicationArchive.aspx?publicationid=724; http://unctad.org/en/pages/PublicationArchive.aspx?publicationid=680).
59 Medard Gabel and Henry Bruner, *Global Inc.: An Atlas of the Multinational Corporations,* (New York, NY: New Press, 2003), 2.
60 Arnoud De Meyer, Roland Van Dierdonck, and Ann Vereecke, "Global Plant Networks in European Multinationals," Working Paper in the INSEAD Working Paper Series (Fontainebleau, France: INSEAD, 1996).
61 See Ivan T. Berend, *Europe Since 1980* (Cambridge: Cambridge University Press, 2010), 88–103.
62 Alfred Sherman, article in *The Guardian,* February 11, 1985.
63 Francis Fukuyama, "The End of History," *The National Interest,* August 27, 1989, 27–46.
64 Robert E. Lukas, Jr., "Macroeconomic Priorities," Presidential Address at the Annual Meeting of the American Economic Association, January 4, 2003 (pages. stern.nyu.edu/~dbackus/.../Lucas%20priorities%20AER%2003.pdf).
65 Piketty, *Capital in the Twenty-First Century,* 13–15.
66 Archive of European Integration, Karel Lannoo and Arman Khachaturyan, "Reform of corporate governance in the EU," CEPS Policy Brief, no. 38 (October 2003).
67 Piketty, *Capital in the Twenty-First Century,* 435, 64.
68 Walter Leisner, *Demokratie, Selbstzerstörung einer Staatsform* (Berlin: Duncker und Humblot, 1979), quoted in Iring Fetscher, ed., *Neokonservative und "Neuer Rechte". Der Angriff gegen Sozialstaat und liberale Demokratie in den Vereinigten Staaten, Westeuropa und*

der Bundesrepublik (Munich: Verlag C.H. Beck, 1983), 108; Thomas Piketty called our attention to the book *De la liberté du travail* by the French economist Charles Dunoyer. Dunoyer argued similarly, in 1845, about what he called "natural inequality": "Reduce everything to equality and you will bring everything to a standstill." For this see Piketty, *Capital of the Twenty-First Century,* 85.

69 I have to note at this point that the economic history of the early twenty-first century has made clear that business cycles, against the declaration of neoliberal economists, have not been eliminated. De-industrialization, over-financialization, and deregulation have exacted a high price. This new trend simply led to a new crisis: the 2008 financial crisis, or Great Recession, the worst and largest since the Great Depression of the 1930s. Around the turn of the millennium, very few economists, politicians, or business people believed this could or would happen. On this, see Ivan T. Berend, *Europe in Crisis, Bolt from the Blue?* (London: Routledge, 2013).

70 Harlan Cleveland, *Nobody in Charge: Essays on the Future of Leadership* (New York: John Wiley and Son, 2002); Commission of Global Governance, *Our Global Neighborhood. The Report of the Commission of Global Governance* (Oxford: Oxford University Press, 1995); Lawrence S. Finkelstein, "What is Global Governance?" *Global Governance* 1, no.3 (1995): 367–72, here 368–70.

71 George Soros, *The Crisis of Global Capitalism* (New York, NY: Public Affairs, 1998), xxiii, xxvii.

72 Emmanuel Mourlon-Druol and Federico Romero, eds., *International Summitry and Global Governance. The Rise of the G-7 and the European Council, 1974–1991* (London: Routledge, 2014), 41.

73 Ibid., 25.

74 Ibid., 92.

75 Mihály Simai, "Global Economic Governance," *Society and Economy in Central and Eastern Europe* 35, no. 3 (2013): 303.

76 OECD, *Structural Adjustment and Economic Performance,* 29–31.

77 Ibid., 230–1.

78 European Union, *Tableau de bord des aides d'état, Commission of the European Union* (Brussels: EU, 2002).

79 Burgess, *Federalism and European Union: The Building of Europe, 1950–2000,* 149.

80 Ibid., 157. Burgess states: "In the mid-1980s a new consensus was found among member state governments about the decline in Europe's ability to compete, in both domestic and world markets, with the United States, Japan, and emerging other Asian countries."

81 Stanley Hoffman, "The European Community and 1992," in Stanley Hoffman, ed., *The European Sisyphus. Essays on Europe (1964–1994)* (Boulder, CO: Westview Press, 1995), 231.

82 Hayward, ed., *Industrial Enterprise and European Integration,* 4.

83 Geoffrey Owen, "Industrial Policy in Europe Since the Second World War," London School of Economics. ECIPE Occasional Paper, no. 1/2012, 8–9: "Ministers and advisers considered that many British industries were too fragmented and that the necessary rationalization was unlikely to take place without government intervention."

84 Ibid., 8.

85 Ibid., 11–12.

86 Frank Fishwick, *Multinational Companies and Economic Concentration in Europe,* 14, 36.

87 Joseph Harrison, *The Spanish Economy in the Twentieth Century* (London: Croom Helm, 1985), 149–53.

88 Jack Hayward, ed., *Industrial Enterprise and European Integration. From National to International Champions in Western Europe* (Oxford: Oxford University Press, 1995), 12.

89 Sandholtz, *High-Tech Europe,* 104, 105.

90 Ibid., 112, 160.

91 Sandholtz and Zysman, "1992: Recasting the European Bargain," 95.

92 Barry Eichengreen, *The European Economy Since 1945. Coordinated Capitalism and Beyond* (Princeton, NJ: Princeton University Press, 2007), 257–8. In 1975, according

to the European Commission's European Economic and Social Committee: Europe and the New Technologies: Research and Development, Industry Special Aspects, the ten countries of the European Community have spent only 1.81 percent of their GDP for research and development (R&D). At that time, the American investment in R&D accounted for 2.4 percent of the GDP and the Japanese more than 2 percent. Less than a decade later, in 1983 the ten countries' R&D investments reached more than 2 percent of their aggregate GDP. However, American and Japanese expenditure to R&D had also increased to 2.7 and 2.6 percent of GDP, respectively. For this, see Archive of European Integration (aei.pitt.edu/view/eusubjects/socasp.default.html), 9–10.

93 (archive.unu.edu/unupress/unubooks/un09ue0d.htm).

94 Archive of the European Integration, The European Economic Community and Changes in the International Division of Labour. Report of an Expert Group on the Reciprocal Implications of the Internal and External Policies of the Community, III/1367-78-EN (January 1979).

95 Sandholtz, *High-Tech Europe,* 174.

96 Maria Green Cowles, "The Changing Architecture of Big Business," in *Collective Action in the European Union. Interests and the New Politics of Associability,* eds. Justin Greenwood and Mark Aspinwall (London: Routledge, 1998), 112.

97 Ibid., 163, 164, 166.

98 "Europe 1990," quoted in Sandholtz and Zysman, "1992: Recasting the European Bargain," 117.

99 On aspiring corporations, see Greenwood and Aspinwall, eds., *Collective Action,* 13, 23–4.

100 Sandholtz and Zysman, "1992," 116.

101 Adam Harmes, *The Return of the State. Protestors, Power-brokers and the New Global Compromise* (Vancouver, BC: Douglas and McIntyre, 2004), 126.

102 See Adam Smith, *An Inquiry into the Nature and Causes of the Wealth of Nations,* Vol. 1 (London: Mathuen, [1776] 1904); Book II, Chapter V; Karl Marx, Das Kapital, Vol. 1, Chapter 14.

103 Schneider, "Organized Interests in the European Telecommunication Sector," in *Organized Interests and the European Community,* ed. Justin Greenwood, Jürgen R. Grote, and Karsten Ronit, (London: Sage Publications, 1992), 42–68.

104 Sandholtz, *High-Tech Europe,* 159.

105 Archive of European Integration, Report of the Ad Hoc Committee for Institutional Affairs to the European Council (Brussels, 29–30 March 1985), 11, 13, 32.

106 Maria Green Cowles, "The 'Business' of Agenda-Setting in the European Union" (paper presented at the Fourth Biennial International Conference of the European Community Studies Association, Charleston, South Carolina, May 11–14, 1995), aei.pitt.edu/6916/1/cowles_maria_green2.pdf.

107 Terrence R. Guay, "Interest Groups and European Union Policymaking: The Influence of Defense Industry Interests" (paper presented at the European Community Studies Association Conference, Seattle, Washington, May 29–June 1, 1997), aei.pitt.edu/2603/1/002820_1.pdf, 5, 7, 8, 10, 12.

108 Archive of European Integration, Maria Green Cowles, "The Changing Architecture of Big Business," (paper presented in 1997 at the 5th Biennial ECSA Conference in Seattle, May 29, 1997), 23. The author describes a later stage of corporate organization when they established sectoral and trans-sectoral groups focused to the regulatory process. Among them the ENER-G8, the coalition of eight energy-intensive manufacturing corporations in 1995–6 and the International Communications Roundtable.

109 David Coen and Jeremy Richardson, eds., *Lobbying the European Union: Institutions, Actors, and Issues* (Oxford: Oxford University Press, 2009), 6.

110 Archive of European Integration, Jenny Fairbrass, The Europeanization of Interest Representation: A Strategic Decision-Making Analysis of UK Business and Environmental Interest (November 29, 2002).

111 Archive of European Integration, David Coen, The Role of Large Firms in the European Public Policy System: A Case Study of European Multinational Political Activity (1997).

112 Archive of European Integration, Communication from the Commission to the Council and the European Parliament on Standardization and the Global Information Society: The European Approach, COM (96) 359 final (24 July 1996), 3.

113 Archive of European Integration, The Single Market and Tomorrow's Europe. A Progress Report from the European Commission, 10.

114 Archive of European Integration, Commission Statement on the European Automobile Industry. Structure and Prospects of the European Car Industry (1981), Commission communication to the Council presented on 16 June 1981, COM (81) 317 final, 42.

115 Archive of European Integration, European Motor Vehicle Industry: Situation, Issues at Stake, and Proposals for Action. Communication from the Commission to the Council, the European Parliament and the Economic and Social Committee, COM (92) 166 final (8 May 1992).

116 See George Ross, *Jacques Delors and European Integration* (Oxford: Basil Blackwell, 1995); Ken Endo, *The Presidency of the European Commission under Jacques Delors. The Politics of Shared Leadership* (Houndmills, UK: Macmillan Press, 1999).

5

CREATING A EUROPEANIZED ECONOMY WITH CORPORATE ASSISTANCE

The Single Market and common currency

Introduction of the Single Market

In the European Community's forward leap into Europe, which, as we have seen in Chapter 4, was a step advocated strongly by the big corporations and François Mitterrand who led the way. This socialist president of France, who assumed his office in 1981, found his best ally in the conservative Christian democrat, Helmut Kohl, who was elected in 1982 as chancellor of Germany. These two men, despite their strongly opposed political persuasions, realized that cooperative work to find the answer to the challenge of globalization was unavoidable. In other words, they continued the tradition of Franco–German reconciliation and cooperation that had been followed since 1950. Both wanted to revitalize the European Community and its domestic corporations. Mitterrand wanted to have at the head of the European Commission a confident and efficient politician who shared his views about integration. At a breakfast meeting with Kohl at the Fontainebleau Summit of June 25–26, 1984, he recommended appointing Jacques Delors to the European Commission presidency. Kohl agreed. This decision proved to be a turning point in the history of the European Community.[1] Delors, who had been serving in Mitterrand's Administration as the minister of economics, finance, and budgetary affairs since 1981, was a European federalist. He became the most effective and innovative of the Commission presidents to date, serving ten years over three terms. The Mitterrand–Kohl–Delors troika, working with corporate Europe, found the answer to the globalization challenge and relaunched Europe.

Although the Treaty of Rome had set up the common market as a vehicle for attaining the free movement of goods, persons, and capital, those goals had proved elusive. Three decades later, Delors's political skill would succeed where the earlier treaty had failed: he persuaded the European Community governing bodies to restructure Community institutions in favor of the greater federalization necessary to a single European market. As Stanley Hoffman rightly noted, Delors acted as a "policy entrepreneur."[2] Under Delors's guidance, the Commission embraced policies that the corporations had been advocating since the 1970s. It succeeded in obtaining necessary EC political support, in part because the corporate-inspired policies it was championing also happened to accord with the thinking of none other than Altiero Spinelli, then serving as president of the European Parliament. Spinelli, one of the authors of the early federalist Ventotene Manifesto, had already worked out a new federalization plan, the "Draft Treaty Establishing the European Union," which had been accepted by the European Parliament in 1984 but never formally adopted.

Delors's draft for what became the Single European Act drew from that plan, as well as from the "Europe 1990" plan of Philips CEO Wisse Dekker. Article 47 of the draft, "Internal Market and Freedom of Movement," contained these words:

> The Union shall have exclusive competence to complete, safeguard and develop the free movement of persons, services, goods and capital within its territory . . . . This liberalization process shall take place on the basis of detailed and binding programmes and timetables laid down by the legislative authority in accordance with the procedures for adopting laws . . . . The Union must attain: within a period of two years . . . the free movement of persons and goods; this implies in particular the abolition of personal checks at internal frontiers, within a period of five years . . . the free movement of services including banking and all forms of insurance, within a period of 10 years . . . the free movement of capital.[3]

Delors followed up his draft with the publication of an action program "seeking to abolish, within seven years, all physical, technical and tax-related barriers to free movement within the Community. The aim was to stimulate industrial and commercial expansion within a large, unified economic area."[4]

In June 1985, the European Council, meeting in Milan, discussed a Commission White Paper, "Completing the Internal Market." This document began with the fact that

> during the recession [of the 1970s] . . . [non-tariff barriers] multiplied as each Member State endeavoured to protect what it thought was its short-term interest . . . Member States also increasingly sought to protect national markets and industries through the use of public funds to aid and maintain non-viable companies.

The Commission convincingly criticized those obsolete "defensive" national policies. As an alternative it recommended "setting the stage for a new type of association" with governance by uniform legislation, which would ease joint activities by enterprises from different Member States, permit cross-border mergers, and generally

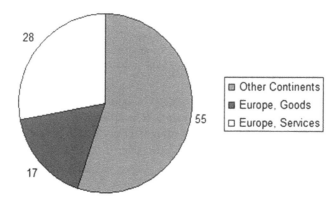

FIGURE 5.1 Intra-European trade as a percentage of world trade 2006

Source: Based on statistics from *OECD Factbook 2006* (Paris: OECD, 2006).

"create an environment or conditions likely to favour the development of coop-eration between undertakings."[5] With this document, the European Commission, in the summer of 1985, provided a plan for what European big business had been requesting for at least a decade: policies that would allow them to "redefine their 'home' market as the *European* as opposed to *national* market."[6] Nine countries accepted the Single European Act in February 1986, but—because of some diffi-culties of ratification in Denmark and Ireland—the act only came into force in July 1987. After two decades of stagnation in the integration process, Delors had brought about the first ambitious revision of the Treaty of Rome; the European Single Market had finally become a reality.[7]

A press release from the EU describes the Single Market as follows: " . . . the common area . . . where goods, services, capital and persons can circulate freely." It goes on to state that "the Single Market also ensures that European citizens are free to live, work, study and do business where they want in the EU . . . ".[8] But the Single Market has brought even more. With barriers removed and national markets opened, more firms now compete against each other. This means lower prices—and wider choice—for the consumer. Figures for 2006 show that firms selling on the Single Market had unrestricted access to nearly 500 million consumers in the EU (see Figure 5.1). It was estimated that between 1992 and 2006, the Single Market had generated 2.75 million jobs and 2.15 percent of extra growth for the European economy—that is €518 extra for every person in the EU in 2006 alone. In that year, intra-European trade accounted for 17 percent and 28 percent of world trade in goods and services, respectively.

Corporate assistance to create a single market

Under the umbrella of the Single European Act, the Community proceeded to eliminate several restrictions that had formerly blocked the road towards a single market. Both the Commission and Parliament worked closely together with the corporate world in pursuit of this goal. Top representatives and experts of the big multinational firms were invited to sit on advisory bodies and expert committees working out the exact plans and regulations. The European Commission needed badly the direct contribution of the corporate world. The Community had a surprisingly small bureaucracy. Less than 3,500 senior administrators were charged with drafting thousands of policy and regulatory documents, each of which required a huge amount of information and special expertise. A Commission document stated the situation clearly: "Drafting legislative proposals is a highly complex and lengthy process in which the Commission needs a considerable amount of expertise. Since the Commission is notoriously understaffed, it is highly dependent on external expert knowledge to draft policy proposals."[9] One consequence? "Expert groups mushroomed" in number.[10] In 1985, there were 700, but by 1988, 1,336. The elimination of market barriers, for example, was helped along by "bringing together all relevant stakeholders to analyze the overall market access situation for a given sector." The stakeholders belonged to two groups, the Market Access Advisory Committee and Market Access Working Group, which met on a regular basis. The work was done by "the partnership between Commission, Member States and business."[11]

The European Parliament had already gained joint decision-making right, but it also had very few experts and advisors on staff, and the highly technical issues under consideration required tapping outside expertise. Lobbyists acquired an expanded presence in the legislative and regulatory process, with rather predictable consequences. As one policy brief explained: "Lobbyist therefore welcomed guests in the office of busy M[ember of] E[uropean] P[arliament]s. Most MEPs, assistants and parliamentary policy advisors cannot imagine doing their work without information provided by lobbyist groups." The same brief quoted a source as saying:

> We cannot do our work without information from interest groups ... Sometimes it is very tempting to copy and paste their amendments ... It is reported that representatives of European associations have written large parts of the rapporteur's report ... about 80 percent of all amendments launched directly from interest representatives ...[12]

In the EU legislative process, regulations being proposed by the Commission and the Parliament are open for amendments. In the preparation of the Single Market, the Commission considered 1,052, and the Parliament 1,724 amendment suggestions to the proposed Single Market laws. In the end, the European Council accepted 719 of them.[13] When the Commission crafted its security proposal, for instance, it took over the recommendations of three high profile bodies, the Group of Personalities on Security Research, the European Security Research Advisory Board, and the European Security Research and Innovation Forum. These bodies were comprised of top executives of major European defense and security companies such as Siemens, Ericsson, BAE System among others.[14]

An article in a professional journal of biotechnics describes the connection between big business and the institutions of the European Community by unfolding that originally more than 600 European firms established the European Multinational Biotech Companies or EuropaBio Group in 1996. This group "worked closely with the European Commission . . . achieved modification of regulations and worked as "an advisory and monitoring group . . .". It went on to say: "Multinationals have established very close links with EU institutions in the last two decades to be involved in decision making process."[15]

It cannot be doubted that the thousands of regulations worked out in the second half of the 1980s and early 1990s to eliminate barriers for a real single market served the interest of the big corporations.[16] In the market for telecommunications, for example, the Community abolished most restrictions imposed by member countries on so-called consumer premises equipment. Directive 88/301/EEC (May 16, 1988), ordered the withdrawal of various restrictions against foreign companies' activity in other member countries' telecommunications markets. The Community also re-regulated the mutual recognition of tests and licenses from June 1990; with a service directive of 1990, it eliminated all exclusive rights. Following the "logic of the Single Market," the Community also directed that public telecommunication operators (PTOs) that were considered to have strategic importance and were strictly national enterprises, could now expand to other EC countries.[17] In general, for all sectors, regulations removed all special and exclusive rights to work in national markets; they also introduced general Community standards and initiated patent and trademark legislation, all in the service of completing the construction of a unified internal market. Internationalization, at least Europeanization, was the order of the day.

An insider who worked in the Brussels bureaucracy, describing the birth of the single market laws on financial services during the five years of the single market legislation preparation, remarked that the process was carried out essentially with the close collaboration with "the European Banking Federation, the European Stock Exchange Federation, [and] the various insurance federations." The so-called reciprocity clause of the Second Banking Directive, he noted, was based on the "detailed drafting proposal" of the banking group.[18] In another instance of collaboration between EU legislative bodies and the business targets of a given piece of legislation, the Committee of Common Market Automobile Constructors established in 1972 became one of the most influential organizations to closely shape all-European standards for cars.

Corruption, perhaps inevitably, sometimes tainted this "public–private" collaborative process. At the tip of the iceberg, two cases that echoed across Europe stand out. In the first, Ernst Strasser, member of the European Parliament and a former Austrian minister of interior, was arrested in 2011 on bribery charges and sentenced to four years in prison; he had been caught on camera offering an amendment to European legislation in return for cash. In the second case, the John Dalli case, the European Health Commissioner was forced to resign over bribery involving tobacco rules. The findings of EU Ombudsman P. Nikifouros Diamandouros also reverberated widely and loudly, namely, that five of thirteen former EU Commissioners had moved from public office to lucrative jobs in private businesses. American-style "revolving-door" practices, giving the private sector direct access to senior officials at EU institutions, had clearly taken root in the EU.[19]

From national towards "European Companies"

The Single Market regulations strengthened European transnational companies and underwrote a "sharp movement" by both the Community and its individual member countries "away from the traditional 'national enterprise' approach."[20] The Community initiated mutual investments, cross-border mergers, and joint ventures across national boundaries within the EU framework; and the member countries turned towards each other, not only by increasing trade, but also by making direct investments in each other's enterprises. All these actions became important components of the growing foreign direct investment (FDI) inflow into Europe. The yearly average total inflow of €313 billion between 1995 and 2000 increased to €531 billion by 2006.[21]

Even before the Single Market Act, EC multinationals were considered "crucial instruments and allies in the achievement of the EC's goals of market integration and improved international competitiveness."[22] That assessment would not change after the passage of the Single Market legislation. The reasons can be seen easily in the following statistics: up until 1965, European multinationals had established 585 subsidiaries outside Europe, but only 68 in European Community countries and 119 in other European countries. The figures changed after 1965 as big corporations realized the importance of the European area. Multinationals soon had 434 affiliates within the EC, 311 others within greater Europe, and 908 across the rest of the world.[23] German FDI, 38 percent of which had gone to developing countries in 1961, was redirected to Europe. European Community countries had received only 14 percent in 1961, but that figure grew to 36 percent in 1972 and 41 percent in 1990, while the share of all other countries dropped from 29 to 15 percent in the same period.[24] Dutch multinationals were strongly Europe-oriented: in 1989, 41 percent of their investments went to other Community countries, but only 5 percent to Asia and Africa combined. In 1986, 60 percent of the employees of Swedish multinationals worked in Western Europe, and only 12 percent in Latin America, 5 percent in Asia and Africa, and 21 percent in North America.[25]

Other business statistics display similar trends. In 1987, EU firms employed 53 percent of their employees in their home country and 25 percent in other EU countries. By 1997, the latter figure increased to 32 percent. Sales in home countries, meanwhile, dropped from 42 to 35 percent while assets located outside the home country, but in other European nations, increased from 17 to 25 percent in the decade around the introduction of the single market. In general, then, Europe became the dominant area of business for EU companies: by 1997, 82 percent of their combined assets, 79 percent of employees and 70 percent of sales were realized in the Community. "These results imply that European multinationals redeployed their assets and employment across Europe in response to opportunities from the SMP [Single Market Pact]."[26] Put another way, the Single Market encouraged a special form of international strategy: Europeanization.

This process was helped by regulations that facilitated capital movement within the Community. In April 1985, as the Commission's Program stated, this was a "top priority" of the Community, which wanted "to achieve the unconditional and effective liberalization throughout the Community of the capital operations most directly necessary for the proper functioning of the common market."[27]

Mergers, as will be explored in Chapter 6, progressed rapidly in the late 1980s. Among the 1,000 larger firms, mergers in 1982–83 numbered 117; in 1988–89, 303; in 1987–88, 383; in 1988–89, 492; and in 1989–90, 662. Together these increased European companies to sizes comparable with the American giants.[28] Besides, a great number of minority acquisitions (in 1986–87, 117; 1988–89, 159; 1989–90, 180) and joint ventures (111, 129, 156, in the aforementioned years), especially among high-tech firms, also created large, competitive companies. The Single Market initiatives were working.

It is important to note that to foster these trends the Brussels leadership made special efforts, best exemplified by the introduction in 1989 of a new sort of corporative form, pan-European in scope, the so-called European Company (Sociétas Europaea). In May 1991, the Commission amended the original SE program to additionally initiate the SE Holding Company, European Cooperative Society, European Mutual Society, and European Associations, institutions all licensed for transnational activities.[29] By 2011, more than 700 Sociétas Europaea had been registered. Various directives facilitated the growth of these entities. The Council Directive of July 23, 1990 (90/434/EEC), for example, eliminated double taxation in case of intra-Community mergers; the Directive of Cross Border Mergers (2005/56/EC, Article 14) facilitated pan-European mergers and simplified cross-border business activities. Community provisions legalized "the carrying out of cross-border mergers," stipulating that "none of the provisions and formalities of national law . . . should introduce restrictions on freedom of establishment or on the free movement of capital."[30] The 2004/25/EC Takeover Bids Directive of April 2004 introduced common rules to strengthen legal certainties for cross-border takeovers; Directive 2007/44/CE of the European Parliament and Council allowed 50 percent shareholding in European banks without the host country's notification. All of these innovations eased and simplified the creation and operation of Europeanized businesses.

More than 300 binding directives were issued to create and regulate the internal European market, mostly by eliminating non-tariff barriers, by partially liberalizing telecommunications, banking, and transportation, and by harmonizing social and environmental regulations. These alone, however, could not address all the obstacles to the smooth functioning of the newly created market entity. Thus, in 1991, an Intergovernmental Conference—a newly introduced institution charged with preparing new European Community rules and agreements by representatives of the member countries—began working to prepare amendments to the Single

European Act. This reform process culminated at the December 1991 European Council meeting in Maastricht with the signing of the Maastricht Treaty or, as it came to be called, the Treaty on European Union, which came into effect on November 1, 1993.

Under the banner of neoliberalism

The relaunching of the European Economic Community (EEC) embodied in the Single Market occurred in conjunction with major shifts in the 1970s and 1980s, in the general cultural–ideological environment of the Western world. I have touched upon this development in the previous chapter; here I further examine its implications and effects. The Keynesian economics that had dominated in postwar Western Europe, and the state intervention and regulation it had prescribed as solutions, were now declared to be the problem. New ideologies, rooted in the socio-economic sensibilities of post-industrial consumer middle classes, successfully challenged the policies of Left-leaning parties, which had served the European postwar recovery so well. The Left parties lost their self-confidence, as well as their mass support, and subsequently they shifted their political platforms to the center. The 1970s and 1980s essentially incubated a new political culture and *Zeitgeist*, an amalgam of triumphant neoliberalism, neoconservatism, and postmodern culture and ideology.

During the 1980s, the now-dominating neoliberal ideology seriously questioned two postwar institutions—the mixed economy and the social welfare system—which particularly distinguished the European economic model from other Western forms of capitalism. The mixed economy, with its 20–25 percent state sector, had arisen in Western Europe with the major wartime and postwar nationalizations. The state sector, working in a market environment and acting accordingly, had played a strategic role in bringing about the modernization and economic growth of the postwar "miracle" era.[31] Now, following the imperatives of neoliberalism, Europe eliminated this principal pillar of its postwar economic architecture; however, despite attacks and curbs, the other pillar—the welfare system—survived; so did the pension systems, albeit in strongly modified form. In the end the European social model was mostly preserved, albeit in altered and in some cases, in limited form.

Besides eliminating the state sector, the Community adjusted to the neoliberal era by deregulating the economy, especially the financial markets, and generally moving towards a laissez-faire system. The main economic trend, the transformation from a regulated to an unregulated market system, had actually emerged first in the US, followed closely by Britain. The European action was, therefore, part of a broader "Western" phenomenon. The countries of the Western half of the continent deregulated their banking systems and entered into vast international financial transactions.[32] Their foreign assets and liabilities increased by five times during the 1990s, and then doubled again in the single decade between 1998 and 2008.

By 2004, Europe had actually become the most globalized region of the world, with Belgium the most globalized country of all. According to the Swiss KOF globalization index issued in 2013, which assessed the economic, social, and political aspects of 122 countries, the first sixteen of the most globalized countries are European, with scores between 80 and 92 out of 100. Among the top twenty countries, only four—including the US and Canada—are non-European.[33] Without a doubt, the European Community has adjusted to global capitalism.

Europeanization of research and development

As a major element of the Community's all-European answer to globalization and relative technological backwardness, the Commission followed European corporations in embracing cooperative research and development (R&D). The failure of the national policies of adjustment had been connected, in part, with fragmented, isolated, inefficient R&D practices. One of the earliest cooperative efforts came in 1980 when the Commission set up a complex program for science and technology. The Commission's "communication" to the European Council on the subject suggested introducing a systematic evaluation of the Community's R&D programs along with an assessment of the actual utilization of research results. It also suggested that Member States cooperate and coordinate their R&D programs.

The focus on joint R&D, "to strengthen the scientific and technological basis of European industry and to encourage it to become more competitive at international level," was a leitmotif of further EU integration.[34] Two hundred eighty-two detailed supplemental measures facilitated the attainment of the goals.[35] Additional major reforms in the mid-1980s further encouraged cooperation and development. The EC Commission also adopted new rules for R&D agreements. Between 1975 and 1984, 215 such agreements were signed, 70 between two countries, 15 between three, 26 intra-EC, and 74 extra-EC.[36]

The Commission reported that between 1973 and 1980 the Community had already increased its spending on R&D by 336 percent, from 70.5 to 306 million European Currency Unit (ecu). Now, the Community focused on "several programs to assist with catching-up technologically with the United States and Japan."[37] Among the initiatives was the European Strategic Programme for Research and Development in Information Technology (ESPIRIT), launched in 1985 with joint public–private financing, €750 million in EC funds that had to be matched by the participating companies; the Research in Advanced Communications for Europe (RACE), also started in 1985 and financed by ecu 970 million; and also the Basic Research in Industrial Technologies in Europe/ European Research in Advanced Materials, funded from 1985 to 1992 with ecu 1.21 billion. The European Community invested altogether ecu 63.3 billion between 1984 and 2006 in various research and technology programs.

The amount of Community investment during this period was designed to provide, not full funding, but rather seed money that would promote a change of direction and orientation for economic activity. Community financing totaled only about 5 percent of the member countries' rising expenditures. Denmark and Germany, nearing American levels, spent about 2.5–2.6 percent of their GDP for

R&D financing. Sweden and Finland dedicated more, spending 3.5 percent of their GDP, therefore approaching the Japanese level, which was the world's highest. The EU average, however, at 1.9 percent investment of GDP, was still behind the levels of the US and Japan. The number of employed researchers averaged only 6 per 1,000 in the EU (10.4 and 9.6 per 1,000 employees in Japan and the US, respectively), but member countries such as Finland and Sweden stood at the highest level internationally with 17.3 and 11.0 per 1,000 employees, respectively.[38] By 2005, thirteen West European countries already numbered among the twenty most innovative countries.

Corporate efforts and the European Community's assistance succeeded in integrating key R&D activities within the Community. For example, Dutch Philips, German Siemens, and the French Thomson agreed to run a joint semiconductor research program. Multinational pharmaceutical companies also "set up R&D facilities in each other's countries." Of the thirty largest pharmaceutical companies, twenty-three had R&D facilities in other countries, sixteen in Britain, eleven in France, seven in both Germany and Italy. One analysis maintained that "research is more integrated than production" in that area.[39] Statistics for 2004 reveal even more Europeanized research and development activity by multinationals. Nearly two-thirds of the foreign-located research centers created by French companies had been founded in the immediately preceding decade. By 1999, 27 multinational groups had 35 percent of their research globalized, with most of it invested in EU countries or future member countries. This trend is the strongest in chemical–pharmaceutical and electronics–telecom industries. These groups control 148 out of 214 research centers abroad. All-European R&D is more prevalent in the early twenty-first century than American and Japanese R&D.[40]

Assisting infrastructural renewal

To increase competitiveness—the core requirement for success in the globalized world—the EU turned to improving infrastructure. Richard Burke, the Commissioner responsible for infrastructure, called attention to this issue in 1980 when he stated that transportation infrastructure was "unjustifiably neglected" and he noted that transportation bottlenecks "hindered free and easy contact between member states." The Commission followed up by adopting the policy, outlined in "A Transport Network for Europe," of coordinating national planning and aiding programs "more valuable to the Community as a whole."[41] In 1996, the Commission issued guidelines for the development of a trans-European transport network. The freeway system, for example, was significantly increased: in the mid-1970s, freeways stretched 22,000 kilometers across seventeen West European countries, but by 2005, the figure had reached 57,000 kilometers. EU member countries with few or no freeways, such as Finland, Greece, Ireland, and Portugal, began extensive construction projects; even France and the Scandinavian countries had 3–6 percent annual increases of their networks. Highway miles per square kilometer of landed area in the EU grew to nearly four times the figure for the US.

The Single European Program, therefore, brought an integrated trans-European transport system into being. The Essen Council meeting in 1994 assented to a plan of fourteen priority projects with 2010 target completion dates. This plan was amended in 2003 in connection with the eastward enlargement of the EU, at which time thirty priorities were formally accepted, two for inland water transportation, eighteen for high-speed, high-capacity railroads, two for water transportation, and the remainder for automobile roadways. The main goal was the elimination of transportation bottlenecks around big cities, at border crossings, and in mountainous regions. Another central goal was the integration of railroad, water, and air transportation by means of better connections between train stations, ports, and airports. Missing links in the EU system were to be closed through the construction of 4,800 kilometers of roads and 12,500 kilometers of railroad lines. To create a better radio navigation system, thirty satellites were launched. The EU provided 10–20 percent of financing for all these ambitious programs. For the priority projects alone, the EU spent at least ecu 600 billion.

The railroad system was spectacularly renewed. In borderless Europe, Eurail and Eurostar permits guaranteed unlimited travel in twenty countries. Railways connected Britain with the continent in 1994 via the Channel Tunnel, a pioneering transportation project, but also a symbolic project that ended the "splendid isolation" of Britain. Railroad electrification and dieselization were accomplished in the 1980s and from then on, new high-speed trains began running at 400–500 kilometers (250–300 miles) per hour in France. Italy and Germany quickly ordered the new super trains. Germany, meanwhile, also created the efficient Intercity System (ICE). The renewed railroad network competed with car and air transportation in a pan-European system that far surpassed what could be found in the US.

The air transportation system received significant attention and upgrades. The successful Airbus program was further developed with the launching of the A380 project in 2002. The first of these giant, 555-seat planes started service in 2005. By this time, Airbus employed 57,000 people at sixteen sites in France, Germany, and Britain. In 2001, the European Commission introduced the Single European Sky Program, a joint EU air-control system to supplement national systems. It controlled the upper air space above 7.5 kilometers, thereby separating high-altitude from short-haul air traffic.

As part of the infrastructural renewal, the energy sector also entered a new age. In 1985, the Commission informed the public that, as a consequence of a concentrated effort, the percentage of total Community electricity output attributable to nuclear energy production had risen from 26 percent in 1984 to 32 percent in 1985. Statistics by countries for 1985 show that nuclear production accounted for 60 percent of electricity output in France and Belgium; also that its role in Germany had doubled in just two years to 30 percent, and in Spain it had increased from 9 to 22 percent.[42] Later, renewable energy sources, such as hydro, geothermal, solar, wind, tide, wave, biomass, and water, gained ground. This later set of developments is still in its infancy. In the EU-15 in 1995, only 5 percent of the energy production on average was produced by renewable sources. The EU's plan was to reach a 20 percent share by 2020, but at the end of the first decade, in 2004, the share had increased only to 6.4 percent. Some countries, such as Sweden, Finland, Austria, Denmark, and Portugal, however, produce significant amounts of energy via renewable sources: 28, 23, 22, 16, and 13 percent, respectively. Germany initiated the most ambitious *Energiewende*, or energy transformation program, in all of Europe. In 2000, only 6.3 percent of the country's electric energy came from renewable sources, but by 2012, that share stood at 25 percent. The country's first offshore wind farm, 45 kilometers off the North Sea coast, supplies thousands of households. According to the plans, by 2020 Germany wants to produce 35 percent of energy by renewable sources; by 2030, this share would be increased to 50 percent, and by 2050 to 80 percent.[43] Scientists believe that 100 percent is possible—and even earlier than 2050. The German Renewable Energy Act "has been an export hit: 19 out of the EU's 27 member states are now using this model for their own energy transformation."[44] Europe is making impressive progress in this area.

Schengen Agreement: eliminating borders

In connection with the Single European Act, a ground-breaking agreement was signed by five member countries—France, Germany, and the three Benelux countries—on a boat next to a Luxembourgian village named Schengen. They agreed in June 1985 to abolish all their common borders and border controls. The resulting effective creation of a single external border containing five still-sovereign countries was a revolutionary step in uniting the continent. The signatory countries harmonized common rules and procedures at their old borders. They also agreed on some "compensatory measures," including police cooperation to fight crime. The Schengen Information System, an international database, was set up to facilitate this cooperation. The really free movement of persons and the idea of a borderless Europe was very attractive and soon most EU member countries joined the Schengen Agreement: Italy in November 1990, Spain and Portugal in June 1991, and in 2007, even the newly accepted former communist countries. Moreover, in the early 2000s, some non-member countries, such as Iceland, Norway, and Switzerland, also partly joined, with associated member status. The Schengen Agreement imposes strict external border security, and signatories must accept a specific border control system. The Schengen system became a formal EU system when, in 1997, as a protocol of the Amsterdam Treaty, it was adopted as EU law.[45]

The free movement of persons, including the right to take a job in any other member country, required and generated the harmonization of education. One of the major initiatives was formulated in 1998 by France, Germany, Italy, and Britain. Their Sorbonne Declaration called for the "harmonization of the architecture of the European Higher Education System." The very next year, twenty-nine European countries launched the so-called Bologna Process, which introduced a uniform system with three levels, the BA, MA, and PhD. The unification created a system that would enable credit transfer and exchange among universities throughout the

EU and even beyond. The Bologna Process actually includes forty-six countries, several of which lie outside the borders of the EU.[46] Another initiative, the Copenhagen Process of 2002, widened the harmonization to include vocational education and training. The declaration stated: "Economic and social developments in Europe over the last decade have increasingly underlined the need for a European dimension to education and training." As with university education, this cooperation spread beyond the EU's borders. Not much time passed before thirty-three European countries joined.[47]

The EU then followed up with programs to facilitate mobility in education. In 1987, it launched the first of these programs, the Erasmus Program for student exchange, followed by the Leonardo da Vinci Program, co-founded by the EU and several major companies, which allows students to pursue vocational education and training for a few months in another country.[48] These programs not only created greater mobility but also stronger European identity and the new, so-called Erasmus- and Leonardo da Vinci-generations.

Introduction of the common currency

Further integration, as a pillar of the single market creation, had a twin, the introduction of the common currency. As the European Commission rightly notes on its EU legislation website, "the EMU [European Monetary Union] puts the finishing touches to the single market."[49] This program has a long history in the European Community. The Werner Plan first placed it on the agenda in 1970;[50] nevertheless, the common currency had to wait for three more decades. The corporations, ever more transnational with large networks of subsidiaries and value-chains based on the Single Market, badly needed a common currency to simplify and cheapen their trans-European business activities. The normal fluctuation of the exchange rates of European national currencies made business more risky and less predictable. The introduction of the common currency eliminated the cost of exchange, allowing the companies to increase their earnings by about €20–25 billion per year. This was equal to 0.3–0.4 percent of the EU's aggregate GDP. Additionally, the currency union made European prices transparent and encouraged growth in the euro-zone trade. The zone began enjoying 4–10 percent increases in the coming decade. One of the greatest winners of the common currency introduction was the finance sector, which became much more integrated and profited from the removal of barriers to capital flow.[51]

In the matter of the common currency, as in the case of market unification, corporate interests accorded with federalist fervor. Delors, who had argued passionately for a true federation in Europe, also expressed his belief that "economic and monetary union is the *interface between economic and political integration* . . . It is time, then, for a new political initiative . . . The Community is faced with the challenge of making a telling contribution to the next phase of our history."[52] Michael Burgess has observed that the post-1985 European renaissance began as a market-based revival but has moved beyond that to state-building.[53]

Whatever the federalist enthusiasm and motive, the common currency would never have been realized had it not harmonized with the central political interests of key member states. The three decades required to bring the common currency into being—after it was first recommended—can be largely connected to national resistance. In 1989, however, political circumstances in Europe changed. In that year, as EU-relaunching was moving forward, the Soviet Bloc, including the German Democratic Republic, collapsed, sending shock waves across the continent and around the world. The "German Question"— that prime mover of postwar European cooperation and early integration—once more reared its head. The collapse of the Soviet Bloc and the withdrawal of the Soviet Army from the region automatically put reunification of the two postwar Western and Eastern German states on the European agenda. Old fears and hostility quickly resurfaced. Virtually all the key European powers opposed German unification. Margaret Thatcher, François Mitterrand, Giulio Andreotti, and Michael Gorbachev were all strongly against it.

The process of German reunification nevertheless was unstoppable. The West found itself in a "rhetorical trap": for four decades during the Cold War era, Western leaders had blamed the Soviet Union for dividing Germany and had called for unification. Moreover, the right of self-determination, as they repeatedly announced, belonged among basic Western democratic principles. Given this rhetoric, openly opposing unification against the will of the Germans was virtually impossible, and only an aggressive character, such as Margaret Thatcher, did it. Behind the scene, machinations, which President Mitterrand tried in East Berlin and Moscow, did not work.

In the end it was Chancellor Kohl, whose check-book diplomacy in fatally weakened Moscow and assurances to Western allies of Germany's desire to anchor itself in an integrated Europe persuaded both the Russians and the West to allow reunification. He began his diplomatic campaign by proposing a very gradual progress towards a solution—the best would be a confederate arrangement of two independent German states—and he also guaranteed the Oder-Neisse border of Germany. During his visit to Moscow, he told Gorbachev that "the NATO naturally will not move to the territory of the German Democratic Republic."[54] But he also stressed that "the German development has to be embedded in a European architecture." He used skillful diplomacy to attain his goals: it is recorded that he described the path to success as "a kind of slalom-tour."[55]

The American Bush Administration immediately accepted the strengthening of Germany, its most important European ally. The record of Kohl's thirty-five exchanges with President Bush (meetings, telephone conversations, letters) makes this absolutely clear. Secretary of State Baker confirmed the American acceptance with Kohl, but he also indicated that the Bush Administration wanted a "new European architecture and a closer connection between the United States and the European Community, and also a stronger European Community . . . and the NATO with a bigger political role."[56] The critical year between the fall of 1989 and the fall of 1990 was probably the busiest year ever in the diplomatic history of

Europe. Chancellor Kohl alone had more than 100 meetings, telephone talks, or letter exchanges with Bush, Mitterrand, Gorbachev, Delors, and Thatcher.[57]

Kohl had a strong and convincing argument to present to Gorbachev when the two met in Moscow in February 1990: "a dramatic development that no one had foreseen, in the last four, five weeks dramatically changed the situation."[58] He was referring to the mass emigration of mostly young and well-trained East Germans to West Germany. In the last weeks of 1989, 380,000 people had moved to the West, and then in January 1990, another 200,000. Gorbachev acknowledged that although "at the end of December you spoke about several years-long process . . . [however] people will make the decision with their feet."[59] In January 1990, having tried unsuccessfully to block the road for German reunification, President Mitterrand told Kohl: "If I were a German I would make the reunification as fast as possible."[60] In March, the East German elections delivered a victory for Kohl that clearly documented the East Germans' wish to reunite, and that made that wish a *fait accompli*.

The pragmatic Mitterrand saw in further European integration a means to limit the potential threat that a reunified Germany might pose for Europe. Unlike the rigid Thatcher, he found a novel way to satisfy French security interests by trying to anchor a now greatly enlarged and strengthened Germany into a more vigorous, more permanent, organic form of European Community. Actually, this was easy to achieve because Kohl was ready to pay the price for his reunification victory. He argued that a reunified Germany embedded within a unified Europe would serve the causes of Europe even more effectively than would a divided country. "Germany," Kohl stated in the European Parliament, "will be completely united only if progress is made towards the unification of our old continent. Policy on Germany and policy on Europe are completely inseparable." He emphasized that "we are already making preparations for the further development . . . with Political Union as our goal."[61] The chancellor said the same at the Bundestag: that "German and European unification were intertwined and that the process of German unification would function as a 'catalyst' for the acceleration of Europe's integration in the direction of a political union."[62] One of Kohl's closest aides noted that after the collapse of the Berlin Wall, Kohl found himself "in the situation of having to approve practically every French initiative for Europe."[63]

The Mitterrand–Kohl tandem, in other words, worked excellently. Mitterrand embraced both the project of monetary unification and the introduction of the common currency as a kind of guarantee to bind Germany to Europe, while Kohl was more than happy to go along with the French president to demonstrate Germany's readiness to be incorporated more strongly into an integrated Europe.[64] So too, did the Mitterand–Kohl–Delors troika: Delors saw German unification as an excellent opportunity, a "catalyst" to move Europe towards monetary and political unity, and thus to greater integration. It was against this backdrop that the European Commission initiated the Monetary Union as the logical next step.[65]

The breakthrough came in the negotiations of 1989, with Delors once again playing a critical role, this time as chairman of the committee charged with designing a common currency plan. The governors of the various central banks, whose own work of a quarter-century was reflected in the new Delors Committee report, astonishingly did not expect that report to have any greater impact than earlier recommendations, even as they signed the document. Robin Leigh-Pemberton, the head of the Bank of England, recalled that "most of us, when we signed the Report in May 1989, thought that we would not hear much about it. It would be rather like the Werner Report of 1970." The German representative, Karl Otto Pöhl, maintained that the report was "a confused piece of work," with some "wild ideas in it." The Italian banker, Tommaso Padoa-Schioppa, "did not think the outcome would be very significant."[66] These superb financial experts did not understand the implications and potential of the political situation, but Delors did, and he exploited it expertly. On account of his support and excellent diplomatic maneuvering, his committee's recommendations did not suffer the fate of the 1970 Werner Report. Instead, they found a place in the 1992 Maastricht Treaty, which laid out three steps for introducing the "euro," which was to take place between January 1, 1999 and January 1, 2002.[67]

Under the terms of the EMU agreement, before member countries could join the common currency, they had to meet certain "convergence criteria."[68] Alongside the EMU, the Maastricht Treaty set up a new supranational institution, the European Central Bank (ECB), to administer common monetary policy. Together with the national central banks, the ECB formed the European System of Central Banks.[69] With these changes, a major part of national sovereignty was shifted to supranational control. The introduction of the common currency was thus a major *political* step, as well as a response to economic necessity. One of the indicators of a political origin is the fact of the major "birth defect" of the common currency: monetary unification without economic convergence and fiscal unification.[70] The experts clearly recognized the requirements of economic convergence and fiscal unification as prerequisites for the introduction of the euro,[71] and yet all these warnings were neglected in the political rush to anchor a reunited Germany strongly to Europe.[72]

The Single Market and common currency, however, did target one central economic goal: increasing the global competitiveness of the European corporate world. Jacques Santer, who followed Delors as president of the European Commission, recognized that changes needed to be made if European products were to be able to compete with the rising export of developing countries. Among the problems facing Europe in the 1980s was the increasing structural unemployment. Santer appointed a Competitiveness Advisory Group in 1995 and suggested further deregulating the economy, especially the financial and infrastructural sectors, to follow the example of the US.[73]

Serving corporate Europe by endless enlargement

Twenty-three days before the fall of the Berlin Wall in November 1989, Delors delivered a speech in Bruges. He was aware that given the peaceful regime change in Poland and the announcement of free elections in Hungary, the likelihood of collapse of the entire Soviet Bloc was great, and his speech effectively challenged the European Community to expand its vision of Europe beyond its original Cold War-determined boundaries. The European Community, he stated,

> did not want Europe to be cut in two at Yalta . . . They did not, nor do they close the door to other European countries willing to accept the terms of the contract in full. The present upheavals in Eastern Europe are changing the nature of our problems. It is not merely a matter of when and how all the countries of Europe will benefit from the stimulus and the advantage of a single market . . . The West is not drifting eastward, it is the East that is being drawn towards the West. Will the Community prove equal to the challenge of the future?[74]

Business interests motivated the European Community to enlarge its sphere of influence. In the remaining part of this chapter, I will discuss its impact. In the early 1970s, the Community had made plans for incorporating the Mediterranean countries into its business activities, many of which, like Greece, Spain, Portugal, and Turkey, were controlled military–fascist dictatorships. Nevertheless, the Community's plan, as the *Washington Post* reported in November 1972,

> calls for a larger free trade zone for industrial goods between the European Community and the Mediterranean countries by 1977. Greece and Turkey have negotiated agreements which are intended to lead to a customs union and eventually to full membership in the Community.[75]

This bold enlargement of the Community gained momentum in the following decade with the accession of these countries.

Competitiveness in the globalized world economy required more than a common market of twelve developed West European countries: the larger the European markets the better. A bold EU enlargement drive had actually started a few years earlier, with the inclusion of three Mediterranean countries: Greece, Spain, and Portugal. These additions on the Southern European periphery had provided European multinational companies with new hunting grounds where they could find low-wage labor pools, deepen their value chains, and broaden their subsidiary networks. In Spain, for example, in the decade after the death of Franco, foreign-controlled companies represented nearly half of the turnover of the major Spanish industries and employed 43 percent of the industrial labor force. In certain modern key industries this share was much greater—81 percent of the turnover of Spanish industries occurred in the vehicle and transportation equipment industries, 79 percent in electric machinery, and 78 percent in chemicals—and foreign-controlled companies employed 66–82 percent of the labor force in these sectors. Similarly, foreign affiliate companies in Greece overall produced one-quarter of industrial products in the first years of Greek EU membership, but 56–58 percent in chemical and metal industries and 52–53 percent in electrical machinery and transport equipment industries. In Portugal, even before membership, 36 percent of industrial output was being produced by European Community subsidiaries: 858 firms had foreign participation, 357 in manufacturing, and 106 in banking and insurance.[76]

The collapse of the Soviet Bloc also affected the markets of non-member countries. During the Cold War, neither Austria or Sweden (both politically neutral) or Finland (quasi-neutral) had chosen to join any international bloc or organization, but between 1989 and 1991, they, together with Norway, changed course and sought European Community membership.[77] What caused their rush to join? Their big corporations and banks definitely pushed this advance. Finland offers a very telling example. With the disintegration of the Soviet Union in 1991, a solid market for one-fifth of Finnish exports collapsed, and Finland declined into a severe economic crisis. GDP dropped by 11 percent in three years and unemployment jumped to 18 percent. Europe offered the only escape. Economic restructuring and the establishment of new export industries became extremely urgent needs.[78] As a corollary, so did EU membership.

Evidence of the legitimacy of this point of view can be found in the Nokia experience. In 1991, at the old Nokia factory, the new president and CEO, Jorma Ollila, decided to restructure the company to concentrate on mobile phone and telecom systems manufacturing.[79] The new industry miraculously developed into a top export industry and was soon producing one-quarter of the country's exports. Export industries, of course, tend to thrive in a world market, and therefore, the fact that the Nokia Group and Ollila emerged as the main proponents of joining Europe and the common currency is quite understandable; membership would help them to gain entrance into a greater market. Historically, however, in general, major developments usually have several motivations and connections. This was the case here as well: Finland had a major security consideration as an additional motive. "Neighboring Russia—with a 1,300 kilometer-long border with Finland and a 150-year history of bad relations with the Finns—declined into a dangerous chaos after 1991."[80] Security for Finland in this situation was equal with EU membership. As *The Economist* maintained, "EU membership has strengthened Finnish sovereignty, by anchoring Finland in Europe."[81]

Sweden also changed its position. The political elite of the country, the long-dominant Social Democratic majority, had long opposed joining the West European integration. Tage Erlander, prime minister between 1946 and 1969, expressed one element of the Social Democratic Party's argument as follows: "It would be a dreadful mistake to allow economic factors to determine Swedish foreign policy."[82] The Social Democratic Party won the election in 1990 with the promise to actively defend the Swedish Welfare Model in the rising neoliberal age. That was the unshakeable position of the Ingvar Carlsson Government in the spring of 1990. In early 1994, 70 percent of Social Democratic Party members still opposed joining the EU. The new Carlsson Government, however, changed its mind, called for a referendum in November 1994, and applied for membership. Why? The pressure to join the EU began to mount during the 1970s . . . almost exclusively the goal of political conservatives . . . whose interests tend to coincide with those of big business, saw in the EEC a device for prying the country loose from what they considered to be its dangerous isolation.[83]

From the 1970s, the influential Swedish Employers' Confederation and the Federation of Swedish Industries had been lobbying for joining the EU with the argument that "the country was falling behind economically and could no longer afford the delusion of independence . . . [and] nostalgic attachment to 'the Swedish model.'" They accused previous governments of having failed to provide a "level playing field in matters of economic competition." Even the Social Democratic leadership accepted this argument and appealed to "loyalty" of their members, and in case of voting, they argued, a "no" would be an "impending economic disaster."[84]

In the decades of globalization, the leader of the Conservative Party, Carl Bildt, expressing the interests of the business circles, declared "that the nation-state was for all intents and purposes dead as an independent actor on the world scene." In 1994, Carlsson adopted this point of view: "National politicians have a formal decision-making power over an increasing powerlessness." Two months after the election, the new government strongly stressed the requirements of the globalized world economy: "We cannot accomplish anything on our own. We have to go out and join Europe in order to prevent disaster. It was a 180-degree change of course." The same Social Democratic Party started "maneuvering the ship of state into an enterprise that had long been regarded as an instrument of the rich and powerful," explained Per Olov Enqvist, the Swedish journalist–writer.[85]

Austria had been satisfied with the earlier European Free Trade Association (EFTA)–EEC agreement and with being part of a free trade area, but started seeing actual membership in the European Community as a highly desirable, even necessary advantage in a globalized economic environment. When the systemic change of Eastern Europe began, joining the EU became urgent. Austria applied for membership on June 17, 1989.[86] From its earlier position on the edges of the Western bloc, Austria now "moved into the centre of unified Europe, fully involved in the 'mini-globalization' triggered by eastern transformation and EU enlargement."[87] Austria's export to the ten Central and Eastern European countries that became EU candidates and then members increased from 7.3 percent of total export to 17.5 percent by 2008. The country's direct investments abroad increased from 0.5 to 10.0 percent of its GDP: Austrian companies, which had had no real presence in other European countries before joining the EU, were investing roughly €15 billion in Central and Eastern Europe by 2008 and took over a great part of the region financial institutions.

The fact that the collapse of the Soviet Bloc had enhanced the appeal of EU membership is evidenced in the ensuing rush to join by the whole group of non-member countries: Austria applied for membership in 1989; Cyprus and Malta in 1990; Sweden in 1991; and Finland, Switzerland, and Norway in 1992.[88] Accession negotiations were opened by the EEC in 1992–93 and closed without difficulty in the spring of 1994. Membership for Cyprus and Malta was postponed, but Austria, Sweden, and Finland were admitted, effective in 1995. In the end, Switzerland and Norway decided not to join.

Business circles of both the old and new advanced member countries gained advantages from this influx, but the more significant benefit, for both business and member countries, came with the addition of Central and Eastern Europe to the membership roster. The Community and its member states rushed in immediately after the Soviet withdrawal to stabilize Eastern Europe. Chancellor Kohl, at a meeting with European Commission President Delors in early October 1989, had stressed already that a failure of the reform process in Hungary would be "a catastrophe" and observed that "Europe will not remain divided forever."[89] In December of that same year, he had told Secretary of State Baker that in the future "the Czechs as well as the Hungarians and Poles will join the European Community." Baker had agreed and stressed immediately the "extraordinary role of the European Community in the entire process [of East European transformation] since it is the 'Art Magnet' for Eastern Europe."[90] Kohl also guaranteed Gorbachev that the Germans would help "private initiative to work" in Russia and that they would encourage investments to flow into the Soviet Union, Poland, Hungary, Bulgaria, and Romania.[91]

Just a few months after the collapse of communism, the Dublin meeting of the European Council approved the outlines of association agreements with the former communist countries. Political dialogue began on economic, cultural, and financial cooperation, and the EU offered immediate financial assistance.[92] When the European Council met in Maastricht in December 1991, two years later, the EU had already signed the so-called Europe Agreement—a new version of earlier association agreements—with Poland, Hungary, and Czechoslovakia. In May 1992, similar negotiations began with Romania and Bulgaria, and somewhat later with Slovenia and the three Baltic states. At the Copenhagen meeting in 1993, something happened that had never happened before: the former communist countries were practically invited to join: "The associate countries in central and eastern Europe that so desire shall become members of the European Union . . . as soon as . . . [they have fulfilled] the obligations of membership by satisfying the economic and political conditions required."[93]

Despite early initiatives, the incorporation of the former communist countries was extremely difficult. These countries were economically backward. In most cases, their economic level, measured by per capita GDP, had never reached more than half the West European level in modern history, and now it was sinking. By 1993, in five former Soviet Bloc countries, the composite average industrial production was 37 percent below the 1989 level, and the animal stock halved.[94]

In several countries of the region the decline reached an unprecedented scale: in 1994, Lithuania's industrial production dropped to little more than one-third of the 1991 level. Bulgaria's agricultural output decreased by more than 50 percent in 1992 and 1993. Unemployment jumped from virtually 0 percent to 16 percent in Poland and Bulgaria, and to 29 percent in Albania and Macedonia. In the early 1990s,

Central and Eastern Europe's per capita GDP was one-quarter less than in 1989. Average per capita income level declined from 37 to 27 percent of the Western European level, a historical nadir. Even in 2004, when eight of these countries (Poland, Hungary, Czech Republic, Slovakia, Slovenia, Estonia, Latvia, and Lithuania) were taken into the EU, their average per capita income level was only $9,240, and the two (Romania and Bulgaria) accepted in 2007 had a US$4,000 level: a stark contrast to the EU's per capita average of US$29,000. Notably, all the former Soviet Bloc countries had lost their financial–economic balance and suffered from high inflation: in 1992, Estonia, Lithuania, and Macedonia experienced 1,000 percent hyperinflation; Croatia's inflation reached 1,500 percent in 1993; Poland had 600 percent inflation in 1990; Romania 250 percent in 1993.[95]

Almost all these countries were heavily indebted. Their aggregate debt burden increased from US$6 billion in 1973 to US$100 billion five years later. Meanwhile, originally low interest rates increased steeply. Poland, Yugoslavia, and Bulgaria soon became unable to repay and had to ask for rescheduling.[96] The hazard associated with the abrupt regime change in the region was amplified by this tragic economic situation, as well as by their non-capitalist economic structures and traditionally non-democratic political forms.

To help the accession process, in 1993 the Copenhagen European Council drafted specific political and economic conditions for joining the EU. The Essen meeting of the Council in December 1994 worked out an exact pre-accession strategy and drew up the *acquis communautaire*, a thirty-one-chapter, nearly ten-thousand-page document specifying the tasks to be completed before acceptance. Between 1994 and 1996, Hungary, Poland, Estonia, Latvia, Lithuania, Bulgaria, the Czech Republic, and Slovenia all applied for membership. The European Agreements took effect between 1994 and 1996. They stipulated that for a decade, an asymmetric progress towards free trade would be allowed. Under these terms, for six years, the EU decreased its own general tariffs faster and earlier than the applicant countries. Meanwhile, the applicant countries started to adjust their political, economic, and legal systems to EU standards. All these steps aimed at bringing into reality what the European Commission had stated in 1994, that "the goal for the period before accession should be the progressive integration of the political and economic systems . . . to create an increasingly unified area."[97] Negotiations began with the five best-prepared countries in March 1998, and with the other five in February 2000. The processes ended in 2004 and 2007. Ten former communist countries were now members of the EU.

The rush for membership by the economically devastated former Soviet Bloc countries was more than understandable. But why, it must be asked, was the EU ready to accept economically bankrupt countries emerging from non-market, centrally planned economic systems and one-party, non-parliamentary, political regimes? (See Table 5.1 and Figure 5.2.) Why did the EU choose to include countries with the highest pollution of Europe?[98] Why was the EU more than ready to include countries that had rather different historical experiences and cultural backgrounds? Why, in other words, did the EU choose to dilute its relative

TABLE 5.1 Central and Eastern Europe's economic growth, 1950–92

Region	Annual growth rate: 1950–73	Annual growth rate: 1973–1992	Eastern Europe in % of West: 1950–1992
Central and Eastern Europe	3.79	−0.7	1950 = 46
Soviet Union and Successor States	3.36	−1.4	1973 = 43
Western and Mediterranean Europe	4.8	2.0	1992 = 37

Source: Based on Angus Maddison, *Monitoring the World Economy 1820–1992* (Paris: OECD, 1995).

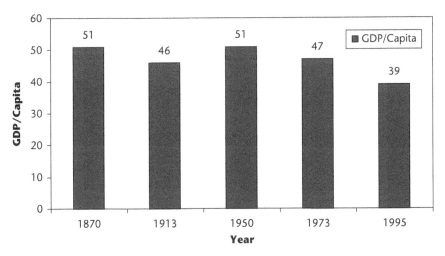

FIGURE 5.2 Central and Eastern Europe's GDP in percentage of Western Europe

Source: Based on Ivan Teodorovic, Zeljko Lovrincvzevic, Davor Mikulic, Mustafa Nusinovic, and Stjepan Zdunic, eds., *The Croatian Economic Development, Transition Towards the Market Economy* (Zagreb: Institute of Economics, 2005).

homogeneity in order to embrace countries that departed so markedly from the community norm? "Why," as one of the popular textbooks on the EU asks, "has it [the EU] been so willing to open its doors to applicants . . . Why was the EU—a highly successful organization in most respects—willing to risk enlargement to CEECs [Central and Eastern European countries]?"[99]

Most Central and Eastern European nations had been governed for centuries by centralized, non-democratic regimes, and during the post-Soviet transformation decades, authoritarian political tendencies actually gained ground, at least in some places. The Mečier Government in Slovakia, the Kaczyinski regime in Poland, several Romanian governments up to Victor Punta, as well as the Viktor Orbán Government in Hungary are clear examples of the permanently present undercurrent of what Orbán calls "illiberal democracy"—that is, authoritarian limitation of democracy, strong state control of political and economic life, including renationalization of previously privatized companies.[100] All these countries departed culturally from the West in significant ways.

As in peripheral countries everywhere in the world system, high levels of clientelism and corruption characterized the Eastern European countries. The Corruption Perception Index of 2013, which evaluates the relative corruption of 177 countries, clearly illustrates the problem. On a scale where a high ranking indicates absence of corruption, the Western EU members all ranked above 70, with the Northern European countries the cleanest, at about 90. The Mediterranean and Central European countries ranked in the 50s—evidence of severe corruption. Several, including Italy, Romania, Bulgaria, and Greece, show up in the zone of the 40s, the zone of dangerous corruption. But the most tragic are the countries of the former Soviet Union, Russia, Belarus, Ukraine Tajikistan, Uzbekistan, and others, which lie in the zone of the 20s. The corruption index is extremely low in several Asian, African, and Latin American countries as well.[101]

So why did the EU choose to embrace such countries? Several interpreters of the eastward enlargement speak of the determining effects on EU policies of moral commitments, including those associated with "Yalta guilt," the guilt presumed to have arisen from having allowed Central Europe to be sovietized after World War II. To this argument they add the influence of the moral discomfort associated with failure to support anti-Soviet revolts in 1956, 1968, and 1980–81 after having encouraged them. There is also the argument about the rhetorical trap, which we have already explored. The West, this argument continues, could not escape its moral responsibility: as Frank Schimmelfenning puts it: "The West talked itself into a commitment to admit countries that share its liberal values—and this 'rhetorical entrapment' has subsequently sustained enlargement."[102]

In reality, the various EU countries quite naturally had differing reasons for voting to accept new members from the eastern flanks of the continent. Although Germany and Austria certainly expected most of the gain to arise from their proximity to a new market, in regions where they had close historical contacts, Britain hoped that by accepting such a diverse area, they would block the road of further supranational integration.[103] Furthermore, it is even difficult to speak about "German," "British," or "Austrian" national interests. Certain globalized business circles and their political representation looked for the lavish business opportunities (described earlier) in virgin territory, while average citizens thought about new and cheap vacation possibilities, or about paying their guest-worker cleaning ladies less, or about the "Polish plumber" whose fees were so much lower than his Western counterpart's. Therefore, behind the enlargement rush, more than one motive may be found and must be considered.

The creation of a peaceful continent, however, was among the most important of motives. The Balkan Peninsula was a tinderbox and the disintegration of Yugoslavia in a bloody civil war in the first half of the 1990s, followed by the Kosovo crisis at the end of the century, warned ominously of the potential for violence and chaos. Russia, a humiliated great power, remained a challenge as well.

With its nuclear arsenal and uncertain future, it still represented a potential danger. A Central and Eastern European EU-affiliated zone between the West and Russia, it seemed, would create a major security guarantee.

To exploit this situation, NATO rushed into the region along with the EU. Just a few months after the collapse of communism, the countries of the region were invited to participate as associate members in NATO's Parliamentary Assembly. In 1997, Poland, Hungary, and the Czech Republic were actually invited to join NATO, and they became members in 1999. Three years later, the three former Soviet republics in the Baltic, along with Bulgaria, Romania, Slovenia, and Slovakia, were also invited to join, which happened in 2004. The former Soviet Bloc thus became part of the Western military alliance during the process of joining the EU. The two procedures were closely connected and mutually strengthening.

Returning to the question of moral obligations: probably the West felt some uneasiness after encouraging revolts and promising, but not providing, assistance. They could also have had some unpleasant feelings of moral responsibility. Such factors, however, rarely play a decisive role in politics. The enlargements, it would appear, arose from the overlapping and sometimes reinforcing "interested" calculations of private corporations, the EU, and NATO.

Enlargement towards the Eastern peripheries was definitely a central goal of the Western corporate world, for reasons we have indicated already.[104] Immediately after the collapse of communism, multinational companies therefore started building up their affiliate networks in the region. Attracted by the low-wage environment, they established medium–high-tech—and even high-tech—industries and created new export sectors. Major West European banking institutions acquired almost the entire banking system in the transforming countries. As a consequence of these changes, Central and Eastern Europe found itself remade as a dual economy; that is, as an economy with a relatively backward sector producing for the domestic market, and an advanced multinational sector consisting of finance, several services, and modern technology that exported to the West. In effect, the transforming countries became low-wage producers for the Western European markets—a border land or backyard of the EU. The Ukrainian crisis in 2014 shows these impulses at work in ways that have produced unintended and, to date, negative consequences. As the special subcommittee of the British Parliament concluded in its nine months investigation on the failure of the Ukrainian policy,

> Britain and the EU made a catastrophic misreading of Russia ... and sleep-walked into the Ukrainian crisis, treating it as a trade issue rather than as a delicate foreign-policy challenge ... Member nations [were] insensitive [to the political consequences, when they chose] to negotiate a closer political and economic relationship, known as an 'association agreement' with Ukraine.[105]

Looking for new and better business possibilities, the EU stepped into a dangerous nest of snakes. This step generated the Ukrainian crisis.

Indeed, there was, and seemingly is, a kind of permanent enlargement-hunger among the business circles of the EU that is inseparable from globalization—a relationship already evident in the Cold War enlargement of the 1980s. According to the Community's Economic and Social Committee (a representative of the various interest groups and business circles), the Mediterranean enlargement "was endorsed by virtually all the Community's major economic and social interest groups."[106] Even more telling, the EU's Council of Ministers in 1996 had already envisioned incorporating Ukraine into the EU orbit: the EU, it stated, "wishes to see the Partnership and Cooperation Agreement . . . [to] establish the fundamental basis for a privileged partnership with Ukraine."[107] A few days earlier, the European Commission had also unequivocally expressed the desire to add Ukraine to "the European architecture drawn up by the Copenhagen European Council, to develop partnership relations with Ukraine." From the EU's perspective, the integration of Ukraine would create political conditions that would prevent "any possible return to the former ways," or that would "loosen the grip of dependence upon their powerful neighbor [Russia]."[108] In other words, after the collapse of the Soviet Bloc, the high stakes competition of the Cold War simply dressed itself in new garb.

In April 2007, the Commission presented a new initiative to the Council and the Parliament: a "Black Sea Initiative." The Commission noted that "the Black Sea region is a distinct geographical area rich in natural resources and strategically located at the junction of Europe, Central Asia and the Middle East," and it argued that the EU's presence in the Black Sea region "opens a window on fresh perspectives and opportunities."[109]

In search of more satisfactory and illuminating answers to the question why the EU rushed to enlarge well beyond its original borders, it is important first to try to sketch aspects of the rush to invest in the former Soviet Bloc countries. Capital inflow began almost immediately after the barriers came down. Starting in the mid-1990s, most of the region's countries issued "eurobonds" and easily sold them in the West. Altogether, these brought in about US$5–$6 billion to Eastern Europe by the end of the century. International bank lending also began in the mid-1990s and averaged US$5–$15 billion per year during the preparations for membership. These credits covered about half of corporate funding in the area. In the decade after the Soviet collapse, about 26 percent of capital inflow took the form of loans; the other 19 percent consisted of portfolio investments. The most important form of capital inflow, however, was foreign direct investments (FDI).

With FDI, the facts are extremely telling: in the first one-and-half decades until 2005–2006, Central and Eastern Europe and the Baltic states received US$204 billion FDI, equaling 3–5 percent of their GDP. This amount was significantly larger in relative terms than the FDI in the newly accepted Mediterranean countries in the 1980s—equal to only 1–3 percent of their GDP. The main winners were the Czech Republic, Hungary, and Poland. These three countries received US$135 billion from the total US$204 billion. Foreign, mostly European, multinational companies became dominant in the region. In Hungary, they employed

47 percent of industrial employees, and delivered 73 percent of sold products and 89 percent of industrial exports. Foreign companies provided 82 percent of total industrial investments. In Poland, their employment share was 29 percent and they delivered 59 percent of the country's export. In the Czech Republic, 27 percent of industrial employment, 61 percent of exports, and 53 percent of investments were made by foreign companies. By 2003, the FDI stock was equal to 49, 29, and 23 percent of the Croatian, Bulgarian, and Romanian GDP, respectively.[110]

An additional advantage of investing in the peripheries derived from the EU's policy of assisting backward regions. The Cohesion Policy and Structural Fund assistance for backward regions offered subsidies for peripheral investments. When IBM opened its technology service–delivery center in Wrocław, Poland, as a special subsidy for its US$198 million investment, it received €20 million from the EU. FIAT applied for €25 million for its Polish subsidiaries, and CocaCola gained subsidies for its bottling site established in Hungary. Poland received €67 billion from the Structural Fund to attract multinational investments. As Johannes Hahn, Commissioner for Regional Development stated: "There is a global contest. If we don't participate in this contest all the production sites will go out of Europe."[111]

Western European multinational companies, with manifold motivations, thus flooded into the void of Central and Eastern Europe. Some invested for *market-seeking* reasons—that is, to sell their products or enlarge their retail networks. Nine of the world's top fifteen retail giants and most of the major European retail chains, among them the Belgian Delhaize, the German Metro, the British Tesco, and the French Carrefour, built shopping malls and supermarkets in the region. In the case of the Czech Republic, they built nearly one thousand hypermarkets and by 2002 monopolized 55 percent of the retail sales of the country. They were definitely contending with an American presence: PepsiCo, investing US$1 billion in the region, opened bottling plants as well as retail outlets; McDonald's established a dense network throughout the former Soviet Bloc; and Philip Morris took over three-quarters of the Czech market. To return to the European companies: the Austrian Julius Meinl delicatessen chain bought up a part of the formerly state-owned Hungarian Közért supermarket chain. Swedish IKEA opened seven superstores and a dozen factories in the region. The retail giants often established factories in the countries to secure supply on-the-spot. The German Bertelsmann Company bought up major dailies and magazines in Hungary, Slovakia, and Poland. The Swedish Bonnier owned Latvian publications, and the German WAZ bought media in Bulgaria, Romania, and Serbia. In the Czech Republic, Estonia, and Hungary, Western European companies controlled 85 percent of daily newspaper circulation and the majority of television audience shares.[112] Almost all the major international hotel chains, whether European or American, bought or built hotels, and virtually all of the five-star hotels in the region are now in their hands.

One of the most important market penetrations occurred in the telecom market. The Ameritech-Deutsche Bundespost consortium bought 67 percent of the Hungarian state telephone company. Five leading telecom multinationals made a US$1 billion deal in the Czech Republic. A great part of the Polish telecommunications sector was bought by Ameritech-France Telecom, and the Baltic telecom systems bought by the Swedish Telia and Finnish Sonera companies.

Probably the most significant market-seeking investment activity occurred in the financial sector of Central and Eastern Europe. Almost the entire banking and insurance industry of the region was either established or bought up by leading West European companies such as the Italian Banca Commerciale, the Austrian Erste Bank, the Belgian Société Générale, a consortium of UniCredito and Allianz, as well as by French, German, Swedish, and Finnish banks. The Central and Eastern European region absorbed 25 percent of international financial investments while Asia received only 16 percent. Only 10 percent of the financial capital in the region was in foreign hands in 1990, but by 2004, on average, the figure was 87 percent. In the Czech Republic, Slovakia, and Estonia, the share equaled 96–7 percent. The pay-off with these investments could be significant. Austrian banks, for example, invested 16 percent of their assets but earned one-third of their profits from Central European businesses.[113]

Some European industrial companies focused on *labor-seeking* investments and hurried to Central and Eastern Europe to buy or establish companies. This happened most extensively in labor-intensive production branches, such as textiles, clothing, and furniture, which were eager to exploit the tremendous wage difference between the West and the region. Just after the collapse of the communist regime, the Central and Eastern European wage level, on exchange-rate parity, was only 7 percent of the Western level; a decade later, it was still only 15 percent. In 2004, an autoworker in Slovakia in the Volkswagen factory earned US$5.40 per hour, while at the same company's factory in Germany a similar worker's wage with the high benefits was US$40. Western companies often contracted and sub-contracted certain parts of their production. The export of "light" consumer industries, because of foreign investments, increased during the first years of transformation from 7 percent to 21 percent in Poland, from 11 to 18 percent in Hungary, and from 6 to 15 percent in Czechoslovakia. Every second piece of furniture sold in Germany in the mid-1990s was produced in the German Steinhoff Company's Polish factory. Meanwhile, German clothing factories outsourced so much production eastward that post-communist countries accounted for 60 percent of their output; in Romania 70 percent of the workers in the clothing industry were employed by Western companies. Between 1988 and 1996, outward processing exports from Eastern Europe to the EU increased by 24 percent per year.

In the Central European area, the role of such cost-reduction investments declined sharply in later years. In 1993, 70 percent of foreign investment targeted the consumer goods area in the Czech Republic; in 2002 this share dropped to 16 percent. What had changed? Primarily, the fact that Western companies were starting to exploit new resources in the Central European region—specifically the well-trained cheap labor force in these relatively more advanced countries. The level of labor competence, especially under Western management, made it possible to impose Western technological culture in those countries. Companies started targeting medium–high-tech sectors and locating new factories in areas no more than 500 kilometers (300 miles) from their Western headquarters. In the cases of Slovenia, Hungary, the Czech Republic, and Slovakia, multinationals increasingly channeled their investments into complementary specialization projects.

Several multinational giants bought out technologically obsolete companies and modernized them. General Electric, for example, bought the Hungarian Tungsram Electric Company, and the Volkswagen Company took over the Czech Škoda Works and modernized it. Others, making so-called greenfield investments, built new factories in the region, for example General Motors introduced car production in its brand new Szentgothard factory in Hungary; Volkswagen established a factory in Győr, Hungary and produced engines for Audis for the entire European market; Volkswagen Bratislava in Slovakia became a major producer of the Tuareg SUV and Polo, as well as of bodies for Porsche Cayenne SUVs.

The cost-reductions were substantial. With its Slovakian factories, for example, Volkswagen saved US$1.8 billion on wages and connected expenditures per year. After China, the fastest growing auto-making center in the world was located in Central Europe, which had US$24 billion in multinational investments. Nearly 20 percent of the West European car output was eventually shifted to former communist countries. Volkswagen and FIAT delivered 22 and 10 percent, respectively, and the ten leading multinationals together delivered 82 percent of the Central and East European car production. The auto supply industry also built up a huge network in the region. Two leading companies, Delphi and Visteon, closed five factories in Western Europe and opened fifteen in the East. Sixteen international auto suppliers established firms in Poland in the Volkswagen Company's thirty-one-hectare supply park five kilometers from Poznań.

High-tech multinationals also entered the region. The American General Electric, the Dutch Philips, and the German Siemens built production networks in Hungary for consumer electronics. IBM and Nokia also invested in the country. Sony subcontracted in Poland, Hungary, and Slovakia, and Samsung established a major TV and radio factory. The Japanese Panasonic and the Taiwanese First International Computer started production in the Czech Republic. Bosch and Siemens chose Poland, where the Swiss Brown-Boveri also opened thirteen subsidiaries. By 1997, half of Estonian exports were produced by foreign-owned, mostly Swedish and Finnish, companies and one-third of the Hungarian export was produced by four Western multinationals.[114]

As these statistics demonstrate, investment in Central and Eastern Europe brought multiple and significant advantages and opportunities to Western European multinationals. The rush to invest simply reflects attempts by these companies to capture the competitive advantages offered by countries with good educational systems, acceptable infrastructure, geographical proximity, and extremely low wages; in short the rush shows their determination to acquire and build up an economic backyard.[115] Tapping a population of more than 100 million people for its consumption potential and labor brought the profits associated with economies of scale to European corporations. Transporting labor-intensive branches of industry to a low-wage backyard and significantly enlarging the presence of service branches, including financial services, in that area enabled the EU to rearrange its overall division of labor and cut production costs. All these contributed to bringing about the restructuring of European corporations that was urgently needed to preserve their profits and positions. It seemed evident to the EU that countries offering such economic benefits ought to be incorporated organically into the integrated EU system, first by association and ultimately through full membership, and that such incorporation offered the most reliable way to secure these important economic investments, connections, and effects.

Put another way, this first post-Soviet enlargement eliminated a major disadvantage for Western Europe in worldwide competition. The EU's main rivals in the global economy—the US and Japan—already had important backyards in Latin America and Asia that served all the functions we have outlined earlier. Western Europe, before 1989, had nothing of the sort. With the enlargements, Europe's disadvantage disappeared.

Globalization enlargement is not yet finished and doubts have emerged about the wisdom of accepting anymore former Soviet Bloc nations into the EU. Croatia, for example, which became the twenty-eighth member country of the EU in 2013, just one year earlier, had to jail a former prime minister, Ivo Sanader, for corruption. Was this country really ready for full membership in a union formed by Western political practices?[116] Bulgaria, another example, joined the EU in 2007, but suffers from poverty, lawlessness, and high corruption. Sofia, in July 2013, experienced major demonstrations in which protesters, quietly supported by EU officials, expressed lack of trust in the government.[117] Romania has had similar difficulties. In all three countries, there are reasons to ask whether the significant EU aid has been properly used. Were they really ready for EU membership?

What about the Balkan countries, other than Croatia, Bulgaria, and Romania? Albania, Kosovo, Serbia, Macedonia, Montenegro, and Bosnia-Herzegovina are all either official candidates or waiting to be so designated. Albania and Serbia both applied for membership in December 2009 and, according to the European Commission, may be accepted in 2015; however, acceptance was postponed and the Commission declared that it will not happen in the coming five years. The Serbia–Kosovo Agreement in the spring of 2013 opened a road for both countries to join. Montenegro, having applied at the end of 2008, became a candidate in 2010 and may become a member before 2020.[118] Future acceptances of all these countries definitely requires considerations of security and peace, and also promises yet another extension of the EU backyard with all the economic advantages that has brought to the EU. However, acceptance is problematic.

Of all the EU applicants, Turkey is the most controversial. The story of its acceptance for candidacy reaches back to the Cold War enlargement process and to the Ankara Agreement of 1959. Having been judged unacceptable in the Cold War period, its official candidacy was postponed, only to resurface again in the more recent globalization enlargement period.

Turkey became part of the EU's customs union in 1996, and an official candidate at the end of 1999.[119] Open-ended negotiations stopped in 2005, but were renewed in 2012, only to be delayed again in the summer of 2013 because of the oppressive actions of the Recep Erdogan government against a demonstrating political opposition. According to the Commission, the negotiations now cannot be completed for another ten to fifteen years.

Considering the entire further enlargement program, with all of the Balkan candidates and Turkey, we find the same characteristics and problems as in the 2004–2007 enlargement rounds (see Figure 5.3). The candidacies of Turkey and the

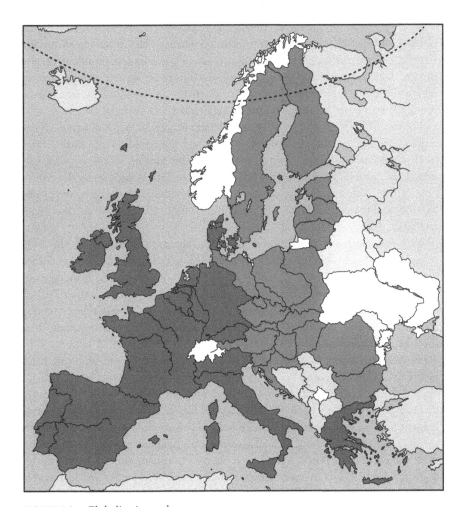

FIGURE 5.3 Globalization enlargement

Notes:
Dark gray: EU members at the end of the 1980s: France, Germany, Belgium, the Netherlands, Luxembourg, Italy, Britain, Ireland, Denmark.
Medium gray: New members of the 1990s and 2000s: Sweden, Finland, Austria, Czech Republic, Poland, Hungary, Slovenia, Slovakia, Estonia, Latvia, Lithuania, Romania, Bulgaria, Croatia.
Light gray: Associates: Iceland, Albania, Serbia, Montenegro, Bosnia-Herzegovina, Macedonia, Turkey.

West Balkans represent an area of great potential with 100 million inhabitants—another large backward market but with an even lower level of economic development than in Central Europe. The poor countries have huge populations and high rates of reproduction, and thus a limitless labor force and an extremely low wage level. Turkey's population has increased eight-times faster than the EU's since 1990. The country's GDP per capita level is only 30 percent of the EU average, and more than one-third of the labor force works in agriculture. The minimum hourly wage is only US$3.14 in Turkey, but in Albania, Kosovo, Serbia, and Bosnia-Herzegovina it is even lower at US$1.20–$1.30. Although the inclusion of Turkey is more than controversial and there is strong opposition within the EU, the official German and British policy definitely favors acceptance. This extension of the EU across the Bosporus would crown the process of globalization enlargement. For Britain, the inclusion of a marginally European country would be a strong guarantee against further deeper integration, and for Germany, it would offer a tremendous additional economic advantage by providing markets and cheap labor.

For the EU as a whole, security considerations play an important role. In this respect, Turkey, a country bordering Russia and the Middle East, with enough local power and authority to act as a bridge to the Muslim world, is potentially extremely valuable. So, too, are the Balkan countries, and consequently the resolution of the explosive Balkan conflicts between Serbia and Croatia, Serbia and Kosovo, and the consolidation of the peninsula under EU auspices are also major end goals.

The economic advantage provided by the opportunity to enlarge the EU's cheap-wage "backyard" towards the Southeast is also evident. When Turkey became part of the European common market, the multinational car manufacturers rushed in to establish new capacities, and today they sell 68 percent of their Turkish production on the European markets. As happened in Central Europe, future accession of the West Balkans immediately attracted huge direct investments from the core countries of the EU. In 2002, the region received US$2.1 billion and by 2008 it had received $13.3 billion in foreign investments. Croatia alone absorbed nearly half of that amount.[120]

Will the Balkan enlargement and Turkey's probable acceptance end the enlargement rounds? This is an open question. Several former Soviet republics are waiting before the door, having already signed so-called Partnership Agreements offered by the EU. The very first to sign such an agreement was Ukraine in June 1996, followed shortly thereafter by Russia. These agreements envisioned the creation of a free trade zone, which was to have come into being in 1998. The EU and its member countries assisted the transformation of the partner countries by sending financial support. Ukraine and Russia together received €4 billion between 1991 and 1997, either directly from the EU (€1.5 billion) or from member states acting individually. The EU wanted a peaceful transformation and friendly contacts with the region.[121]

Ukraine, Moldova, Georgia, and other successor states of the Soviet Union want more than loose association. They look for a new home in the EU. As Nicolae

Timofti, the president of Moldova, phrased it: the signing of a political and free trade agreement with the EU "is the only chance that Moldova has in order to develop itself as a European country and in the European spirit."[122]

These former Soviet republics are far from being prepared for EU participation. Some are quite distant geographically from the EU. Moreover, Russia has not hesitated to take action to reestablish its sphere of interest by open, often brutal political pressure on, and blackmail of, these countries whenever they seem to be moving too close to the EU. In August 2013, for example, as a kind of warning, Putin stopped imports from Ukraine, stating that the situation might become permanent if Ukraine signed a further agreement with the EU. It was even suggested, through an aide, that signing such an agreement would be "suicidal." Russia also banned wine imports from Moldova and threatened to stop exporting oil if that country signed an agreement, a step that the Russian deputy prime minister Dimitri O. Rogozin said would be a "grave mistake." Russian Government officials have been trying to persuade these countries that joining with Russia, Kazakhstan, and Belarus in a new Eurasian customs union would be more productive. Armenia, strongly dependent on its huge neighbor, recently gave up years of work towards EU partnership and, in August 2013, chose that customs union instead.[123]

In Ukraine in November 2013, when President Viktor Yanukovych declined to sign the association agreement offered by the EU and turned to Russia instead, endless demonstrations began playing out, leading to the outbreak in February 2014 of a revolution that ousted Yanukovych from the presidency.[124] The pro-Europe demonstrators in Kiev proclaimed: "We want to live in Europe." But the dream of EU membership harbored by the majority of the population of western Ukraine is not shared in the strongly ethnically Russian eastern and southern Ukraine, or in the ethnically Russian-dominated Crimean Peninsula. Some groups in these regions prefer being rejoined to Russia. The Putin Government first reacted to Yanukovych's ouster by sending Russian troops for military exercises to the Ukrainian–Russian border. Then Russian troops entered Crimea. Although this move violates international principles, Russia has explained it as the annexation of a genuinely Russian territory, a defense of its military base and of the Russian population, which represents a 60 percent majority.

From the Russian perspective, Ukraine lies in the historic and current Russian sphere of interest. Russian actions in this instance differ little from past US policies, for example in Central America where the "Hemispheric Defense" alliance was initiated in 1947, or in Grenada where the US military intervened in the early 1980s, or in Panama in 1989. Unfortunately, the EU has not taken into account the fact that Ukraine, an independent country only for twenty-three years and an area historically merged with Russia, is ethnically and religiously sharply divided: the western parts are West-leaning and Catholic, the eastern and southern parts are pro-Russian and Orthodox.

In 2002, during the US presidency of George W. Bush, NATO, the organization of the Western military alliance, had already made a major mistake when, as a clear provocation to Russia, it offered a Membership Action Plan to Ukraine—in other words, a quasi-invitation to enter the alliance. In 2008, on behalf of Ukraine, then President Viktor Yushchenko and Prime Minister Yulia Tymoshenko signed a statement of intention to join NATO. In the summer of 2010, however, the Ukrainian Parliament voted down this plan. French and German opposition contributed to its cancellation. By offering associate membership to Ukraine in 2013, the EU repeated the kind of mistake made by NATO, albeit not in the realm of military defense. Unfortunately, the EU remained silent when the new Ukrainian Parliament, a politically heterogeneous body that includes fundamental Ukrainian nationalists, chose as one of its very first actions to abolish the official status of the Russian language, thereby endangering the Russian minority's citizenship status, or at least raising the specter of such endangerment. The 2014 Ukrainian civil war and the Russian intervention created an international political crisis. If over-enlargement of the EU is more than controversial in general, then attempting to include a stridently divided and extremely unstable Ukraine just might be suicidal.

The so-called *Mediterranean Challenge*, the relation of the EU with the southern Mediterranean area, might also open new enlargement rounds. In November 1995, the foreign ministers of fifteen EU member states and twelve southern Mediterranean countries met in Barcelona and initiated the "Barcelona Process," a Euro–Mediterranean partnership with Morocco, Algeria, Tunisia, Egypt, Jordan, Palestine, Lebanon, and Syria to establish a common Euro–Mediterranean Area. In March 2000, Mohammed VI, the new king of Morocco, stated during his official visit in France: "After the acceptance of the Turkish candidate, EU membership for Morocco is no longer taboo." The author of a study about the possibility of the southern Mediterranean enlargement, who quoted the King of Morocco, argues: "For the sake of Europe's own interest . . . the EU could and should systematically envisage membership for the Muslim South and South East of the Mediterranean world."[125] Péter Balázs, former EU Commissioner, speaks about "exactly thirty-six countries . . . as potential EU members."[126]

On the other hand, as has been indicated previously, the 2004–2007 enlargements have generated major doubts and opposition. Is there a possibility of a break up of the EU under the impact of previous and potential future enlargements? In the 1990s, an alternative eastern enlargement strategy was suggested to integrate the post-communist countries in "an outer free trade area."[127] Some experts speak about a "'vicious spiral' of continuous enlargements that might overstretch the Union . . . Increased heterogeneity may cause spill-back and a loose Union . . . Further enlargement will cause disintegration and deconstruction of the Union we see today."[128] Acceptance of Bulgaria, Romania, Croatia, and Turkey "may overburden the capacities of the Union and stretch the integration process to breaking point."[129]

Further eastward enlargement is already rejected by some Central and East European countries. Several countries firmly believe that they are the very last real Europeans, while the eastern neighborhood already "belongs to the Balkans," a term long used in a pejorative way. That was the view of a great many Hungarians about the Romanians and of the Croats about the Serbs and Bosnians. The well-known Croatian writer Slavenka Drakulic, in her article, "Heim in den Westen"

(Home in the West), which was published a few days before Croatia joined the EU, speaks about her genuinely Mediterranean country—only an insignificant part of which belongs to the western Balkans—as a place that "returns" to Europe. For her, it is a "homecoming" to civilization and social welfare. The Croats from now on will "play the piano and not the gusla, the typical Balkan instrument." Beyond Croatia's eastern borders, according to Drakulic, people belong to the Balkan's "orthodox culture of the Serbs . . . and the Islamic culture of the Bosnians" instead of the Christian culture of the Croats and the EU.[130]

Giscard d'Estaing, former president of France, speaking on the 2004 eastward enlargement, argued "that this enlargement will water down the community is not a risk but a certainty."[131] Has the predicted danger come into being since the onset in 2008 of the still-ongoing European economic crisis? Could the EU proceed with association and free trade agreements instead of additional enlargements? That certainly is being explored. The EU has launched negotiations with most countries of the world. In the middle of 2013, it had free trade or associate membership negotiations with eighty-five countries of the world and had already signed preferential trade agreements with forty-six countries on six continents. Such an arrangement with the countries now seeking membership could well serve trade and economic interests without exposing the EU to the risks entailed in further enlargement. All these issues remain open to discussion. The newly appointed president of the European Commission, Jean-Claud Junkers, reacting to the gathering criticism and opposition, has stated that "negotiations would continue, but no further enlargement will take place over the next five years."[132]

This does not necessarily mean the end of the enlargement drive, but continued enlargement may indeed endanger the entire EU as we know it. It will definitely further undermine EU homogeneity and block the way of further deepening the integration process. And if the latter were to occur, then enlargement for the EU would have transmuted from nurturing to death-dealing force.

Notes

1 Thomas Pedersen, *Germany, France and the Integration of Europe: A Realist Interpretation* (London: Pinter, 1998), 97.
2 Stanley Hoffman, "The European Community and 1992," in *The European Sisyphus. Essays on Europe (1964–1994),* ed. Stanley Hoffman (Boulder, CO: Westview Press, 1995), 231.
3 "Draft Treaty Establishing the European Union," www.spinellisfootsteps.info/ treaty/47.html.
4 "Single Market Act—Frequently Asked Question," europa.eu/rapid/press-release_ MEMO-10-528_en.htm?locale=en.
5 For the complete text of this Commission document, see Archive of European Integration, "Completing the Internal Market," White Paper from Commission to the European Council, Milan 28–29 June 1985, COM (85) 310 final (14 June 1985). Here I have paraphrased as well as quoted the original.
6 Archive of European Integration, Maria Green Cowles, "The Changing Architecture of Big Business," presented in 1997 at the 5th Biennial ECSA Conference in Seattle (May 29, 1997).

7 Four years later, Delors acknowledged in a speech that the new act would not have been possible without the draft treaty and Spinelli's initiative (see Address by Mr Jacques Delors, President of the Commission of the European Communities (Bruges, October 17, 1989), accessed July 28, 2015, europa.eu/rapid/press-release_SPEECH-89-73_en.htm?locale=FR).

8 See "Single Market Act II—Frequently Asked Question," EU press release, October 3, 2012, europa.eu/rapid/press-release_MEMO-12-734_en.htm?locale=en.

9 Archive of European Integration, Heike Kluever, "Interest Group Influence on EU Policy-making. A Quantitative Analysis Across Issues" (2009).

10 Ibid.

11 Archive of European Integration, "Trade and Investment Barriers Report 2011: Commission Staff Working Document Accompanying the Report," SEC (2011) 298 final (10 March 2011).

12 Archive of European Integration, Maja Kluger Rasmussen, "Lobbying the European Parliament: A Necessary Evil," CEPS Policy Brief No. 242 (May 2011).

13 *The Economist* (November 10, 1990), quoted by Sonia Mazey and Jeremy Richardson, eds., *Lobbying in the European Community* (Oxford: Oxford University Press, 1993), 4, 11.

14 Archive of European Integration, Didier Bigo and Julian Jeandesboz, "The EU and the European Security Industry, Questioning the 'Public–Private Dialogue'," INEX Policy Brief No. 5 (February 2010).

15 Dilek Demirbas, "The EU Regulation on GMOs, Multinational Biotechnology Companies and their Lobby group, EuropaBio," *Eubios Journal of Asian and International Biotechnics* 13 (2003): 11–15.

16 See Beate Kohler-Koch, "Changing Patterns of Interest Intermediation in the EU," *Government and Opposition* 29, no. 2 (April 1994): 166–80 for information about the positive effects of Community directives in the information technology sector. Kohler-Koch describes the Community's research and technology policy as "a good example of successful cooperation between EC Commission and private interests . . . Despite initial opposition from member governments . . . the information technology industry was able to shape the new EC policy according to its own needs."

17 Mark Thatcher, "Regulatory Reform and Internationalization in Telecommunication," in *Industrial Enterprise and European Integration. From National to International Champions in Western Europe,* ed. Jack Hayward (Oxford: Oxford University Press, 1995), 255, 256.

18 Robert Hull, "Lobbying Brussels: A View from Within," in Mazey and Richardson, eds., *Lobbying in the European Community.*

19 "EU Lobbyists Wield their Influence in Brussels," accessed February 18, 2013, www.dw.de/eu-lobbyists-wield. . .brussels/a-16607385.

20 Thatcher, "Regulatory Reform," 239.

21 See UNCTAD World Investment Report 2007, 2, accessed October 16, 2007, unctad.org/en/Docs/ wir2007_en.pdf.

22 On the survey, see John H. Dunning and Peter Robson, eds., *Multinationals and the European Community* (Oxford: Basil Blackwell, 1988), 8, 19.

23 United Nations, *From the Common Market to the EC92. Regional Economic Integration in the European Community and Transnational Corporations* (New York, NY: United Nations Department of Economic and Social Development, 1993), 19.

24 Geoffrey Jones and Harm G. Schröter, *The Rise of Multinationals in Continental Europe* (Aldershot, UK: Edward Elgar, 1993), 41.

25 Ibid., 80.

26 Neil Fligstein, *Euro-Clash. The EU, European Identity and the Future of Europe* (Oxford: Oxford University Press, 2008), 79–80.

27 Archive of European Integration, "Programme for Liberalization of Capital Movements in the Community. Communications from the Commission to the Council, COM (86) (23 March 1986).

28 Andrew Cox and Glyn Watson, "The European Community and the Restructuring of Europe's National Champions," in Hayward, ed., *Industrial Enterprise and European Integration*, 322.

29 Archive of European Integration, "Second Report on the Application of the Council Decision of 28 July 1989 on the Improvement of the Business Environment and the Promotion of the Development of Enterprises, and in Particular Small- and Medium-sized Enterprises in the Community," 1991, SEC (92) 764 final (11 June 1992).

30 Dirk Van Gerven, ed., *Cross-Border Mergers in Europe, Vol. I* (Cambridge: Cambridge University Press, 2010), 328.

31 Neoliberals attacked the state-owned sector and advocated universal privatization. The first steps were taken in Britain by Margaret Thatcher, who transferred more than £5 billion and 400,000 jobs from state to private ownership. Mitterrand's France fol-lowed, in 1986 and 1987, by privatizing all the previously nationalized French companies. Next in line came post-Franco Spain, where a privatization wave began in 1984. Italy, too, sold off the holdings of its previously dominant state sector to private companies. On this see J.-J. Santini, "Les privatizations à l'étranger, Royaume-Uni, RFA, Italie, Espagne, Japon," Etudes coordonnées (Paris: La Documentation Françoise, 1986).

32 Paul Krugman, *The Return of Depression Economics and the Crisis of 2008* (London: Penguin Books, 2008).

33 For the KOF globalization index, see Globalization.kof.ethz.ch/media/filer. . ./rankings_2013.pdf, accessed March 26, 2013.

34 See Article 130F of the Single European Act.

35 Activities of the European Union. Summaries of Legislation, europa.eu/scadplus/treaties/singleact_eu.htm.

36 J.L. Muchielli, "Strategic Advantages for European Firms," in *Multinationals and Europe 1992. Strategies for the Future,* B. Bürgenmeier and J. L. Muchielli, eds. (London: Routledge, 1991), 42–3.

37 Ivan T. Berend, *Europe Since 1980* (Cambridge: Cambridge University Press, 2010), 177–8.

38 *OECD Factbook: Economic, Environmental and Social Statistics* (Paris: OECD, 2007), 149.

39 John Cantwell, "The Reorganization of European Industries after Integration: Selected Evidence on the Role of Multinational Enterprise Activities," in *Multinationals and the European Community*, eds. John H. Dunning and Peter Robson (Oxford: Basil Blackwell, 1988), 36, 38.

40 Bernadette Madeuf and Gilliane Lefebvre, "Globalization of R&D and Local Scientific Systems: Regional Patterns and Local Integration," in *Economic Integration and Multina-tional Investment Behaviour. European and East Asian Experience*, ed. Pierre-Bruno Ruffini (Cheltenham, UK: Edward Elgar, 2004), 55–56.

41 Archive of European Integration, "Commissioner Richard Burke's statement in London on the Channel Tunnel (12 March, 1980)," 1–2.

42 Archive of European Integration, "Eurofocus: A Newsletter for Journalists, weekly no. 8/86 (24 February–3 March 1986).

43 *OECD Factbook*, 110–11; *Der Spiegel,* July 14, 2013.

44 *DE Magazin Deutschland*, no. 1. (2013): 67.

45 eur-lex.europa.eu/summary/glossary/free_movement_persons.html.

46 www.eua.be/eua-work-and-policy-area/. . .the. . ./bologna-basics.aspx.

47 ec.europa.eu/education/pdf/doc125_eu.pdf.

48 http://ec.europa.eu/education/tools/llp_en.htm.

49 Summary of EU legislation, eur-lex.europa.eu › . . . › EU law and publications › EUR-Lex.

50 The first steps were made in the 1960s when the French commissioner, Raymond Barre, responsible for economic and financial affairs, recommended the elimination of the fluctuation margins of member countries' currencies. In December 1969, the heads of member states' governments met in The Hague and accepted the idea of targeting the introduction of monetary union—in the longer run. In March 1970, a special study

group, headed by Pierre Werner, the prime minister and minister of finance of Luxembourg, was appointed to make recommendations on the matter. Because Werner already had a plan for the European monetary policy, the report was ready in October. It recommended a three-stage program to introduce the common currency over a ten-year period. The Werner Plan, however, was shelved. A currency management system was only introduced in 1972, binding the member states' currencies to each other, rather than to the US dollar. In January 1979, a new agreement was made to introduce the European Monetary System. This was based on the recommendation of Roy Jenkins, then president of the European Commission, with approval from the French president, Valéry Giscard d'Estaing, and the German chancellor, Helmut Schmidt. The agreement introduced a European Currency Unit (ecu) to which the European Community exchange rate was bound. Although this reform minimalized exchange-rate fluctuations among the member countries by setting a rate and a band around which it could fluctuate, it was not sufficient enough after the introduction of the Single Market.

51 ec.europa.eu › . . . › Economic and Financial Affairs, accessed December 16, 2015.
52 Ibid., emphasis added. Some of Delor's eloquent pro-federalist statements can be found in Charles Grant, *Delors, Inside the House that Jacques Built* (London: Nicholas Brealey, 1994), 70, 135: "We're not here," he declared, "just to make a single market—that doesn't interest me—but to make a political union . . . My objective is that before the end of the millennium [Europe] should have a true federation. [The Commission should become] a political executive."
53 Michael Burgess, *Federalism and European Union: Political Ideas, Influences, and Strategies in the European Community, 1972–1987* (London: Routledge, 1989), 173: the union was constructed "as a market-based revival . . . [There was however] a gradual shift from market building to state-building . . . [coordinated] social policy, regional economic redistribution, EMU and a single currency, a common foreign and security policy and, ultimately, political union (which meant federal political institutions)."
54 Gespräch des Bundeskanzler Kohl mit Generalskretär Gorbatschov, Moskau, 10 Februar 1990, in *Dokumente zur Deutschlandpolitik. Deutsche Einheit, Sonderedition aus den Akten des Bundeskanzleramtes 1989/90*, bearbeitet von Hanns Jürgen Küsters und Daniel Hofmann (München: R. Oldenbourg Verlag, 1998), 799.
55 Gespräch des Bundeskanzlers Kohl mit Aussenminister Baker, Berlin (West), 12 December, 1989, in *Dokumente zur Deutschlandpolitik*, 637.
56 Ibid.
57 The already cited *Dokumente zur Deutschlandpolitik* contains more than 450 documents on the diplomatic events of German unification in the year of 1989–90.
58 Horst Teltschik, *329 Tage: Innenansichten der Einigung* (Berlin: Siedler, 1991), 61, 228, quoted in Pedersen, *Germany, France and the Integration of Europe,* 131.
59 Gespräch des Bundeskanzlers Kohl mit Generatsekretär Gorbatschow, Moskau, 10. Februar 1990, in *Dokumente zur Deutschlandpolitik*, 796, 799. All translations from this source are mine.
60 Gespräch des Bundeskanzler Kohl mit Staatspräsident Mitterrand, meeting at Latché (4 Januar 1990), in *Dokumente zur Deutschlandpolitik*, 685–86. Mitterrand added that he is French and they have to be careful not to undermine Gorbachev and open the door for a hard liner military dictatorship in Russia.
61 Kohl speech in the European Parliament, Debates of the European Parliament, DEP 3-383, 156–59, November 22, 1989, quoted in Burgess, *Federalism and European Union*, 193.
62 Ibid.
63 Teltschik, *329 Tage*, 61, 228, quoted in Pedersen, *Germany, France and the Integration of Europe*, 131.
64 Recalling the process by which the Economic and Monetary Union came to be accepted by his country, Kohl stated at an interview after he was already out of office: "I wanted to bring the euro because to me it meant the irreversibility of European

development . . . for me the euro was a synonym for Europe going further." Knowing "that I could never have won a referendum here in Germany" about replacing the D-mark with the euro, "[I acted] like a dictator." For these statements, see Valentina Pop, "Kohl Confesses to Euro's Undemocratic Beginnings," a 2002 interview, April 8, 2013, https://euobserver.com/political/119735.

65 Burgess, *Federalism and European Union*, 86–87.

66 Quoted by Harold James, *Making the European Monetary Union* (Cambridge, MA: Belknap/Harvard University Press, 2012), 211.

67 In 1999, the euro was introduced as "book" money while national currencies were still in circulation. The financial market, however, immediately used the euro in cashless operations. Dual pricing appeared in shops, and on January 1, 2002, €144 billion banknotes replaced the withdrawn national currencies of 300 million people.

68 They had to have a high degree of price stability; inflation rate could not surpass the rate in the three best-performing states by more than 1.5 percent. They also could not have undergone currency devaluation for at least two years before joining the euro. They had to show stable long-term interest rates, not exceeding the rates of the three best-performing countries by more than 2 percent. And finally, they had to have a budget deficit of no more than 3 percent and a national debt no greater than 60 percent of national GDP. By 1999, eleven countries qualified for the introduction of the euro.

69 Within this system, the national central banks were clearly subordinate to the European Central Bank. Their governors became members of the Governing Council of the European Central Bank, which also included an appointed, six-member Executive Board.

70 James, *Making the European Monetary Union*, 212, 232.

71 Karl Otto Pöhl of the German Bundesbank, for example, explained at a press conference in 1988 that "European monetary union would be a failure if it were not accompanied by convergence in economic, financial, regional, and social policy." He also stressed, in a statement, that "in a monetary union with irreversibly fixed exchange rates the weak would become ever weaker and the strong ever stronger. Many of the bank governors stressed similar considerations. Alexandre Lamfalussy, the first president of the European Monetary Institute, argued the need "of a Community-wide macroeconomic fiscal policy which would be the natural compliment to the common monetary policy." See James, *Making the European Monetary Union*, 249.

72 James, *Making the European Monetary Union*, 249.

73 Jacques Santer, "Preface," in *Europe Competing in Global Economy. Reports of the Competitiveness Advisory Group*, eds. Alexis Jacquemin and Lucia R. Pench (Cheltenham, UK: Edward Elgar, 1997), 2–4.

74 Address by Mr Jacques Delors, President of the Commission of the European Communities, Bruges (October 17, 1989), accessed October 26, 2015, europa.eu/rapid/press-release_SPEECH-89-73_en.htm?locale=FR.

75 "Common Market Plans Joint Policy in Mediterranean," *Washington Post*, November 11, 1972.

76 For these statistics, see Archive of European Integration, Peter J. Buckley and Patrick Artisien, "Policy Issues of Intra-EC Direct Investment: British, French and German Multinationals in Greece, Portugal and Spain, with Special References to Employment Effects," 11, 116, 118.

77 With the Soviet Bloc collapse, a rush to join the EU swept through the whole group of non-member countries: Austria applied for membership in 1989, Cyprus and Malta in 1990, Sweden in 1991, and Finland, Switzerland, and Norway in 1992. Accession negotiations were opened by the EEC in 1992–93 and closed without difficulty in the spring of 1994. Membership for Cyprus and Malta was postponed, but Austria, Sweden, and Finland were admitted, effective in 1995. In the end, Switzerland and Norway decided not to join.

78 Finland, after two wars with the Soviet Union, the Winter War of 1939 and the Continuation War after 1941, made a deal with the Soviet Union and signed the agreement

of Friendship and Cooperation and Mutual Assistance in April 1948. Due to the Doctrine of Juho Kusti Paasikivi, Finland voluntarily pledged not to challenge Soviet foreign policy interests in return for Soviet promises to preserve Finnish national sovereignty and independence. In other words, Finland adopted neutrality during the Cold War decades. To characterize this political situation, in contrast to the "sovietization" of Central and Eastern Europe, German political debates introduced the new term "finlandization" in the 1960s.

79 The Nokia Company was established in 1865 as a paper mill, later altered to produce rubber boots and tires. After the World War II, the company gradually switched to TV set manufacturing, but it nearly became bankrupt during the 1980s.

80 Fundamental nationalism appeared in Russia. Vladimir V. Zhirinovsky, a rising political star, founded the Liberal Democratic Party and came in third in the 1991 presidential elections, and received nearly one-quarter of the votes in the 1993 parliamentary elections. He wanted to reconstruct the 1900 borders of the Russian Empire, which would have included Finland and Poland. It is claimed by some that he "assisted the Finns to make up their minds by making radical statements about the annexation of Finland by the Russian federation. See Yrjö Venna, "EU–Finland, First Year Impression," accessed 1995, http://aei.pitt.edu/828/1/2.htm.

81 "Finland and the EU. In and Happy," *The Economist* (October 9, 1997).

82 For the path to EU membership in Sweden, see "Sweden in the European Union, A Doubtful Referendum," 3, *Nordic News Network*, based on November 2, 2014 referendum, www.nnn.se/n-model/eu/vote1.htm.

83 Ibid.

84 Ibid., 7.

85 Ibid., 2–3. See also Lee Miles, *Fusing with Europe? Sweden in the European Union* (Aldershot, UK: Ashgate, 2005).

86 For Austria's path to EU membership, see Fritz Breuss, "15 Years of Austrian EU Membership," *Austrian Economic Quarterly* 2 (2010): 166 and 169 especially.

87 Ibid., 171–4, 178.

88 Norway's Government lost the referendum on the question of membership—for the second time since 1967—and the country remained outside, but, as a government report put it, as the "most integrated outsider," bound to the Union by several agreements and laws. Switzerland also declined to join, but then entered into several bilateral agreements with the Union and became a kind of "connected outsider."

89 Gespräch des Bundeskanzlers Kohl mit Präsident Delors, Bonn, 5 Oktober 1989, in *Dokumente zur Deutschlandpolitik*, 1998, 443

90 Ibid., 640. Additionally, see Gespräch des Bundeskanzlers Kohl mit Aussenminister Baker, Berlin (West), 12 December, 1989, in *Dokumente zur Deutschlandpolitik*, 1998.

91 Schreiben des Bundeskanzlers Kohl an Generalsekräter Gorbatschow, Bonn 14 Dezember 1989, in *Dokumente zur Deutschlandpolitik*, 1998, 649.

92 In November 1989, the Commission of the European Union hosted a meeting of twenty-four advanced countries who pledged a US$6.5 billion PHARE (Poland and Hungary: Assistance for Restructuring their Economies) aid package for the two pioneer-heroes of transformation. They also promised to provide US$27 billion over three years, until the end of 1991, and altogether US$62.5 billion over a five-year period for the entire region. In reality, these generous pledges remained a promise, and only US$11 billion was disbursed to six of the region's countries during the first four years of transformation. Including the debt-burden relief to Poland, the only country whose debt burden was severely reduced, the aid package provided to the transforming countries was US$19.1 billion. On this see Krzysztof J. Ners and Ingrid Buxell, *Assistance to Transition Survey* (Warsaw: PECAT, 1995), 34.

93 The European Councils, *1993: Conclusions of the Presidency 1992–1994, Report of the European Council in Copenhagen 21–23 June 1993* (Brussels: European Commission, 1995).

94 Based on Brian R. Mitchell, *International Historical Statistics: Europe 1750–1993*, 4th ed. (London: Macmillan, 1998).

95 Based on The Economist Intelligence Unit, Quarterly Country Reports in Estonia, Latvia and Lithuania, 1st quarter, 1996; European Bank of Reconstruction and Development, *Transition Report* (London: EBRD, 1996); European Bank of Reconstruction and Development, *Transition Report 2000, Employment, Skills and Transition* (London: EBRD, 2000).

96 *The Economist Pocket World in Figures* (London: Profile Books, 2006), 42–3. Indebtedness actually accompanied the entire first stage of transformation. In the early twenty-first century, the debt burden in Hungary and Bulgaria was equal to 80 percent of their GDP; in Estonia, Lithuania, and Croatia to even more, 112–16 percent. Poland's debt service consumed 44 percent of its export income.

97 European Commission, *The European Agreements and Beyond: A Strategy to Prepare the Countries of Central and Eastern Europe for Accession* (Brussels: The European Commission, 1994).

98 In 2011, the ten most polluted cities in the European Union were all Bulgarian and Polish cities. Krakow in Poland and Plovdiv in Bulgaria have more than ten times the air pollution of Paris. Nowy Sacz, Zabrze, and Katowice in Poland are four to five times more polluted than Berlin, Brussels, Amsterdam, or Birmingham. For these figures, see "Bulgaria's Air is Dirtiest in Europe, Study Finds, Followed by Poland," *New York Times* (October 15, 2013).

99 Neill Nugent, *The Government and Politics of the European Union,* 7th ed. (London: Palgrave Macmillan, 2010), 47, 48.

100 For renationalization in Hungary, see Péter Mihályi, "A privatizált vagyon visszaállamosítása Magyarországon 2010–2014," Discussion Papers, MTA Közgazadasági-és Regionális Tudományi Kutatóközpont, Közgazdaság-Tudományi Intézet, Budapest, 2015), MT-DP – 2015/7. The author presents the story of renationalization of more than 200, previously nationalized banking, energy, manufacturing, and other companies by the Orbán Government that look to Putin's Russia as a model.

101 www.transparency.org/research/cpi/overview, accessed 2013.

102 Frank Schimmelfenning, "The Community Trap: Liberal Norms, Rhetorical Action, and the Eastern Enlargement of the European Union," *International Organization* 55, no. 1 (Winter, 2001): 47–80.

103 Backward regions that were eligible for EU assistance had to have less than 75 percent income level than the EU's average. The average GDP level of the EU decreased with the acceptance of the low GDP level of East European countries. Consequently, some regions that previously had a GDP level lower than 75 percent now surpassed that limit and were not any longer eligible for EU aid.

104 Andrew Moravcsik, one of the most well-known political scientific experts on the EU, rejects idealistic explanations: "EU leaders promote accessions because they consider enlargement to be in their long-term economic and geopolitical interest." See Andrew Moravcsik and Milada A. Vachudova, "National Interest, State Power, and EU Enlargement," *East European Politics and Society* 17, no. 1 (February, 2003): 42–57. Richard Baldwin and his co-authors calculated that in the longer run, the EU-15 countries will profit 10 billion dollars from the eastward enlargement (see Richard E. Baldwin, Joseph F. Francois, and Richard Portes, "The Cost and Benefits of Eastern Enlargement: The Impact on the EU and Central Europe," *Economic Policy* 12 (April 1997): 125–76.

105 "Britain and Europe 'Sleepwalked' Into the Ukrainian Crisis, Report Says," *New York Times* (February 20, 2015). The journal's article was based on the report of European Union External Affairs Subcommittee of the British House of Lords.

106 Archive of European Integration, Conference on the Enlargement of the European Community (Brussels, 26 and 27 June 1980), Extract, Economic and Social Committee.

107 Archive of European Integration, "Action Plan for EU Relation with Ukraine, Extract from the Council of Ministers," press release (6 December 1996). The statement dates back to the time of preparations for the admittance of the original ten former communist countries.

108 Archive of European Integration, "Action Plan for Ukraine. Communication from the Commission to the Council," COM (96) 593 final (20 November, 1996).

109 Archive of European Integration, "Black Sea Synergy—A New Regional Cooperation Initiative," Communication from the Commission to the Council and the European Parliament COM (2007) 150 final (11 April, 2007).

110 UNCTAD, World Investment Report 2004 (New York, NY: UNCTAD, 2004), 371.

111 "Multinational Cash In on EU funds," The Bureau of Investigating Journalism, November 29, 2010, www.thebureauinvestigates.com/. . . .

112 Václav Štětka, "The Rise of the Tycoons. Economic Crisis and Changing the Media Ownership in Central Europe," Visegrad Insight 1, no. 3 (2013): 30–1.

113 András Bethlendi, "Foreign Direct Investment in the Banking Sector," Development and Finance, no. 1 (2007); Wall Street Journal (June 2 and November 7, 1995; March 30 and April 5, 1998); Österreichische Nationalbank, June Report (Vienna: ÖN, 2006).

114 Ivan T. Berend, From the Soviet Bloc to the European Union. The Economic and Social Transformation of Central and Eastern Europe since 1973 (Cambridge: Cambridge University Press, 2009), 123–31.

115 Constanze Kurz and Volker Wittke speak of the "twin process of transformation in the East and structural adaptation in the West." For this, see Constanze Kurz and Volker Wittke, "Using Industrial Capacities as a Way of Integrating Central and Eastern European Economies," in Enlarging Europe: The Industrial Foundation of a New Political Reality, eds. John Zysman and Andrew Schwartz (Berkeley, CA: University of California Press, 1998), 64.

116 Ivo Sanader "was jailed for ten years for taking bribes" (see "As Croatia Struggles, Some Wonder if It Won Entry to European Union too Soon," New York Times (July 24, 2013)).

117 For the protest in Sofia, see "Bulgarian Police Break Up Protest Outside Parliament," New York Times (July 25, 2013).

118 "EU Enlargement: The Next Seven," BBC News Europe (July 1, 2013), accessed September 2, 2014, www.bbc.co.uk/news/world-europe-11283616.

119 Archive of European Integration, Annabelle Littoz-Monnet and Beatriz Villanueva Penas, "Turkey and the European Union. The Implications of a Specific Enlargement," Egmont European Affairs Papers (April 2006).

120 Based on UNCTAD World Investment Report, accessed June 24, 2014, unctad.org/en/Pages/. . ./world%20Investment%20Report/WIR-Series.asp.

121 Hermann Clement, "The Case of Russia and Ukraine," in Economic Convergence and divergence in Europe. Growth and Regional Development in An Enlarged European Union, eds. Gertrud Tumpel-Gugerell and Peter Mooslechner (Cheltenham, UK: Edward Elgar, 2003), 415.

122 "Russia Putting a Strong Arm on Neighbors," New York Times (October 23, 2013).

123 Ibid.

124 "Ukraine and the European Union. Day of the Gangster Pygmy," The Economist (November 30, 2013).

125 Arno Tausch, "Towards a New EU Policy for the Mediterranean South?" in Economics and Politics of Europe, ed. Kemal H. Ferthold (New York, NY: Nova Science Publisher, 2008), 2, 3, 7.

126 Wojciech Przybylski, "History Beyond Nations, Interview with Péter Balázs," Visegrad Insight 1, no. 3 (2013): 44.

127 Jürgen Elvert, "The Institutional Paradox: How Crises Have Reinforced European Integration," in Crises in European Integration. Challenges and Responses, 1945–2005, ed. Ludger Kühnhardt (New York, NY: Oxford University Press, 2009), 54, 56.

128 Wolfgang Wessels and Thomas Traught, "Opportunity or Overstretch? The Unexpected Dynamics of Deepening and Widening," in Crises in European Integration. Challenges and Responses, 1945–2005, ed. Ludger Kühnhardt (New York, NY: Oxford University Press, 2009), 81.

129 Michael Gehler, "Challenges and Opportunities: Surmounting Integration Crises in Historical Context," in *Crises in European Integration. Challenges and Responses, 1945–2005*, ed. Ludger Kühnhardt (New York, NY: Oxford University Press, 2009), 109.
130 Slavenka Drakulic, "Heim in den Westen," *Süddeutsche Zeitung* (June 26, 2013).
131 *Frankfurter Allgemeine Zeitung* (October 12, 2005).
132 "The western Balkans and the EU. In the queue," *The Economist* (September 27, 2014).

6

TOWARDS A EUROPEANIZED
ECONOMIC STRUCTURE OF EUROPE

Although the European Community's Single Market, common currency, and enlargement-created backyard owe their existence to joint action by supranational institutions, committed federalist leaders, member states' governments, and big business, the transformation of formerly national economies into a Europeanized economic structure has largely been the product of the actions of a single category of actor, self-transforming European companies that are gripped by "merger mania." "Mania" applied to business mergers is a term that came into use at the end of the nineteenth century to describe the frenzied transformations affecting American business. Mergers themselves, however, are a logical and normal phenomenon in a capitalist economy.[1] In Europe during the 1960s and 1970s, mergers served nation-states as they sought to enhance competitiveness by creating "national champion" companies. Mergers also decisively contributed to the creation of the first cross-border European multinationals in the early twentieth century, but the most intense wave in Europe started in the late 1970s and continued through to the first decade of the twenty-first century. European multinational companies started to expand, to create bigger, more optimal size firms able to take advantage of economy of scale by producing for the entire vast European Community market. The announcement of the Single Market project in 1985 provided a major impetus to this process. Among the results was the expansion of the concept of a home- or domestic-market to cover the new Europe-wide market—this kind of market is the presumed springboard for international competitiveness.

To exploit the potential of this newly defined "domestic" market, national companies went after its consumers and started building up Europe-wide networks of subsidiaries and value chains. They moved their subcontracting to neighboring countries and made "greenfield" investments—that is, they built new factories outside their own borders, in other countries of the Community. Most of all, they engaged in mergers, acquisitions, and organized cooperative ventures, all of which mushroomed in number. Among the results of these expansions was an increased rationalization of production: fewer but bigger firms, well-organized value chains, new patterns of labor division within a specific corporation, specialized production of various components of end products, and the provision of support services to the entire European market all cut production costs and increased productivity. In manufacturing, this dramatic reorganization made corporate Europe competitive. Mergers often led to the building up of enormous corporate empires that employed tens- and hundreds-of-thousands of employees, operated in several branches of the economy in many countries, and, especially in the case of the banking industry, owned enormous assets that were greater than the GDP of their home countries. All the giant corporations in banking, manufacturing, and services took part in this European "merger mania."

Among the giant multinational corporations that did business throughout Europe, the biggest banks of key West European countries played the leading role. The banking and insurance industries had become genuinely more international since the second banking revolution, which had introduced the Crédit Mobilier-type of Belgian and French banking in the 1830s.[2] This was even more apparent after the third banking revolution of the 1860s–70s created the German-type mixed investment banks, which built up huge economic empires within the nation-states, but also across frontiers in Europe.

From the 1960s on, the leading European banks within the EU, especially the French, British, German, and Italian institutions, but also the banks of smaller countries such as Austria or Sweden, turned to all-European businesses instead of limiting themselves to the narrower national market. This process was advanced not only by mergers and acquisitions, but also by branch openings throughout the entire EU.

Europeanizing the banking system

The transformation from national to pan-European company structures began in the financial sector. Until the 1960s, banks in Europe and America restricted their foreign transactions to lending and investing. In that decade, they also began to establish subsidiaries and branches abroad—that is, they internationalized their regular banking activities. American banks took the lead in internationalization. In 1960, only eight American banks had foreign branches with a total US$3.5 billion assets, but by the mid-1970s, 125 US banks had such branches or subsidiaries, with a combined total of US$181 billion in assets. This US phenomenon clearly signaled a new trend and banks in Europe soon followed suit: "Concentration and expansion across the borders characterized the history of both banking and insurance since the 1960s. Dutch banks, for example, had 25 percent of their liabilities in foreign business already in 1965."[3] The City, the banking center of London, followed closely in the American footsteps. Some of the multinational banks formed cross-border consortiums and with their new partners they penetrated the markets of other countries.

In the early 1970s, the area that later became the euro-currency market suddenly and unexpectedly became invigorated. The US$12 billion (later) euro-currency market of eight Western European countries in 1964 grew to US$300 billion by 1977. In the 1970s, after the first oil-shock and the consecutive indebtedness and even financial bankruptcy of several non-oil producing less-developed peripheral countries, multinational banks became very cautious about doing business with them. They turned instead to opportunities in advanced countries. A similar turn had occurred with the collapse of colonialism. The winners were the financial markets of advanced countries.[4] European multinational banks sought out the safety and stability of European Community markets.

Deutsche Bank was one of the major European banks that first reinterpreted the concept of "domestic market" to mean the European instead of national market. At the end of World War II, this major German bank was broken up into ten regional banks. To escape the disadvantages of smallness, these regional entities merged in 1952 into three banks: Norddeutsche Bank, Süddeutsche Bank, and Rheinisch-Westfälische Bank. Five years later, these three united to reestablish Deutsche Bank. Together with some of its domestic rival banks, Deutsche Bank embarked on a policy of international expansion in the 1970s. The large German banks established offices (*Repräsentanzen*) abroad, for example in 1952 Dresdner Bank opened an office in Istanbul and by 1977 it had eighteen outside Germany. Commerzbank and Deutsche Bank also opened eight and eleven offices in other countries, respectively. These offices were transformed into full-service branches during the 1960s, and by 1967 these three German banks had sixteen equity interests in banks in fifteen countries. In 1973, the German banks had twenty-seven subsidiaries and twenty-three branches abroad, but by 1980, these numbers had increased to 101 representations, eighty-four participations, fifty-two subsidiaries, and seventy-four branches.[5] In 1977, Deutsche Bank opened offices in Milan, and then in Moscow, London, Paris, and Tokyo.

However, conditions were not yet satisfactory for the business world. In 1966, the European Commission appointed an expert committee of bankers and financial experts to analyze the Community's financial markets. This committee presented its 380-page report in November that year. "The Treaty [of Rome]," the report clearly stated, "has done no more than fix the objectives . . . and indicate the procedure to be followed in freeing capital movements . . . New laws and regulations of various types will be needed to speed the establishment of an integrated European capital market." It stated later: "In fact, the common market for capital is at present little more than a preliminary plan."[6]

The report painted a disappointing picture of a European financial market where medium- and long-term capital movements were relatively modest. In Belgium, for example, only 10 percent of the bank reserves were invested abroad. Foreign securities were not permitted to exceed 20 percent of the reserves:

> Banks could extend their operations to other member countries by setting up subsidiaries or branches and by collaborating more closely with institutions in

these countries. It would appear, however, that the founding of subsidiaries and branches is not likely to be undertaken on any great scale in the near future.[7]

Several national differences and restrictions blocked the development of the capital market. In some countries financial institutions and insurance companies either were not allowed to invest abroad or needed government authorization for such investment, but "in most cases they are not even interested in doing it."

This situation changed considerably in the mid-1980s after the European Community launched the Single Europe project. It was this act that opened the floodgate for the Europeanization of the banking industry. "The logic of the European financial system," stated the Commission in its proposal to the European Council in 1986, "inevitably leads to the ending of all restrictions on capital movements." Financial loans, money market operations, deposits, and balances on current accounts were all liberalized. The goal was not only a financial free trade system, but rather "the establishment of a Community-wide integrated financial system." Such a system needed standardization of laws and rules governing financial activities.[8] Three years later crucial new regulations, including the Single Banking License or Single Passport in 1989 and then the First and the Second Banking Directive, did indeed transform the environment for finance and open up the flow of money across national boundaries.[9] Definitive steps towards a unified European financial market had been taken.

The principle of "mutual recognition," introduced by the European Court of Justice in its famous Cassis de Dijon ruling in 1979, which was made operational by the Council Resolution of October 1999 and Community Regulation No. 764/2008, simplified the task of harmonizing laws and standards by requiring the acceptance by one Community country of other member countries' rules and regulations.[10] The Single Passport for banks was an application of that principle and meant that a bank licensed in one Community country had the right to do business, including establishing branches and subsidiaries, in all the member countries. This principle, which became a law in the Community, led to the creation of a single body of finance law and regulations applicable throughout the Community.[11] By 2010, 166 French banks operated under European Passport; there were only 106 in 2000. In 2010, twenty-nine foreign bank branches operated in Sweden, Deutsche Bank was the largest after the acquisition of the Oestgoeta Enskilda Bank in 1997.[12]

The introduction of the euro in 1999 eliminated another set of risks associated with currency exchange fluctuations and provided a further push towards financial integration. In this new environment, the main form of expansion became mergers in the European banking sector. Both the removal of currency risk and the legal and regulatory convergence associated with the implementation of the principle of mutual recognition explained the marked increase—40 percent—in cross-border financial activity in the euro area.[13] Directive 2007/44/CE of the EU Parliament and the European Council eliminated another important legal obstacle for cross-border mergers by allowing 50 percent shareholding without the host country's notification. In 2008, the creation of the Single European Payment Area established the same conditions for payments.[14]

National banks became highly Europeanized. As the European Banking Industry Committee stated, "bank mergers in small countries [became] less attractive on the basis of a narrow definition of 'national market' . . . [national banks] not large enough to compete at the European Union level."[15] Bankers at Deutsche Bank, for example, recognized that opportunities were greatest if the focus moved beyond the national domestic arena to Europe as a whole.[16] Indeed, in the 1980s, the bank launched an aggressive expansion with acquisitions in Italy, Spain, Britain, and several other countries within the Community. As a consequence Deutsche Bank became "the largest asset managing bank in the EC."[17]

In the crucial period beginning in the mid-1980s and ending in 2013, a significant enlargement transformed the European Community from a union of ten countries to one of twenty-eight countries. Now the West European giant banks could extend their networks into the less developed peripheral regions of Europe, and they jumped to take advantage of the situation by launching an aggressive expansion campaign: "Cross-border raids multiplied in the late 1980s and early 1990s. Crédit Lyonnais, for example, spent $1 billion in foreign acquisitions between 1987 and 1991."[18] In 1998, 28 percent of all banking mergers were cross-border mergers, but by 2007, the figure had reached 45 percent.[19] In 1986, Deutsche Bank bought Banca d'Americae d'Italia, the Italian subsidiary of the Bank of America, gaining with this acquisition a huge branch network in another European Community country. In 1994 and 1995, Deutsche Bank took further major steps to dominate the Italian financial market by acquiring Banca Popolare di Lecco and Finanza & Futuro Banca. Further expansion within the European Community markets was signaled by the inclusion into the Deutsche Bank Group of the British Morgan, Grenfell & Co. in 1989 and, ten years later, the American Bankers Trust. Banco de Madrid was swallowed in 1993, and five years later the Crédit Lyonnais of Belgium.

After the collapse of communism, Deutsche Bank opened branches and subsidiaries in Warsaw and Budapest. In 2002 it absorbed the Swiss Rüd Blass & Cie and the Russian United Financial Group in 2006. By 2002, the bank had 1,711 branches world-wide, although it still gained 67 percent of its revenue from the "European home market" where 71 percent of its employees worked. It has been noted that "although Deutsche Bank has customers in 76 countries . . . it is not a global company, but a home-region company with a significant presence [in the world]."[20] As the bank's 2013 Annual Report documented, Deutsche Bank had built up a huge corporate empire. At the end of 2012, it had total assets of more than €2 trillion spread throughout Europe in almost 3,000 branches, one-third of them outside Germany; and close to 100,000 employees somewhat less than half of whom worked in Germany. In its shareholding, the bank also had become European. In 2012, 45 percent of its shareholders were Germans and 39 percent EU and Swiss.[21]

The French BNP Paribas also emerged as a pan-European bank. Its existence goes back to the mid-nineteenth century when Comptoir National d'Escompte de Paris was founded. This bank was nationalized in 1945, together with the Banque Nationale pour le Commerce et l'Industrie. In 1966, the two financial institutions merged to become the Banque Nationale de Paris (BNP). This state-owned bank was reprivatized in 1993. In the 1870s, almost a quarter of a century after the founding of Comptoir National, a new bank, the Banque de Paris et des Pays-Bas (Paribas), started activity. With thirty-nine other banks and two financial companies, Paribas was nationalized in 1983 during the leftward turn of the Mitterrand Government, but it was reprivatized in January 1987. In 2000, these two leading French banks—BNP and Paribas—merged to create BNP Paribas. With nearly €2 trillion in assets, it was the world's fourth largest bank in 2012. The bank's official "domestic market" is France, Italy, Belgium, and Luxembourg, but within Europe, it has also operations in several other countries. It acquired the Belgian Fortis Bank to form the BNP Paribas Fortis and also the Fortis Bank Netherlands. In Italy, BNP Paribas took over the Banca Nazionale del Lavoro and its 810 Italian branches. BNP Paribas Cetelem was established in Germany in the 1990s. Its Cetelem network moved into Turkey through the Turk Ekonomi Bankasi, into Ukraine through the UkrSibbank, into Poland through the Bank Gospodarski Żywrosćiowej, and into Bulgaria through its Sofia branch. The bank is also present in Spain, the Czech Republic, Slovakia, Serbia, Portugal, Bulgaria, Denmark, Norway, and Britain. The Magyar Cetelem Bank and the Russian Standard Bank and Sperbank also belong to the network.

Today the BNP Paribas empire is present in seventy-eight countries and employs 200,000 people, 145,000 of whom work in Europe. Although 23 percent of its business activity is in North America, Asia, Africa, and the Middle East, BNP Paribas is a par excellence pan-European bank—31 percent of its business is in France and 46 percent in other EU countries.[22]

The four giant British banks are entirely global with a vital world importance, but they are also strongly European. The largest of these banks, HSBC Holdings, founded in 1865, grew from origins in colonial trade. In the early twenty-first century, it had US$2.67 trillion assets and 6,200 offices in seventy-four countries, and served 95 million customers. HSBC took over the Crédit Commercial de France and today it operates 800 branches in France and another 336 branches in Turkey. The second largest British bank, Barclays Bank, operates in fifty countries and serves more than 50 million clients. It has assets of £1.312 trillion. The value of the assets of the Royal Bank of Scotland Group is US$2.3 trillion, and of the Lloyd Banking Group, £0.84 trillion.

Since the late 1980s, the merger process has advanced by means of cross-border acquisitions. Indeed, mergers might be described as having mushroomed. We have already seen that cross-border mergers represented 23 percent of total merger volume in 1998, but 45 percent in 2007.[23] Among the most high-profile cases were the takeover of Erste Bank in Austria and of Hypobank in Germany by the Italian UniCredito. The UniCredito Group itself had been established by the mergers of several Italian banks in 1998. With 9,000 branches and 148,000 employees, and with divisions in London, Munich, Budapest, and Warsaw, it had also built up a strong presence in the European Community. In Germany, two Bavarian banks formed the German HVB group in 1988, and then, in 2000, merged with the Austrian Creditanstalt. Other significant mergers include the takeover of Abbey National in Britain by the Spanish Banco Santander and the takeover of the Dutch Amsterdam–Rotterdam Bank (AMRO) by collective action of the Belgian Fortis, Royal Bank of Scotland, and Banco Santander in 2007. Like its fellow historical institutions, the Société Génerale, founded in 1864, became a pan-European bank by a collective action, this time of Belgian, French, Italian, and British groups.

The West European countries France, Germany, Britain, Switzerland, and the Netherlands, and the European subsidiaries of American multinational banks together owned about half of the cross-border European banking assets before the 2008 financial crisis. The leading European banking groups not only operated throughout the EU, but they also became all-European by ownership. Investors from foreign countries owned a huge part of their assets: foreign share of the assets of Deutsche Bank accounted for 82 percent, 64 percent for the Spanish Santander, 62 percent for the Italian UniCredito, 41 percent for BNP Paribas, and 29 percent for Société Générale. Each of these banks now has at least 100 majority-owned subsidiaries and more than half have over 500 subsidiaries.[24] As all these statistics hint, European banking is now highly concentrated. According to a report of the European Central Bank (2007) and the European Commission (2008), in 2005 there were forty-six EU banking groups (formed from the total of 8,000 banks) holding 68 percent of total EU banking assets. Of these, sixteen major banks held at least 25 percent of their assets in other EU countries. These major banks have been important drivers of enhanced financial integration at the EU level.[25]

When communism collapsed and the Community started its preparations for enlargement, the leading West European banking groups rushed in to Central and Eastern Europe to invest and build networks. This expansion contributed significantly to the Europeanization of the EU banking sector. Bank lending to Eastern Europe, averaging US$5–$10 billion annually, started in the mid-1990s. By the 2010s, cross-border bank loans were providing about 40–50 percent of corporate funding of the region, and in Albania, Bulgaria, Hungary, Latvia, Lithuania, and Romania, more than 50 percent of private sector loans.[26]

Central and Eastern Europe offered the best business opportunities for Western banks during this post-Soviet period and, consequently, investment capital (US$15–$30 billion per year) flowed into the region. In the Czech Republic, Estonia, and Hungary, it equaled 10–15 percent of national GDP; in other countries about 5 percent. A significant part of these investments was dedicated to financing the acquisition of the backward and poor banks of the region. Italy's Banca Commerciale bought the Croatian Privredna Banka; the Austrian Erste Bank acquired the Czech Česká Spořitelna Bank and also three Croatian banks; the Belgian KBC swallowed the Československá Obchodni Banka and a few years later the Slovene Nova Ljubljanska Banka. Three Bulgarian banks were sold to the

Société Génerale and a consortium led by the Italian UniCredito and the German Allianz.[27] By 2011, the Italian bank UniCredito had a market share of 17, 27, and 14 percent in Bulgaria, Croatia, and Poland, respectively. Austria's Erste Bank had 14, 10, 24, and 21 percent in Croatia, Hungary, Romania, and Slovakia, respectively. By 2011, Austria's Raiffeisen-RZB had 30 percent market share in the banking industry of Albania, 22 percent in Bosnia, and 17 percent in Slovakia. The Österreichische Nationalbank reported in 2006 that Austrian banks had 16 percent of their assets invested in the region, and that "they earned more than one-third of their total profits from Central and Eastern Europe."[28] By 2010, Austria had 842 banks and 4,180 branches, geographically focused in Albania, Bosnia, Bulgaria, Belarus, Serbia, Montenegro, Czech Republic, Croatia, Hungary, Poland, Romania, Russia, Slovakia, and Ukraine.[29] Meanwhile, in the Baltic countries formerly part of the Soviet Union, Scandinavian banks came to dominate: Swedbank had a 62 percent share in Estonia's banking industry, 27 percent in Lithuania, and 21 percent in Latvia, while the Swedish SEB owned 29 percent of Estonian, 16 percent of Latvian, and 37 percent of Lithuanian banking.[30] All-in-all Central and Eastern Europe absorbed one-quarter of all international banking investment of the period from 1989 to 2007.

By 2004, after the EU had taken in eight new countries 80–97 percent of the total assets of local banking were in the hands of West European banks. The Central and Eastern European banking industry had become the most Europeanized within the EU. Foreign-owned shares in the EU averaged 29 percent. In several countries, however, this share was much higher: in Ireland it was 53 percent, in Britain 52 percent, and in Belgium 37 percent.[31] In Estonia, this share was 97 percent, in the Czech Republic and Slovakia 96 percent, and in Hungary 83 percent. German banks were strong in Hungary, Belgium, and the Czech Republic, and Dutch banks in Poland. Austrian groups owned 30 percent of banking assets of the entire region.[32] In other peripheral regions of the world, foreign banking participation was much lower: 39 percent in Latin America and 15 percent in Asia.[33]

Another clear sign of Europeanization of the financial market is that 60 percent of the bonds in the residents' international portfolios are the issues of other euro-area countries. It is estimated that "bilateral holdings [have risen] between member countries by 97 percent for bonds and 62 percent for equities." A typical citizen of the EU-15 holds 35 percent of his equity portfolio in assets issued abroad and his spending is 14 percent for imported goods, and yet the probability that he resides abroad is only 1.6 percent. "Over the last 10 years," a Bruegel Institution analyst has concluded, "there has been a remarkable advance in financial integration in the EU . . . European financial markets today are more integrated than product markets and by a very wide margin more integrated than labour markets."[34] An analysis by the Washington DC-based Brookings Institution added a qualitative judgement: "Europe's monetary union can . . . be seen as the ideal case study for full integration as the optimal treatment of international capital flows."[35]

After this huge wave of mergers and expansion, the top layer of the Europeanized banking industry gained tremendous strength. The top twenty-five banks increased their assets by six times in the two decades between 1990 and 2009. In Europe, fourteen banks had more than €1 trillion in assets. In 1990, no bank had a balance sheet larger than their home country's GDP, but by 2007 seven did.[36] According to the European Banking Federation, of the 8,878 banking entities of Europe 78 percent operate in the EU-27 area and the leading banks have 229,000 branches in the euro-zone. The banking sector employed 3.1 million people in 2011. Sector assets were valued at €46.34 trillion, nearly four times the value of the combined GDP of the 28 countries of the EU. As a clear reflection of the progressive Europeanization of the system, 72 percent of these assets were located in the euro area. The value of loans and deposits accounted for 144 percent and 135 percent, respectively, of EU's aggregate GDP; three-quarter of those loans went to the euro area. The amount of interbank lending was €0.84 trillion; the value of household mortgages per each EU inhabitant was €11,400; deposits per inhabitant were €12,000.[37]

The Europeanizing trend came to a halt with the financial crises of 2008–2009. In 2007, European banks spent US$115 billion on mergers and acquisitions, mostly at the national level. Between 2009 and 2014, the figure did not exceed US$10 billion, and for two of those years, it hovered around US$5 billion. In 2014, inter-European mergers hardly happened at all. February and March 2015 brought stirrings of new life with two inter-European mergers—the Spanish Caixa Bank's acquisition of the Portuguese BPI (for US$1.2 billion) and the Spanish Sabadell's acquisition of the British TSB (for US$2.5 billion), both outside the European core. As one of Sabadell's representatives stated, "cross-border consolidation will come to Europe one day . . . But for the moment . . . mergers are likely to be rare, and confined to markets where banks have too little capital to stand alone."[38]

Despite travails and setbacks, the giant multinational Europeanizing banking industry is the strongest and richest banking sector in the world. Assets are three times the value of those of the US banking sector and four times those of the Japanese. In 2009, one-third of the 1,000 largest European banks held more than one-half of world-wide banking assets and half of the top 100 banks were European institutions. The six largest banking groups, including the four British banks, BNP Paribas Group, and the Deutsche Bank Group, had combined assets of nearly €12 trillion (about US$16 trillion), a figure almost equal to the GDP of the US. The giant pan-European banking groups are much stronger and richer than the European nation-states. Some examples: Paribas's assets equal the national GDP in Russia and Italy; HSBC's assets exceed the value of French GDP; the British Barclays Bank holds assets equaling the combined GDPs of the most developed Central European EU member countries—Poland, Czech Republic, Hungary, Slovenia, and Slovakia; and finally, the combined assets of Paribas and Deutsche Bank equal Spanish, Swedish, Dutch, Polish, Belgian, Danish, and Finnish GDP combined.[39]

Together with banking, the insurance industry also Europeanized. In Europe, this industry is dominated by French, German, British, Italian, Dutch, and Swiss companies. Regarding assets, the French AXA and the German Allianze are the biggest, but the top ten European companies together had more than US$1 trillion in assets at the end of 2011. The companies belong to Insurer Europe, a federation of the European insurers employing about one million people in thirty-four countries. Their annual premium intake is €1.1 trillion and they invest €8.5 trillion.[40] The top companies operate throughout Europe.[41] A European Commission document in 1996 registered that "the Single Market for insurance has now been operational for just over one year . . . German customers are now benefitting from increased competition among insurers selling motor insurance . . . Belgian customers are now buying capitalization life insurance products marketed by French insurance companies."[42]

Europeanizing corporate manufacturing empires

Developments similar to those in banking characterized manufacturing as well. To achieve economies of scale, lower the costs of production, and become internationally competitive, companies targeted mergers and acquisitions as a way of initiating concentrations and building up huge corporate empires. Cross-border mergers, however, were blocked by legal and administrative obstacles. As a report stated in 2008, "cross-border mergers have not been recognized in some EU members until 2003. That was the case in Germany, the Netherlands, Sweden, Ireland, Greece, Finland, Denmark and Austria. By 2007, cross-border mergers were accepted by all member states."[43]

Foreign subsidiaries, therefore, were not widespread in Western Europe. Moreover, because the US had embarked on globalization earlier, many of the foreign subsidiaries that did exist were partly American owned. Ford and General Motors, as well as several other American companies, occupied huge parts of the European market. Greece offers a good example: between 1953 and 1984, US$5 billion was invested in this country, 73 percent of it in the manufacturing industry. During 1953–76, 44 percent of the investments were American transactions. Later, however, European participation increased and the share of the US declined to one-quarter of the total, while France and Germany each had a 30 percent share. Sales of foreign affiliates' products within the European Community represented 25 percent of industrial production. In the chemical and metal industries, this share was 56–58 percent, in electrical machinery and transport equipment 52–53 percent.[44]

Concentration in the 1950s and 1960s, however, took place mostly within national borders, but in the 1970s the number of national mergers declined.[45] Nevertheless, the great interest in mergers expressed by European manufacturers inspired the European Commission to establish a Business Cooperation Centre in 1976 to organize "collective contacts, sector by sector, between Community industrialists and their counterparts." In 1983, a seminar was organized on "cross-border cooperation between firms of Europe."[46] But the merger process would not take off again until later in the 1980s.

Mergers and acquisitions started a process of restructuring in West European industry. Until the late 1970s, the Netherlands was the leading foreign investor in

Europe. Dutch or partly Dutch–British multinationals such as Shell, Unilever, and Philips played the leading role. The latter had established subsidiaries in France, Greece, Poland, Britain, and Ireland. Dutch foreign direct investment (FDI) in Europe doubled between 1975 and 1985. Germany remained behind until 1975.[47] A horizontal merger boom gathered speed and progressed rapidly.

The defense industry provides an excellent example. After the Cold War, "defense contractors around Europe were prepared to join together in mergers . . . This has produced . . . joint product alliances of defense firms across Europe . . . There are three large firms in Europe and an even larger number of alliances that cross-cut the industry."[48] Governments at first preferred joint ventures and subsidiaries instead of direct mergers. Countries turned to single weapon systems, and they pooled research and production. In 1993, French and German defense cooperation started; three years later, Italy and Britain joined in; and later still Belgium and Spain. They established the Organisation Conjointe de Coopération en Matière d'Armament in 1996 to facilitate cooperative production. This organization started managing seven weapon programs, among them the Boxer armored vehicle, the Cobra radar system, and the FSAF surface-to-air-missiles programs. In 1998, Britain, France, Germany, Italy, Sweden, and Spain agreed on rationalizing the defense industry by cross-border mergers, and in 2004 they formed the European Defence Agency. Several important cross-border mergers happened around the turn of the millennium. The French Thomson-CSF bought the British Link-Miles and part of Pilkington Electronics, and also parts of Philips. Four European companies, GEC, Daimler-Benz, Alenia, and Saab, established the Eurofighter program to build new fighter planes.[49] Mergers supported the Europeanization of the aerospace industry. Deutsche Aerospace—part of the Daimler-Benz conglomerate—purchased 51 percent of mostly Dutch state-owned Fokker's stock and reorganized production: the German company produced the 50-, 150-, 400-, and bigger-seaters, and Fokker the 50-, 70-, and 100-seater planes.[50] Nothing could signal the new pan-European industrial merger and alliance trend better than the cooperation of the previously strictly national military industries.

In the 1960s, concentration of industry increased in the entire Community. In Germany, the top fifty firms' market share jumped from 30 percent in 1959 to 39 percent in 1966, while the share of the top 100 companies increased from 37 to 45 percent. Between 1950 and 1960, concentration was fastest in Britain where the largest 100 companies produced 33 percent of output in 1958, compared to 22 percent in 1948. By 1976, concentration in manufacturing was such that the 100 largest corporations in the Community produced about 30 percent of output and employment; they were also responsible for 30 percent of European Community's exports. The fifty largest companies alone increased their share of manufacturing output from 15 percent in 1965 to 25 percent by 1979.

In the car industry, between 1970 and 1986, there were twenty-three horizontal mergers and acquisitions and thirty-three major joint ventures. General Motors and Volkswagen led the way with six joint ventures each, followed by FIAT with five and Ford Europe with four.[51] Between France, Germany, Italy, and Britain, in the years between 1975 and 1986, 954 collaborative agreements were signed, 50 percent of them among European Community firms, another 25 percent between Community and American firms, and 13 percent between Community and Japanese firms.[52] Even before 1975, subsidiaries from other West European (and American) companies played an important role in manufacturing in the Community: in 1974, 44 percent in Belgium; 25 percent in Germany; 21 percent in France; and 14 percent in Britain. Outside the Community, the shares were somewhat lower: 23 percent in Austria; 11 percent in Spain; 4 percent in Finland; and 6 percent in Sweden.

The participation of other countries' subsidiaries varied from one industrial branch to another. In the French chemical industry, it accounted for 30 percent, in mechanical engineering 24 percent, and in electrical goods 22 percent. In Germany, 40 percent of iron and steel, 30 percent of electrical goods, and 24 percent of motor vehicles. In Italy, 25 percent of mechanical engineering, 23 percent of chemicals, and 21 percent of food, drinks, textiles, and clothing.

Foreign companies provided 52 percent of the sales of agricultural machinery in France, 83 percent in Britain, and 23 percent in Germany. In the mid-1970s, in electrical products and electronic appliances 37 percent and 18 percent of sales, respectively, in France were accomplished by foreign subsidiaries; 51 and 73 percent in Germany; 45 and 62 percent in Italy; and 77 and 54 percent in Britain. In Germany, 23 percent of sales of all industrial goods were sold by non-German companies. In Britain this share was also 23 percent in 1973.[53] One author writing in the early 1990s, said:

> The great increase in mergers in Europe during the 1970s has now made the largest European firms comparable to the largest American ones . . . Unlike the US trend the European merger boom was predominantly one of horizontal merger between competing firms in the same industry.[54]

Observing globalization from the vantage point of the mid-1990s, another author wrote that "rapid internationalization is running amok: corporate investments across frontiers grew four times faster than world output, and three times faster than world trade between 1983 and 1990."[55] Far from being restricted to Europe, this internationalization was a world-wide phenomenon, but after the Single Market project was launched in Europe, cross-border mergers and acquisitions gained a special importance and significant new impetus. The United Nations Department of Economic and Social Development reported: "Since 1985, there has been a surge of cross-border acquisitions involving EC firms."[56] Already in the very first years between 1985 and 1987, there were fifty-seven important mergers and the top nineteen firms bought thirty-one of them. Additionally, forty-three joint ventures began operations during those years. The top nineteen firms were involved in twenty-eight joint ventures, 84 percent of them targeted joint production and marketing, and 16 percent joint research.[57] Among the 1,000 largest firms, 117 mergers occurred in 1982–83, but 383 in 1987–88, 492 in 1988–89, and

662 in 1989–90. Purely national mergers declined by nearly 20 percent. Mergers within industries were the most numerous in the high-tech sector and more than 40 percent in the industrial sectors, while only 16–25 percent in other sectors. At the end of the 1980s, for the first time in history, American takeovers were fewer in number than their European counterparts in every single European Community country.[58]

Quite characteristically, this Europeanization started first in the most competitive high-tech industries where the failure of national policy became evident very quickly. The aircraft and satellite launcher industries offer telling examples. Wayne Sandholtz, in his study on high-tech cooperation, described this early all-European industrial cooperation: "European collaboration in space technologies began after purely national space programs proved untenable. The sheer scale of national investment required to join the space race led national policy-makers to return to cooperation."[59] As early as 1964, the European Launcher Development Organization and the European Space Research Organization were ratified. In the Ariane Program, the first rockets were launched in 1979. Twenty years later, with the contribution of the leading West European countries and French leadership, it had conquered half of the international market for commercial satellite launchers. Similarly, French Aérospatiale and Deutsche Aerospace jointly established the Eurocopter Company to produce helicopters. British Aerospace, Alenia, and CASA joined these two companies to produce military transport planes. Aero-engine production was also Europeanized: in the early twenty-first century helicopter engines are produced by Rolls-Royce and Turboméca, and small plane engines by Rolls-Royce and BMW.[60]

The high-tech aircraft industry had a similar development. Britain started with its Comet program, but failed. Germany only had the possibility of entering this area with cooperation from other Western countries. The Report of the Committee of Inquiry into the Aircraft Industry, chaired by Lord Plowden (Plowden Report), which was discussed in the House of Commons in Britain in December 1965, concluded "that the only hope for British civil aviation lay with European collaboration. The French reached a similar conclusion and Airbus was born." The idea emerged at the Paris Air Show in 1965, and on December 18, 1970, the Groupement d'Intérêt Économique was founded. The French Sud Aviation, the German Airbus, and the British Hawker-Siddeley established a cooperative production plan. The German share was 37.9 percent, the French 37.9 percent, the British (after having left and then returned in 1979) 20 percent, and the Spanish Constucciones Aeronauticas 4.2 percent.[61]

The collaborating countries started building the A-300 Airbus for 250–270 passengers. France produced the cockpit, flight control, and the lower center section of the fuselage. Britain produced the wings, Germany the forward and backward fuselage sections and the upper center section, the Netherlands the spoilers and flaps, Spain the horizontal tailplane, and Rolls-Royce the engine. However, they had to import 40 percent of the parts from the US. The A-300 started flying in 1973.

By the time the A-320 Airbus project started in 1988, imports of American parts had dropped to only 8 percent. By 1984, Airbus had penetrated 18 percent of the world market, but Boeing, the previously unchallenged American company, still had a dominant 54 percent share.[62] Airbus's newest project, the A-380, challenged Boeing by producing the largest airliner, a double-decker 40 percent bigger than Boeing's 747-8. By 2013, more than seven thousand Airbuses were in operation. Airbus, with half of the world's orders, now truly shared the market with Boeing.

In 1992, the European Commission analyzed the situation in the European aircraft industry and found that this industry, with its several thousand factories and national champions supported by member states, had an economy of scale more limited than in the US. Its prescription was more thorough integration. The report showed that within the EU there were seven aeronautical research centers. It evaluated the rate of duplication as 20–30 percent and the consequent loss due to excess expenditure as 20 percent. European standardization, the report surmised, might reduce production costs by another 20 percent. It estimated that 10,000 of the existing standards were necessary, but that two-thirds of those were company standards, 20 percent national, and only 10 percent EU. By 2000, it argued, half of the standards ought to be European and international, while national standards ought to have disappeared.[63]

Cooperative research and production produced positive results, not least of which was the merger mania that swept through Western Europe. Siemens and UK's GEC jointly acquired the British Plessey, and the French Carnaud and the British Metal Box merged to form CMB Packing. French corporations led the way in the frenzy of the late 1980s and early 1990s, with 775 deals worth £37 billion. American multinationals had 886 deals with £30 billion value in Europe; Britain had 982 deals with £20 billion value. Britain became a major target: France had 925 deals with a value of £23 billion; Germany 901 deals worth £22 billion; and Spain 489 deals worth £4 billion. In 1989, French state-owned companies spent 11 billion francs on British acquisitions.[64] Among the many examples that might be given, I offer these: French and Italian groups battled for control of Société Général de Belgique in the late 1980s and for the Perrier Company in 1992. In Germany, the Feldmühle packing company, the Hoesch steel factory, and the Sabol lawnmower manufacturer became foreign controlled. The Italian Finmeccanica, part of IRI holding company, acquired 45 percent of SGS-Thomson, the French public semi-conductor enterprise.[65] Air France took majority share of the Belgian airline, Sabena, and in 2004, in one of the biggest mergers of the airline industry, joined with the Dutch KLM to establish Air France–KLM. The result of this giant merger is an airline group that employs 100,000 people and with 573 planes, carrying 77 million passengers per year to 103 countries.[66] In 1999, the giant British Steel merged with the Dutch Hoogovens and the new joint company became the biggest steelmaker of Europe. A series of mergers followed in the European steel industry.[67]

An article on the ceramics industry, titled "From Giants to Mega-Giants," tells a typical, and by now familiar, story about mergers in the 1990s:

> As with other industries, the ceramic industry has undergone much change over the last few years, with a myriad of mergers and acquisitions. 1996 was

no exception ... Saint-Gobain continued its domination of the advance ceramics industry with its acquisition of Carbomudum. In fact, Saint-Gobain could be considered the world leader in ceramics and glass overall.[68]

The Flare Group acquired several other suppliers for ceramics industry: CMS a supplier of ultraviolet light ceramics printing technology; Bricesco, the largest ceramics kiln builder in the UK; Gibbons Refractory Ltd, a UK manufacturer; and Thermic Design Ltd, a manufacturer of ceramic dryers.

By 1995, as was reported in a collection of papers on European integration, the European Commission was already aware of a dramatic increase in the numbers of mergers and acquisitions "in the run up to [and after] the completion of the internal market."[69] Between 1990 and 2011, 4,857 merger and acquisition notifications were sent to the European Commission. In 1990, there were only eleven; in 1995 110; but 300 annually between 1998 and 2000. More than 90 percent were accepted and approved.[70] Cross-border purchases increased from US$86.5 billion in 1990 to US$386.8 billion by 2005. In 2005, in giant cross-border mergers (deals of US$1 billion or more each), Europe dominated the world. Only twenty-six such mergers happened in America and Asia combined, but 107 within the EU.[71]

Major European multinationals often launched wild acquisition battles within Europe. A good example is the case of Electrolux, which acquired 200 units in fifteen countries, including large units such as Zanussi, White, Thorn EMI, and Appliances.[72] Another exceptional example is the Sanofi Group, headquartered in Paris, which was the world's fifth largest pharmaceutical company (in terms of prescription drug sales) in the early twenty-first century. It was established by the merger in 2004 of Aventis and Sanofi-Synthélabo, the second and third largest French pharmaceutical firms. The history of this giant corporation is actually a series of mergers. Sanofi-Synthélabo (founded in 1999) had the pre-histories of Sanofi, which was founded in 1973 as a subsidiary of the French oil company Elf Acquitaine, and also of Synthélabo, founded in 1970 by the merger of two French laboratories and then swallowed by L'Oreal. Aventis, the other branch of the 2004 deal that created the Sanofi Group, had been founded in 1999 as an outcome of the merger of the French Rhône-Poulenc with the German Hoechst Marion Roussel, the latter a company established in 1995 by Hoechst together with the French Roussel Uclaf and the American Marion Merrell Dow. The Sanofi Group spent US$17 billion between 2008 and 2010 on further acquisitions and mergers and strengthened its consumer healthcare and generics businesses. In 2008, the company bought the Prague-based Zentiva and, in 2010, the Polish Nepentes Pharma, a cosmetic firm.[73]

As a consequence of this frenetic activity, the value of FDI in the EU-27 region, which was only US$5,128 million in 1970, surged to US$857,118 million by 2007. EU countries investing in each other accounted for a lot of this increase. Even Denmark and Britain, both of which invested less outside their own borders than other EU members, channeled 69 and 72 percent, respectively, of the FDI they did make into the EU-27 region. Other EU countries made 89 percent of foreign investments in France and 77 percent in Germany. These shares were even higher in the EU peripheries. In Portugal, since its acceptance by the European Community, for example, 69 percent of FDI came from the Community countries.[74] In the recent candidate countries on the peripheries, the pattern was even more pronounced: in the Czech Republic 92 percent of foreign investments originated from EU countries; in Poland 91 percent; and in Slovakia 94 percent. Between 1998 and 2010, 136 large mergers and acquisitions happened in Croatia; 380 in Romania, and 194 in Bulgaria. Between 1998 and 2010, a total of 43,391 mergers happened in the EU, more than two-thirds of the 60,180 mergers in the entire world.[75] "The largest European corporations," an analyst concluded in 2008, "have made most of their investments in the past twenty years within Europe . . . The interlocking of the economies of Western Europe . . . has gone a great distance."[76]

During the 1990s, the EU attracted 40 percent of the world FDI and became the "largest recipient of multinational activity. Multinationals account for a grow-ing share of gross fixed capital formation in Europe (from 6 percent in 1990 to over 50 percent in 2000)." The majority (60 percent) of the multinationals that are working throughout Europe are from Europe. The authors of the study from which I have taken these statistics sum up the outcome of their research by saying "country borders do not matter." They quote the 2012 Eurostat report that 72 percent of total inward FDIs during the 1990s have been intra-EU flows.[77]

As they proceeded with their mergers and acquisitions, European industrial companies also built up large, all-European value chains. By 2001, according to a 2013 European Central Bank study, foreign value added in corporate output "was to a major extent sourced from other euro area countries." In intra-EU trade, 32 percent of imports were parts and components in 1990, and 36 percent in 1997. In 2011, 30 percent of the parts in EU export products were actually "imports" from companies' own value chains. Between 2000 and 2008, the Global Value Chain Participation Index significantly increased, a change "which points to an increase in the vertical specialization of production." The European Central Bank study concluded:

> Internationalization of production and, more specifically a higher degree of vertical integration into global value chains provided in recent years critical stimulus to the European economy. First, it fostered an industrial restructur-ing both across the European economies . . . which allowed European firms to vertically specialize in those activities in which they have a comparative advantage.[78]

A European Commission document of 2012 presents a similar picture of an inter-nationally "increasingly fragmented" manufacturing production in Europe, one in which the end products of a company are not produced by one or a few factories any longer, but consist of parts produced in dozens of factories in networks flung far and wide across Europe. Imported intermediaries are the highest in the chemical and electrical industries where nearly one-quarter of parts come from the foreign value chains. The food industry exhibits the lowest level of such Europeanization, with imports from non-domestic value chains accounting for only 8–9 percent of total product. In most EU countries, this share in the manufacturing industry in general is 30 percent, with regional variations: in Germany, Italy, France, and Britain this share increased from 15 to 20 percent between 1995 and 2008; and in the Netherlands, Belgium, Slovakia, and Hungary it jumped from 25 to more than 40 percent. Regional value chain contribution to output in the world is the highest in the EU, nearly 30 percent; in the US and East Asia this share is only 16 and 10 percent, respectively. The global value chain income in Europe totaled US$2.5 trillion (in Germany US$0.65 trillion; Italy US$0.36 trillion; France US$0.31 trillion; Britain US$0.27 trillion), in the US US$1.4 trillion and in China US$1.1 trillion.[79]

In the all-European value chains, the small- and medium-sized companies gained prominence and a great many companies from this category, in spite of their small size, also became Europeanized. This was especially true in the high-tech sector where several small- and medium-sized companies were, one might say, "born-global." But even in older sectors like clothing, several Italian small family companies, for example, were internationalized by production agreements.[80]

The *Supply Chain Standard Magazine* reported in 2008 on the outstanding case of the Nokia–Siemens Network. The merger of the two companies' networks was accepted by the Commission in 2006. This created an "end-to-end supply chain" that reduced installation cost per installed system by 50 percent and service installation cost by 20 percent, while it increased installation engineering productivity by a factor of 2–3.[81] This started in Germany and followed in other countries.[82]

Giant European multinationals, built by mergers and acquisitions into huge corporations with widespread foreign value chains, were the first to transform themselves into true pan-European companies. The initial formative processes were already underway in the nineteenth century, as I have already indicated, but the development of true pan-European status would have to wait until the establishment of the Single Market to bear fruit for the European economy.

The famous Bayer Group, as one example, originated from the firm that was established in 1863. It owed its success to the invention of aspirin, the most successful medicine in history. Bayer was already an international corporation between the 1880s and 1914. In 1925, it merged together with BASF and Agfa to establish I.G. Farben Industries. Because of the company's role in the Nazi war economy and genocide, the Allied Forces dissolved the company and mostly confiscated its assets. In 1951, however, Bayer was reconstructed and by the end of the century had already several sub-groups, for example Bayer Healthcare, Bayer Crop Science, and Bayer Material Science. The company established a huge European network of subsidiaries: a factory in Antwerp, its largest research facility in Turku, Finland, and the Lyon Crop Science unit. Bayer had five production facilities in Italy, eight in the Netherlands, units in Newbury and Berkshire in Britain, and also subsidiaries in Spain, Switzerland, and, after the collapse of communism, in Poland, Hungary, and Serbia. In 2013, the Bayer Group owned 150 companies in Europe and employed 53,600 people, more than 18,000 of whom were outside Germany. The company's European sales surpassed €15 billion in that year. Bayer had become an all-European company.[83]

One of the world's most powerful multinational firms is the ThyssenKrupp Corporation. The history of this mega-company goes back to the early nineteenth century when Friedrich Krupp started his mining and iron producing firm in 1811. Half a century later, August Thyssen started his coal and iron business, and by 1871 was the owner, with his brother Joseph, of Germany's major heavy industrial firm. By 1925, Fritz Thyssen absorbed several coal, iron, and steel companies in the Ruhr area into the Thyssen Group. Parallel with that, Krupp, Germany's leading military industrial company, also enlarged dramatically. Both companies served the Nazi regime and Hitler's war efforts. After World War II, both were consequently put under the control of the Allies and placed on the list for dismantling. This program, as discussed before, stopped in 1949, and the companies were given back to the two families in 1953. Further enlargement and mergers followed. Krupp, for example, acquired the major Ruhr iron and steel company, Hoesch AG in 1992. In 1999, Thyssen and Krupp merged into ThyssenKrupp. The new corporation engaged in an impressive multinational expansion, including in the US and Brazil. By 2009, ThyssenKrupp operated in eight business areas, owned 670 companies in eighty countries, and employed 150,000 employees worldwide. Beginning in the later twentieth century, the corporation, like other European multinationals, turned strongly towards Europe: it started producing stainless steel in Italy and elevators in Spain. Overseas operations remained important but accounted for barely more than one-fifth of the company's worldwide activities. Based on revenue, one-third of ThyssenKrupp's operation occurred in Germany, a total of 61 percent within the EU.[84]

The Siemens Group is another multinational raised in 1847 from nineteenth-century beginnings. By World War I, it became a giant firm with 34,000 employees. Between 1985 and 2012, Siemens incorporated several other companies, at least one per year. Its four divisions—Industry, Healthcare, Energy, and Infrastructure and Cities—employ 360,000 people in 190 countries; its R&D section alone employs nearly 28,000 people. The Siemens Group dominates the European markets.[85]

The French company L'Oreál gradually launched a bold merger and acquisition drive and became the owner, among others, of Cacharel, Garnier, Helena Rubinstein, Lancôme, Vichy, the American firms Maybelline and Kiehl's, and the Japanese Shu Uemura. In 130 countries, the company has 238 subsidiaries and employs 50,000 people. Sixty-eight percent of them work outside France. Its main market, however, is Europe where it sells half of its production. L'Oreál is listed as 415th among the world's top 500 companies.[86]

The history of the Daimler-Benz company also follows a typical trajectory—a transition from a single branch (car producer) to a diversified corporation and from a national to an international, European corporation. Without reciting the story from its beginning with the foundation of the company in 1890 and its later development, it seems enough to start with the company's immediate postwar situation. During the war years, the company produced products for the army, its income doubled, and by 1943–44, its workforce increased by 50 percent to nearly 65,000. As a consequence of the war, however, the company's income in 1945–46 dropped to one-tenth of that of the most profitable war year, and the number of employees to one-fifth of that level. By 1949, as part of the most successful reconstruction of the country, Daimler-Benz's situation improved, its income climbed to one-third of the final war year's level, and the labor force to half of it.

After the rapid postwar reconstruction, the company started to internationalize from the 1950s on. Initially, exports were important: in 1950 only 13 percent of Daimler-Benz's production was exported, but by 1957, exports had increased to 42 percent. From its exports, 38 percent went to other European countries. The company's first foreign subsidiaries were established in Argentina (1951), Brazil (1953), and in India later in the decade. A major breakthrough came during the 1960s when Daimler-Benz became a real international corporation by building up a network of subsidiaries and production sites abroad. In the rise of the company, as one chronicler of the firm stated, the "foundation of the EEC and EFTA played a determinant role." Subsidiaries were established in Spain and Turkey, and somewhat later in Belgium and Switzerland and several other countries. Production and employment abroad, which did not exist before 1960, had already a 14 and 13 percent role in the work of the corporation a decade later, respectively. Whereas Daimler-Benz owned only forty-one foreign companies in the late 1970s, its foreign holdings increased to 102 by the mid-1980s. These foreign subsidiaries employed about 20 percent of the labor force of the multinational company and produced one-third of its total production. The same Daimler-Benz that had invested less than 10 percent of its total investments abroad in 1970 had increased its share of foreign investments to more than 30 percent by 1985.

To maintain and even improve its place in the global competition, Daimler-Benz also diversified its production. Besides its original car business, the company also entered into airplane production (with 63,000 workers) and joined French, British, and later Spanish and other companies in the most successful European Airbus program. Through its 80 percent ownership of AEG, the corporation also entered into the electronics industry (with nearly 73,000 employees) and changed its name to AEG Daimler-Benz Industry. In 1990, a service and financial arm was established as well.

Diversified international operations led to doubling the annual sales income in ten years between 1985 and 1995. The company's labor force jumped from 231,000 to 311,000 in that decade, but the share of auto production in the output of the corporation declined from 93 to 68 percent. Although traditional multinational operations continued on various continents, especially in North America where 19 percent of the corporation's production originated, the real center of operation became Europe. More than 64 percent of the turnover of the corporation was produced in the old continent (including Germany's 37 percent share). The corporation's Eurocentrism is clearly expressed by the fact that the affiliated foreign companies were 70 percent European, 15 percent North American, and another 15 percent Asian, African, Latin American, and Australian together.[87]

The market of the 100 largest European companies is, as a Bruegel Policy Brief presented,

> increasingly Europe as a whole rather than any particular country within it. The companies' revenue comes by 65 percent from Europe. This share is the same as with US top-100 companies' revenue from US ... German companies are among the frontrunners of both Europeanization and globalization ... French companies have Europeanized rather than globalized.[88]

It pays to take a closer look at the especially interesting case of the European car industry. This industrial sector, endangered by American and Japanese competition in the European markets and losing their overall market share to invading rivals, was one of the forerunners of the expansionist renewal in Europe. In a 1976 study of the auto sector, the European Commission strongly underlined the need for further transnational concentration and cooperation among European companies. It would be important, the analysis stressed, to set up assembly production in low wage countries. It also noted that financial assistance from the EC would be needed for forward-looking research and development, especially in the development of electric cars.[89]

In 1981, the Commission returned to the topic and concluded that between 1970 and 1980, while the European car industry remained stagnant and its exports declined by nearly one-quarter, the rival overseas industries had made significant progress. The cost of production in the Japanese car industry had dropped 20 to 30 percent lower than in Europe. The leading Japanese corporations had built up a huge network of value chains and subsidiaries and were subcontracting 65–80 percent of the work within their networks, while the top European carmakers were subcontracting only roughly half of the production of parts and accessories for the cars they manufactured. In America and Japan, the report noted, the two top producers controlled 75 percent of the market. European car companies were just not big enough. Although the American General Motors produced 8.5 million cars and Ford 5.2 million, Volkswagen and Peugeot–Citroën produced only about 2.5 million each. Unit cost would drop by half if 500,000 vehicles were produced instead of 100,000. Productivity, the report observed, was much lower in Europe where the assembly of a car in some companies required more than 55 hours and averaged about 35.3 hours, more than twice as much as Japan's 16.8 hours. In Japan, 350 companies were producing components for cars; in Europe component producers were smaller and fragmented, and there were 1,750 such producers. Reorganization, the report noted, was badly needed. European carmakers would have to

> start to think in Community rather than national terms, particularly as far as component manufacture concerned ... Cooperation between European

companies would thus seem to be the best way of achieving these aims at present ... Only if this condition is fulfilled can economies of scale be fully exploited.

A homogenous internal market would give "an important advantage for the Community automobile industry." To help this process, the 1981 analysis concluded that the Community had to introduce "all-European standards, eliminate heterogeneous regulations and the huge differences in vehicle purchase taxes ... [The Community rejects the] compartmentalized conception of the various markets."[90]

During the 1970s and early 1980s, however, in spite of the Commission's realistic evaluation of the situation, the European Community could not really make radical changes to these conditions. In contrast, the corporate world could and did. As in other sectors, mergers, including cross-border mergers, and the establishment of subsidiaries and value chains in several member countries, including in the low-wage peripheral European countries, started in the 1970s. In the case of the auto industry, huge internationally competitive industrial empires were the result. Between 1970 and 1986, twenty-three horizontal mergers occurred in the car industry and thirty-three major joint ventures were formed. Among the world's twenty largest corporations, Volkswagen rose to nineteenth place.[91]

When the European Commission returned to the situation of the car industry one-and-half decades later in 1996, it found rather different conditions. Europe's share in world car production—29 percent—surpassed both the American (24 percent) and Japanese (21 percent) contributions. Several major carmakers had established subsidiaries in the new member countries on the European peripheries. The first one had been founded in Ireland, others followed in the 1980s in Spain and Portugal, and after the collapse of communism, from the early 1990s, in Central and Eastern Europe. The Community's carmakers were producing 80 percent of their total production within the Community.

Significant concentration characterized the first-tier supplier industry as well. The number of companies—10,000 in 1970—had dropped to 3,000 by 1996 and, as the Commission forecast, shrank to 500 by 2000. The European companies invested 6 percent of their turnover; the Japanese only 4 percent. Community standards for vehicle types had at last replaced national standards.[92] By 2007, the top European automakers were already producing for the entire European market. In the previous two to three decades they had also become competitive outside Europe. In the early twenty-first century, the German BMW's sales outside Germany represented 81 percent of its total sales. Daimler-Benz's sales in other than German markets were 78 percent of total sales, and Volkswagen's 83 percent. This share was 78 percent for the French Peugeot, 74 percent for Renault, and 63 percent for the Italian FIAT.[93]

The huge investments of German, French, and Italian carmakers in Central Europe after the collapse of the Soviet Bloc meant that the corner where Austria, Hungary, Slovakia, and the Czech Republic meet acquired eleven new auto plants from the early 1990s on; this cross-border region was dubbed the "Detroit of

Eastern Europe"—before the bankruptcy and collapse of Detroit.[94] A European Commission document from 2004 underlines the importance for the car industry on the acceptance of the East European countries into the Community: besides providing a significantly expanded market for cars, "enlargement has been a very important development for the European automotive industry . . . Investments there reinforce the European value chain by adding to it lower cost locations."[95]

The German Volkswagen Corporation offers a typical example. The company has had a stormy history. Hitler's pet project in the newly built township, *Kraft durch Freude Stadt* (named after the Nazi organization), started producing in the late 1930s but almost immediately became a major military supplier during the war. It suffered a devastating allied bombing attack that destroyed two-thirds of the factory. After the war, in the renamed city, Wolfburg, the remnant of the factory was put under British military management, with Major Ivan Hirst in control. The newly produced car was called the Volkswagen, the people's car. The prototype of this car, however, had been initiated by the visionary creator Ferdinand Porsche, technical director and then general director of the Austro Daimler between 1906 and 1923. He had convinced Hitler in 1933 to build the factory that produced the first Käfer (Beetle), the most successful car in the entire history of automotive industry. Because the company also produced for the Wehrmacht during the war, Porsche, together with his son Ferry and son-in-law, Anton Piëch, were arrested in 1945 and sent to prison for two years.

The company, however, survived. In 1948, it was given back to Germany as a state-owned firm, and in 1960 it was partially privatized and subsequently returned to the family. Porsche's son Ferry inherited the German part of the firm, and his daughter, Louise Piëch, the Austrian part of the firm. At the head of the Volkswagen Corporation Ferdinand Porsche was followed by Ferry, and then by his grandson Ferdinand Piëch.[96] Expansion had already started in the 1950s and 1960s. By the mid-1970s, Volkswagen had eight huge factories in Germany, and in 1953 it opened its São Paulo firm in Brazil. In 1962, the Mexican factory was opened, followed by other factories on various continents. By 1972, the company employed 200,000 workers and was a dominant multinational. In 1980, Volkswagen's empire employed four times more workers abroad than at home.[97] In the second half of the 1980s, two-third of Volkswagen cars were produced abroad.

Although a genuine multinational, with production facilities on virtually all continents, including China, South Africa, and Latin and North America, Volkswagen, in parallel with the European Community enlargements, would become a *par excellence* European corporation. The company belonged to the forerunners in investing in Mediterranean Europe and then, after 1989, in Eastern Europe. It took its first steps during the Franco era in Spain in 1968 when Seat S.A. was acquired. This was followed by several new establishments in Portugal and Spain: AutoEuropa–Automóveis Lda. (Portugal); Volkswagen Navarra, S.A. (Spain), and Gearbox del Prat, S.A. (Spain). In 1991, as regimes were changing across Eastern Europe, Volkswagen bought a third of the well-known Czech Škoda factory, and in a few years, the entire factory became part of the Volkswagen Empire. Volkswagen also made several greenfield investments in Slovakia, Hungary, and Poland. Slovakia was nicknamed "Volkswagen Land" because three major plants were established there. In 1991, Volkswagen bought the Bratislavské Automobilové Závody and with huge investments created a major factory with an assembly hall as big as twenty-one football fields. This became the world's only factory to produce five different car brands. The Martin plant produced components and exported their products to other Volkswagen plants in Europe. The Košice plant in 2004 produced cars for the Russian market. In Bratislava, a large part of the Cayenne model was produced and the Tuareg SUV production was started.[98]

In the west Hungarian city, Győr, Audi Hungaria Motor Kft was founded in 1993. The establishment of the new factory was 30–40 percent cheaper than if it had been in Germany. Production cost was 60 percent lower. After three years, the capacity of the factory was doubled, and after 1997–98, 2,200 engines and later 6,900 engines were produced daily: "Győr became the engine producing leader in the VW Empire."[99] In 1998, an engine production assembly line was built as well. The auto bodies were delivered from the Ingoldstadt factory in Germany and assembled in Győr. By 2007, 57,000 vehicles were being produced.[100] The company also established a new factory in Poznań, Poland, and a second one in Wrzesnia, and it built Volkswagen-Sarajevo in Bosnia-Herzegovina[101] The Volkswagen Corporation had forty-seven production plants in eleven European countries by 2006. Europe became the rock solid base for building up a wide, cross-border value chain network. For the Volkswagen Passat, forty-nine suppliers produce parts and accessories; for the Volkswagen Golf, fifty-one suppliers operate in Europe.[102]

In 1998, Volkswagen bought Bentley, Lamborghini, and Bugatti, and later the motorcycle producer Ducati. During the first two decades of the twenty-first century, the company's empire enlarged by the acquisition of the car designer Italdesign Giugiaro, the commercial vehicle producer MAN SE, the Scandinavian Scania AB, and Porsche. By 2011, the Volkswagen Group—in 100 plants with 550,000 employees—produced 9.3 million vehicles (twelve brands, 280 models) world-wide, and occupied more than 10 percent of the world market. Within the EU-27, Volkswagen produced nearly 4 million units and occupied more than 21 percent of the market.[103]

Among the giant European carmakers, the Fabbrica Italiana di Automobili Torino, or FIAT as it has been known for more than a century, followed a different route towards multinationalization and Europeanization. The company was established in Turin in 1899 by a cavalry officer, Giovanni Agnelli, and it originally operated with fifty employees. By 1914, 4,000 employees were producing 4,000 cars per year. In 1966, the founder's grandson Gianni Agnelli took over the direction of what had already become a giant corporation.[104] The company then proceeded over the next few years to acquire smaller sports car producers, such as Lancia (1968), Ferrari (1969), Alfa Romeo (1986), and Maserati (1993). In addition, it also expanded its activity to civil engineering, cement, newspaper, merchant shipping, and the food industry. The company employed 130,000 people who produced

1,335,000 cars per year, as well as trucks, motors, tractors, airplanes, and diesel engines. The company's total annual turnover was equivalent to 5 percent of Italy's GDP. Expansion, including the aforementioned acquisitions of Alfa Romeo and Maserati, exploded during the 1980s and into the 1990s. At the end of the 1980s, FIAT employed 350,000 workers in an international empire comprising 569 subsidiaries and 190 associated companies in fifty countries. Only 100,000 of the employees worked in Turin.[105] As a consequence of enlargement and fragmentation into several kinds of businesses, by 2001 FIAT's total sales were €58 billion, but less than half of that figure, €24.4 billion, came from the car business.

Around the turn of the millennium, partly because of sharp competition and partly because of business policy mistakes, FIAT declined into a deep crisis. Between 1993 and 2003, FIAT's car output had decreased by 40 percent. At its biggest plant, Miafiori, only 40 percent of capacity was being used. The company's share on the Italian car market had dropped from 60 percent in the 1980s to 30 percent by 2000. In one decade during the 1990s, FIAT's share in the European market declined from 14 to 7.4 percent. Heavy borrowing to finance acquisitions to diversify the business, meanwhile, left the company heavily indebted (in 2001 its debts amounted to €35.5 billion, 62 percent of its total turnover).[106] After a century of carmaking, FIAT actually wanted to get out of the auto business; its position had been weakened lethally by European and international competition. Buyers were sought and offers received from the American General Motors and the German–American Daimler–Chrysler.

In March 2000, at a news conference, the merger with General Motors was announced: General Motors acquired a 20 percent stake in FIAT, and FIAT became the single largest stakeholder of General Motors. After this transaction, FIAT became the seventh largest carmaker in the world. In 2002, nevertheless, FIAT was close to bankruptcy. Its CEO, Paolo Cantarella, had to resign for having neglected the car business in favor of financial and insurance businesses.[107] A radical restructuring was still needed. This happened in February 2003 when Umberto Agnelli appointed a former Pirelli executive, Giuseppe Morchio, as new CEO. Morchio wanted to retain the car business and started selling other sectors, such as the company's airline engine division FIAT Avio, its insurance unit Toro, and the majority shares of Fidis, the company's financial arm. The truck production and farm equipment sector were also sold. By June 2003, Morchio announced a turnaround plan to return to net profit making by 2005. Following the dictates of this plan, FIAT closed twelve out of 138 plants world-wide, but the income derived from these sales was radically decreased as debts associated with the sold units were paid off. In response, FIAT started investing in research and new car models, focusing once again on the company's original idea of designing autos to fill gaps in the small car market. The entire production was reorganized by creating a broad value chain and outsourcing a higher percentage, 50–70 percent of total product value, to its suppliers. To cut costs, the majority of the activities to develop new models were also outsourced—up to 70 percent of design and engineering of the new products. FIAT also reduced the number of its suppliers from 1,200 (1988) to 350 (1997).[108]

The first success, a new small car called Panda, became European Car of the Year in 2004.[109] The relationship between FIAT and General Motors was dissolved by General Motors in 2005. FIAT then moved to acquire a majority share in the troubled American automaker Chrysler. The combined FIAT–Chrysler, under a single management team from the end of July 2011, had become the world's sixth-largest automaker and planned to make 6 million cars by 2014.[110]

The company's annual report of December 2012 presents an impressive picture of this complex multinational corporation. FIAT operates in sixty-one countries, owns 1,063 companies, and employs 223,000 people (111,000 outside Italy). Within the EU, it also occupies an important place with its 186 car and auto component production and service subsidiaries—fifty in France, twenty-six in Britain, thirty in Germany, seventeen in Spain, and ten in Poland. Nearly 89,000 FIAT employees work in Europe and 52 percent of its seventy-seven R&D centers are located there.[111]

Europeanization of services

Along with manufacturing and finance, the latter including financial services, banking, and insurance, various services sectors have been Europeanized and transformed into a single market. Among them were several strictly national services. For example, the Community's Electricity Directive, accepted in 1996, opened EU-wide competition on the electricity markets, allowing companies to operate anywhere within Community boundaries. The same had happened earlier in the natural gas market in 1988.[112]

Europeanization of the aircraft industry advanced hand in hand with the Europeanization of air transport. Again the traditional national character of an industry was nudged aside in favor of the international. Although the Treaty of Rome (Article 84(2)) targeted a common air transport policy, implementation did not happen until the late 1980s. The EU liberalized air transportation in the early 1990s and any airline gained the right to offer service in all the member countries. Air France, Alitalia, British Airways, and Lufthansa began forming mutual alliances. Air France took 37.5 percent share of Sabena and, with partners, 40 percent in the Czech airline; Lufthansa took 26 percent of Air Lauda; British Airways took 49 percent of French TAT and opened Deutsche BA, a subsidiary in Germany.[113]

Giant French, British, German, and other retail chains also crossed frontiers and spread across the European Community. Among them was Carrefour. As one researcher stated in 2005, "anyone observing French retail giant *Carrefour* over the last three decades must concede that international expansion is a key part of its strategic plan."[114] The company, established as a discount shop by three families, opened its first business in Annecy, France, in 1960. In two years, supermarket chain-building began in France. From 1973, the company started opening hypermarkets in Spain, Brazil, and Argentina. It acquired several retail chains, and opened businesses in the US and Asia in 1989. Its major European expansion occurred between the early 1990s and early 2000s when it established Carrefour hypermarkets in Greece, Italy, Turkey, Poland, Portugal, Belgium, Romania, the Czech Republic, and Slovakia.[115] This process has continued in the twenty-first century: the *New York Times* reported at the end of 2013 that Carrefour had sold 150 malls in France "to help finance its push into other European countries," including the purchase of "127 malls, especially in Spain and Italy."[116] The company became a *par excellence* European retailer. "Today, it has 6,132 stores in 29 countries. Yet . . . only 13 percent of Carrefour's sales originated outside its European home region . . . Carrefour is the number one retailer in Spain, Portugal, and Greece, and the second largest in Italy."[117]

The British Tesco provides yet another example of retail Europeanization. This company started in 1919 in the East End of London with a stand that was set up by a demobilized soldier, Jack Cohen. His first shop in North London opened a decade later. The successful shop embarked on an aggressive expansion after World War II. During the 1950s–60s purchases included seventy William stores, 200 Harrow stores, and ninety-seven Charles Philips stores. Gradually Cohen's little shop emerged as the country's leading supermarket chain. By 2010, Tesco had become the world's third biggest retailer with 3,146 shops in twelve countries and employing 330,000 people. A great part of this status derived from the occupation of the Central European markets just a few years after the collapse of the Soviet Bloc. Tesco opened supermarkets in Poland, the Czech Republic, Slovakia, and Hungary and conquered their markets.[118]

The German retail and wholesale giant Metro Group, another instructive example, was founded by the merger of three major German retail companies in 1996. It immediately became one of the twenty largest publicly listed companies in the country. Shortly after its creation, Metro started its European and international expansion: by 1998 more than 35 percent of its turnover originated from abroad, and this share increased to more than 42 percent by 2000. The group focused primarily on the Central and Eastern European countries. It has stores in Poland, Russia, Ukraine, Serbia, Montenegro, Romania, Turkey, Greece, Luxembourg, and Kazakhstan. It has also made strategic alliances with sixteen international companies and organizations. By 2004, this German corporation employed 250,000 employees in thirty-two countries (including China, India, and Pakistan) and was the fifth largest retail chain in the world and, together with the British Tesco and French Carrefour, belonged to the three largest in Europe.[119]

The European Community Green Paper of 1997 registered: "Retail chains are increasingly undertaking cross-border activities." Three-quarters of the Community's food retailing was controlled by the corporations of just three countries, Germany, France, and Britain.[120] The European Commission reported in 1999 that Europeanization of retailing was part-and-parcel of an increased integration of services. Service providers expanded their markets by "widening their network of outlets . . . branches and subsidiaries." Overall, the share of services in intra-EU direct investments increased to more than 73 percent after the introduction of the Single Market.[121]

Notes

1 See Alfred D. Chandler, *The Visible Hand: The Managerial Revolution in American Business* (Cambridge, MA: Harvard University Press, 1977); Naomi R. Lamoreaux, *The Great Merger Movement in American Business, 1895–1904* (New York, NY: Cambridge University Press, 1985).
2 The first banking revolution accompanied the British Industrial Revolution and was characterized by the foundation of the British National Bank and commercial banks that limited their business for short-term crediting.
3 Geoffrey Jones and Harm G. Schröter, *The Rise of Multinationals in Continental Europe* (Aldershot, UK: Edward Elgar, 1993), 58, 86. By 1980, this share increased to 45 percent. In 1984, forty out of the total sixty-three Dutch insurance companies were doing business throughout the entire European Community.
4 Stephany Griffith-Jones, "The Growth of Multinational Banking, the Euro-Currency Market and their Effects on Developing Countries," *Journal of Development Studies* 16, no. 2 (January 1980): 204–23, here 205.
5 Jones and Schröter, *The Rise of Multinationals*, 174, 176.
6 Archive of European Integration, "The Development of a European Capital Market. Report of a Group of Experts Appointed by the EEC Commission," (November 1966), 39, 46.
7 Ibid., 18, 24, 31, 278, 280.
8 Archive of European Integration, "Programme for the Liberalization of Capital Movements in the Community," Communication from the Commission to the Council. COM (86) 292 final (23 May 1986), 8, 11.
9 Franklin Allen, Thorsten Beck, Elena Carletti, Philip R. Lane, Dirk Schoenmaker, and Wolf Wagner, *Cross-Border Banking in Europe: Implications for Financial Stability and Macroeconomic Policies* (London: Center for Economic Policy and Research, 2011), ix, www.voxeu.org/sites/default/files/file/cross-border_banking.pdf.
10 The Court of Justice ruled according to the complaint of the German retailer Rewe-Zentral AG against the German Government, which prohibited selling the French blackcurrant drink, Cassis de Dijon, on the German market because it did not meet German standards. See Archive of European Integration, Council Resolution of October 1999, Official Journal C 145 of 19.5.2000; Regulation (EC) No. 764/2008.
11 Neil Murphy, "European Union Financial development: The Single Market, the Single Currency and Banking," accessed October 29, 2004, www.fdic.gov/bank/. . ./ banking . . ./ . . . .
12 Emiliano Grossman, "Europeanization as an Interactive Process: German Public Banks Meet EU State Aid Policy," *Journal of Common Market Studies* 44, no. 2 (2006): 325–48.
13 Isil Erel, Rose C. Liao, and Michael S. Weisbach, "Determinants of Cross-Border Mergers and Acquisitions," *The Journal of Finance* LXVII, no. 3 (June 2012): 20.
14 Archive of European Integration, Banking Consolidation Directive, 2006/48/EC.
15 European Banking Industry Committee (EBIC) Response to the European Commission's Inquiry in Retail Banking. Interim Report II, ec.europa.eu/competition/ sectors/. . ./inquiries/. . .report_2/ebic.pdf.
16 See Grossman, "Europeanization as an Interactive Process," 343.
17 Jones and Schröter, *The Rise of Multinationals*, 37.
18 Vincent Wright, "Conclusion: The State and Major Enterprises in Western Europe: Enduring Complexities," in Jack Hayward, ed., *Industrial Enterprise and European Integration. From National to International Champions in Western Europe* (Oxford: Oxford University Press, 1995), 346. Hayward's edited volume is hereafter cited as Hayward, ed., *Industrial Enterprise and European Integration*.
19 Erel *et al.*, "Determinants of Cross-Border Mergers and Acquisitions," 1045.
20 Alan M. Rugman and Simon Collinson, "Multinational Enterprises in the New Europe: Are they Really Global?" www.bus.indiana.edu/. . ./bepp2005-12-rugman-collins.

21 Deutsche Bank Annual Report, 2013, www.db.com/ir/en/content/reports_2013.htm.
22 www.bnpparibas.com/en, accessed February 16, 2016.
23 Erel *et al.*, "Determinants of Cross-Border Mergers and Acquisitions," 1045.
24 Allen *et al.*, *Cross-Border Banking in Europe*, 2.
25 Ibid., 27.
26 European Bank of Reconstruction and Development, *Transition Report* 2000 (London: EBRD, 2000), 84–6; Gregory Impavido, Heinz Rudolph, Luigi Ruggerone, "Bank Funding: Central, Eastern and South Eastern Europe Post-Lehman: a New Normal?" IMF Working Papers 13/148, 13, www.imf.org/external/pubs/. . ./wp13148.pdf.
27 Ivan T. Berend, *From the Soviet Bloc to the European Union. The Economic and Social Transformation of Central and Eastern Europe since 1973* (Cambridge: Cambridge University Press, 2009), 120.
28 Österreichische Nationalbank, *June Report 2006* (Vienna: ÖNB, 2006).
29 *European Banking Sector. Facts and Figures* (Brussels: European Banking Federation, October 2012), 32.
30 Gregory Impavido, *et al.*, "Bank Funding".
31 Nicole Lindstrom and Dóra Piroska, "The Politics of Privatization and Europeanization in Europe's Periphery: Slovenian Banks and Breweries for Sale?" *Competition and Change* 11, no. 2 (June 2007): 119, 125.
32 Ibid., 18–19.
33 Impavido *et al.*, "Bank Funding," 10.
34 Archive of European Integration, Jean Pisani-Ferry, "Financial Integration and European Priorities," Bruegel Third-Party Papers (November 2006), 1, 2. The Bruegel Institution is a think tank based in Brussels.
35 Brookings Institution, "Banks and Cross-Border Capital Flows: Policy Challenges and Regulatory Responses. Committee on International Economic Policy and Reform" (Washington, DC: Brookings Institution, September 2012), 3; http://www.brookings.edu/~/media/research/files/reports/2012/9/ciepr/09%20ciepr%20banking%20capital%20flows.
36 Archive of European Integration, Karel Lannoo, "Europe 2020 and the Fiscal System: Smaller is Beautiful," CEPS Policy Brief, no. 21, 9 July 2010. The assets of J.P. Morgan, the largest American bank, are only 15 percent of US's GDP.
37 *European Banking Sector: Facts and Figures*, 2012.
38 "European Bank Mergers. Passport Check," *The Economist* (March 28, 2015).
39 United Nations Statistics Division, December 2013, unstats.un.org/unsd/selbasicFast.asp; *World Economic Outlook*, IMF, April 2014, www.imf.org/external/pubs/ft/. . ./2014/01. The *New York Times*, in its May 22, 2014 edition, listed the wealth of the top European banks as follows: HSBC US$2.74 trillion, Paribas US$2.58, Crédit Agricole US$2.36, Barclays US$2.26, Deutsche Bank US$2.24, Société Génerale US$1.74, Royal Bank of Scotland US$1.70, Group BPCE US$1.56, Lloyds US$1.40, and UniCredit US$1.15. Two Swiss banks, the UBS and Credit Swiss also have around US$$1 trillion assets.
40 World Top Insurance Companies, www.relbanks.com>insurance; www.insuranceeurope.eu/; www.insuranceeurope.eu/facts-figures/. . ./total-business.
41 As a typical case, in the mid-1980s, forty out of sixty-three Dutch insurance companies already worked throughout the European Community. See Jones and Schröter, *The Rise of Multinationals*, 86.
42 Archive of European Integration, "The Single Market in 1995," COM (96) 51 final (20 February 1996), 35.
43 Archive of European Integration, "Corporate Taxation and the European Company Structure, CEPS Task Force Report" (16 January, 2008), 7.
44 Peter J. Buckley and Patrick Artisien, "Policy Issues of Intra-EC Direct Investment: British, French and German Multinationals in Greece, Portugal and Spain, with Special Reference to Employment Effects," in *Multinationals and the European Community*, eds. John Dunning and Peter Robson (Oxford: Basil Blackwell, 1988), 111.

45 Archive of European Integration, Marc Koster, "Competition, concentration and competitiveness in the Common Market: Towards an EC Merger Control Regulation," Second International ECSA conference, George Mason University (May, 1991), 23–27.

46 Archive of European Integration, Business Cooperation Centre—Eighth Progress Reports (years 1980–83) COM (84) 169 final (28 March 1984).

47 Jones and Schröter, *The Rise of Multinationals*, 13. By 1990, Germany had the largest stock of investment in the Continent. Jones and Schröter note that the realization of overseas superiority, "which was attributed by several analyses to the small size of European firms . . . [gave] a greenlight for mergers which transformed the corporate structure of the European industry in the 1960s."

48 Neil Fligstein, *Euro-Clash. The EU, European Identity, and the Future of Europe* (Oxford: Oxford University Press, 2008), 89–90.

49 Ibid., 94–8.

50 Arthur F.P. Wassenberg, "European Alliance: on the Art and Science of Directing Interfirm Strategies," in *Changing Business System in Europe. An Institutional Approach*, eds. Jules J.-J. van Dijck and John P.M. Groenwegen (Brussels: VUB Press, 1994), 77.

51 J.L. Muchielli, "Strategic Advantages for European Firms," in B. Bürgenmeier and J.L. Muchielli, eds., *Multinationals and Europe 1992. Strategies for the Future* (London: Routledge, 1991), 40.

52 Archive of European Integration, Marc Koster, Competition, concentration and competitiveness in the Common Market, 1991.

53 United Nations, *From the Common Market to EC92. Regional Economic Integration in the European Community and Transnational Corporations* (New York, NY: United Nations Department of Economic and Social Development, 1993), 25.

54 Muchielli, "Strategic Advantages for European Firms," 36.

55 Wright, "Conclusion: The State and Major Enterprises in Western Europe," 344.

56 United Nations, *From the Common Market to EC92*, 25.

57 Ibid., 40, 41.

58 Andrew Cox and Glyn Watson, "The European Community and the Restructuring of Europe's National Champions," in Hayward, ed., *Industrial Enterprise and European Integration*, 322, 324, 327. Minority acquisitions also increased in 1986–87 to 117, 1988–89 to 159, in 1989–90 to 180. The same is true regarding joint ventures. In the same years their numbers were 111, 129 and 156.

59 Wayne Sandholtz, *High-Tech Europe. The Politics of International Cooperation* (Berkeley, CA: University of California Press, 1992), 104.

60 Pierre Muller, "Aerospace Companies and State in Europe," in Hayward, ed., *Industrial Enterprise and European Integration*, 168, 172, 176, 185.

61 Sandholtz, *High-Tech Europe*, 100–2.

62 Ibid.

63 Archive of European Integration, "The European Aircraft Industry: First Assessment and Possible Community Actions," COM (92) 164 final (29 April 1992), 7, 8, 14, 20, 21.

64 Wright, "Conclusion: The State and Major Enterprises in Western Europe," 345, 346, 349.

65 Ibid.

66 http://www.klm.com/corporate/en/about-klm/profile/, accessed December 15, 2015.

67 Nam-Hoon Kang and Sara Johansson, "Cross-Border Mergers and Acquisitions: Their Role in Industrial Globalization," OECD Science, Technology and Industry Working Papers, 2000/01, OECD Publishing, 24, http://dx.doi.org/10.1787/137157251088.

68 "From Giants to Mega-giants," *Ceramic Industry* 147, no. 9 (August 1997): 14.

69 Cox and Watson, "The European Community and the Restructuring of Europe's National Champions," 35.

70 The EU Merger Regulation, 38, accessed March 2015, www.slaughterandmay.com/. . ./the-eu-merger-regulation . . .

71 Fligstein, *Euro-Clash*, 84, 85.
72 M.J. Earl and D.F. Feeny, "Information Systems in Global Business: Evidence from European Multinationals" in Michael J. Earl, ed., *Information Management. The Organizational Dimension* (Oxford: Oxford University Press, 1996), 86.
73 en.sanofi.com>our company, accessed 2014.
74 Peter J. Buckley, *The Challenge of International Business* (Houndmills, UK: Palgrave Macmillan, 2004), 259.
75 Davor Filipović, Najla Podrug and Jasna Prester, "Cross-border Mergers and Acquisitions in Southeast Europe: Cases from Croatia, Romania and Bulgaria," *International Journal of Management Cases* 14, no. 3 (2012): 32–40, here 35, Management Database.
76 Fligstein, *Euro-Clash*, 62.
77 Roberto Basile, Davide Castellani, and Antonello Zanfei, "Location Choices of Multinational Firms in Europe: The Role of National Boundaries and EU Policy," accessed 2004, https://ideas.repec.org/p/wiw/wiwrsa/ersa04p37.html.
78 Filippo di Mauro, Hedwig Plumper, Robert Stehrer, "Global Value Chains: a Case for Europe to Cheer Up," European Central Bank, Component Policy Brief 03/2013 (August 2013), www.ecb.europa.eu/. . ./policy-brief-3-global-val . . .
79 World Input Output Database (WIOD), "New Measures of European Competitiveness: A Global Value Chain Perspective," Background paper for conference on April 16, 2012, Seventh Framework program, accessed April 10, 2012, www.wiod.org/conferences/brussels/Timmer_background.pdf.
80 Lorenzo Berra, Laura Piatti, and Gianpaulo Vitali, "The Internationalization Process in the Small and Medium Sized Firms: A Case Study on the Italian Clothing Industry," *Small Business Economics* 7, no. 1 (February 1995): 67–75.
81 *Supply Chain Standard Magazine* (December 2008): 46.
82 *Autonews*, europe.autonews.com/. . ./Peugeot-and-Citroen-national . . ., accessed April 20, 2012.
83 www.bayer.com/en/bayer-group.aspx, accessed February 5, 2016.
84 www.thyssenkrupp.com/, accessed February 12, 2016.
85 www.bsh-group.com/index.php?page=100325.
86 Rugman and Collinson, "Multinational Enterprises," 20.
87 Elfriede Grunow-Osswald, *Die Internationalisierung eines Konzerns. Daimler-Benz 1890–1997* (Vaihingen/Enz, Germany: Nieman and Feldenkirchen, 2006), 178, 284, 286, 346, 358–59, 365–67, 373, 376).
88 Archive of European Integration, Bruegel Policy Brief, "Farewell National Champions," 2006/04 (2006).
89 Archive of European Integration, "The Future of the Community's Car Industry," Commission of the European Communities, Brussels, SEC (76) 4407 final (17 December 1976).
90 Archive of European Integration, Commission Statement on the European Automobile Industry. Structure and Prospects of the European Car Industry (1981), 4, 28, 29, 33, 39, 42–44, 50. Commission Communication to the Council Presented on 16 June 1981, COM (81) 317 final.
91 W.J. Reader, *Fifty Years of Unilever 1930–1989* (London: Heinemann, 1980), 89.
92 Archive of European Integration, European Automobile Industry 1996, Communication from the Commission to the Council, the European Parliament, the Economic and Social Committee and the Committee of the Region, COM (96) 327 final (10 July 1996), 2, 5, 7, 16.
93 Stefan Schmid and Philipp Grosche, "Managing the International Value Chain in the Automotive Industry," *Bertelsmann Stiftung*, 16, http://www.bertelsmann-stiftung.de/fileadmin/system/flexpaper/rsmbstpublications/download_file/3424/3424_1.pdf.
94 Ibid., 119.
95 Archive of European Integration, European Competitiveness Report 2004. Commission Staff Working Document, SEC (2004) 1397 final (8 November 2004), 14.

96 Ferdinand Piëch, *Auto. Biographies* (Hamburg: Hoffmann und Kampe Verlag, 2002), 25, 49.
97 For the early history, see Jerry Sloniger, *The VW Story* (Cambridge: Patrick Stephens, 1980).
98 en.volkswagen.sk/en/Company/plants.html; www.volkswagenag.com/content/. . ./ the_group.html, accessed December 31, 2014.
99 Schmid and Grosche, "Managing the International Value Chain," 111.
100 Ibid., 83, 106, 110.
101 *Automotive Manufacturing Solution* 15, no. 3 (May/June 2014): 11.
102 *Automotive News Europe* 10, no. 5 (3/7/2005): 24.
103 Volkswagen, *2012 Annual Report*, accessed February 22, 2013, www.volkswagenag. com/ir/Y_2012_e.pdf.
104 For the early years, see Alan Friedman, *Agnelli: Fiat and the Network of Italian Power* (New York, NY: New American Library, 1989).
105 Jennifer Clark, *Mondo Agnelli. Fiat, Chrysler, and the Power of a Dynasty* (Hoboken, NJ: John Wiley & Sons, 2012), 89, 94.
106 Among FIAT's many acquisitions—this one to enlarge its agricultural machinery business—was its purchase of Case New Holland for US$4.6 billion.
107 Luciano Cira Vegna and Giuliano Maielli, "Outsourcing of New Product Development in Mature Industries: A Longitudinal Study of FIAT during Crisis and Recovery," *International Journal of Innovation Management* 15, no.1 (February 2011): 69–93, here 81.
108 Ibid., 85.
109 Ibid., 95, 168.
110 Ibid., 309.
111 FIAT Annual Report, December 31, 2012, accessed December 31, 2012, www.fiatspa. com/. . ./FiatDocuments/. . ./FiatGroup_Annual_Report_20 . . . FIAT also produces materials for cars, and owns large iron foundries and aluminum producing companies.
112 Archive of European Integration, "Second Report from the Commission to the Council and the European Parliament on the State of Liberalization of the Energy Market," COM (99) 198 final (4 May, 1999), 3, 5.
113 See Hussein Kassim, "Air Transportation: Still Carrying the Flag," in Hayward, ed., *Industrial Enterprise and European Integration*, 206–7.
114 Rugman and Collinson, "Multinational Enterprises," 6.
115 www.carrefour.com/content/carrefour-stores-worldwide, accessed December 2015.
116 "Carrefour of France in Deal to Buy 127 Malls," *New York Times*, December 17, 2013.
117 Rugman and Collinson, "Multinational Enterprises," 6.
118 *BBC News Magazine*, September 9, 2013; *Telegraph*, January 1, 2015.
119 www.metrogroup.de/en/company/history.
120 Archive of European Integration, Green Paper on Vertical Restraints in EC Competition Policy, COM (96) 721 final (22 January 1997).
121 Archive of European Integration, Economic reform: report on the functioning of community product and capital markets. Presented by the Commission in response to the conclusions of the Cardiff European Council, COM (99) 10 final, 20 January 1999.

EPILOGUE

Quo vadis European Union?

During the entire half-a-century, postwar Europe successfully adjusted to new challenges, and during various crises, the member countries of the European Community always escaped by going ahead towards further integration. There were strong builders of the integration process. After World War II, the bitter lessons of the war mobilized peoples and leaders to draw the conclusions from the historical lesson and create an integrated Europe not to repeat previous tragedies. The nation-states and conflicts among them, however, were still decisive forces. Britain, France, and Germany certainly could never have agreed to go down the road towards federalization of Europe. However, the danger of a new war between the West and the East, this time frightening with nuclear confrontation and devastation, occupied the central role. The two allied victorious superpowers in the war against Hitler—the US and the Soviet Union—turned against each other. The lack of trust and fear about each other, trying to guarantee their own security and gain advantage, led to more suspicion and, soon after the end of the war, confrontation in the Cold War.

The US, the unquestioned leader of the Western world, was strong and determined enough to initiate and also assist and push European integration ahead to strengthen their common Atlantic front against the Soviet Union and the Soviet Bloc.

The American attempt met with the enthusiastic contribution from federalist European elite and some of the leaders of the European nation states. This alliance led to the historical breakthrough of the integration process that emerged during the 1950s and progressed through the 1960s.

When the US changed its international strategy during the 1970s and opened towards China and the Soviet Union, Cold War tension—which had already started to weaken after 1963—was gradually replaced by détente. Meanwhile, Western Europe and the European Economic Community (EEC) dramatically strengthened and gradually emerged economically as a rival and competitor of the US. Europe became much less dependent on the US and in several areas even conflicted with it.

However, when American policy changed towards Europe during the 1970s, a new age of technological revolution and globalization created a dramatically changed international economic environment. The most successful reconstruction and growth period in postwar Europe was suddenly replaced by crisis and stagnation. Europe started losing ground in modern technology and in the sharpened international competition. Moreover, even its own domestic market was invaded by the much stronger American, Japanese, and other competitors.

In this new situation, the big European corporations entered the arena and demanded, planned, and pushed further integration to create a real common all-European market, to be competitive again and independent from American tutelage and the US dollar. They took the role that the US had before in building Europe. The big corporations needed a more organically integrated European economy where they could build all-European networks by cross-border mergers, acquisitions, and establishing a chain of subsidiaries. This process created huge, even internationally exceptional, corporative empires in Europe. The concentration in banking and manufacturing reached or even surpassed the American level by the early twenty-first century. European big corporations became increasingly powerful. The leading all-European banks possessed greater financial power than most of the European nation-states, or the entire European Union (EU). Somewhat similar, wealth accumulated in the hands of giant industrial and service corporations. Their all-European manufacturing networks and Europeanized value-chains, together with the Europeanized services and retail networks, created a solidly re-inforced concrete base and frame that served to keep the Europeanized economy and the EU together.

During the 2010s, however, a major historical question emerged. After a quarter of a century of American and then another quarter of a century of European corporative push for integration, will these forces advocate further integration, or will they be replaced by other forces? The US certainly wants to keep the Atlantic alliance alive, but has no interest to work with a federal Europe. As far as the big European corporations are concerned, the process of further Europeanization of business is still important and required. The impressive progress of building a real single market Europe is not yet ended. The corporate world needs a further homogenized Europe to exploit the unique advantage of a market of half-a-billion people.

The 2008 financial–economic crisis, however, hit Europe uniquely hard and opened a new chapter of the history of integration. This became very clear during the 2010s when several new crises emerged, especially by a war-ridden, burning Eastern and Southern neighborhood of the European Community. The Ukrainian crisis generated a new Russian challenge of European security. The chaotic Middle East and Africa led to a mass migration of millions of mostly Muslims to Europe. All these were combined with the expanded financial–economic crisis and undermined European solidarity and the EU's legitimacy. All the hidden weaknesses of the previous integration process came to the surface and exhibited severe contradictions and dangers. Will Europe be able to go further on the road of integration, or the opposite: will disintegration follow?

This book is about the past, about those who built the EU. Writing in a time of still unresolved crises, in 2015–16, when all the possibilities, from disintegration to further integration, are open, I try to draw some conclusion from the past to the foreseeable future. Are the builders of the EU still on track to cure the malaise? Nowadays there are very few enthusiastic federalists; the handful of their last Mohicans cannot make future history. Are the nation-states going to try together to find an exit from the crisis or are they going to turn inward and even turn against each other?

Most of all, do we have an international political challenge serious enough as during the Cold War period to hammer stronger ties in the Western alliance again? Do we have intact the reinforced concrete base of strong corporate networks and economic Europeanization? Do we have builders who are ready and able to repair and strengthen the shattered walls of the building of the EU?

For a more well-based answer to these questions, let's have a bird's-eye view look at the crisis situation first. The collapse of the American Lehman Brothers mortgage bank in 2008 kicked off the liquidity crisis that caused banks and countries to stop lending. An international financial crisis emerged, and the recession of the real economy followed. Unlike in other countries, however, in Europe this collapse undermined the common currency, the euro, the main symbol of the European integration process. Nine countries of the EU became bankrupt and required bailouts by the EU and the International Monetary Fund (IMF). Moreover, the liquidity and financial crises led to a long two- or in some countries even a three-dip-recession, which, in 2016, is still not entirely over even after six years. Such a frightening crisis had never happened in the more than sixty-year history of the EU.

One of its episodes, the uniquely deep and dangerous Greek debt crisis that led to three bailouts between 2009 and 2015, the first time in the history of integration, put on the agenda the exit of one of the countries from the euro-zone, or even from the EU. Solidarity among the member states was strongly challenged. On top of this long-lasting economic turmoil, several unrelated parallel challenges also shocked the EU and undermined its cohesion.

For the first time since the end of the Cold War, European security was also endangered. A mistaken and overambitious further enlargement attempt provoked the Ukrainian crisis and civil war and a confrontation with Russia. President Vladimir Putin overreacted, became involved in the civil war in Ukraine and engineered unacceptable border changes by occupying the Crimean Peninsula from Ukraine. Russian provocation in air and sea near or even across the EU's borders openly endangered European security again. Elements of the Cold War were beginning to reemerge. Russia started to build new, non-, or even anti-Western alliances with China and Iran and tried to reestablish parts of the former Soviet empire. As part of the Russian strategy, impressive military actions and an exhibition of military strength were shown in Syria. The security crisis spread into other areas and generated an energy crisis in the form of dependence on Russian oil and gas deliveries, which Russia already used as a blackmailing tool against certain countries. Energy independence became a burning European issue.

Beside the northern neighborhood of the EU, the southern neighborhood, North Africa and the Middle East also erupted in wars and chaos, which led to the rise of frightening terrorist organizations and attacks. That burning region also generated another major crisis: millions of endangered people started escaping from war zones in Syria, Iraq, Afghanistan, and even from Africa to Europe. Among the millions of migrants who crossed the Mediterranean Sea and marched throughout the Balkans, targeting the most prosperous countries of the EU, hundreds of thousands were not endangered refugees, but wanted to find jobs, a better life, and lucrative welfare institutions. An uncontrollable, chaotic invasion of the EU by mostly Muslim migrants generated the most dangerous cracks in solidarity and cooperation in Europe. The building of the EU was severely damaged.

These complex crises put the EU on trial. The devastation they caused became more serious because all the elements of the crisis required rapid actions and healing. The decision-making mechanism of the EU is known to be very slow and it was severely tested. Inaction for years deepened the crisis and sharpened inner conflicts to a degree that alienated a great part of the population, and thus undermined the legitimacy of the EU. Anti-immigration, anti-integration, and anti-common currency right-wing nationalist, populist forces appeared and strengthened in some of the countries. From 2014, these forces occupied nearly one-third of the seats of the European Parliament. Their strength and increased popularity, especially in some member countries such as Britain and France and in countries where they had already gained majority and elevated into the government such as in Hungary and, in the fall of 2015, in Poland, represent a fatal danger to the future of integration. British exit from the Union also became a real possibility in 2016. Will the EU survive or disintegrate? If it survives, will it be able to go further along the road of integration, towards "ever closer" union, or will it have to do just the opposite and step backward to lesser integration?

Politicians, scholars, and journalists alike enthusiastically make forecasts about the future of the euro and the EU, but there is no consensus among them on outcome. Some of the prophecies leave scarcely any or even no place for positive solutions. The historian Walter Laqueur, published his gloomy forecasts—as the titles of his books clearly express—in his *The Last Days of Europe: Epitaph for an Old Continent* (2007), and four years later in his *After the Fall. The End of the European Dream and the Decline of the Continent*.[1] In late 2011, Larry Elliott, the economic editor of the *Guardian*, entertained the possibility of the break-up of the euro-zone.[2] He was not alone then, but looking back from the vantage point of 2015, he was also clearly wrong. Robert Bideleux argued more specifically that the euro-zone perhaps was not serving the interests of the peripheries, in particular Ireland and the countries in the South, and he speculated that a smaller unified monetary zone might be the better configuration in Europe. He also feared that the euro-zone was in danger of breaking up in response to problems in the peripheries.[3]

None of the peripheral countries, however, drew the same conclusion. In fact, since 2007, during this serious recent crisis, the opposite has happened in the peripheries. Slovenia, Slovakia, Malta, Latvia, and Estonia have all rushed to join the euro area. The euro looks anything but "beyond rescue."

As a general guide to the process by which the euro-zone might break up, Roger Bootle, an economist and columnist for London's *Daily Telegraph*, offered this:

> The euro could be reduced to something like the Northern core ... through the process of the Southern countries leaving, either individually or *en bloc*. But it would be possible for the euro-zone to break up via the departure of the strong core economies to establish their own union.

He added that "it would be in the interest of the 'stronger' countries that remain in the euro to support the exit of their weaker partners."[4] No one as yet has chosen Bootle's political guide. Martin Feldstein, Harvard economist, also writing in 2012, was blunter: "The euro should now be recognized as an experiment that failed." From his perspective, the failure was "inevitable."[5] Today, in 2016, it is doubtful that anyone would want to sign on to this statement.

Nothing is unthinkable, warns the Bulgarian political scientist Ivan Krastev.

> Soviet disintegration was perceived as unthinkable in 1985 and declared to have been inevitable in 1995. This leap from the 'unthinkable' to the 'inevitable' is a useful footnote to the current discussion on the future of Europe ... After all, the present crisis has powerfully demonstrated that the risk of the EU disintegrating is not just a rhetorical device, a toy monster used by scared politicians to enforce austerity on their unhappy voters. It is not only the European economies, but also Europe's politics that are in turmoil. The financial crisis has sharply reduced the life expectancy of governments, regardless of their political colour, and has made room for the rise of populist and protest parties. The public mood is best described as a combination of pessimism and anger.[6]

Bernhard Clemm had a similar forecast:

> The future of an 'ever closer' Europe is increasingly uncertain ... Old animosities between Europeans are reappearing with alarming seriousness ... All this makes questions about a possible European disintegration plausible ones to ask ... Europe will disintegrate when people are fed up with the EU.[7]

This forecast seems ominous in the light of Eurobarometer's poll results in 2012 and 2013: "fewer and fewer people still think that the EU serves them well ... Only 33 percent of Europeans trust their common institutions and only 30 percent have a good image of the European Union."[8]

Even George Soros, an integration enthusiast who closely watches and analyzes the development and problems of the EU, returned at the end of 2013 to pessimism about the future of the EU: "My worst fears are confirmed. This is what I was afraid of, that the euro would be preserved and it would pervert the venture and destroy the European Union."[9] In his interview book of 2014, with its dramatic title, *The Tragedy of the European Union. Disintegration or Revival?* he repeats a bleak forecast: "The Eurozone is facing a long period of stagnation . . . So I expect the process of disintegration to gather momentum." Soros actually suggested dissolving the euro and establishing a German-led Northern currency-bloc and a second, French-led, Southern currency bloc within the EU.[10] In a similar way, François Heisbourg, in *La Fin du Rêve Européen* (The End of the European Dream), concluded in the fall of 2013 that the only really positive solution would be a federal Europe, but that because such a Europe is politically impossible, the only realistic solution is to cut out the euro-cancer and eliminate the common currency in an orderly manner.[11]

Paul Krugman, already on record with concerns about the possibility of the collapse of the common currency, at the end of May 2014, clearly expressed the worry that the EU itself may not be able to survive this latest round of troubles:

> The euro is still holding together, surprising many analysts—myself included—who thought it might well fall apart . . . the [European] elite has been able to hold things together. But we don't know how long this can last, and there are some very scary people waiting in the wings . . . If we are lucky . . . we may see some real economic recovery over the next few years. This could in turn, offer . . . a chance to get the European project as a whole back on track.[12]

The Economist expressed a partly similar view: "There are two solutions to Europe's problems: economic prosperity and increased democracy." The latter, however, for the British journal, means "returning [more] power to the states and institutions that voters trust . . . [i.e. with] the national parliaments given more say in EU legislation."[13] Anthony Giddens, on the other hand, recommend a bold jump forward by radical reform and even further federalization as the only way to rescue the EU, which "could still founder, even disintegrate, the result of a chain reaction of circumstances that member states were unable to control."[14]

On the surface, some developments since the end of 2013 would seem to support pessimism about the future of Europe as a union. According to a December 2013 Eurobarometer poll, among EU citizens, trust in the EU—57 percent in the spring of 2007—had dropped to less than a third. By January 2014, a *New York Times* article with the title "Europeans United in Hating Europe," alerted readers to the emergence of an alliance among anti-EU right-wing parties. The article reported that "the perception that bureaucrats in Brussels, bankers in Frankfurt and European lawmakers in Strasbourg are haughty and indifferent has made it possible for demagogues to pose as populists who are alone in understanding 'the people'." It went on to note that these parties promise to give back power to the nations "by dismantling the technocratic decision-making power amassed in Brussels and returning powers back to individual member states. They would pause, if not quite reverse, six decades of growing integration."[15]

This alliance turned out to have enough appeal to produce shocking electoral results in the May 2014 European parliamentary elections. In four countries the outcome could be called tragic. Anti-euro and even anti-EU parties gained significant ground. In Greece, the extreme left and right together gained 40 percent. The openly neo-fascist Jobbik Party came in second place in Hungary, the British anti-EU Independence Party (UKIP) attracted 27 percent of the voters, and Marine Le Pen's French National Front won 25 percent of French votes. In the Netherlands, Finland, and Italy, however, anti-integration extremists lost ground. Still, in late 2014 about 30 percent of the European Parliament seats were filled by anti-establishment, anti-integration, and even anti-EU representatives.

The immediate impact of the parliamentary elections in the EU, however, may not be dangerous, given that strongly integrationist, pro-EU party groups occupy 70 percent of the seats—down from 80 percent before but nevertheless representing a strong majority. The real dangers lie in the next national parliamentary elections in some member countries. One of the first shocks came from Poland where the right-populist-nationalist Jarosław Kaczynski's Law and Justice Party was able to exploit the migration crisis and regained power in a landslide victory in the fall of 2015. If the United Kingdom Independence Party, for example, strengthens its influence and cements an alliance with the anti-integrationist members of the Conservative Party, Britain, which faces a referendum in the summer of 2016, may withdraw from the EU. Hurtful though such an event would be to the integration process, it would not fatally wound the EU. A Le Pen victory in the next national elections in France, however, might lead to a French pull out, and that, as *The Economist* phrased it, "would be the end of it."[16]

There can be no doubt that recent complex crises in the EU have nurtured a resurgent nationalism in certain strata of the population in some countries. Opposition to immigration and to the recent enlargements, perceived by some as over-enlargement, are the primary stimuli, but nationalist anti-EU sentiment is also being fed by the economic troubles of the past several years, especially by high unemployment rates and austerity measures that have endangered, and in some countries significantly decreased, the living standard.

One of the most recent and most interesting analyses on the present and possible future of the EU came from the outstanding expert of the topic, the Italian political scientist Giandomenico Majone, who concluded that the EU is "over-integrated" and "over-enlarged."[17] "The depth of the current crisis," he said, "justifies the widespread opinion that integration has gone too far." The euro was a political concept, motivated by the goal of political union, "to make the integration process irreversible" regardless of the economic realities. It failed and its collapse was unavoidable. "The end of the monetary union appears to be only a question of time . . . ."

It pays to summarize Majone's arguments and recommendations in length because they express widespread views in the 2010s: "By the latest enlargement of the EU," he argues, there was "produced . . . [a] high level of socioeconomic heterogeneity . . . Income inequality is today much greater in the socially minded EU than in the supposedly arch-capitalist US." Furthermore, even in the integrationist countries such as Germany, Italy, Spain, and Belgium "there is no agreement about how far integration should go, with the majority of the countries favouring economic, rather than political, integration." However, "the political benefits of monetary union are even more doubtful than the economic ones." The crisis de-legitimized the EU because economic development and prosperity was the main legitimizing factor. "Popular distrust in the European institutions and widespread disenchantment with the very idea of European integration [emerged]." A survey of five euro-zone countries showed that a median of 37 percent believe that the euro is a good thing.

Europe, Majone also argues, has to return dominance to the nation-state. "The search for alternative integration methods . . . must start from the realization that despite globalization and regional integration the nation is still vitally important." "Reducing the autonomy of democratically elected national governments is likely to be self-defeating." Article 50(1) of the Treaty on European Union "acknowledges the right of any member state to withdraw from the Union . . . This means that the present EU is already, de facto, a confederation . . . [but] mimic[s] a federal state."

And he goes on to say:

> Some form of differentiated integration is no longer an option but . . . a necessity . . . [Federalists and scholars] greatly underestimated the effectiveness of the nation state and of its institutions . . . Neither globalization nor European integration have reduced the central role of the nation states in economic development and innovation . . . and hence must avoid too rigid limits on their freedom of action . . . The long century of nationalism . . . was an aberration in European history . . . European history suggests that there is something unnatural in this [federalist] approach.

As Majone sees it, the EU has to step back and look for a less ambitious cooperation restricted to economies because no one wants political integration and federalization any longer. *A looser cooperation of otherwise competing countries would be the solution.*

There are many pessimistic views about disintegration, and suggestions that the only way out from crisis is a return to free trade among fully sovereign nation-states are crowned by the newly elected president of the European Commission, the federalist Jean-Claude Juncker's pessimistic statement: "In a speech to the European Parliament," reported the *New York Times*, "Mr Juncker acknowledged that the next five years . . . would be the '*last chance*' to get citizens of the bloc's member countries to fully support the concept of European unity."[18]

In spite of the quite significant pessimism regarding the future of the EU, one could list several facts that challenge the gloomy forecasts. One of them perhaps is that a single anti-EU block has not been created. The United Kingdom Independence

Party shuns alliance with the French National Front because of the latter's racist stance. Le Pen, for her part, rules out coalition with the Greek and Hungarian neo-Fascist parties. Instead of one significant opposition, there were three relatively small opposition party groupings formed in the European Parliament. Furthermore, the motivations of the anti-EU votes are rather diverse and express the views of barely more than one-third of the potential voters.

Besides, the state of both the EU and euro-zone is not as bad as many experts have described it. Mario Draghi, the president of the European Central Bank, at a press conference in early November 2013 called attention to the economic facts:

> If you look at the euro area from a distance, you see that the fundamentals in this area are probably the strongest in the world. This is an area that has the lowest budget deficit in the world and the highest trade surplus.[19]

The return to the past through the dissolution of the euro currency, or worse, of the EU, is among the least likely of possibilities. The policy of economic nationalism that dominated the interwar decades—national self-defense, protection of national markets, manipulation of currencies, as the chief goals and practices among competing European states—has already failed miserably, with tragic consequences. The leader of the Dutch right-wing opposition Party of Freedom, Geert Wilders, explicitly suggested another alternative in the fall of 2015: "there is a perfectly good alternative to the European Union – it is called the European Free Trade Association, founded in 1960 . . . It does not rob anyone from sovereignty . . . "[20] He certainly does not remember that a simple free-trade zone has already proved its unviability: the European Free Trade Association (EFTA) initiated by Britain in 1960 failed in the competition with the European Community. EFTA members, including its initiator, joined the Community as soon as they could.

The earlier recommended model of functional integration, put forth by Lord Ralf Dahrendorf, and also the idea of *à la carte* integration in which "everybody does what he wants and . . . no one must participate in everything" would degrade the EU, creating a set of temporary organizations of the sort that Majone prescribes: "ad hoc responses to [certain] concerns . . . A Europe of clubs organized largely around functional tasks . . . Not top-down harmonization," as Majone suggests, "but a multiplicity of clubs seems to be the appropriate approach to this problem."[21]

In contrast, key members of the EU, including Germany, want to maintain it as a federalizing, if not federal, entity. They argue and recommend "more Europe" beyond the nation-state and indeed have stepped ahead by establishing a banking union and European Central Bank control of major national banking institutions. The correction of the birth defect of the common currency, creating monetary unification without fiscal unification, is also, in a way, creating a quasi-fiscal union by regulatory measures and legal (constitutional) arrangements. An EU analysis, based on the 2011 Report of Mario Monti, which suggested seven "flagship initiatives," speaks about the "Single Market revival . . . [when] business is back with its insistence on seriously improving the internal market." New initiatives are in the center, including the nearly fully realized introduction of a common EU patent system, an idea that first surfaced forty-eight years ago; the creation of a digital single market; decarbonization of the transport systems; the formation of an energy union, a capital union; and the introduction of a comprehensive labor migration policy.[22] Economic recovery is already on its way. Balanced budgets and economic growth returned. In the mid-2010s, it was already about 1.5 percent per year. Most of the experts are dissatisfied with the moderate growth, but they are wrong: 1.5–2 percent was the norm in long-term economic growth from the nineteenth century and only exceptional periods exhibited higher growth rates. In spite of most of the negative evaluations, austerity policy worked in Ireland, Spain, Portugal—thus in most of the countries. In other words, in spite of the bleak forecasts, the integration process was already renewed. Except for Britain, always a hesitant outsider, and later hesitant inside–outsider, no other member countries are flirting with leaving or weakening the EU.

A telling example is the Greek Syriza Party, which gained power in January 2015 and rejected the EU's austerity policy, demanded the writing off of its huge debts, and started blackmailing the EU by trying to organize a group of opposition countries to Brussels policy. When it failed and Greece had to face the reality to leave the euro-zone, the Greek Syriza Government made a sudden political U-turn, gave up its opposition and accepted even worse conditions for a new bailout than those to stay in. It is well-known that it would be extremely costly and even self-devastating to leave the euro-zone, let alone the EU.[23] As *The Economist* remarks, "a cascade of defaults and lawsuits would follow."[24]

The EU structure provides the best mechanism for stabilizing and keeping peace, and for collaboration among countries of Europe. Therefore, preserving the EU optimally serves the political interests of all these countries. The same is true regarding global competition. If Europe does not want to be eliminated as a world power, then keeping the EU alive is an absolute must. However, who will build Europe? In the dangerous Cold War decades, the US initiated and assisted hammering out an integrated Western Europe. Although the Cold War is over, outside dangers in the form of international fundamental Islamist terrorism, a dangerously destabilized Arabic world, and a humiliated and resurrected more aggressive Russia are already around. In the early twenty-first century, the geographical surroundings of the EU in the South, Middle East, and East are burning. This international political situation is a centripetal force, assisted by the traditional Atlantic alliance and working to keep the EU closely together.

During the 1970s and 1980s, Europe was endangered economically by the globalized world competition that led to its decline and loss of position. Big European corporations advocated a closer integration, a unified single market with common currency, and a backyard containing huge new markets and a cheap labor force. The nation-states embraced these goals as a means of serving their interest in greater integration. Consequently, they supported and constructed the new integrated framework, which in turn led to the "second coming" of the EU. The banking and manufacturing corporate giants, stronger than the nation-states, provided (using this term again) a reinforced concrete base and frame for the EU. Going backward by reestablishing the dominance of the nation-state is strongly against corporate interests. In other words, "builders" of integration are still around and working to promote their own programs. This is well demonstrated by the British business interest and banking that strongly opposed British exit from the Union in 2016.

All these considerations lead to the conclusion that the EU must escape from this crisis, as it has in the past, by driving onward down the road of integration. As Daniel Cohn-Bendit, the German Green Party member of the European Parliament, argued in 2013, "the nation state is fast becoming an obsolete political structure . . . The time is ripe for a transnational, transgenerational, transpartisan, grassroots . . . movement to take European integration to the next level."[25] Even *The Economist*, always a less enthusiastic proponent of integration, argues in a similar way: "A limited version of federalism is a less miserable solution than the break-up of the euro . . . To survive, Europe has to become more federal."[26] Further economic integration, a stable single market with monetary and a quasi-fiscal unification, banking union and supervision, and strong supranational institutions are the guarantees of a prosperous and competitive Europe in the age of the globalized world system. "Either we harness the power and the rich resources of the entire European network, or let the pace of globalization leave us behind."[27] Leaving the euro—or even more, leaving the EU—would be severely counterproductive for any country. Quoting *The Economist* again:

> It is a long agenda; but it is more manageable than trying to redesign Brussels from the top down, and it is less costly than a break-up. Saving the euro is desirable and it is doable. One question remains: will Germans, Austrians and the Dutch feel enough solidarity with Italians, Spaniards, Portuguese and Irish to pay up? We believe that to do so is in their own interests.[28]

Today, two-thirds of a century after the birth of the European Community, asking and answering the question *'quo vadis* Europe' is critical to fighting successfully against euroscepticism and anti-Europeanism within the EU, as well as to clarifying the enlargement policy of Brussels. Without a clear political philosophy, the EU may well continue down the path of over-enlargement, which could injure the federalizing EU seriously, pushing it back towards its earlier status.

During this second decade of the twenty-first century, several advocates of further enlargement have been speaking about "post-Westernization" and "multiple modernities" when "the identity of Europe will become more and more post-western." Rather than being a "single entity," a place of millions of citizens remarkable for their uniformity, the "true face" of post-Western Europe could be "a composite of universal values . . . and regional identities where the West in general and Europe in particular is no longer the main reference point of identity formation." This concept is based on the idea of the end of "a monolithic idea of modernity," and a "cross-fertilization" of various cultures in which, among others, secularism and political Islam may comfortably co-exist.[29]

As appealing as this scenario might be, it is highly artificial and outlandish. Relativizing European values and replacing them with "hybridized" "multiple modernities"—in other words, transforming the EU into an entity of coexisting, differentiated, regional value systems—raises the danger of the end of Europe and the twenty-first century EU. Based on European values and interests, an institutionalized and more flexible two-tier arrangement may serve the future well. This could allow further integration and a limited federalization to occur, at least in some of the core countries. Nowadays, no one speaks any longer about the goal of a United States of Europe, but rather of preserving the *sui generis* form of the EU, its unique status as an entity lying somewhere between the endpoints of confederation and federation. But there are many possible configurations lying in the vast middle of this continuum, and all these would serve the self-interest of the EU's member-states. The facts of the 2010s clearly reflect that, at least the euro-zone is going ahead in further integration. Cautious optimism regarding the future of the EU seems to be reasonable.

Notes

1 Walter Laqueur, *The Last Days of Europe: Epitaph for an Old Continent* (London: Thomas Dunne, 2007); *After the Fall. The End of the European Dream and the Decline of the Continent* (New York, NY: St Martin's Press, 2011).
2 Larry Elliott, "We've Been Warned: The System is Ready to Blow," *Guardian,* August 14, 2011.
3 Robert Bideleux, "European Integration: The Rescue of the Nation State?" in *The Oxford Handbook of Postwar European History,* ed. Dan Stone (Oxford: Oxford University Press, 2012), 379–405.
4 Roger Bootle, "Leaving the Euro: A Practical Guide," www.policyexchange.org.uk/ . . ./wep%20shortlist%20essay%20-%20roge . . .
5 Martin Feldstein, "The Failure of the Euro," *The Foreign Affairs* (January/February 2012).
6 Ivan Krastev, "How Real Is the Risk of Disintegration? The Lessons of the Soviet Collapse," accessed May 2012, http://www.diplomaatia.ee/article/how-real-is-the-risk-of-disintegration-the-lessons-of-the-soviet-collapse/.
7 Bernhard Clemm, "Integration on Trial: EU Disintegration is Still Possible," *European Politics and Society* (January 7, 2013).
8 *Standard Eurobarometer* 78 (Autumn 2012); Stefan Collignon, "Italy and the Disintegration of the European Union," *Social Europe* (February 28, 2013).
9 "Sceptics See Euro Eroding European Unity," *New York Times,* November 12, 2013.
10 George Soros, *The Tragedy of the European Union. Disintegration or Revival?* (New York, NY: Public Affairs, 2014), 44–46, 94. To save the European Union, he suggests, "you may have to break up the currency."
11 François Heisbourg, *La Fin du Rêve Européen* (Paris: Stock, 2013).
12 For Krugman's earlier concerns, see Paul Krugman, "Eurodämmerung," *New York Times,* May 13, 2012. Here Krugman forecast "the endgame" of the euro, ending with a sentence: "and we are talking about months, not years, for this to play out." For his mid-2014 views, quoted here, see Paul Krugman, "Crisis of the Eurocrats," *New York Times,* May 23, 2014.
13 "Europe's Angry Voters Bucked Off," *The Economist,* May 31–June 6, 2014, 12.
14 Anthony Giddens, *Turbulent and Mighty Continent. What Future for Europe?* (Cambridge: Polity Press, 2014), 220.

15 "Europeans United in Hating Europe," *New York Times*, January 3, 2014.

16 "Europe's Angry Voters Bucked Off," 12.

17 My quotes in this paragraph and the next three are taken from Giandomenico Majone, *Rethinking the Union of Europe Post-Crisis. Has Integration Gone Too Far?* (Cambridge: Cambridge University Press, 2014), 19, 38–40, 110, 210, 228, 265, 279, 297, 322.

18 "European Union's Executive Branch Approves Slate of Commissioners," *New York Times,* October 23, 2014.

19 "Sceptics See Euro Eroding European Unity."

20 Geert Wilders, "Let My People Vote," *New York Times,* November 20, 2015.

21 Giandomenico Majone, *"European Integration: From Collective Good to Club Good,"* paper presented at the Hertie School of Governance in Berlin on May 15, 2013, 6, 8, 15.

22 Archive of European Integration, Jack Pelkmans, "Thinking Ahead for Europe. Single Market Revival," Center for European Policy Studies (17 March 2010), 23, 37.

23 In 2013, a study by Germany's Bertelsmann Foundation showed that "a return to the German mark would cost some US\$1.6 trillion over 13 years, paring back Germany's gross domestic product by an average of 0.5 percentage points between 2013 and 2015."

   According to the Britain-based Centre for Economics and Business Research, the orderly break-up of the common currency would cost 2 percent of the aggregate GDP of the EU, about US\$300 billion; a disorderly break-up could cost 5 percent or US\$1 trillion. The media have published calculations that vary in significant respects, based on different research results from various financial institutions. These calculations univocally warn about the high cost of a break-up. The return to the national currencies of old would devaluate them by about 60 percent and cause losses equaling €9,500–€11,500 per citizen in the first year, and €3–€4,000 per citizen per year for the following several years. All experts agree that saving the euro is cheaper than dropping it. Bailing out all the Mediterranean countries, for example, has so far cost only €1,000 per EU citizen. Among these costs could be the collapse of stock markets, major capital flight from weaker countries, bank runs that decapitalize the financial institutions, steeply increased costs for debt repayments, major recession, even depression (see www.cbsnews.com/8301-505123. . ./leaving-the-euro-what-would-it cost). See also John Palmer, "The EU Crisis: Integration Or Gradual Disintegration?" http://www.eurozine.com/articles/2011-08-31-palmer-en.html.

24 "The Future of the European Union. The Choice," *The Economist,* May 26, 2012.

25 Daniel Cohn-Bendit and Felix Marquardt, "The Fix for Europe: People Power," *New York Times,* September 3, 2013.

26 "The Future of the European Union. The Choice," *The Economist.*

27 Cohn-Bendit and Marquardt, "The Fix for Europe: People Power."

28 "The Future of the European Union. The Choice," *The Economist.*

29 Hasan Turunç, "The Post-Westernisation of EU–Turkey Relations," in *New Perspectives on Turkey–EU Relation*, ed. Chris Rumford (London: Routledge, 2013), 81–5. See also *European Stability Initiative,* 19 September, Berlin–Istanbul, http://esiweb.org/pdf/csi..document_id_69.pdf, 20 October 2010; Chris Rumford, "Rethinking Turkey's Relationship with the EU: Postwestern Turkey Meets Postwestern Europe," in *Politics and International Relations,* Working Paper 3, November 2006.

BIBLIOGRAPHY

Primary sources (archives, published volumes of documents, documents on the Internet)

American National Archive. Confidential US State Department Central Files, France, Foreign Affairs 1945–1949. College Park, MD: National Archives and Record Administration.

Archick, Kristin, and Vincent L. Morelli. "European Union Enlargement." Congressional Research Service, February 19, 2014. www.fas.org/sgp/crs/row/RS21344.pdf.

Archive for European Integration. European Commission, Directorate-General for Economic and Financial Affairs, Issue 17, December 2012.

Archive of European Integration. "Action Plan for EU Relation with Ukraine, Extract from the Council of Ministers." Press release (6 December 1996).

Archive of European Integration. "Action Plan for Ukraine. Communication from the Commission to the Council." COM (96) 593 final (20 November 1996).

Archive of European Integration. "Black Sea Synergy: A New Regional Cooperation Initiative." Communication from the Commission to the Council and the European Parliament COM (2007) 150 final (11 April 2007).

Archive of European Integration. "Commissioner Richard Burke's statement in London on the Channel Tunnel (12 March 1980)."

Archive of European Integration. "Completing the Internal Market." White Paper from Commission to the European Council, Milan 28–29 June 1985, COM (85) 310 final (14 June 1985).

Archive of European Integration. "Corporate Taxation and the European Company Structure, CEPS Task Force Report, 16 January 2008".

Archive of European Integration. Eurofocus: A Newsletter for Journalists, Weekly No. 8/86 (24 February–3 March 1986).

Archive of European Integration. "Europe: a Time to Choose." European Parliament Document, 1985.

Archive of European Integration. "Programme for Liberalization of Capital Movements in the Community. Communications from the Commission to the Council." COM (86) (23 March 1986).

Archive of European Integration. "Second Report from the Commission to the Council and the European Parliament on the State of Liberalization of the Energy Market." COM (99) 198 final (4 May 1999).

Archive of European Integration. "Second Report on the Application of the Council Decision of 28 July 1989 on the Improvement of the Business Environment and the Promotion of the Development of Enterprises, and in Particular Small- and Medium-sized Enterprises in the Community." 1991, SEC (92) 764 final (11 June 1992).

Archive of European Integration. "The Community's Relations with the Outside World." Bulletin from the European Community for Coal and Steel No. 20 (December 1956).

Archive of European Integration. "The Development of a European Capital Market. Report of a Group of Experts Appointed by the EEC Commission." November 1966.

Archive of European Integration. "The European Aircraft Industry: First Assessment and Possible Community Actions." COM (92) 164 final (29 April 1992).

Archive of European Integration. "The Future of the Community's Car Industry." Commission of the European Communities, Brussels, SEC (76) 4407 final (17 December 1976).

Archive of European Integration. "The Single Market in 1995." COM (96) 51 final (20 February 1996).

Archive of European Integration. "Trade and Investment Barriers Report 2011: Commission Staff Working Document Accompanying the Report." SEC (2011) 298 final (10 March 2011).

Archive of European Integration. Robert J. Licher, "The European Union and the United States." ACES Working Paper Series.

Archive of European Integration. Address by Roy Jenkins, President of the Commission of the European Community to Meeting of the Bundeskommitee Europe-Wahl, Frankfurt (24 April 1979).

Archive of European Integration. Annabelle Littoz-Monnet and Beatriz Villanueva Penas, "Turkey and the European Union. The Implications of a Specific Enlargement." Egmont European Affairs Papers (April 2006).

Archive of European Integration. Annual Economic Report 1980–81, Communication of the European Commission of the European Community to the Council (15 October 1980).

Archive of European Integration. Athens Ceremony for EEC-Greek Associations. Bulletin from the European Community No. 48, July 1961.

Archive of European Integration. Banking Consolidation Directive, 2006/48/EC.

Archive of European Integration. Bruegel Policy Brief, "Farewell National Champions." 2006/04 (2006).

Archive of European Integration. Business Cooperation Centre: Eighth Progress Reports (years 1980–83) COM (84) 169 final (28 March 1984).

Archive of European Integration. Commission Proposes Community Research Programme in Biomolecular Engineering, Information Memo P-7/80 (January 1980).

Archive of European Integration. Commission Statement on the European Automobile Industry. Structure and Prospects of the European Car Industry, 1981. Commission Communication to the Council, presented on June 1981, COM (81) 317 final.

Archive of European Integration. Communication from the Commission to the Council and the European Parliament on Standardization and the Global Information Society: The European Approach, COM (96) 359 final (24 July 1996).

Archive of European Integration. Conference on the Enlargement of the European Community (Brussels, 26 and 27 June 1980), Extract, Economic and Social Committee.

Archive of European Integration. Council Resolution of October 1999, Official Journal C 145 of 19.5.2000; Regulation (EC) No. 764/2008.

Archive of European Integration. David Coen, The Role of Large Firms in the European Public Policy System: A Case Study of European Multinational Political Activity, (1997).

Archive of European Integration. Didier Bigo and Julian Jeandesboz, "The EU and the European Security Industry, Questioning the 'Public–Private Dialogue,'" INEX Policy Brief No. 5 (February 2010).

Archive of European Integration. "Economic reform: report on the functioning of community product and capital markets." Presented by the Commission in response to the conclusions of the Cardiff European Council, COM (99) 10 final. 20 January 1999.

Archive of European Integration. EU Commission Working Document. The 1980s: The Decade for Technology? A Study of the State of Art of Assembly of Apparel Products (1979), 1.1.

Archive of European Integration. EU Diplomacy Papers, 2/2006, December 2006, Günter Burghardt, "The EU's Transatlantic Relationship."

Archive of European Integration. Eurofocus: A Newssheet for Journalists. Weekly No. 7/86 (17–24 February, 1986).

Archive of European Integration. European Automobile Industry 1996, Communication from the Commission to the Council, the European Parliament, the Economic and Social Committee and the Committee of the Region, COM (96) 327 final (10 July 1996).

Archive of European Integration. European Competitiveness Report 2004. Commission Staff Working Document, SEC (2004) 1397 final (8 November 2004).

Archive of European Integration. European Motor Vehicle Industry: Situation, Issues at Stake, and Proposals for Action. Communication from the Commission to the Council, the European Parliament and the Economic and Social Committee, COM (92) 166 final (8 May 1992).

Archive of European Integration. Frances G. Burwell, "Transatlantic Cooperation and Influence: The Virtue of Crisis and Compromise."

Archive of European Integration. George W. Ball, "The Common Market: The Period of Transition." The 400th Meeting of the National Industrial Conference Board, New York, 21 January 1960. aei.pitt.edu/14940/.

Archive of European Integration. Green Paper on Vertical Restraints in EC Competition Policy, COM (96) 721 final (22 January 1997).

Archive of European Integration. Heike Kluever, "Interest Group Influence on EU Policymaking. A Quantitative Analysis Across Issues" (2009).

Archive of European Integration. IES Working Paper (2/2007), Youri Devuyst, "American Attitude on European Political Integration. The Nixon–Kissinger Legacy."

Archive of European Integration. Improving Competitiveness and Industrial Structure in the Community. Commission Communication to the Council, COM (86) 40 final (25 February 1986).

Archive of European Integration. Interview of Three European Community Presidents, P. Paul Finet (High Authority of the ECSC), P. Etienne Hirsch (Commission of Euratom) and P. Walter Hallstein (Commission of the EEC), National Pan Club, Washington, DC, 11 June 1959.

Archive of European Integration. Jack Pelkmans, "Thinking Ahead for Europe. Single Market Revival." Center for European Policy Studies (17 March 2010).

Archive of European Integration. Jean Pisani-Ferry, "Financial Integration and European Priorities." Bruegel Third-Party Papers (November 2006).

Archive of European Integration. Jenny Fairbrass, The Europeanization of Interest Representation: A Strategic Decision-Making Analysis of UK Business and Environmental Interest (29 November 2002).

Archive of European Integration. Karel Lannoo and Arman Khachaturyan, "Reform of corporate governance in the EU." CEPS Policy Brief No. 38 (October 2003).

Archive of European Integration. Karel Lannoo, "Europe 2020 and the Fiscal System: Smaller is Beautiful." CEPS Policy Brief No. 21 (9 July 2010).

Archive of European Integration. Maja Kluger Rasmussen, "Lobbying the European Parliament: A Necessary Evil." CEPS Policy Brief No. 242 (May 2011).

Archive of European Integration. Marc Koster, "Competition, concentration and competitiveness in the Common Market: Towards an EC Merger Control Regulation." Second International ECSA conference, George Mason University (May 1991).

Archive of European Integration. Maria Green Cowles, "The Changing Architecture of Big Business." Paper presented in 1997 at the 5th Biennial ECSA Conference in Seattle (29 May 1997).

Archive of European Integration. No. 1614/November 2013: Konstantin M. Wacker: On the Measurement of Foreign Direct Investment and its Relationship to Activities of Multinational Corporations (Frankfurt, Germany: European Central Bank, 2013).

Archive of European Integration. Peter J. Buckley and Patrick Artisien, "Policy Issues of Intra–EC Direct Investment: British, French and German Multinationals in Greece, Portugal and Spain, with Special References to Employment Effects."

Archive of European Integration. Report of the Ad Hoc Committee for Institutional Affairs to the European Council (Brussels, 29–30 March 1985).

Archive of European Integration. Roy Jenkins, President of the European Commission, Address to the Nuremberg Chamber of Commerce and Industry (4 December 1980).

Archive of European Integration. Speech [on European unity] by Mr Helmut Burckhardt, Vice President of the Consultative Committee of the European Community for Coal and Steel, at the Duquesne Club, Pittsburgh, 22 October 1954.

Archive of European Integration. Stephanie B. Anderson, "Developing Europe into a Third Great Power Bloc: the US, France and the Failure of European Defense Community" (2005).

Archive of European Integration. Terrence R. Guay, Interest Groups and EU Policy Making: The Influence of Defense Industry Interests (1997).

Archive of European Integration. The Community's Role in the World. Lecture by Mr Roy Jenkins, President of the Commission of the European Community at the Institute Royal des Relations Internationales, Brussels (6 November 1980).

Archive of European Integration. The European Economic Community and Changes in the International Division of Labour. Report of an Expert Group on the Reciprocal Implications of the Internal and External Policies of the Community, III/1367-78-EN (January 1979).

Archive of European Integration. The Single Market and Tomorrow's Europe. A Progress Report from the European Commission.

Archives Direct. Sources from the National Archive, UK, FCO, 82/287, Political relations between the USA and Europe, (Folder 7) 18 October, 1973.

Aus der Regierungserklärung der Bundeskanzlers Kiesinger vor dem 5 Deutschen Bundestag. 1968. *Dokumente zur Deutschlandpolitik*, V. Reihe, Band 1, 1 Dezember 1966 bis 31 Dezember 1967. Bearbeitet von Gisela Oberländer, Bundesministerium für Innerdeutsche Beziehungen. Frankfurt: Alfred Metzner Verlag.

Automotive Manufacturing Solution 15, no. 3 (May/June 2014): 11.

Automotive News Europe 10, no. 5 (3/7/2005): 24.

Bureau of Investigating Journalism. "Multinational Cash In on EU funds." November 29, 2010.

Deutsche Bank Annual Report 2013. www.db.com/ir/en/content/reports_2013.htm.

"Directive to Commander-in-Chief of United States Forces of Occupation regarding the military government of Germany, April, 1945, JCS-1067." http://usa.usembassy.de/etexts/ga3-450426.pdf.

Draft Treaty Establishing the European Union. www.spinellisfootsteps.info/treaty/47.html.

Draft Declaration of the European Resistance Movement (20 May 1944). ucparis.fr/index.php/download_file/view/748/235/.

European Commission. "Single Market Act – Frequently Asked Questions." EU press release October 27, 2010. europa.eu/rapid/press-release_MEMO-10-528_en.htm?locale=en.

European Commission. "Single Market Act II – Frequently Asked Questions." EU press release October 3, 2012. europa.eu/rapid/press-release_MEMO-12-734_en.htm?locale=en.

Marshall, George. "Fourth Meeting of the Council, of Foreign Ministers, Moscow, March 10 to April 24, 1947. Report by Secretary Marshall, April 29, 1947." Yale Law School Lillian Goldman Law Library. Accessed 18 February, 2016. http://avalon.law.yale.edu/20th_century/decade23.asp.

Morelli, Vincent L. "European Union Enlargement: A Status Report on Turkey's Accession Negotiations." Congressional Research Service, August 5, 2013. www.fas.org/sgp/crs/row/RS225.

National Archive. 504/4-2347, April 23, 1947.

National Archive. Acheson's Message to McCloy, October 28, 1949, 862.00/10-2849.

National Archive. Acting Secretary of State Telegram of December 23, 1947, 862.00/12-1747.

National Archive. Altaffer Consul Reports from Bremen, January 31, 1949, 862.011/1-3149.

National Archive. Ambassador Caffery's Memorandum to the Secretary of State, May 12, 1945, 751.00/5-1245.

National Archive. Ambassador Caffery's Message to the State Department, 851.00/4-446.

National Archive. Ambassador Caffery's Telegram for the Secretary of State, August 17, 1945, 751.00/8-1745.

National Archive. Ambassador Jefferson Caffery's Report to the Secretary of State, May 8, 1945, 711.51/4-2045.

National Archive. American Embassy in London, October 4, 1949, 862.01/10-449.

National Archive. Barbour's Message to Secretary of State, October 20, 1949, 862.00/10-2049.

National Archive. Brussels Embassy Reports, February 1, 1945, 862.014/2-145.

National Archive. Bureau of German Affairs. From Henry A. Byroade to Mr Joce, December 15, 1949, 711.5162/12-1549.

National Archive. Caffery Report on March 27, 1948 to Secretary, 862.00/3-2748.

National Archive. Caffery's Report from Paris to Secretary of State, May 10, 1949, 862.00/5-1049.

National Archive. Caffery's Report to the Acting Secretary of State, May 5, 1945, NIACT 2381.

National Archive. Charles Bohlen's Letter to Representative John M. Folger, March 1, 1948, 862.00/3-148.

National Archive. Charles E. Bohlen's Answer to La Follette's Article, 862.00/1-1749.

National Archive. Chief Naval Intelligence to State Department, July 3, 1946, 864.01/7-346.

National Archive. Committee Report on foreign economic administration, October 22, 1945, 862.60/10-2245.

National Archive. Communist Penetration in the Mannheim Area, September 14, 1949, 862.00/9-1449

National Archive. Confidential US State Department Central Files. France. Foreign Affairs, 1945–1949, 711.51/4-2045.

National Archive. Consul Altaffer's Report from Bremen, October 8, 1947, 862.00/10-847.

National Archive. Consul General Altaffer's Message to the Secretary of State, September 24, 1947, 862.00/9-2447.

National Archive. Consul General Altaffer's Report from Bremen, November 17, 1947, 862.00/11-1747.

National Archive. Consul General B. Tomlin Bailey's Report from Munich, August 16, 1948, 862.00/8-1648.

National Archive. Consul General Edward M. Groth's Report from Hamburg, January 17, 1947, 862.00/1-1747.

National Archive. Consul General Edward M. Groth's Report from Hamburg on the Change in German Mentality, April 6, 1948, 862.00/4-648.

National Archive. Consul General in Hamburg to the Secretary of State, January 23, 1948, 862.011/1-2348.

National Archive. Consul General Maurice Altaffer's Report from Bremen, May 5, 1948, 862.00/5-548.

National Archive. Consul General Maurice W. Altaffer's Report on his Meeting with Adenauer, Bremen, January 5, 1947, 862.00/6-547.

National Archive. Consul General Richard M. Groth's Report from Hamburg, December 5, 1946, 862.00/12-546.

National Archive. Consul Hillenbrand's Report Attached to Consul General Altaffer's Message to Washington, October 14, 1947, 862.00/10-1447.

National Archive. Consul Martin J. Hillenbrand's Report from Bremen, March 29, 1948, 862.00/3-1548.

National Archive. Consul Maurice W. Altaffer's Report from Bremen, February 5, 1947, 862.00/2-247.

National Archive. Consul Maurice W. Altaffer's Report on Denazification to Secretary of State, December 24, 1946, 862.00/12-2446.

National Archive. Consular Report from Bremen about the Congress of the CDU, September 8, 1948, 862.00/9-848.

National Archive. Consular Report to the Secretary of State, May 22, 1949, 862.00/5-1549.

National Archive. Dana Hodgen, Consul General in Stuttgart, Report, May 23, 1947, 862.00/5-2347.

National Archive. Draft Letter to Foreign Minister Schuman Concerning German Development from H.A. Byroade to Secretary of State, October 28, 1949, 862.00/10-2849.

National Archive. Embassy Report from Paris to Secretary of State, September 3, 1949, 862.00/9-349

National Archive. Embassy Report on the Media Reaction on the Byrnes Speech, Montevideo, October 4, 1946, 862.00/10-446.

National Archive. Ernest de W. Mayer Consul's Report from Baden-Baden, March 31, 1948, 862.00/3-3148.

National Archive. Ernest de W. Mayer US Consul's Report of October 10, 1947, 862.00/10-1047.

National Archive. Frederick J. Mann, Consul in Stuttgart, Report on July 26, 1948, 862.00/7-2848.

National Archive. Frederick J. Mann, Consul in Stuttgart, Report of August 20, 1948, 862.00/8-2048.

National Archive. From Brussels to Secretary of State, August 24, 1948, 862.00/8-2448.

National Archive. From Mr Oppenheimer to Mr Fahy, December 10, 1946, 862.00/12-1046.

National Archive. From the State Department to US Consular Officer in Charge, Stuttgart, 862.00/3-248.

National Archive. From Wayne G. Jackson to J.D. Hickerson, March 25, 1/949, 862.00/3-2549.

National Archive. George Kennan's memorandum, April 1, 1946, 711.51/4-146.

National Archive. High Commission and Federal Government Agreement, signed by Adenauer, McCloy, B.H. Robertson, and A. François Poncet, November 24, 1949, 862.00/11-2449.

National Archive. High Commissioner McCloy's Letter, October 28, 1949 to James E. Webb, 862.00/10-2849.

National Archive. James F. Byrnes Letter to Georges Bidault, President of Provisional Government, Against French Unilateral Action to Annex the Saarland, September 25, 1945, 862.014/9-2546.

National Archive. James Wilkinson, Consul General in Munich, Report of May 6, 1947, 862.00/5-647.

National Archive. John Edgar Hoover, Director of the FBI, to the State Department, February 7, 1946, 862.01/2-746.

National Archive. John J. McCloy, Telegram No. 962, for Acheson and Byroade, August 3, 1950, in Record Group 466, Top Secret General Records, Box No. 2, File August 1950, J.J. McCloy Papers.

National Archive. Kalergi's Letter to John D. Hickerson, Director of the Office of European Affairs, March 11, 1948, 862.00/3-1148.

National Archive. Leon Blum Message to Ambassador J. Caffery, January 23, 1946, 851.00/1-2346.

National Archive. Letter to the Secretary of State, March 30, 1948, 862.01/3-3048.

National Archive. Material Prepared for the Secretary's Press Conference, November 30, 1948, 862.014/11-3048.

National Archive. Maurice Altaffer, American Consul General's Report from Bremen, October 22, 1948, 862.00/10-2248.

National Archive. McCloy to Secretary of State, October 26, 1949, 862.00/10-2649.

National Archive. McCloy's Report on an Informal Meeting Between the Federal Chancellor and the Council of the Allied High Commission, October 27, 1949, in Bonn-Petersberg, September 27, 1949, 862.00/9-2749.

National Archive. McCloy's Report on December 22, 1949, 862.014/12-2249.

National Archive. McCloy's Report to Secretary of State, October 26, 1949, 862.00/10-2649.

National Archive. Meeting About How to Deal with Postwar Germany, April 27, 1945, 862.00/4-2745.

National Archive. Memorandum "What Worries the French." March, 1945, 711.51/3-2145.

National Archive. Memorandum for the Secretary of State from Ambassador Jefferson Caffery, May 12, 1945, 751.00/5-1245.

National Archive. Office Memorandum, 711.51/1-245.

National Archive. Paris Embassy's Report, March 22, 1946, 751.00/3-2246.

National Archive. Proposal for Meeting Anglo–French Security Desires with Respect to Germany, December 9, 1948, 862.00/12-948.

National Archive. Records of the US House of Representatives, HR-77 A-D13, Record Group 233. www.ourdocuments.gov/doc.php?doc=71.

National Archive. Report of Ambassador Murphy on Governor Conference in Berlin, April 1, 1948, 862.00/4-148.

National Archive. Report of Consul Martin J. Hillenbrand, Attached to Consul General Altaffer's Letter, October, 13, 1947, 862.00/10-1447.

National Archive. Report of Robert Murphy, September 15, 1948, 862.00/9-1548.

National Archive. Report of the American Consul in Bremen about the Congress of the CDU, 862.00/9-848, September 8, 1948.

National Archive. Report of the American Legation in Bern, August 26, 1946, 862.00/8-2646.

National Archive. Report of the US Consulate in Hamburg, January 13, 1948, 862.00/1-1348.

National Archive. Report on Bevin's Foreign Affairs Speech, by Douglas, November 17, 1949, 862.00/11-1849.

National Archive. Report on the Danger of Neo-Nazism, Berlin, June 17, 1948, 862.00/6-1748.

National Archive. Robert A. Lowett's Message on November 26, 1947, 862.00/11-2647.

National Archive. Robert Murphy's Report on May 2, 1947, 862.00/5-2147.

National Archive. Robert Murphy's Report to the Secretary of State, July 28, 1948, 862.00/8-648.

National Archive. Sam E. Wood, Consul General in Munich, Report of October 16, 1947, 862.00/10-1647.

National Archive. Some Aspects of Renazification in Bavaria, Clarence M. Bolds, Acting Land Commissioner, to J. McCloy, Munich, November 1, 1949, 862.00/11-149.

National Archive. Telegram from the State Department to Moscow (Kennan), May 8, 1945, 862.00/5845.

National Archive. Telegram from Wiesbaden to Secretary of State, April 5, 1949, 862.00 (W)/4-1549.

National Archive. The Acting Secretary's Report on the Meeting of Truman, Bidault, Admiral William D. Leahy, and Acting Secretary Grew, May 2, 1945, 711.51/5-1845.

National Archive. The Allied High Commissioners' Meeting with Representatives of the German Federal Government on November 15. McCloy's Report of November 16, 1949, 862.00/11-1549.

National Archive. "The evolution of US denazification policies in Germany." Report of the Political Advisor of the Military Government in Germany, May 5, 1948, 862.00/5-1148.

National Archive. US Embassy in The Hague Reported (Baruch) on March 8, 1949, 862.011/3-349.

National Archive. US Embassy Report from Mexico City on the Echo of Byrnes Speech, September 9, 1946, 862.00/9-946.

National Archive. US Initial Post-Defeat Policy Relating to Germany, March 23, 1945.

National Archive. Walter R. Sholes's Consul General Report "The Communist Threat in Germany" from Basel, August 28, 1945, 862.00/8-2845.

The Churchill Centre. "Speeches." www.winstonchurchill.org/resources/speeches.

This Day in History. "Eisenhower gives famous 'domino theory' speech." April 7, 1954.

US Department of State, Bulletin (July 23, 1962), 131–3.

Volkswagen. *2012 Annual Report*. www.volkswagenag.com/ir/Y_2012_e.pdf.

World Input Output Database (WIOD). "New Measures of European Competitiveness: A Global Value Chain Perspective." Background paper for the WIOD project presentation at the high-level conference on "Competitiveness, trade, environment and jobs in Europe: Insights from the new World Input Output Database (WIOD)." April 16, 2012. Seventh Framework Program. www.wiod.org/conferences/brussels/Timmer_background.pdf.

Books and studies

Adenauer, Konrad. *Erinnerungen, Vol. I, 1945–53*. Stuttgart, Germany: DVA Verlag, 1965.

Allen, Franklin, Thorsten Beck, Elena Carletti, Philip R. Lane, Dirk Schoenmaker, and Wolf Wagner. *Cross-Border Banking in Europe: Implications for Financial Stability and Macroeconomic Policies*. London: Center for Economic Policy and Research, 2011. www.voxeu.org/sites/default/files/file/cross-border_banking.pdf.

Anderson, Perry. *The New Old World*. London: Verso, 2009.

Andrianopoulos, Argyris G. *Western Europe in Kissinger's Global Strategy*. New York, NY: St Martin's Press, 1988.

Archick, Kristin. "European Union Enlargement." Congressional Research Service, February 4, (2013): 1, 10.

Aron, Raymond. "Europe and the United States: The Relations Between Europeans and Americans." In *Western Europe: The Trials of Partnership*, edited by David S. Landes. Lexington, DC: Heath and Co., 1977.

Balabkins, Nicholas. *Germany Under Direct Controls. Economic Aspects of Industrial Disarmament, 1945–1948*. New Brunswick, NJ: Rutgers University Press, 1964.

Balassa, Bela. *The Theory of Economic Integration*. Westport, CT: Greenwood Press, 1961.

Baldwin, Richard E., Joseph F. Francois, and Richard Portes. "The Cost and Benefits of Eastern Enlargement: The Impact on the EU and Central Europe." *Economic Policy* 12 (April 1997): 125–76.

Ball, Donald A. and Wendell H. McCulloch Jr. *International Business*. Plano, TX: Business Publications, 1985.

Basile, Roberto, Davide Castellani, and Antonello Zanfei. "Location Choices of Multinational Firms in Europe: The Role of National Boundries and EU Policy." Accessed 2004. https://ideas.repec.org/p/wiw/wiwrsa/ersa04p37.html.

Baun, Michael J. *An Imperfect Union. The Maastricht Treaty and the New Politics of European Integration*. Boulder, CO: Westview Press, 1996.

Baydar, Yavuz. "Turkish–European Relations and the Importance of Visa Liberalization." *Südosteuropa Mitteilungen* 01 (2013): 90–4.

Beloff, Max. *The United States and the Unity of Europe*. Washington, DC: The Brookings Institution, 1963.

Berend, Ivan T. *An Economic History of Nineteenth-Century Europe*. Cambridge: Cambridge University Press, 2006.

—. *Europe in Crisis, Bolt from the Blue?* London: Routledge, 2013.

—. *Europe Since 1980*. Cambridge: Cambridge University Press, 2010.

—. *From the Soviet Bloc to the European Union. The Economic and Social Transformation of Central and Eastern Europe since 1973*. Cambridge: Cambridge University Press, 2009.

—. *The Economic History of Twentieth-Century Europe: Economic Regimes from Laissez-Faire to Globalization*. Cambridge: Cambridge University Press, 2006.

Berger, Helge and Albrecht Ritschl. "Germany and the Political Economy of the Marshall Plan, 1947–52: A Re-revisionist View." In *Europe's Post-War Recovery*, edited by Barry Eichengreen. Cambridge: Cambridge University Press, 1995.

Berlin, Isaiah. *The Power of Ideas*. Princeton, NJ: Princeton University Press, 2000.

Bernstein, Barton J. and Allen J. Matusow, eds. *The Truman Administration. A Documentary History*. New York, NY: Harper and Row, 1966.

Berra, Lorenzo, Laura Piatti, and Gianpaulo Vitali. "The Internationalization Process in the Small and Medium Sized Firms: A Case Study on the Italian Clothing Industry." *Small Business Economics* 7, no. 1 (February 1995): 67–75.

Besong, Valery. "Coup d'etats [sic] in Africa. The Emergence, Prevalence and Eradication." Stanford University, Summer 2005.

Bethlendi, András. "Foreign Direct Investment in the Banking Sector." *Development and Finance*, no. 1 (2007): 61–71.

Beugel, Ernst Hans van der. *From Marshall Aid to Atlantic Partnership. European Integration as a Concern of American Foreign Policy*. Foreword by Henry A. Kissinger. Amsterdam: Elsevier, 1966.

Bideleux, Robert. "European Integration: The Rescue of the Nation State?" In *The Oxford Handbook of Postwar European History,* edited by Dan Stone. Oxford: Oxford University Press, 2012.

Blair, Alasdair. *The European Union since 1945*. Harlow, UK: Pearson Longman, 2005.

Bóka, Éva. "The Idea of Solidarity in the European Federalist Thought. A Historical Survey." Working Paper. Accessed December 3, 2011. www.grotius.hu/doc/pub/ECICWF/boka_eva_idea_subidiarity.pdf.

Bootle, Roger. "Leaving the Euro: A Practical Guide." http://www.policyexchange.org.uk/images/WolfsonPrize/wep%20shortlist%20essay%20-%20roger%20bootle.pdf.

Borrus, John and John Zysman. "Globalization with Borders: The Rise of Wintelism as the Future of Industrial Competition." In *Enlarging Europe. The Industrial Foundation of a New Political Reality*, edited by John Zysman and Andrew Schwartz. Berkeley, CA: University of California Press, 1998.

Breuss, Fritz. "15 Years of Austrian EU Membership." *Austrian Economic Quarterly* 2 (2010): 165–83.

Brinkley, Douglas and Richard T. Griffiths, eds. *John F. Kennedy and Europe*. Baton Rouge, LA: Louisiana State University Press, 1999.

Brookings Institution. *Major Problems of the United States Foreign Policy, 1949–50*. Washington, DC: The Brookings Institution, 1949.

—. "Banks and Cross-Border Capital Flows: Policy Challenges and Regulatory Responses. Committee on International Economic Policy and Reform." Washington, DC: Brookings Institution, September 2012.

Brown, Lester. *World Without Borders*. New York, NY: Random House, 1972.

Brugmans, Henri. *Prophètes et fondateurs de l'Europe*. Bruges, Belgium: College of Europe, 1974.

Buckley, Peter J. *The Challenge of International Business*. Houndmills, UK: Palgrave Macmillan, 2004.

Buckley, Peter J. and Patrick Artisien. "Policy Issues of Intra-EC Direct Investment: British, French and German Multinationals in Greece, Portugal and Spain, with Special Reference to Employment Effects." In *Multinationals and the European Community*, edited by John Dunning and Peter Robson. Oxford: Basil Blackwell, 1988.

Bürgenmeier, B. and J. L. Muchielli, eds. *Multinationals and Europe 1992. Strategies for the Future*. London: Routledge, 1991.

Burgess, Michael. *Federalism and European Union: Political Ideas, Influences, and Strategies in the European Community, 1972–1987*. London: Routledge, 1989.

—. *Federalism and European Union: The Building of Europe, 1950–2000*. London: Routledge, 2000.

Burwell, Frances G. "Transatlantic Cooperation and Influence: The Virtue of Crisis and Compromise." European Union Studies Association Biennial Conference (1646), Pittsburgh, Pennsylvania, 1999 (6th), June 2–5, 1999. http://aei.pitt.edu/2233/.

Calvo-Gonzales, Oscar. "Neither Carrot nor Stick: American Foreign Aid and Economic Policy Making in Spain during the 1950s." *Diplomatic History* 30, issue 3 (June 2006), 409–38.

Cantwell, John. "The Reorganization of European Industries after Integration: Selected Evidence on the Role of Multinational Enterprise Activities." In *Multinationals and the European Community*, edited by John Dunning and Peter Robson. Oxford: Basil Blackwell, 1988.

Cawson, Alan. "Interests, Groups and Public Policy-Making: The Case of the European Consumer Electronics Industry." In *Organized Interests and the European Community*, edited by Justin Greenwood, Jürgen R. Grote, and Karsten Ronit. London: Sage Publications, 1994.

Chace, James. "American Jingoism." *Harper's*, March 1976, 37–44.

Chandler, Alfred D. *The Visible Hand: The Managerial Revolution in American Business* Cambridge, MA: Harvard University Press, 1977.

Churchill, Randolph S., ed. *In the Balance. Speeches 1949 and 1950 by Winston Churchill.* London: Cassel, 1951.

Churchill, Winston. *His Complete Speeches 1896–1963. Vol. VII: 1943–1949.* Edited by R. Rhodes James. London: Chelsea House Publisher, 1974.

—. *The Second World War, Vol. IV: The Hinge of Fate.* London: Cassel & Co, 1950.

—. *The Second World War, Vol. VI: Triumph and Tragedy.* Boston, MA: Houghton Mifflin, 1953.

Cira Vegna, Luciano and Giuliano Maielli. "Outsourcing of New Product Development in Mature Industries: A Longitudinal Study of Fiat during Crisis and Recovery." *International Journal of Innovation Management* 15, no. 1 (February 2011): 69–93.

Clark, Jennifer. *Mondo Agnelli. Fiat, Chrysler, and the Power of a Dynasty.* Hoboken, NJ: John Wiley & Sons, 2012.

Clement, Hermann. "The Case of Russia and Ukraine." In *Economic Convergence and Divergence in Europe. Growth and Regional Development in an Enlarged European Union*, edited by Gertrud Tumpel-Gugerell and Peter Mooslechner. Cheltenham, UK: Edward Elgar, 2003.

Clemm, Bernhard. "Integration on Trial: EU Disintegration is Still Possible." (January 7, 2013) http://blog.politics.ox.ac.uk/integration-theory-on-trial-eu-disintegration-is-still-possible-and-the-theory-behind-supernational-governance-offer-little-guidance/

Cleveland, Harlan. *Nobody in Charge: Essays on the Future of Leadership.* New York, NY: John Wiley and Son, 2002.

Coen, David and Jeremy Richardson, eds. *Lobbying the European Union: Institutions, Actors, and Issues.* Oxford: Oxford University Press, 2009.

Coleman, David. "The Berlin–Korea Parallel: Berlin and American National Security in Light of the Korean War." *Australasian Journal of American Studies* 18, no. 1 (July 1999): 19–41.

Collignon, Stefan. "Italy and the Disintegration of the European Union." (February 28, 2013) www.socialeurope.eu/2013/02/italy-and-the-disintegration-of-the-european-union/

Commission of Global Governance. *Our Global Neighborhood. The Report of the Commission of Global Governance.* Oxford: Oxford University Press, 1995.

Cooper, Richard. *The Economics of Interdependence. Economic Policy in the Atlantic Community.* New York, NY: McGraw-Hill, 1968.

Cowles, Maria Green. "The 'Business' of Agenda-Setting in the European Union." Paper presented the Fourth Biennial International Conference of the European Community Studies Association, Charleston, South Carolina, May 11–14, 1995.

—. "The Changing Architecture of Big Business." In *Collective Action in the European Union. Interests and the New Politics of Associability*, edited by Jastin Greenwood and Mark Aspinwall, 112. London: Routledge, 1998.

Cox, Andrew and Glyn Watson. "The European Community and the Restructuring of Europe's National Champions." In *Industrial Enterprise and European Integration. From National to International Champions in Western Europe*, edited by Jack Hayward. Oxford: Oxford University Press, 1995.

Crafts, Nicholas and Gianni Toniolo. "Les trente glorieuses: From the Marshall Plan to the Oil Crisis." In *The Oxford Handbook of Postwar European History*, edited by Dan Stone, 356–78. Oxford: Oxford University Press, 2012.

Dallek, Robert. *Franklin D. Roosevelt and American Foreign Policy, 1932–1945.* Oxford: Oxford University Press, 1995.

Dassbach, Carl H.A. *Global Enterprises and the World Economy. Ford, General Motors, and IBM, the Emergence of the Transnational Enterprise.* New York, NY: Garland Publishing, 1989.

De Meyer, Arnoud, Roland Van Dierdonck, and Ann Vereecke. "Global Plant Networks in European Multinationals." Working Paper in the INSEAD. Fontainebleau, France: INSEAD, 1996.

Dell, Edmund. *The Schuman Plan and the British Abdication of Leadership in Europe.* Oxford: Oxford University Press, 1995.

Delors, Jacques. President of the Commission of the European Communities, Address (Bruges, October 17, 1989). Accessed July 28, 2015. europa.eu/rapid/press-release_SPEECH-89-73_en.htm?locale=FR.

Demirbas, Dilek. "The EU Regulation on GMOs, Multinational Biotechnology Companies and their Lobby group, EuropaBio." *Eubios Journal of Asian and International Biotechnics* 13, issue 1 (2003): 11–15.

Di Mauro, Filippo, Hedwig Plamper and Robert Stehrer. *Global Value Chains: A Case for Europe to Cheer Up.* European Central Bank, Component Policy Brief 03/2013 (August 2013).

Dosemeci, Mehmet. "How Turkey Became a Bridge between 'East' and 'West': The EEC and Turkey's Great Westernization Debate, 1960–1980." In *The East–West Discourse: Symbolic Geography and its Consequences*, edited by Alexander Maxwell. Bern: Peter Lang, 2010.

—. "Turkish Opposition to the Common Market: An Archeology of Nationalist Thought, 1964–1988." *South European Society and Politics* 17, issue 1 (2012): 87–107.

Dulles, Allen W. *The Marshall Plan.* Oxford: Berg, [1948] 1993.

Dunning John H. and Peter Robson, eds. *Multinationals and the European Community.* Oxford: Basil Blackwell, 1988.

Earl, M.J. and D.F. Feeny. "Information Systems in Global Business: Evidence from European Multinationals." In *Information Management. The Organizational Dimension*, edited by Michael J. Earl. Oxford: Oxford University Press, 1996.

Eichengreen, Barry. *The European Economy Since 1945. Coordinated Capitalism and Beyond.* Princeton, NJ: Princeton University Press, 2007.

Eichengreen, Barry and Andrea Boltho. "The Economic Impact of European Integration." *The Cambridge Economic History of Modern Europe. Vol. 2: 1870 to the Present*, edited by Stephan Broadberry and Kevin H. O'Rourke. Cambridge: Cambridge University Press, 2010.

Eichengreen, Barry and Jorge Braga de Macedo. *The European Payments Union: History and Implications for the Evolution of the International Financial Architecture.* Paris: OECD Development Center, 2001.

Elliott, Larry. "We've Been Warned: The System is Ready to Blow." *Guardian*, August 14, 2011.

Elvert, Jürgen. "The Institutional Paradox: How Crises Have Reinforced European Integration." In *Crises in European Integration. Challenges and Responses, 1945–2005*, edited by Ludger Kühnhardt. New York, NY: Oxford University Press, 2009.

Endo, Ken. *The Presidency of the European Commission under Jacques Delors. The Politics of Shared Leadership.* Houndmills, UK: Macmillan Press, 1999.

Erel, Isil, Rose C. Liao, and Michael S. Weisbach. "Determinants of Cross-Border Mergers and Acquisitions." *The Journal of Finance* LXVII, no. 3 (June 2012): 1045–82.

"EU Enlargement: The Next Seven." *BBC News Europe* (July 1, 2013). Accessed September 2, 2014. www.bbc.co.uk/news/world-europe-11283616.

European Bank of Reconstruction and Development (EBRD). *Transition Report*. London: EBRD, 1996.

—. *Transition Report 2000, Employment, Skills and Transition*. London: EBRD, 2000.

—. *Transition Report 2000*. London: EBRD, 2000.

European Banking Industry Committee (EBIC). Response to the European Commission's Inquiry in Retail Banking. Interim Report II. http://ec.europa.eu/competition/sectors/financial_services/inquiries/replies_report_2/ebic.pdf

European Banking Sector. *Facts and Figures*. Brussels: European Banking Federation, October 2012.

European Central Bank, Filippo di Mauro, Hedwig Plumper, and Robert Stehrer. "Global Value Chains: a Case for Europe to Cheer Up." Component Policy Brief 03/2013 (August 2013).

European Commission. *The European Agreements and Beyond: A Strategy to Prepare the Countries of Central and Eastern Europe for Accession*. Brussels: The European Commission, 1994.

European Cooperation Administration. Bulletin No. 232 (October 18, 1948): 156–7.

European Councils. *1993: Conclusions of the Presidency 1992–1994, Report of the European Council in Copenhagen 21–23 June 1993* (Brussels: European Commission, 1995).

European Stability Initiative. 19 September, "Berlin–Istanbul, October 20, 2010."

European Union (EU). *Tableau de bord des aides d'état, Commission of the European Union*. Brussels: EU, 2002.

Feldstein, Martin. "The Failure of the Euro." *The Foreign Affairs* (January/February 2012).

Fetscher, Iring, ed. *Neokonservative und "Neuer Rechte". Der Angriff gegen Sozialstaat und liberale Demokratie in den Vereinigten Staaten, Westeuropa und der Bundesrepublik*. Munich: Verlag C.H. Beck, 1983.

Fieldhouse, D.K. *Unilever Overseas. The Anatomy of a Multinational 1895–1965*. London: Croom Helm, 1978.

Filipović, Davor, Najla Podrug and Jasna Prester. "Cross-border Mergers and Acquisitions in Southeast Europe: Cases from Croatia, Romania and Bulgaria." *International Journal of Management Cases* 14, no. 3 (2012): 32–40.

Findley, Ronald and Kevin H. O'Rourke. *Power and Plenty. Trade, War and the World Economy in the Second Millennium*. Princeton, NJ: Princeton University Press, 2007.

Finkelstein, Lawrence S. "What is Global Governance?" *Global Governance* 1, no. 3 (1995): 367–72.

Fishwick, Frank. *Multinational Companies and Economic Concentration in Europe*. Aldershot, UK: Gower, 1982.

Fligstein, Neil. *Euro-Clash. The EU, European Identity and the Future of Europe*. Oxford: Oxford University Press, 2008.

Fontaine, André. *History of the Cold War. From the October Revolution to the Korean War, 1917–1950*. New York, NY: Pantheon Books, 1968.

Friedman, Alan *Agnelli: Fiat and the Network of Italian Power*. New York, NY: New American Library, 1989.

"From Giants to Mega-giants." *Ceramic Industry* 147, no. 9 (August 1997).

Fukuyama, Francis. "The End of History." *The National Interest*, August 27, 1989, 27–46.

Gabel, Medard and Henry Bruner. *Global Inc.: An Atlas of the Multinational Corporations*. New York, NY: New Press, 2003.

Gareau, Frederick H. "Morgenthau's Plan for Industrial Disarmament of Germany." *The Western Political Quarterly* 14, no. 2 (June 1972): 242–69.

Garrett, Geoffrey and George Tsebalis. "An Institutional Critique of Intergovernmentalism." *International Organization* 50, no. 2 (Spring 1996).

Garton Ash, Timothy. *The Free World: America, Europe and the Surprising Future of the West.* New York, NY: Vintage Books, 2004.

Gauron, André. *European Misunderstanding.* New York, NY: Algora Publishing, 2000.

Gehler, Michael. "Challenges and Opportunities: Surmounting Integration Crises in Historical Context." In *Crises in European Integration. Challenges and Responses, 1945–2005*, edited by Ludger Kühnhardt. New York, NY: Oxford University Press, 2009.

Gerbert, Pierre. *La Construction de l'Europe.* Paris: Notre Siècle, 1983.

Giddens, Anthony. *Turbulent and Mighty Continent. What Future for Europe?* Cambridge: Polity Press, 2014.

Görtemaker, Manfred. "The Failure of EDC and European Integration." In *Crises in European Integration. Challenges and Responses, 1945–2005*, edited by Ludger Kühnhardt. New York, NY: Berghahn Books, 2009.

Graham, Helen and Alejandro Quiroga. "After the Fear Was Over? What Came After the Dictatorships in Spain, Greece, and Portugal." In *The Oxford Handbook of Postwar European History*, edited by Dan Stone. Oxford: Oxford University Press.

Grant, Charles. *Delors, Inside the House that Jacques Built.* London: Nicholas Brealey, 1994.

Greenwood, Justin and Mark Aspinwall eds, *Collective Action in the European Union: Interests and the New Politics of Associability.* London: Routledge, 1998.

Greenwood, Justin and Karsten Ronit. "Established and Emergent Sectors: Organized Interests at the European Level in the Pharmaceutical Industry and the New Biotechnology." In *Organized Interests and the European Community*, edited by Justin Greenwood, Jürgen R. Grote and Karsten Ronit. London: Sage Publications, 1992.

Greenwood, Sean. *Britain and European Cooperation Since 1945.* Oxford: Blackwell, 1992.

Griffith-Jones, Stephany. "The Growth of Multinational Banking, the Euro-Currency Market and their Effects on Developing Countries." *Journal of Development Studies* 16, no. 2 (January 1980): 204–23.

Griffiths, Richard T. *Europe's First Constitution: The European Political Community 1952–1954.* London: Federal Trust, Kogan Page, 2000.

Grossman, Emiliano. "Europeanization as an Interactive Process: German Public Banks Meet EU State Aid Policy." *Journal of Common Market Studies* 44, no. 2 (2006): 325–48.

Grunow-Osswald, Elfriede. *Die Internationalisierung eines Konzerns. Daimler-Benz 1890–1997.* Vaihingen/Enz, Germany: Nieman and Feldenkirchen, 2006.

Guirao, Fernando, Frances M.B. Lynch, and Sigfrido M. Ramírez Pérez, eds. *Alan S. Milward and a Century of European Change.* London: Routledge, 2012.

Haas, Ernst B. *The Uniting Europe. Political, Social, and Economic Forces, 1950–1957.* Notre Dame, IN: University of Notre Dame Press, [1958] 2004.

Harmes, Adam. *The Return of the State. Protestors, Power-brokers and the New Global Compromise.* Vancouver, BC: Douglas and McIntyre, 2004.

Harris, William D. *Installing Aggressiveness. US Advisors and Greek Combat Leadership in the Greek Civil War, 1947–1949.* Fort Leavenworth, KS: Combat Studies Institute Press, 2012.

Harrison, Joseph. *The Spanish Economy in the Twentieth Century.* London: Croom Helm, 1985.

Hayward, Jack, ed. *Industrial Enterprise and European Integration. From National to International Champions in Western Europe.* Oxford: Oxford University Press, 1995.

"Hearing before the Subcommittee on Economic Goals and Intergovernmental Policy of the Joint Economic Committee of the United States, 97th Congress, First Session, July 25, 1983." Washington, DC: US Government Printing Office.

Heisbourg, François. *La Fin du Rêve Européen.* Paris: Stock, 2013.

Henisz, Witold J. and Bennet A. Zelner. "The Hidden Risk in Emerging Markets." *Harvard Business Review*, April, 2010.

Hobsbawm, Eric. *The Age of Empire, 1875–1914*. London: Weidenfeld and Nicolson, 1987.

Hoffmann, Stanley. "The European Community and 1992." *The European Sisyphus. Essays on Europe (1964–1994)*, edited by Stanley Hoffman. Boulder, CO: Westview Press, 1995.

———. *The State of War. Essays on the Theory and Practice of International Politics*. New York, NY: Praeger, 1965.

Hogan, Michael J. *The Marshall Plan. America, Britain and the Reconstruction of Western Europe, 1947–1952*. Cambridge: Cambridge University Press, 1987.

Hull, Robert. "Lobbying Brussels: A View from Within." In *Lobbying in the European Community*, edited by Sonia Mazey and Jeremy Richardson. Oxford: Oxford University Press, 1993.

Hulsink, Willem. "From State Monopolies to Euro-Nationals and Global Alliances: The Case of the European Telecommunication Sector." In *Changing Business Systems in Europe. An Institutional Approach*, edited by Jules J.J. Dijck and John P.M. Groenewegen. Brussels: VUB Press, 1994.

Impavido, Gregory, Heinz Rudolph, and Luigi Ruggerone. "Bank Funding: Central, Eastern and South Eastern Europe Post-Lehman: a New Normal?" IMF Working Papers 13/148, 13. www.imf.org/external/pubs/ft/wp/2013/wp13148.pdf

International Monetary Fund (IMF). *World Economic Outlook, April 2014*. www.imf.org/external/Pubs/ft/weo/2014/01/

James, Harold. *Making the European Monetary Union*. Cambridge, MA: Belknap/Harvard University Press, 2012.

Jenkins, Roy. *Churchill. A Biography*. New York, NY: A Plume Book, 2002.

Johnson, Nancy E., Robert J. McMahon, and Sherrill B. Wells, eds. (William Z. Slany, general ed.), *Foreign Relations of the United States 1955–1957, Vol. 4: Western European Security and Integration*. Washington, DC: US Government Printing Office, 1988.

Jones, Geoffrey. "Multinational Strategies and Developing Countries in Historical Perspective." Working Paper 10-076, Harvard Business School, 2010.

———. *Renewing Unilever. Transformation and Tradition*. Oxford: Oxford University Press, 2005.

Jones, Geoffrey and Harm G. Schröter. *The Rise of Multinationals in Continental Europe*. Aldershot, UK: Edward Elgar, 1993.

Jones, Joseph M. *The Fifteen Weeks, (February 21–June 5, 1947)*. New York, NY: The Viking Press, 1955.

Jørgensen, Knud, Erik Mark A. Pollack, and Ben Rosamond, eds. *Handbook of European Union Politics*. London: Sage Publications, 2007.

Kagan, Robert. "Power and Weakness." *Policy Review*, June/July 2002.

———. *Of Paradise and Power: America and Europe in the New World Order*. New York, NY: Knopf, 2003.

Kang, Nam-Hoon and Sara Johansson. "Cross-Border Mergers and Acquisitions: Their Role in Industrial Globalization." OECD Science, Technology and Industry Working Papers, 2000/01, OECD Publishing. http://dx.doi.org/10.1787/137157251088.

Karamouzi, Eirini. *Greece, the EEC and the Cold War, 1974–1979*. London: Palgrave Macmillan, 2014.

Kashmeri, Sarwar A. "The Sun Never Sets on Britain's Eternal Question: To Be or Not To Be European." Review of David Hannay, *Britain's Quest for a Role. A Diplomatic Memoir from Europe to the UN*. London: I.B. Tauris, 2015.

Kassim, Hussein. "Air Transportation: Still Carrying the Flag." In *Industrial Enterprise and European Integration. From National to International Champions in Western Europe*, edited by Jack Hayward. Oxford: Oxford University Press, 1995.

Keeley, Robert V. *The Colonels' Coup and the American Embassy. A Diplomat's View of the Breakdown of Democracy in Cold War Greece.* University Park, PA: Pennsylvania State University Press, 2010.

Kennan, George. "The Source of Soviet Conduct." *Foreign Affairs* 25, no. 4 (July 1947).

Khanna, Tarun, Krishna G. Palepu, and Javat Sinha. "Strategies That Fit Emerging Markets." *Harvard Business Review*, June 2005.

Kimball, Warren F., ed. *Churchill and Roosevelt, The Complete Correspondence. Vol. III: Alliance Declining. February 1944–April 1945.* Princeton, NJ: Princeton University Press, 1984.

Kissinger, Henry. *World Order.* New York, NY: Penguin Press, 2014.

—. *The Troubled Partnership: A Re-Appraisal of the Atlantic Alliance.* New York, NY: McGraw-Hill, 1965.

—. *The White House Years.* Boston, MA: Little, Brown and Co., 1979.

Kohler-Koch, Beate. "Changing Patterns of Interest Intermediation in the EU." *Government and Opposition* 29, no. 2 (April 1994): 166–80.

Kramer, Heinz. "The Future of Turkish Western Relations." *Südosteuropa Mitteilungen* 1 (2013): 57–72.

Krastev, Ivan. "How Real Is the Risk of Disintegration? The Lessons of the Soviet Collapse."*Diplomaatia*, no. 105 (May 2012) www.diplomaatia.ee/en/article/how-real-is-the-risk-of-disintegration-the-lessons-of-the-soviet-collapse/

Krieger Mytelka, Lynn and Michel Delapierre. "The Alliance Strategies of European Firms in the Information Technology Industry and the Role of ESPIRIT." In *Multinationals and the European Community*, edited by John H. Dunning and Peter Robson. Oxford: Basil Blackwell, 1988.

Krugman, Paul. *The Return of Depression Economics and the Crisis of 2008.* London: Penguin Books, 2008.

Kühnhardt, Ludger, ed. *Crises in European Integration. Challenges and Responses, 1945–2005.* New York, NY: Oxford University Press, 2009.

Kuniholm, Bruce R. "Turkey's Jupiter Missiles and the US–Turkish Relationship." In *John F. Kennedy and Europe*, edited by Douglas Brinkley and Richard T. Griffiths. Baton Rouge, LA: Louisiana State University Press, 1999.

Kurz, Constanze and Volker Wittke. "Using Industrial Capacities as a Way of Integrating Central and Eastern European Economies." In *Enlarging Europe: The Industrial Foundation of a New Political Reality*, edited by John Zysman and Andrew Schwartz. Berkeley, CA: University of California Press, 1998.

Lamoreaux, Naomi R. *The Great Merger Movement in American Business, 1895–1904.* New York, NY: Cambridge University Press, 1985.

Laqueur, Walter. *After the Fall. The End of the European Dream and the Decline of the Continent.* New York, NY: St Martin's Press, 2011.

—. *The Last Days of Europe: Epitaph for an Old Continent.* London: Thomas Dunne, 2007.

Laursen, Johnny, ed. *The Institutions and Dynamics of the European Community, 1973–1983.* Baden Baden: Nomos, 2014.

Leisner, Walter. *Demokratie, Selbstzerstörung einer Staatsform.* Berlin: Duncker und Humblot, 1979.

Lewis, Brian. *'So Clean.' Lord Leverhulme, Soap and Civilization.* Manchester, UK: Manchester University Press, 2008.

Lindberg, Leon N. *The Political Dynamics of European Integration*. Stanford, CA: Stanford University Press, 1963.

Lindstrom, Nicole and Dóra Piroska. "The Politics of Privatization and Europeanization in Europe's Periphery: Slovenian Banks and Breweries for Sale?" *Competition and Change* 11, no. 2 (June 2007): 117–35.

Lipgens, Walter. *A History of European Integration, 1945–1947. Vol. 1: The Formation of the European Unity Movement*. Oxford: Oxford University Press, 1982.

—. *Europa-Föderationspläne der Wiederstandbewegungen 1940–1945*. München: R. Oldenburg Verlag, 1968.

Lipgens, Walter and Wilfried Loth, eds. *Documents on the History of European Integration. Vol. 3: The Struggle for European Union by Political Parties and Pressure Groups in Western European Countries 1945–1950*, European University Institute, Series B. Berlin: Walter de Gruyter, 1988.

Luard, Evan. *The Cold War. A Reappraisal*. London: Thames and Hudson, 1964.

Lukas Jr., Robert E. "Macroeconomic Priorities." Presidential Address at the Annual Meeting of the American Economic Association, January 10, 2003. http://pages.stern. nyu.edu/~dbackus/Taxes/Lucas%20priorities%20AER%2003.pdf

Maddison, Angus. *Monitoring the World Economy 1820–1992*. Paris: OECD, 1995.

Madeuf, Bernadette and Gilliane Lefebvre. "Globalization of R&D and Local Scientific Systems: Regional Patterns and Local Integration." In *Economic Integration and Multinational Investment Behaviour. European and East Asian Experience*, edited by Pierre-Bruno Ruffini. Cheltenham, UK: Edward Elgar, 2004.

Majone, Giandomenico. *"European Integration: From Collective Good to Club Good."* Paper presented at the Hertie School of Governance in Berlin on May 15, 2013.

—. *Rethinking the Union of Europe Post-Crisis. Has Integration Gone Too Far?* Cambridge: Cambridge University Press, 2014.

Martin, James Stuart. *All Honorable Men*. Boston, MA: Little Brown, 1950.

Masclet, Jean-Claude. *L'Union politique de l'Europe*. Paris: Presses Universitaires de France, [1973] 2001.

Maxwell, Kenneth. *The Making of Portuguese Democracy*. Cambridge: Cambridge University Press, 1995.

Mayne, Richard and John Pinder with John Roberts. *Federal Union. The Pioneers. A History of Federal Union*. Houndmills, UK: Macmillan, 1990.

Mazey, Sonia and Jeremy Richardson, eds. *Lobbying in the European Community*. Oxford: Oxford University Press, 1993.

McCormick, John. *Understanding the European Union. A Concise Introduction*. New York, NY: St Martin's Press, 1999.

McGhee, George. "Turkey Joins the West." *Foreign Affairs* 32, no. 2 (July 1954). https:// www.foreignaffairs.com/articles/turkey/1954-07-01/turkey-joins-west

Michalet, C.A. *Les firms multinationals et la novella division internationale du travail*. Geneva: International Labour Office. 1973.

Middelaar, Luuk van. *The Passage to Europe. How a Continent Became a Union*. New Haven, CT: Yale University Press, 2013.

Mihályi, Péter. "A privatizált vagyon visszaállamosítása Magyarországon 2010–2014." Discussion Papers, (MTA Közgazdasági-és Regionális Tudományi Kutatóközpont, Közgazdaság-Tudományi Intézet, Budapest, 2015), MT-DP-2015/7.

—. *Re-Nationalization in Post-Communist Hungary, 2013–2014*. (Budapest: Magyar Tudományos Akadémia, Kozgazdasagtudomanyi Intezet, 2014).

Miles, Lee. *Fusing with Europe? Sweden in the European Union*. Aldershot, UK: Ashgate, 2005.

Milward, Alan S. *Reconstruction of Western Europe 1945–1951*. London: Methuen, 1984.
—. *The European Rescue of the Nation-State*. Berkeley, CA: University of California Press, 1992.
Mitchell, Brian R. *International Historical Statistics: Europe 1750–1993*. 4th ed. London: Macmillan, 1998.
Mitrany, David. *A Working Peace System. An Argument for the Functional Development of International Organization*. Oxford: Oxford University Press, 1943.
Monnet, Jean. *Memoirs*. Translated by Richard Mayne. Garden City, NY: Doubleday, 1978.
Moravcsik, Andrew. *The Choice for Europe. Social Purpose and State Power from Messina to Maastricht*. Ithaca, NY: Cornell University Press, 1998.
Moravcsik, Andrew and Milada A. Vachudova. "National Interest, State Power, and EU Enlargement." *East European Politics and Society* 17, no. 1 (February, 2003): 42–57.
Morelli, Vincent. "European Union Enlargement: A Status Report on Turkey's Accession Negotiations." Congressional Research Service. fas.org/sgp/crs/row/RS22517.pdf.
Morgan, Michael Coley. "The United States and the Making of the Helsinki Final Act." In *Nixon in the World. American Foreign Relations, 1969–1977*, edited by Frederik Logevall and Andrew Preston. Oxford: Oxford University Press, 2008.
Mourlon-Druol, Emmanuel and Federico Romero, eds. *International Summitry and Global Governance. The Rise of the G-7 and the European Council, 1974–1991*. London: Routledge, 2014.
Muchielli, J.L. "Strategic Advantages for European Firms." In *Multinationals and Europe 1992. Strategies for the Future*, edited by B. Bürgenmeier and J.L. Muchielli. London: Routledge, 1991.
Muller, Pierre. "Aerospace Companies and State in Europe." In *Industrial Enterprise and European Integration. From National to International Champions in Western Europe*, edited by Jack Hayward. Oxford: Oxford University Press, 1995.
Murphy, David E., Sergei A. Kondrashev, and George Bailey. *Battleground Berlin: CIA versus KGB in the Cold War*. New Haven, CT: Yale University Press, 1998.
Murphy, Neil. "European Union Financial Development: The Single Market, the Single Currency and Banking." Accessed October 29, 2004. www.fdic.gov/bank/analytical/banking/2000may/2_13n1.pdf.
Nafpliotis, Alexandros. "Britain and Greece: 40 Years Ago." Accessed December 12, 2015. www.academia.edu/242029/Britain_and_Greece_40_years_ago.
—. *Britain and the Greek Colonels: Accommodating the Junta in the Cold War*. London: I.B. Tauris, 2012.
"Nazi Comeback Chance Seen." *Washington Post*, January 17, 1949.
Nelsen, Brent F. and Alexander C-G. Stubb eds. "The Ventotene Manifesto by Altiero Spinelli and Ernesto Rossi." In *The European Union* edited by Brent F. Nelsen and Alexander C-G. Stubb. London: Lynne Rienner, 1998.
Ners, Krzysztof J. and Ingrid Buxell. *Assistance to Transition Survey*. Warsaw: PECAT, 1995.
Neyer, Jürgen. *The Justification of Europe. A Political Theory of Supranational Integration*. Oxford: Oxford University Press, 2012.
Nichter, Luke A. *Richard Nixon and Europe. The Reshaping of the Postwar Atlantic World*. Cambridge: Cambridge University Press, 2015.
Nugent, Neill. *The Government and Politics of the European Union*. 7th ed. London: Palgrave Macmillan, 2010.
Nuti, Leopoldo. "A Continent Bristling with Arms: Continuity and Change in Western European Security Policies after the Second World War." In *The Oxford Handbook of Postwar European History*, edited by Dan Stone. Oxford: Oxford University Press, 2012.
Organisation for Economic Co-operation and Development (OECD). *Factbook: Economic, Environmental and Social Statistics*. Paris: OECD, 2007.

—. *General Report. Gaps in Technology*. Paris: OECD, 1966.

—. *Historical Statistics 1970–1999*. Paris: OECD, 2000.

—. *Structural Adjustment and Economic Performance*. Paris: OECD, 1987.

O'Rourke, Kevin H. and Jeffrey G. Williamson. *Globalization and History. The Evolution of a Nineteenth-Century Atlantic Economy*. Cambridge, MA: MIT Press, 1999.

Orwell, George. *The Lion and the Unicorn*. Harmondsworth, UK: Penguin Books, 1982.

Österreichische Nationalbank (ON). *June Report*. Vienna: ÖN, 2006.

Owen, Geoffrey. "Industrial Policy in Europe Since the Second World War." London School of Economics. ECIPE Occasional Paper No. 1/2012. http://www.ecipe.org/app/uploads/2014/12/OCC12012-revised.pdf

Özdamir, Hikmet. "The Turkish–American Relation Toward 1960 Turkish Revolution." dergiler.ankara.edu.tr/dergiler/44/671/8549.pdf.

Palmer, John. "The EU Crisis: Integration Or Gradual Disintegration?" Eurozine. http://www.eurozine.com/articles/2011-08-31-palmer-en.html.

Parr, Helen. *Britain's Policy Towards the European Community. Harold Wilson and Britain's World Role 1964–1967*. London: Routledge, 2006.

Pedersen, Thomas. *Germany, France and the Integration of Europe. A Realist Interpretation*. London: Pinter, 1998.

Piëch, Ferdinand. *Auto. Biographies*. Hamburg: Hoffmann und Kampe Verlag, 2002.

Pierson, Paul. "The Path to European Integration. A Historical-Institutional Analysis." In *European Integration and Supranational Governance* edited by Wayne Sandholtz and Alec Stone Sweet. Oxford: Oxford University Press, 1998.

Piketty, Thomas. *Capital in the Twenty-First Century*. Cambridge MA: The Belknap Press of Harvard University Press, 2014.

Pop, Valentina. "Kohl Confesses to Euro's Undemocratic Beginnings." A 2002 interview, April 8, 2013. https://euobserver.com/political/119735.

Przeworski, Adam, Michael E. Alvarez, José Antonio Cheibub and Fernando Limongi. *Democracy and Development, Political Institution and Well-Being in the World, 1950–1990*. Cambridge: Cambridge University Press, 2000.

Przybylski, Wojciech. "History Beyond Nations, Interview with Péter Balázs." *Visegrad Insight* 1, no. 3 (2013).

Ranieri, Ruggero. "Unlocking Integration: Political and Economic Factors Behind the Schuman Plan and the European Coal and Steel Community in the Work of Alan Milward." In *Alan S. Milward and a Century of European Change*, edited by Fernando Guirao, Frances M.B. Lynch, and Sigfrido M. Ramírez Pérez. London: Routledge, 2012.

Reader, W.J. *Fifty Years of Unilever 1930–1980*. London: Heinemann, 1980.

Reichlin, Lucrezia. "The Marshall Plan Reconsidered." In *Europe's Post-War Recovery* edited by Barry Eichengreen. Cambridge: Cambridge University Press, 1995.

Robinson, Michael. "Tax Avoidance: Developing Countries Take on Multinationals." *BBC News Business*, May 23, 2013. www.bbc.com/news/business-22638153

Rogoff, Kenneth and Carmen M. Reinhart, "This Time is Different: Eight Centuries of Financial Folly," NBER Working Paper No. 13882, March 2008. Accessed March, 2008. www.nber.org/papers/w13882.

Ross, George. *Jacques Delors and European Integration*. Oxford: Basil Blackwell, 1995.

—. *The European Union and Its Crisis. Through the Eyes of the Brussels Elite*. Houndmills, UK: Palgrave Macmillan, 2011.

Rostow, Walt Whitman. *United States in the World Arena, an Essay in Recent History*. New York, NY: Harper & Row, 1960.

Rothwell, Victor. *Britain and the Cold War 1941–1947*. London: Cape, 1982.

Rugman, Alan M. and Simon Collinson. "Multinational Enterprises in the New Europe: Are they Really Global?" https://core.ac.uk/download/files/153/7080947.pdf.

Rumford, Chris. "Rethinking Turkey's Relationship with the EU: Postwestern Turkey Meets Postwestern Europe." *Politics and International Relations*, Working Paper 3, November 2006. http://www.academia.edu/801659/Politics_and_International_Relations_Working_Paper

Sandholtz, Wayne. *High-Tech Europe. The Politics of International Cooperation*. Berkeley, CA: University of California Press, 1992.

Sandholtz, Wayne and Alec Stone Sweet, eds. *European Integration and Supranational Governance*. Oxford: Oxford University Press, 1998.

Sandholtz, Wayne, and John Zysman. "Recasting the European Bargain." *World Politics* 42, no. 1 (October 1989): 95–128.

Santer, Jacques. "Preface." In *Europe Competing in Global Economy. Reports of the Competitiveness Advisory Group*, edited by Alexis Jacquemin and Lucia R. Pench. Cheltenham, UK: Edward Elgar, 1997.

Santini, J.-J. "Les privatizations à l'étranger, Royaume-Uni, RFA, Italie, Espagne, Japon." Etudes coordonnées. Paris: La Documentation Françoise, 1986.

Sargent, Daniel J. *A Superpower Transformed. The Rethinking of American Foreign Relations in the 1970s*. New York, NY: Oxford University Press, 2015.

Sarotte, Mary Elise. "The Frailties of Grand Strategies: A Comparison of Détente and Ostpolitik." In *Nixon in the World. American Foreign Relations, 1969–1977*, edited by Frederik Logevall and Andrew Preston. Oxford: Oxford University Press, 2008.

Schmid, Stefan and Philipp Grosche. "Managing the International Value Chain in the Automotive Industry." *Bertelsmann Stiftung*. http://www.bertelsmann-stiftung.de/fileadmin/system/flexpaper/rsmbstpublications/download_file/3424/3424_1.pdf

Schimmelfenning, Frank. "The Community Trap: Liberal Norms, Rhetorical Action, and the Eastern Enlargement of the European Union." *International Organization* 55, no. 1 (Winter, 2001): 47–80.

Schneider, Volker. "Organized Interests in the European Telecommunication Sector." In *Organized Interests and the European Community*, edited by Justin Greenwood, Jürgen R. Grote, and Karsten Ronit. London: Sage Publications, 1992.

Schumpeter, Joseph. *Business Cycles: A Theoretical, Historical and Statistical Analysis of the Capitalist Process*. New York, NY: McGraw, [1939] 1981.

—. *Capitalism, Socialism and Democracy*. London: Routledge, 1942.

Schwartz, Thomas Alan. *Lyndon Johnson and Europe in the Shadow of Vietnam*. Cambridge MA: Harvard University Press, 2003.

Servan-Schreiber, Jean-Jacques. *Le Défi Américain*. Paris: Denoël, 1967.

—. *The American Challenge*, English trans. of *Le Défi Américain*. New York, NY: Atheneum, 1968.

—. *Le Défi Mondiale*. Paris: Fayard, 1980.

Simai, Mihály. "Global Economic Governance in the Post-Crisis World." *Society and Economy in Central and Eastern Europe* 35, no. 3 (2013): 299–318.

Singer, Edward N. *20th Century Revolution in Technology*. Commack, NY: Nova Science Publisher, 1998.

Sloniger, Jerry. *The VW Story*. Cambridge: Patrick Stephens, 1980.

Smith, Adam. *An Inquiry into the Nature and Causes of the Wealth of Nations*, Vol. 1. London: Mathuen, [1776] 1904.

Smyser, W.R. *From Yalta to Berlin: The Cold War Struggle Over Germany*. New York, NY: St Martin's Press, 1999.

Soros, George. *The Crisis of Global Capitalism*. New York, NY: Public Affairs, 1998.

—. *The Tragedy of the European Union. Disintegration or Revival?* New York, NY: Public Affairs, 2014.

Spaak, Paul-Henri. *Continuing Battle. Memoirs of a European 1933–1966.* London: Weidenfeld and Nicholson, 1971.

Spanier, John W. *American Foreign Policy since World War II,* New York, NY: Praeger, 1960.

Staab, Andreas. *The European Union Explained: Institutions, Actors, Global Impact.* 3rd ed. Bloomington, IN: Indiana University Press, 2013.

Štětka, Václav. "The Rise of the Tycoons. Economic Crisis and Changing the Media Ownership in Central Europe." *Visegrad Insight* 1, no. 3 (2013).

Stone, Dan, ed. *The Oxford Handbook of Postwar European History.* Oxford: Oxford University Press, 2012.

Stone Sweet, Alec, Wayne Sandholtz, and Neil Fligstein, eds. *The Institutionalization of Europe.* Oxford: Oxford University Press, 2001.

Story, Jonathan and Guy de Carmoy. "France and Europe." In *The New Europe,* edited by Jonathan Story. Oxford: Blackwell, 1993.

Tausch, Arno. "Towards a New EU Policy for the Mediterranean South?" In *Economics and Politics of Europe,* edited by Kemal H. Ferthold. New York, NY: Nova Science Publisher, 2008.

Teodorovic, Ivan, Zeljko Lovrincvzevic, Davor Mikulic, Mustafa Nusinovic, and Stjepan Zdunic, eds. *The Croatian Economic Development, Transition Towards the Market Economy.* Zagreb: Institute of Economics, 2005.

Teltschik, Horst. "329 Tage: Innenansichten der Einigung." In *Germany, France and the Integration of Europe,* edited by Thomas Pedersen. Berlin: Siedler, 1991.

Thatcher, Mark. "Regulatory Reform and Internationalization in Telecommunication." In *Industrial Enterprise and European Integration. From National to International Champions in Western Europe,* edited by Jack Hayward. Oxford: Oxford University Press, 1995.

The British Institute of Historical Research. "Coping with Crisis: Re-Evaluating the Role of Crises in Economic and Social History". https://copingwithcrisisconference. wordpress.com/.

The Economist. May 26, 2012, "The Future of the European Union. The Choice."

—. May 31–June 6, 2014, "Europe's Angry Voters Bucked Off."

—. October 9, 1997, "Finland and the EU. In and Happy."

—. September 27, 2014, "The Western Balkans and the EU. In the queue."

—. March 28, 2015, "European Bank Mergers. Passport Check."

The Economist. Pocket World in Figures. London: Profile Books, 2006.

The Economist Intelligence Unit. "Ukraine and the European Union. Day of the Gangster Pygmy." November 30, 2013.

—. "Quarterly Country Reports in Estonia, Latvia and Lithuania." 1st quarter, 1996.

"The New Germany and the Old Nazis." *New York Herald Tribune,* August 11, 1949.

"The Source of Soviet Conduct." *Foreign Affairs* 25, no. 4 (July 1947).

Thomas, Darryl C. *The Theory and Practice of Third World Solidarity.* Westport, CT: Praeger, 2001.

Toffler, Alvin. *Future Shock.* New York, NY: Bentham Books, 1971.

Tokes, Rudolf, ed. *Eurocommunism and Detant.* New York, NY: New York University Press, 1978.

Trachtenberg, Marc. *A Constructed Peace: The Making of the European Settlement, 1945–1963.* Princeton, NJ: Princeton University Press, 2000.

Truman, Harry S. *Memoirs.* 2 Vols. New York, NY: Doubleday, 1955–56.

Tuber, George M. *John Kennedy and a United Europe.* Bruges, Belgium: College of Europe, 1969.

Turunç, Hasan. "The Post-Westernisation of EU–Turkey Relations." In *New Perspectives on Turkey–EU Relation*, edited by Chris Rumford. London: Routledge, 2013.

UK Parliament. *House of Commons Parliamentary Debates Weekly Hansard* 438, 19.6.1947.

—. *House of Commons Parliamentary Debates Weekly Hansard* 443, 28.10.1947.

United Nations. Assessing Risk in Emerging Markets Infrastructure. Institutional Investor's Infrastructure Investment Forum, New York, June 28, 2007.

United Nations. *From the Common Market to the EC92. Regional Economic Integration in the European Community and Transnational Corporations.* New York, NY: United Nations Department of Economic and Social Development, 1993.

United Nations Conference on Trade and Development (UNCTAD). UNCTAD World Investment Report 2007.

—. World Investment Report. Accessed June 24, 2014. unctad.org/en/Pages/ . . . / world%20Investment%20Report/WIR-Series.asp.

—. World Investment Report 2004 and 2007. unctad.org/en/Pages/ . . . /world%2p/ investment%20Report/WIR-Series.asp;unctad.org/en/Docs/WIR2004_en.pdf.

—. World Investment Report 2004. New York, NY: UNCTAD, 2004.

Uslu, Nasuh. *The Turkish–American Relationship Between 1947 and 2003. The History of Distinctive Alliance.* New York, NY: Nova Science Publisher, 2003.

Van der Breugel, Ernst H. *From Marshall Aid to Atlantic Partnership. European Integration as a Concern of American Foreign Policy.* Amsterdam: Elsevier, 1966.

Van Gerven, Dirk ed. *Cross-Border Mergers in Europe, Vol. I.* Cambridge: Cambridge University Press, 2010.

Van Tulder, Rob, Alain Verbeke and Liviu Voinea. *New Policy Challenges for European Multinationals.* Bradford, UK: Emerald Insight, 2012.

Venna, Yrjö. "EU–Finland, First Year Impression." http://aei.pitt.edu/828/1/2.htm.

Vernon, Raymond. *Sovereignty at Bay. The Multinational Spread of U.S. Enterprises.* New York, NY: Basic Books, 1971.

Von Coudenhove-Kalergi, Count Richard Nikolaus. *Europe Must Unite.* Glarus, Switzerland: Paneuropa Editions, 1939.

Wall, Irwin M. *The United States and the Making of Postwar France, 1945–1954.* Cambridge: Cambridge University Press, 1991.

Ward, Stuart. "Kennedy, Britain and the European Community." In *John F. Kennedy and Europe*, edited by Douglas Brinkley and Richard T. Griffiths, 319–332. Baton Rouge, LA: Louisiana State University Press, 1999.

Wassenberg, Arthur F.P. "European Alliance: on the Art and Science of Directing Interfirm Strategies." In *Changing Business System in Europe. An Institutional Approach*, edited by Jules J.-J. van Dijck and John P.M. Groenwegen. Brussels: VUB Press, 1994.

Weisbrode, Kenneth. *The Atlantic Century: Four Generations of Extraordinary Diplomats Who Forged America's Vital Alliance with Europe.* Boston, MA: De Capo Press, 2009.

Werler, Joseph H.H. *The Constitution of Europe.* Cambridge: Cambridge University Press, 1999.

Wessels, Wolfgang and Thomas Traught. "Opportunity or Overstretch? The Unexpected Dynamics of Deepening and Widening." In *Crises in European Integration. Challenges and Responses, 1945–2005*, edited by Ludger Kühnhardt. New York, NY: Oxford University Press, 2009.

Wilkes, George, ed. *To Enter the European Community 1961–1963. The Enlargement Negotiation and Crisis in European, Atlantic and Commonwealth Relations.* London: Frank Cass, 1997.

Wilkins, Mira. *The Emergence of Multinational Enterprise.* Cambridge, MA: Harvard University Press, 1970.

Wilkins, Mira and Harm Schröter, eds. *The Free-Standing Company in the World Economy 1830–1996*. Oxford: Oxford University Press, 1998.

World Bank. *The East Asian Miracle: Economic Growth and Public Policy*. New York, NY: Oxford University Press, 1993.

——. *World Development Report 1985. International Capital and Economic Development*. New York, NY: Oxford University Press, 1985.

Wright, Vincent. "Conclusion: The State and Major Enterprises in Western Europe: Enduring Complexities." In *Industrial Enterprise and European Integration. From National to International Champions in Western Europe*, edited by Jack Hayward. Oxford: Oxford University Press, 1995.

Zysman, John and Andrew Schwartz, eds., *Enlarging Europe: The Industrial Foundation of a New Political Reality*. Berkeley, CA: University of California Press, 1998.

INDEX